W9-BYM-057

All in the Same Boat

~

*Family
Living
Aboard
and
Cruising*

~

TOM NEALE

INTERNATIONAL MARINE
CAMDEN, MAINE

International Marine/
Ragged Mountain Press

A Division of The McGraw·Hill Companies

10 9 8 7 6 5 4 3 2

Copyright © 1997 Tom Neale.

All rights reserved. The publisher takes no responsibility for the use of any of the materials or methods described in this book, nor for the products thereof. The name "International Marine" and the International Marine logo are trademarks of The McGraw-Hill Companies. Printed in the United States of America.

Library of Congress Cataloging-in-Publication Data
Neale, Tom.
    All in the same boat : family living aboard and cruising / Tom Neale.
      p.   cm.
    Includes bibliographical references. (p.).
    ISBN 0-07-046434-0
    1. Boat living.   2. Family recreation.   3. Boats and Boating.
I. Title.
GV777.7.N43   1997
797.1—dc20   96-35896
                                                              CIP

Questions regarding the content of this book should be addressed to:
International Marine
P.O. Box 220
Camden, ME 04843
207-236-4837

Questions regarding the ordering of this book should be addressed to:
The McGraw-Hill Companies
Customer Service Department
P.O. Box 547
Blacklick, OH 43004
Retail customers: 1-800-262-4729
Bookstores: 1-800-722-4726

All in the Same Boat is printed on 45-pound Editors Eggshell, a recycled, acid-free paper containing a minimum 50% recycled deinked fiber. ♻

This book was typeset in Adobe Meridien and Adobe Gill Sans.

Unless otherwise noted, all photographs by Mel Neale.
Printed by R.R. Donnelley, Crawfordsville, IN
Design by Chris McLarty, Silverline Studio
Production and page layout by Janet Robbins
Edited by John J. Kettlewell, Pamela Benner

CONTENTS

PREFACE

ALL IN THE SAME BOAT is for everyone who dreams of the cruising lifestyle. It is for those who feel trapped by convention and mediocrity and who want to take control of their lives and do something better. And it doesn't just state the obvious: that you should try it. We, the Neale family, go a giant step further. We talk about how we have done it and how *you* can make it work, too. Even if you think you may never break free, read on anyway. You may find that the liveaboard lifestyle is for you after all.

I owned my first boat at age 9; I am 52 as I write this. My family has lived and cruised aboard for well over 17 years, and not one of us wants to stop. But this isn't our only perspective; Mel was a public school teacher and I was a trial lawyer. Although we wanted to make our own way in this lifestyle, we didn't want our children to play in the sand on a pseudo-idyllic island for the rest of their lives; we aren't babbling about a fantasy escape. *All in the Same Boat* tells you how to deal realistically with the world around you as you lead your own lives of freedom on the waters.

The foundation of this book, as it must be with any true taking of control, is pragmatism. So, we write about the tough problems of changing lifestyles. These include reasons for making a change, emotional adjustments, daily-life adjustments, and financial adjustments. Then we get into leaving the old job, handling previous commitments, communicating, educating and raising children, socializing, staying safe, making repairs, preparing for storms and dangers, earning and saving money—doing all the things you must do to be self-reliant. This emphasis on practicality is just a means to adventure, freedom, fun, and a good and meaningful life. We share that with you through stories, wound around the lessons. Come join us.

ACKNOWLEDGMENTS

I'D LIKE TO THANK MY FAMILY for their work on and involvement with this book. Mel, Melanie, and Carolyn not only wrote specific sections for which they are credited in the text, they also helped with discussion, ideas, proofreading, mechanical jobs of text preparation, and provided emotional support. All of the photographs were taken and selected by Mel. I'd also like to thank John Kettlewell of International Marine for his help in the editing process. John and his wife have cruised extensively. They just had another baby, and I hope that one day they will share some of our experiences by cruising with their kids. And I wish to thank my father, who bought my first boat, and my mother, who has anguished ever since then over whether I'd make it back to shore one more time.

▼

A SIMPLE LIFE

Gentle power, a calm sweet push
Tightens the sails in a glorious rush.
The sun on my back is soft and hot
And I watch the speed go up a knot.

Little gusts come and go
Like people who I've been lucky to know.
Some I lost track of, some sailed away
And some I hold dear in my heart today.

And just as I wonder about the next swell,
I wonder about my life and I never can tell
Where I'm going, though I know where I've been,
And will I ever relive this again?

My life's like an ocean with shifting seas,
Rising and falling, pulled by the breeze,
But always moving, never at rest,
And rather unstable it seems I've confessed.

Even so, my stability lies in my close friends,
The few that can cast their souls to the winds
And sail through the ocean, mother of all,
And probably never make a landfall.
                    —Melanie Neale (age 15)

▲

INTRODUCTION

WHAT YOU LEAVE BEHIND

People often ask us why we gave up a comfortable home ashore, and successful careers in teaching and trial law, to move aboard and cruise. They also wonder why we did it with two babies. And then they wonder how it is that we are still doing it, more than 17 years later, with around 5,000 miles per year passing under the keel. The answer doesn't lend itself to cocktail party quips.

We do it because it's fun. We do it because it's beautiful. We do it because we love nature and the sea and the winds and the sky. We do it because it allows us to raise a family the way a family should be raised—and to know our children. We do it because it gives us more control over the way our family lives and survives, over the education and the maturing of our children, over the air we breathe. It gives us more control over our lives.

Most of us live restricted lives, but we are seldom sure of who or what is in control. We do know that it isn't us. We have jobs, the main purpose of which is to support other jobs. Few of these jobs are relevant to our daily well-being, except that they bring in money so we can have things done for us that we could probably do better for ourselves or do without.

Many of us are "required" to do and pay for meaningless things, such as nonsensical clothing. Even in the heat of the summer many men "must" wear a coat, and a long piece of cloth tightly wrapped around their necks. To endure this outlandish attire, we have to fill our buildings and vehicles with cold air. And to afford this luxury, we must work harder.

We are told whether our children can pray; we are told that our children must learn things whether we, as parents, think they are appropriate; we are told that our children must comply with social standards and values established by governmental committees; and we then see that our children haven't learned the basic skills of reading, writing, and arithmetic.

Blackouts tell it all. During a blackout, we often can't get water to drink, we can't get air into the enclosed structures where we work and live, our stored food thaws and begins to rot, our traffic becomes hopelessly snarled, we can't get gasoline from the electric

I
▼

pumps, we can't learn from "the authorities" what to do, and there's not much that we could do anyway.

We are helplessly dependent upon a supply system that, with a hiccup, could leave us starving. What would happen to your family if the convenience store around the corner didn't have food tomorrow? What would happen if the large grocery store in the shopping center didn't open—and the next one down the street? Do you have enough stores in your house to get by for several days? Most of us count on being able to go the grocery store every few days. We never consider buying for a month or more. If the supply were disrupted, we would have very little to get us by, and we'd begin to wonder who in the neighborhood might have what we need.

We live to work rather than work to live. We take jobs to "give the best to our families" and then see our families only a few hours a week. By the time we slow down, our children are gone, having been nurtured and raised by Mother Mall. Mother Mall has the answer to all our important needs, with its artificial smells and never-dying lights. You only have to tender a card, and all is yours. If you don't have a card, they send you one unsolicited. And we walk around breathing the cooled, recirculated breaths of countless thousands with no thought of what would happen if the power were to fail or of how long the little red "EXIT" signs would show, or where they are in the first place.

The family—the building block of civilization—is nearing extinction. We rely on outsiders for social training, education, vocational training, and just about everything else. The outsiders may or may not have the best interests of our children at heart, and they may or may not know what they are talking about. Families no longer work together for a tangible, common goal. We seldom gather together for daily family meals, to eat and talk. Even family gatherings are dominated by lots of people and lots of distractions that prevent meaningful communication. Our houses have lots of separate rooms (a measure of our "success"), replete with televisions and computers with Internet hookups to anything and everything outside the home. Almost nothing in our homes promotes getting together as a family and communicating. Most of the time we aren't even in our homes. And the intelligentsia of our society, in a feeble excuse to justify failure, are now proclaiming in treatises and journals that the family isn't really important anyway.

(text continued on page 4)

"DID YOU HEAR THE NEWS?"

We anchored behind a beautiful and remote island in the Bahamas. The wind was light, the fishing was great, and the sun was warm. We could see the ocean bottom beneath our boat more clearly than we could see the coconut palms along the shore. In the cool night, every star sparkled brilliantly against the sharp, black sky, and then the moon rose over the island, its pale brilliance betraying starfish that moved slowly on the white sand below. The next day some friends sailed by outside the reef, heading up-island. We heard them on the VHF and, of course, we hailed them to see how they were doing. The year was 1986.

"Did you hear the news?" they asked. Thinking "the news" must be about some boat's coming or going or someone's breakdown or grounding, I asked what was up. "Well, it seems there's been a bad nuclear explosion or something somewhere in the Soviet Union. We couldn't get many details, but they say it was in Chernobyl, wherever that is." Stunned and inwardly reeling, I asked them if they knew more. "They're talking about maybe a huge cloud of radioactive gas spreading out; no one knows for sure where it will spread and how far it will go. They're saying maybe around the world. It could be very bad. We've been trying to find out more, but that's all we know now."

They sailed on up the chain, leaving us wondering. We couldn't find out more just then, and the boats around us couldn't find out more either. VHF radio chatter diminished to an occasional query. "Has anybody heard anything?" Occasionally we could decipher scratches of commercial AM transmissions, but the news was vague. Was it deliberately vague? Was it just no big deal? Or was everybody already digging holes? We didn't know and couldn't find out, for more than a day and night—a weirdly surrealistic day and night.

But we had no doubts about what we should do. We immediately set sail for an island that we knew had a full and clean abandoned cistern. The barometer was dropping, the wind was clocking, the air was growing moist. We wanted to fill our tanks and everything aboard with good water before the rains came. From the little information we had, those rains, always so welcome, could be bringing death to the water.

A year's supply of food filled every hole below decks. We hadn't stored it for a nuclear disaster; it was just our regular stock that enabled us to be under way for a long time and to save money. Our stores were mostly wheat and grains and canned goods, but they would do. We wondered about our friends ashore. "What if this is for real? What will they do? What can they do?"

Our plan was to head south. We assumed that this band of dust, if it existed, would be more likely to spread in the northern hemisphere. We didn't know whether our winds would soon be full of radiation; this possibility seemed remote, but delay could be dangerous if our fears were warranted. We felt foolish, but we didn't hear any more news and we weren't going to play around. When we reached the island, everyone in the family, including our children—both under six—pitched in to load up with clean water, several aloe plants, and all the fish that we could quickly catch.

Finally, information began to trickle through. The situation was far less serious than we had feared. We didn't head south. We felt much better, although certainly not good. We sailed away from the experience with yet another reminder that we have so much more control at sea, in what we call the real world.

▼

(text continued from page 2)

TAKE CONTROL

We feel trapped. There is nothing that we can really do to break the mold and create something better for our lives and our family. I frequently talk with people about our life on *Chez Nous*. They say, "Oh, I wish I could do that."

"But you can," I say.

"Oh, no, we don't have the money."

"But you probably do. It doesn't take much money; it takes something else. It takes wanting to do it bad enough and making sacrifices; and you have to do things yourself, not pay someone else. You can do it, but you do have to work hard and give up things you don't need anyway."

Their eyes glaze, they smile wanly, and they change the subject.

But *you* can do it.

You can take control of your existence. You can start doing things for yourself instead of for a "system." You can be a family instead of a splintered group. You can raise your children to understand responsibility, to know self-discipline, and to appreciate real values. And you can know the children you raise. You can breathe clean air. You can see the stars through clear skies. You can fill your days with adventure, and you can walk on white sands and share beautiful sunsets. You and your family can go cruising. But you've got to work at it.

And that's what we do in this book. We work at enabling you to take off in a boat and go cruising. We give practical advice for families with a moderate income who want to begin serious live-aboard cruising for extended periods. Although we address families with children, almost all of what we say will be helpful to families cruising before or after children. Our reference point is the sailboat because that's where *we* live, but what we say is relevant to the cruising trawler as well. Some sections are specifically devoted to that mode of travel. We won't address epic around-the-world cruises, although much of what we say is pertinent to that possibility. We talk about everyday getting along in the real world of live-aboard cruising, and about hard work. But mostly we assert one of the very basic premises of cruising: If it isn't fun, it isn't fun.

A CRUISING FRAME
OF MIND

Chapter One

ATTITUDE ADJUSTMENT

Your attitude may be the single most important factor in determining whether you will enjoy cruising and, believe it or not, whether you can afford it. This is good news, because most of us who want to cruise are already developing the right attitude, and cruising can only further it. But developing a really good cruising attitude takes effort. You can't buy it at the store or borrow it from the bank, and everyone on the boat will need a good dose of it because most failures come from underlying misconceptions of what living aboard and cruising are all about. The right attitude will translate directly into dollars and cents, into comfort, into fun, and into a successful lifestyle.

Although you'll continue to develop your cruising attitude long after you're under way, it is important to think about it from the start: your understanding of it will help you evaluate whether the cruising lifestyle is for you. If you want to try this lifestyle, you'll need to begin changing many of the ways you look at things, and your attitude will affect your planning. But it will also affect, in the long run, how much you enjoy the lifestyle. The following sections will give you a good idea of just what a good cruising attitude is.

LIVING IN THE REAL WORLD OF CRUISING

Sailing away on a false premise is like sailing away in a leaky boat. From the very beginning, you'll need to understand what this lifestyle is and what it isn't. Liveaboard cruising is not a cruising vacation. You have taken your "real world" with you, and it is very different from what it used to be. Boating is no longer a weekend party. You'll have fun and enjoy a better way of living, but you'll also deal with basic, no-frill survival issues every day. You'll work very hard at it. The lifestyle itself, in part, becomes a job.

(text continued on page 9)

"MAYBE NEXT WEEK"

When we first met Donnie around 1983, he had already been cruising with Woofer for a long long time. Donnie was an artist, carving beautiful fishes from selected pieces of wood found on island beaches and in mangrove swamps. Woofer was a gray muzzled attack dachshund, or at least that's the impression he wanted to give if an unknown came too close to their sailboat. Donnie had built the boat of cement and chicken wire (ferrocement), and he had built it well—it floated. At one time its engine was beautifully painted in assorted colors, with an emphasis on lavender and purple. "Might as well do something with it," Donnie said, "since it never works."

It was late February and Donnie hadn't had Christmas. His friends back in the States had sent him a Christmas package, but it hadn't arrived yet. Mail came only once a week by mailboat. It was left off on a pier, usually around 2 A.M., on an island around 10 miles to the south. The boat was always called De Mail, and you would just shrug if your package wasn't on it. You'd think, "Maybe next week." If it was stormy the next week, or if De Mail had broken down, nobody's mail came that week either, and so it was easy for time and lost mail to slide by unnoticed. "That's all right," Donnie had said to Woofer, "we'll just have Christmas when De Mail brings it to us."

We were sharing a harbor up in the mangroves of a lonely island. A long dock stretched from the shore into the deep water, and each of us had tied up to a side. One Wednesday morning Donnie got a call on the VHF. "Hey, mon, you got a pockage on de dock." It took much of a day to get down-island and then back again in the dinghy, but the trip was worth it because Christmas had come. But Donnie wouldn't open the pockage. "Christmas among friends just won't be right without a turkey," he confided. "I'm going to get one."

Getting a turkey in the Out Islands wasn't exactly a next-day event. You had to go back down-island, wait for the one phone, and order the turkey from Nassau. And then it had to come on De Mail. You hoped that it would still be frozen. This depended upon numerous things. First, someone in Nassau had to get it from the store to De Mail when De Mail was in harbor, without any prolonged delays through town and down the dock. Then someone on De Mail had to put it in the freezer—right away. Then the freezer had to be working, and remain working throughout the trip. The crew on De Mail hopefully had not been working too hard on the trip, because that might mean a little bit of extra hunger—and a turkey is a turkey. If De Mail made it to the island, someone had to be at the dock in the dark of morning to receive the turkey and get it back up-island in reasonably good shape. But Donnie wanted a real Christmas, and he ordered his turkey.

About three weeks later it came, and judging from the number of angles on the package, it had only been thawed and refrozen a few times. It was one of the ones you put in an oven and wait for a little signal to pop out. The turkey growers had obviously been thinking of a typical home oven, but with a lot of pots and a good fire going on the shore, Donnie cooked his turkey. Of course, by now he had considerable help.

As evening and the smell of roasted turkey settled over the mangroves, we got ready for Christmas. Donnie wore an ancient, mildewed swallowtail coat, which he stored in his bilge for special occasions. His T-shirt was painted to look like a dress shirt with bow tie and ruffles. His tattered shorts were the same, and only, pair he had worn for the last several years. The rest of us also dressed appropriately.

We had made the unfortunate mistake of opening all our presents on Christmas Day, a couple of months earlier, but we scrounged up some more presents. Our daughters, who were still young at the time, had no problem with the concept of two Christmases. It was a grand event, unlike any Christmas we had ever celebrated. Conch salad, cabbage, bananas, rum in fitting quantities for the adults, and, of course, The Turkey. The Christmas pockage was opened on the dock under the stars, with the sound of palm fronds slatting in the wind. Woofer, not permitted to eat the bones, nevertheless had a Christmas-full look about him. "I guess," said Donnie, "that we'll have Christmas again sometime next year."

▼

(text continued from page 7)

In many ways this job is like your job ashore. You have to train for it, and with experience you will get better. Also, like a shoreside job, you will find that if you don't do it right you may be terminated, but this termination may be more serious than getting fired. Thankfully, you won't have a boss whose main concern is "The Company." You'll be the boss, and your main concern will be your family, your home, and your quality of life. But there will be little room for slack or passing the buck. And there may not be any vacations on the horizon. A vacation would mean getting away from the boat, or tying up for lengthy and expensive stays at marinas where you don't have to worry as much about the mechanical systems, anchors dragging, and weather. When cruising, you won't be splurging on a once-a-year vacation, and, unless you have plenty of money, there may be little opportunity to take a break even when things get bad. And, you will find that you are almost always on duty. Storms don't blow through just from nine to five.

(text continued on page 11)

▼

"IT WAS COMING"

The day began at first light, when we pulled anchor at the southern end of the Alligator River and headed north toward the open water of Albemarle Sound. Although the ICW passage across the sound is only around 15 miles, it can be so rough that large tugs often wait days before crossing. The shallow waters and long fetches turn orderly waves into hard, square battering rams. On this day, the southwesterly winds made a great sail of it, but also a very rough one. When we reached the other side in midafternoon, we anchored in the mouth of Broad Creek in the North River. A strong front with severe storms was on the way, and this is a good anchorage for westerly weather. After securing the sails, we began to relax for the evening, happy in the thought that we were in a good place to comfortably ride out the blow and get some rest.

Then we found that someone had left the lid open on one of the heads. The rolling had shaken a sewing box loose from a shelf, and most of its contents had dumped into the head. As you may know, a marine head doesn't do well with anything except what you've eaten and small amounts of toilet paper. The needles, pins, bobbin wheels, and everything else had to be removed. I wasn't happy. This wasn't my idea of a quiet afternoon. The job required taking apart the pump assembly, removing the "foreign objects" and putting it all back together again. Needless to say, it also involved a lengthy cleanup. The job finally over, and thinking that a short cocktail hour and nice evening meal were going to be very welcome, I went on deck for a breath of desperately needed fresh air.

It was coming. A line squall backed by a cold front packing loads of fresh air was already visible behind the trees ashore and sweeping across the sky. It was coming from the west as expected, and we were in a safe anchorage. Then I noticed small disturbances on the water, all around the boat. Tiny gusts began tugging and tearing at the furled sails, rigging, and "cruising junk" on deck. Looking around I saw that we were in the midst of an active flock of small tornadolike funnels, some connecting with the water and forming spouts. At first I was angry, as buckets and other gear began to get sucked off the deck and into the air. I went forward and actually began pulling things out of the air to stuff into tight places on deck. I had to stop when one playful twister pulled my shirt up over my head and arms.

The world quieted. The wind wall under the roll of clouds hadn't reached us yet, but I could see the leaves on the trees ashore turning white. I heard a loud, strange noise and looked astern. The baby tornadoes had fused. A little over a mile off our stern was one of the largest waterspouts I had ever seen, wide with a thousand explosions, sucking and tearing the water as it headed away. The cold front hit like a brick wall, we careened, the anchor held, the rains cleansed the boat, the air cooled and refreshed, and we went below for dinner, ready to relax. It was growing dark.

Then we heard the high-water bilge alarm. "From the rain," I thought, "or the seas coming down the anchor hole during the crossing." I peered into the bilge to confirm that there was nothing too much amiss, and we began pumping. But the water level didn't go down. And the pump was running too smoothly. Something was wrong. We stopped the pump, I grabbed my tools, and then I began the long task of disconnecting the wiring and hose clamps and loosening the screws. After freeing the pump, I began to take it apart. As expected, debris had become trapped in one of the valves. I cleaned it out and replaced the old valves with new ones. But how did that debris get past the strainer—and would this happen again? I put the pump back together, fit it back into position, and began to hook it up. Then I noticed that the outlet fitting had cracked, obviously due to long-term stress from the curved hose. I had to disconnect the pump, pull it out again, remove the stump of the fitting from the pump body, remove a good fitting from a spare freshwater pump, install it on the bilge pump, and hook it all up again. We don't leave bilge pump problems unsolved, so we next tackled the intake hose in the lowest part of the bilge. Yes, the screen had torn, and yes, we replaced it with a new screen we fortunately had aboard. If we hadn't, the same thing could have happened again with worse consequences.

No, this wasn't a typical evening; but it wasn't atypical either. It was part of our lifestyle.

▼

(text continued from page 9)

A VACATION IT'S NOT

Describing the cruising life to noncruisers can be frustrating. Many think that all we do is lie around while waiters in white jackets serve us piña coladas. Most people, when dreaming of the big plunge, think of boating experiences that compare poorly with liveaboard cruising. Their only contact with this world has been weekends and vacations keyed to escapism, relaxation, and pleasurable pursuits. In this scenario, by the time the family begins to feel crowded and things aboard start to break, it is time to go back home and leave the boat in a marina, where friendly personnel are happy to take care of any really serious problems. The steady income from the job will pay the yard bill. There is nothing wrong with this picture, but it does very little to prepare you for the real world of cruising.

▼

Although a typical sabbatical-leave cruise of a year or so can help prepare you for long-term cruising, such trips are comparable to long vacations. Any type of cruising that has a definite termination is much easier. Many repairs can be put off until the family is back ashore with a good income and a place to live that is far away from the dust and grime of the repair work. On a term cruise, there is a nest egg that needs to last only for a certain period, and expenses can be more easily controlled. If you know how much you have and how long it must last, you can easily tailor your spending to fit. For example, if you find the funds are running low, you can do more sailing and less powering. You can anchor out more and visit marinas less. And, you probably know that when the cruise and savings end, there will be a job waiting for you and new money coming in.

THE MYTH OF THE CURE-ALL CRUISE

One of the most common causes of failing at the liveaboard lifestyle is the belief that a cruise will cure a dysfunctional family. Life doesn't begin anew just because you take off. It continues, carrying with it much of the baggage of the past.

Sometimes people go cruising because their marriage is in trouble. The hope is that sailing away to tropical honeymoon isles will make it right. Don't count on it. It will still take hard work at the basic things that make a marriage successful; being on the boat won't change that. Ashore you can escape from each other rather easily. One or both of you has a job outside the home, and so you must deal with each other only a few hours of the day. Ashore you are accustomed to external stresses. At sea you will have to become accustomed to new ones—storms, a dragging anchor, lack of supplies, and breakdowns.

Some people go on a cruise to mend a broken heart. The theory is that there is nothing like a brave sail around the world to forget a tragedy. A cruising lifestyle can help you focus on new goals, new friends, and new experiences, but the memories seldom fade away over the horizon. And being alone at sea for long periods gives you more time to brood over problems, perhaps making them worse. There's no place like the ocean for thinking. What helps is sharing the loss or the problem with good friends you meet underway. And the same holds true ashore.

Another frequent, and perhaps sadder, reason for choosing the liveaboard lifestyle is to deal with kids who are "in trouble" or "out of control." The popular misconception is that if you get the kid on a boat, the sun and sea will wash away all the bad vibes, and she or he will be obedient, a good student, content to surf and fish—and all will be well again. Unless you work extremely hard at involving your child in these healthier aspects of life afloat and deal directly with her or his problems, you won't find any miracles at sea. Parents often spend most of their time enjoying their new-found paradise, leaving the kids to their own devices. (Later chapters provide details about special things you can do with kids afloat.)

Parents frequently think that the cruising lifestyle coupled with home education will help kids who have "learning disabilities." This term is widely used by professional educators, but sometimes the "disability" is caused by failure of the educational system itself. It's true that many cruising kids who began with a history of poor school performance become very good students. They develop self-confidence and seem happier within a year or so of adopting this lifestyle. But these changes are always achieved through the hard work, dedication, perseverance, and understanding of the parents, who forgo time on the beach and vacation living to be good teachers and good parents. It doesn't happen just because they live on a boat.

Many people adopt this lifestyle right after they have unexpectedly lost their job ashore. They believe that some magical occurrence will find them new jobs and new lives, or that things will be better when they return to shore. If you lose your job and you aren't prepared financially, you are only postponing the inevitable. Your funds may run out, and you may find yourself less employable than before. If you are in this category, think these things through, with your specific circumstances in mind.

Unfortunately, people sometimes choose this lifestyle in an attempt to cure an addiction. Alcoholism is perhaps one of the most common problems. Alcoholics Anonymous and similar groups are available in the cruising community, and in popular harbors it isn't unusual to hear meeting announcements on the VHF radio. But, as is true ashore, there is no easy cure aboard. Recovery requires the same effort and help. At sea, the person may be in a situation where he really needs that help and can't find it.

The bottom line is that you must have your head in the right place, you must have the right attitude, and you must be willing to put effort into solving any problem you bring with you. This lifestyle may help you solve some problems, but it isn't a cure-all.

Chapter Two
LIVING ON THE HOOK

Most of the time you will be on the move or on the hook, with the dinghy as the only way off the boat. Unless you plan to spend a lot of money very quickly, you will seldom tie up at marinas. This confinement can take an incredible amount of adjustment for many people, and normal vacation cruising doesn't prepare you for it. Your life will center around a small boat that, while serving as the key to your freedom, will, paradoxically, limit many of your customary habits.

Elizabeth Harbour, at Great Exuma Island in the Bahamas, is a favorite of many cruisers, yet it provides an excellent case study of cruises gone bad. On one side of the harbor are pretty beaches; on the other side is the quaint village of George Town. But the harbor has a northwest–southeast slant, and when the winds blow strong from either direction the harbor begins to roll. There is an old saying in the Bahamas: "When de wind she blow for one day, den she blow for two. When she blow for two days, den she blow for t'ree. When she blow for t'ree days, den she blow for . . . An' you know, mon, she just keeps on blowing." Often the winds do blow, for days, particularly out of the southeast. Many cruisers find themselves trapped on their boats by high waves, making any dinghy trip something like a ride inside a washing machine. It's entertaining to listen to them on the VHF radio. Some fuss and fight; some tell stories; some have a "joke time" on a particular channel, taking turns telling the best of the worst; some read stories; some even play vintage music over a prearranged channel. People start dreaming about things like pizzas and hoagies, and others start snapping at anyone and everyone within shouting or VHF range. But from some boats, domestic fights boil out from the companionways, spouses threaten to leave as soon as they can get ashore, and sometimes do. A weeklong southeasterly can ruin a lifetime cruise.

ATTITUDE AND LIVING AT ANCHOR

Many experiences that would hardly be noticed ashore can be frightening, and dangerous, out on the hook. And problems that are "no problem" ashore will be big problems at anchor, and vice versa. So, you must prepare yourself to live a very different existence.

Little things like grocery shopping and laundry will become all-day affairs. A weather warning that says a storm is coming and advises you to go inside immediately and seek shelter will have a totally different meaning at sea than it would ashore. The dinghy fun-toy will become one of the most important working possessions you have. Getting mail will sometimes be reminiscent of the days of the Pony Express. Easy things are hard, hard things are harder, but the effort is worth it.

The wrong frame of mind for living on the hook can be a real cruise killer. Some of the basics, with tips for adjusting to this new life, are covered below. Throughout the book you'll learn about many other things that help to make the cruising lifestyle as fun as it ought to be. Remember that as you cruise, you'll be sharing great times with new friends in beautiful and exciting places. But there will also be long passages and stormy anchorages in which you must get along aboard ship in circumstances that are very different from those to which you are accustomed.

Your dinghy will be one of your most important possessions.

WHO DO YOU LIKE?

First, you have to like everyone aboard. You'll also need a high level of tolerance. This may sound simplistic, but think about it. How often do you really spend a lot of time together in that big box of rooms where you live now? And I don't mean just sleeping under the same roof. I mean spending time during which you have to look at each other, talk to each other, deal with each other, and do things with each other whether you feel like it or not. Couples who have been married for years have split soon after beginning their cruise, because they really hadn't spent time together before and didn't get to know each other until the cruise.

Before you set off and while you can still easily abort your plans, eat together, talk together, do things together—just be together. Don't think that this will all "work out" while you are underway. It won't be easy to get to know and appreciate one another when your elbow room suddenly becomes a small fraction of that to which you are accustomed and a new and unfamiliar array of stresses are added to your lives.

Set aside weekends when your family can do something that doesn't involve distractions that make it unnecessary to interact. Have you noticed that most "vacation attractions" are set up so that you don't really have to talk, listen, or do much of anything with family members other than just go there, spend the money, and play the games? Practice being alone together. Set aside a weekend during which you don't leave the house. Then spend another weekend when you use only three rooms of the house, such as the kitchen, bedroom, and bathroom. During these weekends, limit your TV time and plan to do things that necessitate interaction among family members. You must find out if you can make it as a family *before* you go cruising.

ALONE-TIME CRUISES

If you already have a boat, or can afford to charter one, take family vacation cruises. Pretend that you are sailing around in the islands with no marinas and few diversions other than swimming, diving, hiking, or walking the beach. When you're actually cruising, you'll indeed find many other diversions, and friends to share them with. But you'll also encounter long passages, stormy periods, and deserted anchorages, and you'll have to cope together—without outside help. So plan your vacation cruises near remote areas and avoid marinas and shoreside "attractions."

On these preparatory cruises, take along things to do on the boat that involve the whole family. It amazes us when we visit friends who are on vacation cruises and find that almost everything they brought aboard relates to shoreside diversions: restaurant clothes, a television set, tennis and golf equipment—and on it goes. The cruising lifestyle is not made up of wet car trips to resorts where everyone can immediately become immersed in escapist pursuits. Unless you are wealthy, you won't be able to marina hop. Plan a repair or maintenance project the whole family can help with while cruising. The project shouldn't consume the cruise, and it shouldn't destroy the fun of the vacation, but it should be a project you can complete. It may involve polishing the stainless or teak, or maybe just rearranging storage and living spaces. If you can't find a project everyone can do, think of others that individual family members can work on. Reporting back and talking about progress and problems around the dinner table can be a good introduction to shared family living while cruising.

Projects for the kids are particularly important. They should be real jobs of clear importance to the well-being of the family or boat, and they should also involve tasks that are understandable and that can be accomplished in a reasonable time frame. Examples include cleaning the hull, removing equipment from lockers for drying, cooking, food preparation, and foredeck-to-cockpit message relay during anchoring. As the kids get older, they should be entrusted with more responsibility. Rebuilding pumps, changing oil, and changing spark plugs on the outboard are but a few examples. Our girls had rebuilt a carburetor by ages 13 and 15. It is important to explain the why as well as the how. Utilize your kids' special talents and abilities. For example, it shouldn't surprise you if they see much better than you do. Our kids have gotten us out of some real messes just because we had them on watch, looking for obscure buoys and landmarks. You know that little thing you dropped into the tiny space? Maybe your kid can get his hand in. (Be sure it is a safe place.) You will be rewarded by the time you spend with your kids, by jobs well done that relieve you of some of the load, and by a closer family. You will also probably find that your kids, despite occasional bouts of complaining (just like you and me), take pride in their home and family and in the fact that they are important contributing members.

Take along things that will enable family members to have "alone" recreation time while on the boat. These might include good books, favorite hobbies (does someone play the guitar or like

(text continued on page 19)

"IT WAS JUST A LITTLE CUT"

We were once holed up in a safe harbor during a long blow. We were headed back to the States, but slowly. We never rush to leave the islands. One of our evening pursuits during bad weather is to have a team effort at preparing a *Chez Nous* Pizza Supreme. We pull out all the stops, foraging into all corners of the bilge for squirreled-away supplies, and we build the best pizza anyone could ever dream of eating. Of course, as we are doing this, we are telling as many friends as possible about it over the VHF.

On this occasion, to suit me, Carolyn opened a can of anchovies. In doing so she cut her finger on the tin—just a tiny cut. We treated it carefully, as always, and enjoyed the pizza. Two days later we noticed tiny dark spots around the cut, and her arm was painful. The next day the spots had spread slightly. The weather was calming, but there was a lot of sea and reef between us and civilization. Around us were only deserted islands—

Chez Nous *Pizza Supreme.*

beautiful in any other circumstances. We set sail, but were several days away from the coast. We hoped she would be better the next day, but she wasn't.

It had been just a little cut; but it was apparent that she now had blood poisoning or a serious infection of some kind. Ashore, we would have been able to get in the car as soon as we saw the symptoms, drive a few minutes, spend around $30 for a doctor, and have no more worries. In this instance, we would have needed a helicopter to get her to a doctor. We called out on the VHF to find out if a nearby boat had a doctor on board. There were none, but a registered nurse sailing a few miles away answered. She listened to our description and confirmed our fears, but suggested that we watch the cut and continue back to the States.

We decided to give Carolyn strong antibiotics and sailed on, checking the finger every half hour or so, even during the night watches. This time the weather cooperated. We made record time to the east coast of Florida, putting in at Fort Pierce, and went straight to a marina and a doctor. It was just an unusual infection, and the doctor prescribed more antibiotics. We even got a bonus. For $30, we received—in addition to the office visit—two cases of chicken pox. A teenager had visited the same doctor about some of *his* spots. The chicken pox fully manifested itself in both of the girls in due course; we had time to reach a community, however, where it was better to go through the ordeal. We no longer had to worry about the girls contracting chicken pox out in the islands.

▼

(text continued from page 17)

to paint?), a deck of cards, school books and projects, or anything else that fits on the boat and encourages family members to enjoy individual pursuits away from the family psychologically though close physically. Computers have become popular cruising equipment, and can provide educational entertainment as well as perform practical functions. Information on the cruising computer will pop up repeatedly as you read this book. Music can be good for this, but we have noticed that some overdose on headphones for hours, oblivious to people and responsibilities. Keep in mind that if you were long-term cruising, each crewmember would have continuing duties to maintain the well-being of the home and family. Escapes from interrelating should be restorative; they should not encourage avoidance of responsibilities.

Try to live aboard on your mooring or at the marina before casting off. We know many cruisers who have done this, and we recommend it. The sooner you begin, the better. Elsewhere in this book, you'll learn about the different ways in which doing this can help. You would, presumably, be living aboard where you can easily get off and go about shoreside pursuits; thus, the experience won't completely prepare you for full-time living aboard at anchor. But you'll still get a taste of the new experience of close living with your family. If you do this, spend some weekends on the boat during which you don't get off, and try the "alone-time cruises" discussed above.

Chapter Three
CRUISING ISN'T PINK AND BLUE

Equality of the sexes is a stylish concept now. Those successfully going to sea in cruising boats learned this long ago—without the government's help.

ONLY MOTHER OCEAN IS MACHO

One of the most common misconceptions adopted by cruising couples is the "for men only" philosophy. You know the scenario: the macho male is standing nobly at the wheel, his new captain's hat cocked back, yelling at his 120-pound spouse who is up on the bow with a 45-pound anchor and hundreds of pounds of chain. This is a bad way to start, for two reasons: it's unsafe, and it ignores the fact that cruising is a partnership. If one spouse is just along for the ride, both spouses are soon going to be unhappy. This example doesn't imply that women can't do an excellent job on the foredeck; they can and should be equal partners in all duties and responsibilities aboard.

One never knows what will happen at sea. If either partner is unable to perform the jobs that the other customarily performs, the couple might find themselves in deep trouble. The woman may not have the experience or training to do a particular job, and it's true that areas of expertise vary, but if macho man is sick or injured, the woman will have to keep the boat afloat and get it safely back to shore. All crewmembers should try to understand and be able to perform each other's jobs. If the man is the chief engine-room monkey, the woman can watch, help, and ask questions. And the man had better be able to prepare meals at sea, and know where food supplies are stored.

SHARE THE LOAD

As elsewhere in life, it is easy to feel that your efforts aren't appreciated by your cruising family. If, however, they have also done or shared the job, they will respect what you have endured and accomplished. Men (including me) moan about the difficulties of repairing the engine in cramped quarters while rolling around at sea. But some men completely overlook the extra difficulty and the time involved in doing what they consider to be their wife's jobs. For example, grocery shopping from the house may take an hour; it may take a full day when cruising. You have to go ashore with the dinghy, secure it, get to the store (probably walk), do the shopping, get the groceries back to the dinghy, load them, dinghy out to the boat, get the groceries aboard, and—finally—store them. This is usually a two-person or family venture. The same may be true of laundry (see Mel's discussion of this task in chapter 20). Cooking, washing dishes, and storing and retrieving supplies are all more difficult and take more time aboard than they ever did ashore. I'm not suggesting that these are women's tasks. I'm simply pointing out that many families still think this way. And many men are so wrapped up in their new sense of self-importance as "captain of the ship" that they overlook the real world around them and the fact that they need to chip in where and when needed—which may be a place where they weren't needed before.

WHO IS CAPTAIN?

Because both lives and fortunes are at stake, all decisions should be made as a partnership. Spouses and older children should take part, and each person should know enough about a particular subject to make an informed decision.

Sometimes the cruise has commenced with a somewhat reluctant wife who is "doing it for the husband." As difficulties mount and dangers become obvious, the wife will become less happy and more insecure. If, on the other hand, she shares in running the boat (and this works both ways with all shipboard jobs and decisions), the boat will be safer, and the reluctant wife will feel more at ease.

After a seminar, a military man once asked me, "What do you do about the fact that there has to be a captain who takes ultimate responsibility and who must make command decisions in emergencies? How does this fit in with the husband/wife partnership theory of cruising?" That excellent question pointed out a very real concern for most couples. I asked him about his solution. "We take turns. One week I'm the captain, the next week she is." If this works for you, it may be a good solution. It may also help to know that we have experienced few emergencies during which there was no time for discussion. And on a typical cruising boat with only a few people aboard, the designated captain may well be exhausted or sick, or too busy with other matters to make a decision. Cruising boats aren't military or commercial giants where one person can dedicate all of his time to making "ultimate decisions," while officers and crew do everything else. You will have to determine what works best for *you*, but the more each of you knows and can do, including making decisions, the safer and happier you will be.

Full-time cruising gives meaning to the word "partnership" in unimaginable ways.

Chapter Four
ARE YOU READY TO BE DIFFERENT?

Do not expect total support and appreciation from the shoreside community. You are doing something different, and your attitudes will gradually diverge from theirs. This alone bothers some people. Our society is increasingly intolerant of differences. This is one of the reasons you are abandoning a traditional shoreside lifestyle, isn't it?

WHAT THEY THINK OF US

Many shoreside dwellers who think less of cruisers envision luxurious yachts with doting stewards. Many have no concept of the work required to live aboard; they have no concept of anything but the fingertip conveniences our society expects. When you try to explain about fixing the engine in the middle of the night during a rough offshore passage, they don't have a clue.

You may also hear comments implying that yours is a meaningless existence, that you're "irresponsible" and "don't contribute." I still have several lawyer acquaintances who make tons of money. Yet they spend more money than they make, and think nothing of it. "It's my job," they say. They live from spoon to mouth, day to day, buying whatever they want. They spend many thousands of dollars a year to lie around in vacation resorts. They trade their cars in for new ones every two to three years. They move to bigger houses every few years; carpenters and plumbers fix whatever doesn't work. They send their children to exclusive schools, but they don't know who their children are. Every day they spend hours solving paper problems in a paper society, surrounded by artificial climate. If they want to sweat, they spend big bucks to go to health spas and use artificial workout machines. "Only the right one will do." And they think I'm loafing through a meaningless existence. When I see them socially they say, with a polite pause, "And do you still live on a . . . *boat*?" I reply, "Do you still live in a . . . *house*?" These people don't bother me; don't let them bother you. You'll find many other acquaintances and friends who understand and respect what you do, and who realize that it takes work.

LIVEABOARD LAWS

A few shoreside communities attempt to pass discriminatory and illegal restrictions on living aboard. These attempts are based on the assumption that liveaboards would rather move on than fight in court. Unfortunately, this assumption is often correct; but, successful court challenges to these laws are on the increase. Word gets around in the cruising community, and you will probably be well informed about these discriminatory places. We have found that if we respect the legitimate concerns and privacy of those living ashore, we all get along fine. We have also met exceptionally nice folks ashore who are interested in what we are doing, who will help if they can, and who have become good friends.

Problems generally arise when cruisers stop cruising, drop the hook, and begin to live permanently in one anchorage. Some show little respect for the concerns of those ashore, and these cruisers offer no community support but use community services—education, garbage collection, and police protection, to name a few. Hanging clothes, especially underwear, on the lifelines or in the rigging is another habit that upsets some people. Running noisy gasoline deck generators in the quiet of the night near someone's backyard can easily provoke someone's wrath. In my view, navigable waters should be generally free for anchoring as long as it's safe to anchor. But if I had spent a lot of money for a house on shore and then found someone settled in just off my dock, I have to admit that I would get a little testy, too. The solution is simple: be courteous and respectful of other people and their property. Unfortunately, no matter how *you* behave, you may suffer from the effects of the rare discourteous cruiser who preceded you.

A LITTLE HELP FROM YOUR FRIENDS

It helps to find cruising friends who are moving in the same direction, to share times and talks at anchor. You'll be surprised by how friendly other cruisers are, and you'll appreciate the frontier spirit of helping one another, away from the world ashore with all of its built-in safety nets. But how do you meet other cruisers?

Even though you are all moving along in separate boats without telephones, meeting people at sea tends to be much easier than it is ashore. For example, other boats will probably share your anchorage. Anchor a discreet distance away, but do a little exploring in the dinghy before dinner. If your neighbors are sitting in the cockpit, stop alongside to say "hello." Don't tie or hang on to their boat unless they invite you to do so; just stop a few yards off. Most people are delighted to chat, and they might invite you aboard. This will give everyone a chance to appraise one another, to determine mutual interests. You'll make many new acquaintances this way. Remember, however, that all cruisers are not alike. Sometimes you won't want to associate with another cruiser—or he or she with you—just as you don't associate with everyone on shore. Often, you'll want to be alone and enjoy private time at anchor.

We've passed many cruisers as we've sailed or motored along; particularly on the waterways. A pass on the Intracoastal Waterway (ICW), for example, gives you a chance to look over the other boat and all or some of the crew. Most people wave; sometimes we slow down for a few minutes of side-by-side cruising and a chat— if it's safe to do so. Sometimes one cruiser hails another on the VHF with a question about the boat's rig, power, dinghy, or whatever. Sometimes folks just call each other and ask, "Where are you from and where are you bound? Do you know any good anchorages up ahead?" In this way, you'll find new friends quickly.

Most cruisers have favorite anchorages where they gather for the winter, to provision, or to await the weather. In these places, there will be parties on the beach, chats back and forth on the VHF, and other ways to socialize. Some of our favorites on the East Coast are Annapolis, Maryland; Beaufort, North Carolina; Lake Worth at Palm Beach, Florida; Ft. Lauderdale, Florida (there isn't much room for anchoring); the area around Dinner Key and No Name Harbor near Miami, Florida; Marathon, in the Florida Keys; and Key West, Florida. In the Bahamas you'll find large cruising communities around Marsh Harbour, Abaco, and its neighboring islands, and George Town in the lower Exumas.

Cruising magazines, such as *Cruising World,* inform you of news and events; cruising organizations, such as the Seven Seas Cruising Association (1525 S. Andrews, Suite 217, Ft. Lauderdale, FL 33316; 954-463-2431; e-mail: SSCA@BCFREENET.SEFLIN.LIB.FL.US), circulate newsletters and hold seminars and meetings. If you become a licensed amateur radio operator (ham) or use marine single sideband, you will meet many people as you join in on their talk frequencies and attend ham gatherings. (See chapter 6 for more about communications.)

Your existence at sea will indeed be a little like that of the U.S. pioneers. In those days, people relied not only on themselves but also on each other; there was no "Big Brother" to do it for them. At sea, cruisers always lend a helping hand when there's a problem. And when you get together, you have common bonds: basic survival, a love of cruising, and the lifestyle. There is nothing like finding kindred spirits to make you feel comfortable with your choice and to ease the shift from a shoreside mentality to that of the cruiser.

So, good cruising requires and brings about changes in attitude. But this is what you wanted anyway, isn't it?

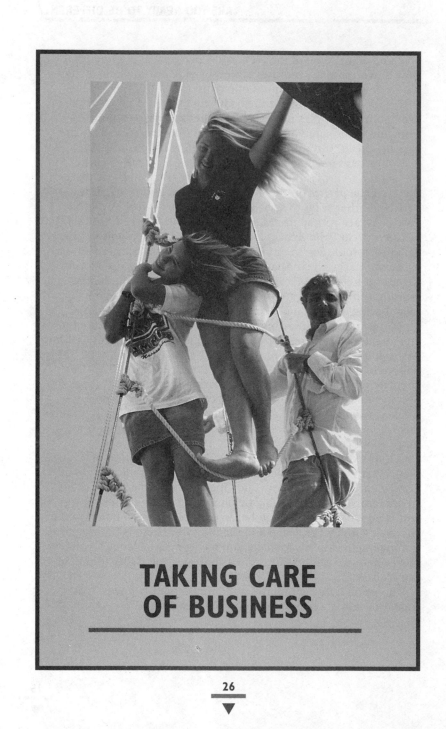

TAKING CARE
OF BUSINESS

Chapter Five

DOLLARS AND SENSE

Perhaps the most frequent questions potential liveaboards ask are "How do you afford it?" and "How much does it cost to cruise for a year?" The answers are seldom satisfying, but they are realistic. To the first we say, "We afford it by not spending money." To the second we say, "It depends on what you spend." People then often roll their eyes. "What a cop-out answer," they think. They don't understand what cruising is all about, and they haven't developed the cruising attitude.

We've all heard the old saying: "If you have to ask, you can't afford it." This isn't applicable to cruising, but a variation of that old saying is applicable: "If you think there is a set figure, you probably aren't suited for cruising." No one should begin this lifestyle if he or she can't swing it financially; but, the bottom line is still your attitude.

THE BOTTOM LINE

Let's get the thirst for numbers out of the way. The typical cruising family of two to four people probably spends between $6,000 and $25,000 per year. Yes, that is a wide range, but these figures are almost irrelevant; they show that the cost of full-time cruising is up to you. As I explain further, you'll see that you can—and must—control your budget.

Your attitude's effect on cost is obvious if you think about it. Do you ask yourself whether you can afford your life ashore over the next few years? Probably not, because it is an ongoing life and you "make do" on a daily basis with earnings and expenditures. The same holds true for cruising, although you can have much tighter control over spending than you do ashore. True, you won't have that wonderful shoreside income, but you won't be spending it either. If, however, you keep your shoreside attitudes and habits, cruising will be prohibitively expensive. For example, couples who complain that they are running out of money shouldn't regularly eat out in restaurants or stop frequently at marinas.

IT'S A JOB

Full-time cruising is not a vacation. It's a full-time job. It is an immensely rewarding job, and it's fun, but it's a tough job that has you on call 24 hours a day and pays in negative numbers. For example, if you put off maintenance and repair of the hundreds of items that need constant attention, even on a simple boat, your expenses will mount when systems start to crash. On the other hand, if you catch your own fish, your savings in food costs may be significant. In the end, your willingness and ability to be self-sufficient will have the most significant effect on your financial survival. Self-sufficiency can save you fortunes. Benjamin Franklin's adage may no longer be politically correct, but it's still true: "A penny saved is a penny earned."

Many variables directly affect the cruising-dollar equation. These include the types of insurance you carry, the size and type of boat, your equipment (the more you have, the more you will have to fix—but some equipment can save money), the number of people in your family, your savings, and your ability to generate income. Other variables affect the equation in more subtle but equally important ways. These include ordering of priorities, self-reliance, and your tolerance for a life without most of the expensive pursuits with which our society ensnares us.

CONTROL YOUR BUDGET

A common denominator for all cruisers is that the lifestyle lends itself to habits that enable you to get by on considerably less income than you would ashore. In fact, the lifestyle is, in part, defined by attributes that give you more control over your financial status than neat columns of numbers would imply; and the issue of whether you can afford it is, to a large extent, a matter of whether you really want to. You pay the "cost" of living aboard and cruising with much more than dollars. Therefore, you won't find a list of items and corresponding costs in this book. These elicit artificial conclusions and automatic decisions. Instead, you'll find information that will enable you to make it work and that lets *you* decide whether the experience is worth the real cost.

Cruisers on sabbatical can benefit greatly from the budgeting lessons of long-term cruising. If you know the length of your cruise and how much savings you have, you can easily tailor your trip to fit your budget. Your cruise can be much less expensive than expected, and you may go home with a sense of genuine accomplishment, a feeling that you've done more than take just another long vacation. You may even decide not to go back.

INSURANCE

For many cruisers, after the boat has been purchased and equipped, the single most expensive item they purchase will be insurance. This huge bite gulps down enormous chunks of a cruiser's assets each year. As a result, many just don't carry it. They say they are "self-insured." The reality is that if they foul on a reef, the cruise ends. If they drag down on someone and damage the other boat, their boat may be seized on the spot to satisfy claims. No one can make this decision for you. We offer only pros and cons from the cruising perspective.

BOAT INSURANCE

As mentioned above, boat insurance is one of the biggest budget items for many cruisers. Predictably, deciding whether to carry it represents one of the toughest decisions cruisers will make. The average cost at this time to insure a cruising boat for $150,000 in hull value and typical personal property for travel on the U.S. east coast and in the Bahamas ranges from $2,000 to $2,500 per year. Factors that influence this number include whether you will be out of hurricane-prone areas during hurricane season (usually north of North Carolina), whether you cruise below 20 to 22 degrees of latitude, whether your home base is in a low-risk area such as the mid-Atlantic states, and whether you agree to be out of ice areas in the winter (no problem in complying with this!).

We have boat insurance because our boat is our home—our estate—and because it holds most of what we have. We also have boat insurance because I don't think I could stand the worry if I didn't have it. If you want coverage, ask for a sample policy, read it, and be sure you understand it. We often get samples from several companies because the differences in cost and coverage can be significant.

Some policies discriminate against liveaboards because many insurance-risk evaluators don't fully understand boating. If a boat is tended and watched daily—if it is the core of a family's life—I know it is a very low risk. But insurance agents and underwriters often don't understand this, so they write in all sorts of exclusions or exceptions. For example, personal property is usually inadequately covered. The typical coverage may be fine for a weekend's worth of property, but hardly for all the "stuff" a typical liveaboard owns. Sometimes you can attach a rider that increases the coverage; check with your agent. Many policies limit coverage to certain geographic areas that are deemed "safe." If your boat will be in Florida, the Bahamas, or the Caribbean during hurricane season, for example, the premiums may rocket upward drastically. Some policies simply exclude liveaboards. As you can see, it is important to carefully study any policy to determine its true worth to you.

It isn't unusual for major companies to change their contract language and coverages regularly, so review your renewal policy each year. And it isn't unusual for companies to stop underwriting the risk and then refuse to renew. Cruising friends of ours have received expiration notices weeks or months after their coverage had expired.

Carriers sometimes decide that they must have a current survey prior to renewal. If your boat is more than 10 years old, you will probably have to do this every three years. If you contemplate heading to an area where obtaining a survey would be difficult, ask your agent if you should obtain one before you leave.

Never assume that you're getting a "good deal" from an insurance company. Any reputable firm is in business to make money. No company can afford to be altruistic if it wants to be profitable. One cruising organization found an insurance company that offered its members policies with good wording and low premiums. Some of our friends jumped. After all, the insurance was "for cruisers." The company went broke. Approach insurance coverage as a business venture, for you and the company. And remember: if you do suffer a loss, you want the company to be solvent so that it can pay. Ask your agent for the latest ratings on the carrier she or he recommends. Have the agent explain the rating system, and look at a second rating system for comparison. The higher rating, the better. Even this isn't a guarantee, however.

Travel outside the United States can complicate insurance coverage. If your boat is damaged in another country, collection—and arranging for repairs—can be difficult.

Despite our concerns, we believe in and recommend insurance. We want to keep cruising and couldn't stand the financial loss if our boat were lost. But we don't let insurance lull us into a false sense of security or into a lax attitude about good seamanship. Unfortunately, it lulls others, and you will need to be alert for them and their boats in mooring and anchorage areas, and sometimes even at sea. If you opt for insurance, find an agent who specializes in marine insurance and tell him or her in writing that you live aboard and where and when you will be cruising during the period of coverage. If you intend to be out of the country with slow mail delivery at renewal dates, notify the agent in writing and provide instructions about coverage renewal. Your agent will then know to protect your interests should your carrier fail to renew. Follow up with a verbal discussion. Letters to insurance agents should always be businesslike and courteous. I get the feeling that many agents are biased against cruisers (and everything else the least bit unusual) anyway. This is a shame, even from their perspective, because narrow-mindedness and short-sightedness cut into profit. But if we let our anger (often well founded) glower through in our letters, we may tip the scale against ourselves. Remember that they are considering whether we are an acceptable risk, and they don't have to insure us.

There is one final thing we'd like to warn you about. Many marina contracts have provisions that could void your boat's insurance coverage. If a marina contract (or any other agreement) stipulates that you agree to hold the marina harmless for any claim relating to your boat, or that you give up various rights to recover damages or assert claims of your own, or that you assume risks, that contract may be in violation of your agreement with your insurance company. Such agreements normally state that you cannot give up such rights or do anything to prejudice their rights without their consent. One can hardly blame insurance companies for including such a provision. They don't want to pay if the loss is someone else's fault, and they want the right to have the issue fairly resolved. It seems absurd that a marina would include contract provisions that void its guests' insurance and possibly leave the marina inadequately covered in a disaster. Most marinas I have asked told me that they didn't realize the implications of the provisions. Many weren't aware of the provision at all. It seems this provision is inserted by marina attorneys who are interested in protecting only themselves rather than their clients. If you pay for vessel insurance, and if you go to marinas, be familiar with your insurance contract and read the marina contract. If there is any question, don't sign it; or, cross out and initial any provisions that may void your insurance coverage. Sometimes we just write over our signature that we don't agree to anything in the marina contract that would in any way impair our insurance coverage.

(text continued on page 33)

▼

"END OF DREAM"

The 38-foot cutter pulled into the harbor just after 3 P.M. A strong wind was picking up out of the southwest, and the couple aboard the cutter were happy to be able to relax and settle into the idyllic cruiser's paradise of the Bahamian Out Islands. We watched them for around 30 minutes as they set two anchors—one into the wind, the other downwind. They were careful to stay well upwind and out of the way of the ketch that had anchored before their arrival. The wind increased during the evening hours until it was gusting to 35 miles per hour, sustained at 25. By around 9 P.M. most cruisers were turning out their reading lights and trying to get a little sleep. A cold front came through, as they so often do, around 2 that morning. The night hid the black row of clouds that preceded the solid wall of wind as it marched across the ocean from the north-northwest. When the wind hit, the vessels in the anchorage veered quickly, straining their anchors from nearly the opposite direction they had a few moments before.

The ketch rapidly swung upwind of the cutter, and as it did, the ketch's bow blew sideways, down and downwind—a sure sign of a dragging anchor. Her owner didn't come up on deck until a moment or so after he heard the crash, and the owners of the cutter yelling for help. They were on their bow, desperately trying to hold off the large boat, as the waves ground it into their bowsprit and anchor rollers. Finally the ketch slid by, banging down the side of the cutter. The dragging anchor snagged the cutter's upwind anchor line, breaking its anchor free. The tangle of two boats helplessly careened downwind toward the reef. The cutter's second anchor, a CQR with an all-chain rode, jerked around but held in the soft sand where it had been buried, saving the two boats.

The captain of the ketch was a gentlemen, if not a good seaman. The next morning he dinghied over to check the damage. He gave the owner of the cutter full insurance information and a letter admitting liability. "That's what insurance is for," the two couples agreed, considerably relieved that the horrible night had ended on a friendly note.

The cutter's anchor rollers had both been bent beyond recognition. Neither could be used. Its bow pulpit, twisted back and around, hampered any pretense of anchoring and fouled the roller-furling equipment. Further cruising was out of the question until repairs could be made. The owners dinghied to the small village, which had a phone.

"Fax us the statement, as well as three appraisals and a qualified survey of the damage, and we will get back with you."

"There aren't any surveyors around—there are only two small island villages within 60 miles. There's only one salvage operation that can make an appraisal, or do the work, for that matter. They are 10 miles down the island chain."

"Well, we'd want you to come in to the States to effect the repairs, and we can send our own surveyor then. We probably wouldn't approve of the prices quoted out there, anyway."

End of cruise. End of dream. At least for a while. And so much for what insurance is supposed to be all about.

▼

(text continued from page 31)

HEALTH INSURANCE

The decision of whether to carry health insurance is so personal that it is pointless to discuss it in detail. We have it primarily because we have children. As a rule, cruisers are healthier than people in the shoreside grind. We usually don't get sick unless we are in the States and tied up somewhere. But a serious illness could wipe us out if we weren't insured. To make the premiums affordable, we opted for a large deductible. This hasn't been too bad because we, thankfully, haven't had to see the doctor often. Even with our coverage, there is always the question of what services and charges the carrier will consider reasonable if the injury or illness occurs in a foreign country. A plan in which you must choose from a list of local doctors and hospitals (many HMOs) is often inappropriate to the cruising lifestyle. We pay higher premiums to get comparable coverage outside our base community.

Your cruising lifestyle may enable you to shop for favorable regional rates. Health insurers charge according to the amount of loss in the group and in the geographical area. Traditionally, for example, carriers have had to make fewer payments per insured in southern rural areas as compared to northeastern high-density urban areas. You may wish to choose your base with this in mind. You must be accurate in any statement about any matter, including domicile or residence. Misrepresentation can void a policy. Rules differ with localities and with applications, but generally a home base must be where you have some substantial connection other than just a post office box. It should be, for example, where you vote, where you return to "lick your wounds," and where you actually consider yourself to be "at home."

You may also want medical evacuation insurance. The best health coverage is worthless if you are in a part of the world that has poor medical facilities. The cost of flying someone home can be staggering. Premiums for insurance to cover this are not unreasonable at this time—around $100 per year per person.

OPTING NOT TO SPEND MONEY

As a new cruiser you will be blessed with a wonderful realization: You don't have to do most of the things you had to do ashore. You have choices. If you choose wisely, you will spend considerably less than you would have ever imagined possible for comfortable living, based on your old shoreside perspective.

MARINAS

Some good friends of ours are marina owners. They work hard at their business and have a difficult time with constant interference from the thousands of governmental agencies and busybody citizen committees who think they know all about everything. Thus, these friends will be less than happy to hear that I think marinas are incredibly overpriced (at least in their transient rates—in the Northeast from $2 to $2.50 a foot per night; $1 to $1.50 a foot per night in the mid-Atlantic; and $0.75 to $1.50 a foot per night in the South). I can't imagine regularly spending the money they charge to tie on to a few pilings.

It is so easy to put over the anchor at night. There are no pilings to bang into while docking. There is no hustling about to find an outlet that wasn't burnt out the night before by the previous power-sucking "guest," no hunting around to find out who and how much to pay, no tipping the dockmaster for getting in your way while you are docking, and no signing away of all rights per the docking agreement, which enables them to take your money. And when you want to leave, you don't have to worry about the current past the pilings and the mega motor box blindly backing out a few slips down. When you're on a mooring or in an anchorage, you just pull up anchor, and go.

If you frequent marinas, you'll quickly run out of money—unless you are so wealthy that you bought this book for your hired, uniformed captain. But if you want to save money, you must be prepared to anchor easily and well. This is one of the prerequisites for successful cruising. The requirements are good

▼

Chez Nous *at anchor off Staniel Cay in the Bahamas.*

▼

ground tackle, a good roller system, good recovery equipment, a self-sufficient boat (a boat with all the systems needed to live aboard indefinitely, away from shoreside facilities), and the knowledge of how to use it and its gear. (More on this in chapter 11.) Suffice it to say for now, these features will pay for themselves quickly if they allow you to give up docking at marinas, except in dire need.

OPTIONAL DRESS

The "dress code" of the cruising world is to wear what is practical and be mindful of others' sensitivities. The money people spend ashore each year on clothing, just to remain in style, is staggering. Take this money out of your budget, and sell most of those clothes. What you should keep depends largely on where you intend to cruise and when. If you head south for the winter, you'll need only one or two sets of warm clothes for cold days. (If you intend to cruise in northern latitudes in the summer, or if you may be late heading south, you may need even more warm clothes, but they don't have to be in style.) Even in the Bahamas, temperatures may occasionally be in the 50s, but usually only for a day. Layering your clothing will enable you to wear the warm-weather clothing you need to bring along anyway, and layering has much the same benefit as an expensive space-consuming coat that you may seldom need. Wool doesn't work well, because it is hard to dry and begins to smell musty in warm, humid environments. Modern fleece clothing does serve well.

You'll also need at least one set of workclothes that you don't mind getting greasy, paint smeared, or dirty. Several bathing suits are in order, and they don't take up much space. You'll be exposed to a lot of hot and dangerous sun in the lower latitudes, so remember to take long-sleeve cotton shirts and long pants. A wide-brimmed hat and sunglasses are everyday wear. A set of foul-weather gear is necessary, but many brands are overpriced. We always buy the less expensive ones (such as "house brand" names) and survive quite well. We do have sea boots because they're helpful on stormy watches when you're heading south in the fall or north in the early spring. Many people do without them altogether. This will depend in part on your choice of sailing areas and seasons. Cruising beautiful New England, for example, normally requires carrying heavier gear. One or two pairs of boat shoes will suffice, especially if the second pair is the leather, dressy type. Sandals are popular, too. Remember, you won't need to wear any shoes most of the time, if you stay where it's warm.

Mel and the girls try to maintain one dressy outfit or a casual nice outfit for stepping out. This would perhaps include a dress or dressy pants with sandals or boat shoes. They avoid material that needs ironing, and choose colors that don't show stains or dirt. Never bring clothing that needs dry cleaning.

We usually buy what few clothes we need in bargain shops. Yes, they are used, but they work. If we can't get what we need in these shops, we go to the super end-of-season sales in the malls. After all, when everyone else is buying winter clothes, you're getting ready to head south. We try not to buy cheaply made clothes, because these fall apart quickly and usually can't be replaced in the islands. You can often find well-made clothes in secondhand stores. When we wear out the cleaner, neater clothing, we move it to the workclothes bin. When it is full of holes, we cut it up for rags, thus saving money on paper towels.

It is important, however, to show respect for the feelings of others in the way you dress. For example, some cruisers think that the lifestyle is an invitation to go nude. And, indeed, the lifestyle does celebrate the philosophy "to each his own." But part of that philosophy includes not spoiling someone else's good time, and some folks are offended by nudity. This is particularly so in island countries, where many boaters, especially those with families, are easily put off. With all the opportunity to go nude privately at sea and in deserted anchorages, it is amazing that a rare few still insist on "flaunting it" in crowded harbors. Then they wonder why the villagers are less than enthusiastic.

It's a good idea to dress cleanly and neatly when dealing with customs and immigration, or when conducting other business with government officials—particularly those of Third World countries. It is perceived as arrogant to show up on their shores, asking for their hospitality, and to appear as though we have no respect for their officials. Again, you needn't be stylish, just reasonably clean and neat when appropriate.

WINTER OR NOT

When you begin cruising, it's hard to believe that you don't have to sit in one place and let the winter consume you. We still pinch ourselves each fall—it feels so good to follow the geese south, fleeing the winter. It seems the only sensible way to live. But this means much more than just comfortable living. It also means savings. As noted above, you save money on clothes, but the list goes on. There is no heating bill. There is also no air-conditioning bill. There is no need to spend money on home insulation or thermal windows. You don't get as many colds and flu bugs because you aren't cooped up with lots of other people in closed buildings, sharing their germs. You don't have to buy snow tires or heat tape for your plumbing. It is very likely that the fuel you burn for the winter will cost considerably less than the fuel you would have needed to heat your house ashore. Going south saves money.

INCOME AND OUTGO

THE OLD JOB

If you maintain some contact with your shoreside job, prepare the groundwork carefully. It usually doesn't work well, but you may need or want to do it. Bosses or fellow workers ashore may begin to get a less than pleasant feeling as they imagine you idling away days in paradise (as they see it) while they tough it out back in the so-called "real world." If you have an understanding that you will have a place in the company when you return, these growing resentments on the part of your coworkers or employer may jeopardize your deal. Your boss may think you've deserted her or him. The best way to continue any relationship with your workplace is to obtain a written record of the understanding. It should clearly spell out what is expected of whom and when. Continue to keep your boss or workers informed as you prepare to leave. The more they participate in preparations for your leaving, the harder it will be for them to divorce their minds from their commitments later on. After you leave, keep regular contact with your old job. You'll grow to hate this, and it may ruin your cruising experience, but maintaining contact will help them keep you in mind. When you do call in, they may try to send you on a guilt trip, or they may try to manipulate you into doing things you can't do. And they will never understand the stresses and demands of your job at sea. Discuss and, if appropriate, include in your written agreement provisions about communications and mailing. Who will pay for telephone calls? They may cost you a minimum of several dollars a minute from overseas. Who will pay for mail? Without the heroic efforts of a special mail carrier, such as Federal Express or UPS, mail may not reach you for months. Will faxes be acceptable? Faxes will streamline communication and costs. Because so many cruisers have serious difficulty maintaining a job back home, or returning to a position at the end of a cruise, I don't recommend keeping your shoreside job unless you have everything tightly under control and in writing.

Running your own business from the cruising scene is perhaps worse than keeping your old job. You'll have to maintain frequent contact, and even then, the employees or partners you left behind may seize more autonomy than you expected or planned for. This may not be a good thing for finances in particular. There will inevitably be decisions only you can make. And this will be hard to do when you aren't on the scene. I don't believe I've met a single cruiser who tried to keep a business back home and still enjoyed the cruise.

As mentioned earlier, maintaining a relationship with your shoreside business may result in insurmountable complications, unless you have a profession you can carry with you (mechanic or welder, for example). One of the worst problems you'll face is communications. Once you leave the U.S. coast, the cost of keeping in touch can be prohibitive. This may change soon (see chapter 6 for more on mail and communications). As it is now, however, you may be in the midst of paradise but worrying about your business because you have little control and scant knowledge of what is going on. And even if you can master the communications problems, keeping one's head in two different worlds seldom works. Besides, the "business" of living aboard requires considerable commitment. And if you fail in that job, you may do a lot worse than go broke.

MAKING MONEY WHILE CRUISING

With the exception of the very wealthy, most liveaboard cruisers take off with the idea lurking around in the back of their minds that they will do something to earn income as they go along. Only those with a specific, marketable skill and who prepare in advance, use it to the maximum, and pursue it diligently tend to succeed. And a marketable skill ashore may not be worth a thing in the cruising world. Most liveaboards are broke—by shoreside standards—and are not looking to hire someone to do a job. They do it themselves. But if you can fill basic needs with skills and equipment not commonly possessed by the cruising community, you will have a better chance of bringing in some income. Obviously, failure to observe local business and employment laws can result in serious problems, particularly in foreign countries. Below are examples of skills that produce some income for those who are proficient.

Highly skilled mechanics with broad experience are always in some demand. Every anchorage has many people who consider themselves mechanics and who, admirably, do much of their own work. But they typically don't have the skills needed to service the already proficient cruising community.

The ability to do skilled machine work is almost always in demand. Parts are often hard to get outside the United States, and if you can repair broken parts or make new ones, you will probably stay busy. This work requires a shop of sorts and special equipment. Most boats don't have room for this, even if the owner has the skill.

Welding, especially if it includes aluminum and stainless, is often needed. Of course, you will want a steel or aluminum boat for this, and you'll need special equipment. Work will probably come in spurts unless you are willing and able to stay in a large cruising community with lots of boats coming and going, especially from far off.

Sail and canvas repair involves purchase of an industrial

machine, as well as the skill to use it. Since most boats don't have a machine of this size, you can probably pick up a few dollars by offering this service.

Refrigeration mechanics, if good, are always in demand. You'll need special equipment, such as pressure gauges and refrigerant supplies.

Believe it or not, I know of some cruisers who bring in extra income by giving haircuts on the beaches in crowded anchorages. I never would have guessed this to be a successful pursuit, but some people go for it. Other cosmetic work, especially in areas where cruisers are only winter vacationers, is often in demand.

Health-related skills are useful. I once heard of a retired dentist who had a dental chair and equipment aboard. Chiropractic skills are frequently in demand, too. Retired doctors and nurses, very much to their credit, will sometimes respond gratuitously to a call for emergency help.

Occasionally a boat delivery job—every cruiser's dream—becomes available. But deliveries are few and far between; you have to luck into them when you can safely and inexpensively leave your boat and someone needs the service.

Many full-time cruisers find temporary jobs ashore. They work for a few months or longer while living aboard at anchor. Because your living expenses are low, low-paying jobs are of more value than they would be ashore. Working as a waitress or waiter, around boatyards and marinas, in the charter business, in the scuba diving business, or for a fast food chain, or doing temporary secretarial work (for those few who still have that skill) are just a few possibilities.

HANDLING CASH

You will need cash. In some places, particularly Third World countries, it is the only method of payment that works well. Most people use ATM machines and travelers' checks. If a locale doesn't accept credit cards, you probably won't be able to use traveler's checks or an ATM card. So, you'll still need to keep a bit of cash on hand. Don't keep too much; if it is stolen or lost, it's gone. Few insurance policies cover lost cash, and I have never seen a boat policy that does. You will need to check the guidebooks for your intended cruising areas to learn where you can use cards and where you must use cash, and then carefully plan your cash withdrawals.

American Express cards have many travel benefits, including relatively large cash advances. They charge a yearly fee, but the convenience can be worth the expense. Remember that customs laws regarding the amount of cash you can take out of or bring into a country without reporting same varies from country to country. As of this writing, the U.S. limit is $10,000, but this could change. Admittedly, few cruisers are likely to exceed that limit.

Chapter Six
COMMUNICATIONS

Whether you hang on to your relationship with your old job or not, you will need to arrange for mail and personal business communications. Unless you plan to stay close to your home area (the U.S. coast if you are a U.S. or Canadian citizen, for example) and anchor in one place most of the time, you'll need help establishing a communications network.

MAIL

In order to get a handle on what you'll need to do, keep a list of the mail you receive for a year before you leave. You'll be amazed at the items that require a quick response. And you'll be amazed at the volume of mail you get, including first class, that you won't even want while cruising. All such mail should be canceled before you leave. Make note of items that have a response deadline. These would include boat decal renewals, car licensing renewals, driver's license renewals, tax events, and many more. Sailing in paradise has a tendency to make you forget things like this, but if you keep a calendar of important items, you'll be more likely to take care of them on time. Be aware that unless you spend perhaps thousands of dollars a year on communications, you simply will not be able to respond daily to time-critical events back home. For example, don't even think of playing the stock market unless someone shoreside does it for you. (You can do it yourself if you're willing to spend at

least $100 a day, plus equipment, on communications.) By the
time you read this book, communications may have improved and
become less costly. Stay up to date on this as you cruise.

SOMEONE YOU TRUST

Find someone you trust to receive your mail and forward it to you
in the manner that you request and to the address that you desig-
nate. Most people prefer to have a relative do this. Many mail
services specialize in this type of arrangement, and some offer a
wide variety of services, but I know many cruisers who left their
business in the hands of such an organization only to have the
outfit go broke or become unreliable. Most services have a toll-free
number (good only within the United States) that can save you
quite a bit. You may have to leave a deposit with them, although
some now accept a credit card number and bill you as needed.
Express mail or express private carrier service costs around $12
and up, depending upon destination and weight (for example, a
four-pound package sent to Venezuela from Florida will cost $30
to $40). Plan in advance when using these services, and be sure that
any service you use is sound, reputable, and has been in business
for a long time. Arrange for a backup should the service fail, and
have this backup authorization recognized in the written agreement
you have with the carrier. There are good services available, so ask
for references and check around. Advertisements in cruising magazines can be a good place to look for these professional services.

PAYING BILLS

Another reason for extra care in your choice of a mail service is
that you may want the service to review certain mail, and perhaps
pay bills. Any notice that you get from your insurance companies,
the IRS and other taxing authorities, and other governmental or
business entities may require immediate attention. If you own a
car, its license and decals will have to be renewed. Your boat documentation or registration also will have to be renewed.

If bills must be forwarded to you out of the country, payment
will be delayed until you mail your check back. When you call to
find out the status of the bills, you may find that your phone credit
card has been cut off because of failure to pay. Bills are one of the
main reasons why many people find a trusted relative or friend to
perform this service. We pay certain bills in advance, including all
insurance payments. For unknown items such as credit card charges

and phone bills, we periodically send a lump sum for credit. Yes, we lose a little interest, but we could lose a lot more. Many cruisers have regular bills deducted automatically from their credit card, mutual fund, or bank accounts. AT&T's telephone credit card allows this and other credit card transactions. You don't get to review the bill before it is paid, but most major retailers and entities such as phone companies will readily credit an overpayment due to erroneous billing. A few people give a general power of attorney to a relative or trusted professional, but I don't recommend this. It means that the recipient could sign your name on just about anything. If you plan well, it probably won't be necessary. You can have a limited power of attorney, but most institutions require an overly broad document.

If you expect income, make arrangements with the payor to send the payments directly to your bank and a copy of the invoice to your mailing address. Send the payor a sufficient supply of deposit slips. If the check must come to you and then go back to your bank, it may be stale before it gets credited.

SENDING AND RECEIVING

Depending on where you are, you may be able to make special arrangements to facilitate mail receipt. In various island communities, a local plane carrier may agree to bring in mail. In some areas you may be able to send out stamped, flat mail with an acquaintance who is flying back to your country. If you have a cruising friend in the harbor who is expecting company, you may be able to prevail upon his or her guest to bring in your flat mail. To arrange this, you would call up your mail service and tell them to fast-forward your mail to that guest's address. When you reach an area in which you intend to remain for a couple of weeks or more, ask the cruising community about local mail practices. Many marinas and marine-related businesses ashore will receive mail and hold it for you, but they won't expedite mail if you are out of your country. Always check with them first before giving out their address. Most guide books should contain current information about places that will receive mail for you and post offices within walking distance from dinghy docks. If you plan to travel along one coastline for a while, you'll be able to receive mail forwarded to these businesses within a couple of weeks of its arrival at your post office, depending on your travel speed and your planning. If you leave the country, mail may take one month or more to reach you— unless you find a special arrangement applicable to the area.

▼

ELECTRONIC MAIL

Electronic mail is becoming faster and cheaper to use. The fax is a problem solver for many cruisers, making it relatively inexpensive to send and receive messages to and from many places in the world. As with mail, businesses that cater to cruisers will receive faxes for you. Again, however, you may need someone at the base to catch the problem in the mail in the first place. E-mail (electronic mail) is now available via ham frequencies and on single-sideband. You can also get telephone hookups through these bands, but this service is expensive. It is generally not permissible under current Federal Communications Commission (FCC) rules to conduct business over the air with a ham license. Satellite transmissions are very expensive but will be getting cheaper. Cellular-phone faxes work fairly well on the continents, but not anywhere else. This will improve as satellite technology improves. Communications options are changing so rapidly that it would be a waste of time to detail what is available as I write. Check up on advancements just before you leave, and make your choice.

HAM AND SSB RADIO

As of this writing, I recommend a combination of ham and single-sideband (SSB) communications. An SSB transceiver is more expensive than a ham transceiver, and some SSBs cover both bands. You don't have to take a test to get an SSB license, and you will be able to talk to people who may not have elected to go the ham route. Another advantage of SSB is that the U.S. Coast Guard stands by on designated SSB frequencies. AT&T High Seas telephone also stands by, providing anytime, anywhere link-up to land phones. AT&T charges around $5 per minute, including long-distance charges. You should register with them and arrange payment before you leave, so you can avoid giving out credit card information on the air. Regular voice SSB transmissions, including those to AT&T operators (and regular ham frequency transmissions), can be easily heard by others. AT&T does have a scrambling program, but it requires special, expensive equipment.

To talk on the ham frequencies you must pass a test to be licensed. At this writing, there are several stages of ham licensing (all require written testing; some require Morse code). The following is a general description of the classes. For full details, contact the FCC, or almost any ham: Novice Element 2 (theory only),

Tech (theory only), Tech Plus (must learn Morse code at a rate of five words per minute), General Theory (must learn code at rate of 13 wpm), Advanced Theory, and Extra Theory (code at 20 wpm). General Theory is required for long-distance high-frequency privileges, but depending on where you are, the lower-level, short-range licenses may be enough to enable you to connect with 2-meter relay systems that provide broad communications. Licensing requirements and coverage are controlled by the FCC and are subject to change. Check for the latest information when you are ready to get your license. Hams are active and helpful in a broad range of communications, and it is very worthwhile to become a ham operator. The Waterway Radio and Cruising Club (P.O. Box 5339, Lighthouse Point, Florida 33074) conducts a network at 7:45 A.M. eastern standard time or daylight savings time that is particularly helpful to those cruising along the lower U.S. east coast and in the Bahamas.

TELEPHONES

Don't forget good old land lines. Even very remote places often have this service now. You may have to wait a bit to get through, but the savings should be worth it. Check locally to determine the cheapest way of calling. Advertisements for AT&T USA overseas direct, for example, imply that you get a good deal using this service from overseas, but the local telephone carrier may be cheaper. At this writing, the first minute of an AT&T call from the Bahamas to the States may cost around $3; every minute thereafter costs more than a dollar a minute. (I cannot be exact about this rate; after wasting lots of time on hold, I found that the typical AT&T agent doesn't know what the company charges.) If you buy a BATELCO (the Bahamas phone company) phone card, you can call anywhere in the States from the Bahamas for a dollar a minute. Rates change daily and locally, so check them out before you call home.

If you communicate via telephone, you'll have to deal with recordings, voice mail, and unenlightened staff who just don't understand that you've gone through minor hell and a year's worth of savings just to get the call through and that there is no way that Ms. Jones can call you back. They don't understand that to call back "tomorrow" you may have to come ashore in a gale. I've taken pains to educate many of the people with whom I do business ashore so that they understand the need to take the call and take care of business—even if it's golfing Wednesday.

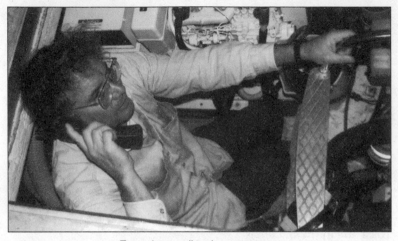

Tom takes a call in the engine room.

▼

CELLULAR TELEPHONES

We also use a cellular phone, and we have a printer for our computer that makes copies and sends faxes via land line or cellular. I hate to admit this, but our life has been significantly improved by this equipment. I probably wouldn't have invested in it if I hadn't needed a printer anyway, or if I were cruising only a few months, or if I weren't in the writing business. Now, if something is extremely urgent, I can try to find a marina with dockside phone connections and get a lot done quickly. Even out in the islands this rig has made the difference between spending a day diving and windsurfing or getting to a village and spending a day finding a copy or fax machine on the island. The dinghy fuel (around $3 per gallon in the Bahamas) I have saved by not having to find these services helps me to justify the cost.

We use a standard bag cell phone, which we plug into our 12-volt batteries, and the type of car antenna with curls that you attach to a car window. The magnet types need a metal ground plane. I had to buy a modem for about $250, which enables the computer and fax machine to interface with the cellular phone. (This setup, incidentally, also lets a regular household phone, including those with portable remotes, interface with the cellular

▼

system. This is truly decadent: you can have a remote phone in the cockpit and avoid missing calls when the motor is running.

Cell phone faxing via modem has been relatively easy on the U.S. east coast. The cost runs around $1.50 a minute, plus a $3 per day/per area connection charge—unless I am in my "home cell" (your designated calling area). Follow Me Roaming is helpful in the United States. With this feature, callers are automatically patched through to you, wherever you are, even though they dialed your "local" number. You'll probably have to pay the long-distance toll from your home cell to wherever you are located, in addition to your cellular air time of around $1 per minute. As you can see, it's easy to run up huge cellular bills unless you are conservative. We reserve the cellular for urgent matters, and keep it short. With a fax, you can say a lot more in a short time, and you don't have to pay to hear the other party's response. Before you sign up with a cellular carrier, find out what coverage it has and with whom it has roaming agreements. Verify their geographical coverage. Today this is rather volatile and confusing. As of this writing, we don't use the cell phone in the Bahamas because the rates are extremely high ($500 just to sign up). In other places in the Caribbean, cell phone charges are more reasonable.

Anywhere you go, it's important to understand the characteristics of your carrier and cooperating carriers. You may need to signal a cooperative carrier when you reach their calling area (by pressing *18, for example), you may need to shift from A to B carriers, or you may have to do something more. Be sure to have your company thoroughly brief you on how to achieve maximum coverage at minimum cost.

In many areas cellular piracy is rampant, and use of PINs (personal identification numbers) and protective codes is inconsistent. Check with cellular carriers (many have a booth at the boat shows) to get the latest.

THEM

You aren't supposed to be out cruising. You're supposed to be in your little cubicle, pushing around trivia, standing up and raising your hand every time you are asked and every time you want to ask. You are supposed to supply "them" with copies anytime they ask. You are supposed to reply within 10 days of receipt of this, that, or the other—whether or not you received it. You are *not* supposed to be doing anything different or unusual. There is no room for it. Wrinkles aren't allowed.

Well, guess what? As hard as they try to stifle it, there are some nonconformist folks who don't toe the line of mediocrity. And you are going to be one of them. But you'll need to obey the shoreside laws and answer the stupid forms, just to stay free. From time to time their obtuseness will drive you crazy, but look at it this way: If you didn't pay taxes and send back forms so that the government could function, society would come tumbling down, and all those mindless bureaucrats and paper pushers might come tumbling and floating out to sea. Talk about pollution! This alone is reason enough to keep them happy.

In the section on mail, covered earlier in this chapter, I discussed having an agent at your home base to review mail and the like. This setup will take care of most of your problems. Some cruisers engage a CPA to whom tax inquiries can be directed. This is expensive, but perhaps worth it. Whether or not you have a CPA, take along whatever tax forms you think may be pertinent, or have your base agent prepared to mail you some on request. There are some computer tax programs that include forms, but these generally need to be updated yearly. Forms for income tax extensions are always pertinent. Under the proper circumstances, you are entitled to a filing extension if you are out of the country; however, you should still pay the taxes you owe on time. Confirm this information before you rely on it; things change. Remember, if the government thinks you aren't paying your taxes, it could seize your assets. You could wake up in paradise and suddenly learn that your credit card doesn't work, and that there is no money available in your bank back home. This is not nice.

There will always be a request for copies of one thing or another, or demand for a phone number where you can be reached next week at 10:32 A.M. Usually you can find a photocopier ashore. If you can't, it's helpful to answer with a letter or fax advising that you are currently traveling (or traveling out of the country), that you are trying to comply with their request, that this is the best you can do, and that you will try to do more as soon as you are able.

Sometimes, ignoring the request will help if a reply isn't required by law or if not replying doesn't waive your rights. Many folks back home just can't handle anything the slightest bit out of the ordinary. When you answer their request or demand with a scenario that prevents them from filling in the blanks, all sorts of problems develop. Then again, sometimes you'll get a real person on the phone, one who is interested and will go the extra mile to help. You'll have to determine this on a case-by-case basis.

One of the most useful tools for dealing with "them" is the shipboard copy machine I mentioned earlier in this chapter. The hassle and inconvenience this can help you avoid is amazing. If you will be mostly cruising along mainland coasts with shoreside amenities, you obviously won't need one as much. But remember, "they" are there, milling around, trying to find things to do to make them feel important. And you want to keep them happy so they'll stay where they are.

Chapter Seven
WHAT DO YOU KEEP?

THE HOUSE

Do you keep the house? This, of course, depends on your long-term plans and state of mind. We tried to keep ours at first by renting it. This turned out to be an incredible pain in the neck and financially unviable. It was difficult, despite careful screening, to find responsible tenants. And when things break they must be fixed. You'll need a reliable agent to administer the rental, the repairs, and the upkeep, and the cost of all this may not be covered by the rent. I've seldom talked to cruisers who were renting their home and who were satisfied with how it was going. If you want to hang on to your house, even if it's just for a while, and renting is your only option, be sure to find a good agent who will handle it all—and perhaps make it an economically viable solution, too.

YOUR STUFF

What about all your stuff? You know, the stuff in the attic, the stuff in the garage, the stuff on the closet shelf, the stuff under the bed? Many feel that they just have to keep it, even though they haven't touched it for years. If you keep your house, you can keep your stuff there. Some cruisers rent storage space. This can be relatively inexpensive, depending on the location, and will give you more

We kept our guitars, which are very important to us.

▼

options, such as retaining furniture that you might want, and financial records that you need. Special storage units and special packing will be necessary for items that can be ruined by bugs, moisture, and temperature extremes. If you plan to return soon, you'll probably want to keep some of your personal possessions, such as clothes. If you're planning a long-term voyage, you'll have not only the expense of storage, you'll also have the nagging thought of "What am I going to do with all that—and when?" It may become a stone around your neck, dragging you down to your past. Or it may be something that really helps you keep your place in time. It's up to you. We had a garage sale and just got rid of most of it. Then we sold the garage, and that big box of rooms next to it.

THE CAR

That American *raison d'être,* the CAR, must be dealt with, both emotionally and physically, before you leave.

Cars are an incredible expense. Some states require you to maintain liability insurance if you maintain your driver's license. Some require you to pay an uninsured motorist fee. You will have to pay licensing fees. Remember that the car will depreciate significantly during this time. You could let a friend drive and maintain it, but be sure the insurance covers your arrangement—and have a written agreement as to who will pay for what. In some areas, rental cars and taxis are inexpensive. On the U.S. east coast, for example, rental cars are cheap in south Florida. Taxis are very cheap in St. Augustine, Florida, and fairly cheap in New York City. In various South American countries both car rentals and taxies are cheap. When you compare the cost of occasionally renting a car or taking a taxi with the cost of keeping your car, you may be surprised to find that renting is cheaper. What you decide will depend on where you intend to cruise and for how long, but do consider the alternatives before keeping that car.

YOUR ADDRESS

How about your home address? This is often referred to as your "domicile," but the definition of "domicile" varies from state to state. (Normally, one's domicile is the place one considers home, and where one maintains some contact such as an address. But don't be surprised if some taxing authority comes up with a new definition.) We hope to avoid confusion by not using that term. As pointed out in the section on insurance in chapter 5, this may be a good time to change your address to a more favorable location. You may want to change it for tax reasons, but investigate thoroughly before doing so. Some states have lower personal-property taxes, some have lower—or no--income taxes, some have lower sales taxes, some have different criteria for liability for personal taxes, and the beat goes on. I would have liked to include a table that compared tax rates among coastal states, but these laws change too frequently to make this practical in a book. States do get their bite in the end, however; for example, a state with no income tax may have a huge and unfair personal-property tax. Some states are, illegally in my view, attempting to tax boats for existing in "their" waters for short periods of time, even when the owner pays taxes or similar fees in another jurisdiction. If you are considering changing your home base or are planning to "hang out" in one area, check out the consequences of making a change. At this writing, you are safe from harassment in most areas if you stay fewer than 90 days.

Don't put yourself in a situation where you could be accused of fraud. If you set up a paper address in an area with low insurance rates, you may have problems if you make a substantial claim. Most people keep their old home address, or at least their post office address. You should also have a street address (maybe that of a relative

"OLD BLUE"

For years we solved the car problem with "Old Blue." As the name implies, she was a rather elderly blue lady, but with a reputation for durability. Every year when we headed south, we drove her up into some woods, on a lot that we purchased when we sold our house. When we came back eight to nine months later, I would take a magnet and a machete and head toward shore, and the thick brush that by then hid her deep within the underbrush. I would claw through the jungle with the magnet extended as far ahead as my reach would allow, until I heard a metallic clump. Then I hacked her free with the machete. Vines had always found their way inside, even with the windows rolled up. After prying up the hood and removing the field mice and their nest from the carburetor air-intake filter (they built their nests using the insulation from under the hood), I hooked up a battery, poured a little gasoline into the carb throat, smiled at the wondrous roar, and crashed out of the foliage—like a phoenix arising, eternal. But I wouldn't advise you to try this with your car, not unless you have one like "Old Blue." She began to have so many problems that I had to take along a change of clothes and a tool box every time I drove her. She finally died on the side of the road; we had a ceremonial parting at a used-car lot. She was sold a few days later, and indignantly burned out her engine when the new owner had driven her about 10 miles from the lot. Most cars don't do well sitting unused. They often do even less well when used by friends and relatives who have them on loan.

▼

or agent), because many governmental agencies and express-mail services require this. It also helps to have a phone number. Those who cash checks and take credit cards aren't prepared to deal with people who don't have a phone number. I know of one cruiser who used to say "123 456 7899"; although it usually worked, I can't recommend doing this. A relative's number will normally suffice. Be aware that if you need to make a major credit card purchase over the phone and your shipping address differs from the record for your card, the vendor may refuse to accept the card because this scenario fits into the profile of credit card fraud. In the past we've asked bank personnel who knew us personally to call and satisfy the vendor. The bottom line is that you will need a home base. Line up a relative, good friend, accountant, attorney, or some other agent.

Whatever you do, take care not to give up your voting rights. We can't complain out here if we don't vote in there.

▼

YOUR NEW
HOME

Chapter Eight
COMFORT: A CRUISING BOAT ISN'T A NIAGARA FALLS BARREL

This is a book about *cruising*, not racing. It's about living aboard, not camping out. Camping out is fine for a weekend, maybe even a few weeks. It isn't fine for six months, a year, or a lifetime. If you think it is, wait till you try it. I'll bet you'll change your mind. Unfortunately, many so-called cruising boats today are not much more than luxurious camping trailers. Some aren't even luxurious. They may be Spartan. They may be tough. They may be fast. They may get you that hoary seaman award the yacht club gives out at the bar every Friday night. But they aren't comfortable. And thus they aren't a realistic choice for cruising.

"Cruising" doesn't imply an epic voyage. Although I greatly respect those who make them, I don't particularly want to sail around Cape Horn in a storm. I don't like to be cold. I don't want to find the eye of a hurricane in a 32-foot boat, or in any boat for that matter. Neither does my family, and I doubt that yours will. This book is about living aboard and cruising for a long time, not taking a brief but furious plunge on a hero's odyssey. This is a lifestyle that involves living and working, eating and sleeping, attending school, having fun, living an enjoyable life—but on a boat, at sea. This means that you avoid storms as much as possible. It means that you hang out on the hook for long periods when you find a spot you enjoy. It means avoiding places you don't like at times that aren't safe. So, you shouldn't look for a boat built to go over Niagara Falls. You should get a boat that is sound and seaworthy, because you never know when you may get hit by the very worst nature can dish out. You should also get a boat that is comfortable, one you can live in for a long time.

Many weekend racer/cruisers you see these days are about as well suited for cruising as a hang glider would be for flying to the moon. When you begin to think about your cruising boat, remember that most of the boat-buying public does not go cruising, except on weekends and short vacations. They don't need the qualities of a good cruising boat; they may have little idea of what these qualities are. And the people who build boats know this. They build for their market, and you can't blame them.

Many new boats are built to convey opulence and luxury when the prospective buyer walks down the companionway for the first time. "Oh, look at all that space. We can entertain so well here." What these buyers probably aren't thinking about at the time is that you cannot store cruising supplies in all the bins and drawers that aren't behind all that hull-to-hull spaciousness. They also don't think about the fun they're going to have in all that space while beating to windward or rolling about on a long offshore passage. Many boats are designed for the dual-purpose buyer. One spouse may want to race; the other may want creature comforts. "This boat does it all—round-the-buoys sailing perfection coupled with enough space to entertain half the yacht club in luxurious splendor after the race. It is also great for anchoring out on a cruise. Screens are included, as is a shower on the transom." And on it goes. If you are to have a successful cruising adventure, you must have a good cruising boat, comfortable and safe. This is a necessity, not an option.

CRUISING COMFORT

Things that may make you comfortable on a weekend outing may not make you comfortable while cruising. They may well contribute to *lack* of cruising comfort. That wonderful wide space in the salon where you can comfortably entertain and comfortably have weekend yacht club rendezvous could be the same space where you break your neck while heaving about in the ocean. That wonderful galley with all the space for blenders and microwaves and "a feeling of airiness that lets you commune with the party" probably doesn't have high fiddles or a place where you can wedge yourself in as you cook on a 20-degree heel.

Some of you may consider the contents of the following pages heretical. Most cruising books and cruising lecturers talk about misery and suffering, of ½-inch overhead clearance, of bunks 2 inches shorter than necessary. The remaining space is devoted to storage of kerosene that will light the lanterns and heat the cabin during an Antarctic circumnavigation. Most of these folks haven't done it for long, and haven't done it with a family.

You'll be living at sea, not just reading about it while curled up in a comfortable chair in front of a fireplace. Few cruisers don't mind being uncomfortable all the time. Unless you and your family are among those fortunate few, start thinking "comfort" as well as sea-worthiness and performance. Of course, you should put seaworthi-ness first, and performance often contributes to seaworthiness. But these qualities, despite popular lore, do not preclude comfort.

SPACES

Cruising boats are, among many other things, a complex combina-tion of spaces with different, sometimes contradictory, functions. They have spaces for equipment; supplies such as towels, rags, linen, suntan lotion, and soap; parts; food; water and fuel; clothing; tools; galley equipment; and items for the pursuit of pleasure—books, videos, and games. All of these spaces, and many more, are around and over and within perhaps the most important spaces of all: the spaces where you'll be living and working.

When you look for a cruising boat, or modify your existing boat, it helps to think of these spaces, the needs each space has to fill, and your priorities. It isn't difficult to determine that you must have a large enough diesel tank to propel your boat at least several hundred miles when the wind fails. And it isn't difficult to deter-mine how much space you'll need for so many pots and pans, the number and size of which you probably already have in mind from experience. But determining how much space you'll need to live and work and relax and play and do everything else is much more difficult. This space is somewhat abstract. How much space do you need to brush your teeth? Does that sound silly? It won't if you wake up one morning and realize that for years to come you must brush your teeth in a dream home with a bathroom that doesn't have enough room between the sink and the bulkhead for your elbow, so that you either drool onto the counter beside the sink or bang your elbow as you brush. How much space do you need to stretch out and be comfortable when reading? How much space do you need to get into or out of a chair or bench that won't pull out from under the table? How much space do you need to turn from the sink to the stove to the refrigerator without spilling something or disrupting the flow of preparing a meal? How much space do you need to prepare a meal, and does all or part of that space include the refrigerator top that you'll need access to as you prepare meals? There are industry norms for many of these spaces; on a boat, however, many of the norms take second, third, or fourth place behind other amenities like that "feeling of spaciousness" or the "deluxe microwave," or the "more than adequate chart table with the luxurious swiveling chair." Besides, norms are norms, and you just may not be normal. You probably aren't, come to think of it. You are going cruising.

As you rebuild or buy your boat, think as hard as you can about this illusive space for your family, and imagine as well as you can what living in that space will be like. Here are some guidelines that will help.

TRY BOATS ON FOR COMFORT

If you already have your cruising boat, you should be familiar with its shortcomings in living space. Any little thing that irritates you as you go about your daily life on a typical weekend cruise will irritate you much more if you must deal with it every day for months or years. If you don't yet have your cruising boat and are looking, keep this in mind as you visit as many boats as you can. It helps to sit, stand, move about—to make believe you are doing things that you would be doing if you lived aboard.

Go to boat shows. I know they are busy and full of hype, but they are still great places to learn what you like and what is available. You don't have to buy a new boat, but looking at new boats will give you a sense of how the experts use space to good effect. Even though it's more expensive to go on the trade days, it's really worthwhile because there are fewer people and you can hang out in the boats you favor. If you go early in the day and stay until closing, you'll avoid traffic and have a better experience. If you're considering a new boat, the dealers will be happy to make an appointment for you to come back when you can spend more time aboard. Of course, you can do this at a dealer's store any time, but the boat shows give you more from which to choose. They offer a great opportunity to narrow down boats into preferable sizes, shapes, and arrangements.

Used boats present great opportunities at better prices, and boat shows bring home the differences between newer boats and older ones. Look at as many as you can, new and used. In newer boats there's a trend toward airy, spacious accommodations and an emphasis on creature comforts. But some of these boats lack good storage space. Newer boats often have thinner hulls and lighter hardware than older ones. They often have lighter diesels. But new construction techniques and materials and advanced design concepts offer many improvements. For example, some older boats were built with balsa-core hulls that later turned to mush; some had poorly laid balsa-core decks that did the same. But the Island Packets, as an example of newer building techniques, have a proprietary deck coring that won't rot. Older boats tend to blister. New boats commonly have at least a five-year warranty (read the fine print). Before you buy, look carefully at old and new.

Another way to check out different boats is to visit your friends' boats. Perhaps they will let you spend a day aboard, just scoping it out. And if you see a stranger's boat along a dock, stop and stare in envy; the owner may invite you aboard. Just say hello and explain why you're looking.

Once you begin to narrow down types of boats you like, there is an even better way to try them out: Take charter vacations. Actually, chartering can help you from the very beginning of your search. You'll be living in the boat, doing many of the things you would be doing if you were cruising (but hopefully not making repairs). Chartering is a somewhat expensive option, but if it helps you to invest your dollars well and to avoid a more expensive, long-term mistake, the cost will be worth it.

SIZE

Many people ask about size. One school believes in starting small, learning what you want to do and how well you like what you are doing, and then moving up. I recommend that you spend at least a year, preferably longer, researching your decision; then start with the largest boat that will meet your financial needs and family size. I've seen many families having a bad time simply because they were too cramped and because the boat didn't provide a sound enough working platform at sea. Remember, we are talking about a *home* at sea. Another problem with beginning your new lifestyle in a small "try it out" boat is that you'll need to equip it for cruising, and it's unlikely that you'll be able to recover your full investment when you sell it to buy a larger boat. You may not be able to afford to lose money and then buy a bigger boat. Despite these considerations, you must make your decision based on your situation and preferences.

Whenever you try on a boat for size, look for features that will make it a good cruising boat. Following are some guidelines.

DESIGN FOR COMFORT

Now let's examine specific parts of the boat and the features that make them good or bad for the liveaboard cruiser.

THE GALLEY, by Mel

There are four basic galley arrangements found on cruising boats: the *companionway galley*, common on both center-cockpit and aft-cockpit boats (galley placed just down the steps to one side or the other); the *passageway galley*, found on some center-cockpit boats (galley placed in the walkway between the main and aft cabins); *main-cabin galley*, found on trawlers and some sailboats, such as the old sailing classic Cal 2-46 (galley placed forward or within the main living area); and the *galley-down* model, found on some sailboats and many trawlers (galley placed forward of the main living area and down a set of steps).

Of these designs, the only one I have not lived with is the passageway galley. Although I have envied the away-from-living-space placement of these galleys, I realize that the cook must move out of the way every time someone wants to get past and that the standing room is frequently in the same space as the engine-compartment entrance. I have stood in this type of galley and become claustrophobic at the thought of performing cruising-cook miracles in such a tunnel-like space, usually without much ventilation. The passageway galley does have the advantage of being in the most stable area of the boat and of being narrow so that the cook will not get thrown about in rough seas.

Being not too neat a cook, I am also thankful that I no longer live with the main-cabin galley on my first small sailboat. It was so small a boat that everything was in the main salon (except the toilet, thank goodness, and the V-berths where we slept). On larger boats with main-cabin galleys, the cook is a part of all the activity, but so is everything she or he is cooking. These frequently have so much open space that it is difficult to cook underway in very rough or rolly conditions.

The galley-down type is what I'm living with now, and I've done it for 18 years. It is forward of the main cabin, down a set of stairs and across from the forward head. It is out of the main traffic area, and it has an open space with a counter between the aft end and the main salon seating area. This allows ventilation and provides a convenient place to pass items up from below. It also pleases the claustrophobic cook. When the kids were little, they used to climb up on the counter and look over into the galley to see what Mom was doing. Once, Carolyn fell from this perch and into the empty (thankfully) sink. There are, however, several disadvantages to this galley placement: it is forward of the center (more stable) part of the boat, so cooking can be difficult in rough conditions. And once the cooking is done, it is exceptionally difficult to get the food across the main cabin and up the steps to the cockpit on the rough days when we must eat there while underway. We solve this problem by leaving the food on the stove and having everybody serve themselves. This layout is a wonderful arrangement at anchor, however, and that is where most cruising boats spend most of their time. Many trawlers and trawler-type motorboats have this arrangement, with a dinette across from the galley.

The most popular galley placement is to either side of the companionway, and with good reason. The cook can pass the food directly up the stairs without walking through open spaces, it is convenient for all crewmembers to get their own drinks and snacks, and this area is usually very stable. If the galley is also a dedicated space, not shared with any other system or activity, this can be the ideal arrangement. As Tom pointed out, clever boatbuilders have often engineered a shared space with one of the mechanical systems, usually the engine-compartment access, and this can have a negative impact on your cruising comfort. Even with this major disadvantage, I think the companionway galley is the most sensible arrangement for most cruising boats.

Galley placement usually cannot be changed without major renovations, so it is an important consideration when choosing a boat. The little things—like shelving, fiddles, and spice racks—can be easily modified or added, so they shouldn't be the primary consideration when you're making this choice. Another important thing that cannot be easily changed is the amount of space available to move around in the galley and whether you can reach all the access spaces. Is there room for more than one person to work (someone to help with dishes)? Can you reach into the back of all the cabinets behind the counters? Can you reach into the bottom of the refrigerator? How much space is wasted behind those pretty little drawers? There's a lot of space on my boat, enough to store a year's supply of powdered milk in 1-quart envelopes for a family of four; I just have to remove the top drawer to get to it. I can also store small canned goods next to the hull behind the other drawers.

The type and placement of the stove and oven are important, too. Having cooked with alcohol and electricity, I was more than pleasantly surprised by how well propane has worked. If you choose compressed natural gas (CNG), be sure to check on its availability in your chosen cruising grounds; it can be extremely difficult to find even in developed areas. I have a three-burner stove, but I often need only two burners; I use the oven daily, but not the broiler—it's not efficient for cooking quantities large enough for a family. Most boat ovens have only one shelf. This can be a disadvantage, especially when you want to make something like a layer cake. You have to cook one layer at a time. Make sure that your chosen stove is gimbaled well, that it has fiddles or retainers to keep the food securely on the burners, that there is enough air space around it to dissipate the heat, that there is a safety rail or bar to keep you from falling onto hot surfaces, and that there is a system for strapping the cook in place when the boat heels. If you have the space and electricity, a microwave is great for warm-ups, heating water, cooking vegetables, and defrosting. I would not consider it as a replacement for a conventional oven on a cruising boat because of the many things it can't do—like bake bread.

Although refrigeration options are discussed in chapter 15, this is a good place to point out that you probably don't need as much refrigerated space as you think you do. Don't go overboard by taking away valuable storage space; and please make sure that access to the fridge is not the only good counter space you have for food preparation. You will become very unhappy very quickly if you have to clear your only counter every time someone wants an ice cube or a drink. I have the upright type similar to a house fridge. It came with the boat, and we couldn't afford the money or the time to retrofit a proper system. We've simply adapted to it. While I don't have the problem with counter space, I find that stuff falls out when I open the fridge in rough weather. Loose items move about, and the open door displaces everyone but me from the galley. Also, the fridge spills cold air every time the door is opened. If you have a side-opening unit, at least hang clear plastic strips down from the top to keep in some of the cold when the door is open. Make sure the fridge is well insulated.

No system is perfect; study the numerous options and remember that the more you depend on it, the more difficult time you will have when it breaks. And it will.

Some small but important galley features are deep double sinks, good fiddles, dedicated storage areas (built-in storage for glasses, mugs, plates, flatware, small items), shelving of different heights to store different-size items, dry storage areas that will stay dry (not right next to the sink), a splash board behind the sink, good ventilation (portholes, hatches, Dorade vents), ample lighting, a place for the trash (can crushers save a lot of space if you use cans), good and easy access to pots and pans, and space and ample electricity for a few chosen appliances (blender, food processor, electric mixer).

You will be spending a lot of time in your galley, so make sure it is comfortable and organized. You'll be living, not camping, so don't plan to use camping equipment. Get some nice dishes (I recommend Corelle by Corning), real wine glasses (stainless, collapsible plastic, or glass), nice stainless flatware, good pots and pans like those you used in your house, a few good serving dishes or trays for entertaining, and anything special you can't do without. Figure out a system for storage of and easy access to food you will be using daily. Tupperware makes the only plastic storage containers that seem to last, and the designs are well conceived for fitting into boat spaces. I use Tupperware to store small amounts of the bulk items I use frequently, and replenish them as needed from the not-so-accessible places where I keep the larger amounts.

Paper items used in excess in many homes these days are best done without, except for good paper towels (Bounty is the overwhelming favorite, and it gets as much use in the engine room as in the galley). In place of paper napkins, we use cloth ones, with matching place mats. There is a different pattern for each family member so that we can use the napkins for several meals, each of us using only his or her own. These are used until dirty and then washed in scant amounts of water (sometimes salt and rinsed in fresh). We do have a small reserve of paper napkins for guests. We don't use paper plates or paper cups, except for infrequent large gatherings or beach events, or when it is just too rough or we're too tired to wash dishes.

Plastic bags, especially Ziploc, are a necessity on boats—both for the galley and mechanical systems and for storage of any other item you might want to keep dry. Freezer bags work best for heavy mechanical items, while the regular sandwich ones are best for galley use. Reusable, recycled plastic containers are preferable to fresh plastic bags for galley use. We use garbage bags frequently, but usually for keeping certain items dry. Each cruising family will work out its dependence on these items, so don't feel that you should scrimp on the amounts you carry before you have determined what your usage will be.

Finally, the galley is the center of activity for a cruising family. Make sure everyone can use it without disrupting your systems and arrangements. If you are the only one who can find the peanut butter, find a better place for it. Your children will want to make cookies and meals when they are older, and you'll want the captain or your mate to share in galley responsibilities. Make it easy for them, and it will be easier for you.

THE HEAD

Go into the head and feel what it would be like to do the things you do in there, including having a seat on the throne. Sometimes I think that boat manufacturers deliberately shortcut the space around the head because they know the customer isn't likely to try it out. I don't suggest that you actually use the thing in every boat in the show (I don't recommend your using it on any boat in the show), but you can at least sit on it and see if you fit into the space. Not only do *you* need to fit there, you need to remain sitting there when the boat is heeling. You need to be able to do all the functions that normal people do there. Think about it. I've seen more than one head where the toilet paper was apparently hung for decoration, because you sure couldn't reach it when you needed to.

Lack of shower space is a serious problem on many boats. Builders today often don't dedicate space for a shower stall because they assume people won't use the shower much. They put up curtains in the head and have you shower in the same space in which you brush your teeth and hair. While their assumption may be true for weekend cruising, its validity rapidly vanishes as you wipe up and close up every day for months and years. Some of these

▼

arrangements are pretty good; some are terrible. If the shower area includes the sink and vanity, forget it, even if the curtain theoretically separates the two areas. Water will go everywhere, even into the cabinets, and you'll have to wipe down most of the head every time you shower. The roll of toilet paper will turn into a big, permanently wet sponge. I'm always amazed at the new and incredibly expensive boats coming off the line in which the toilet paper holder is positioned so that the roll gets wet every time you shower. If they haven't figured that one out, I shudder at what else they don't know about living aboard. And what about the things you keep on the vanity? You won't want to move your hairbrush and makeup and shaving stuff and everything else every time you take a shower. Oh, and incidentally, where do hang your towels while you splash about? That shower curtain will protect everything? Dream on. While you are dreaming, think about the boat heeling as you shower. What will that do to the curtain and to you? Think about those nice tropical breezes that will be blowing through the many portholes and the hatch. Curtains move with breezes. And speaking of breezes, we all know that the head should be well ventilated. Over the years, we've noticed that, no matter how well ventilated this area may be, mildew and moisture—and eventually rot—take hold if you spray fresh water all over it every day. If you do this only on weekends, no problem—maybe. That's why builders get away with this setup. But we aren't talking about weekend cruising.

There is a compromise to this arrangement that works fairly well. The head itself and the shower are at one end of the head-bathroom. The curtain, and preferably a lip in the deck, protect that corner or end from the rest of the items in the head. This setup has the added benefit of constantly keeping the toilet area clean because it is sprayed down every day. Many toilet areas are so cramped that, short of spraying them down, it's difficult to clean around the corners down beside the pump and bowl. This arrangement also makes a good place for all that dirty water to go every time you crack apart the toilet to fix it. Down the sump. As unpleasant as this may seem, it's a lot better than having the waste water flow over that beautiful teak and holly sole that looked so good at the boat show. Boats with this arrangement often have a covered recessed toilet paper holder. Check it out.

We prefer a separate stall dedicated to the shower. This keeps most of the moisture out of the living area of the head and makes each shower much simpler. And this becomes important as you add family members to the equation. Yes, this does take up more space, but you can use that shower space for other things. Use it as a wet locker. Use it to wash clothes. (Make sure it has a deep enough basin; if it doesn't, the water will run out when you are heeling and rolling). Use it to hang clothes to dry when you can't put them on the railing. Use it to store beer. We have found over the years that our separate shower stall has not been a waste of space, but a blessing. Our boat came with two of them, which was a bit extravagant. We made the second into a parts room by adding shelves.

The sump for the shower should have a large enough capacity so that the pump won't need to run all the time. If it doesn't, the pump will be sucking air along with the water, because you won't run the water constantly when you shower. You'll have an on/off valve on the shower head and you'll be wetting yourself, turning off the water at the shower head, soaping and washing, and then rinsing yourself—unless you have a very big watermaker and run it all the time. Most pumps do not last, no matter what the brochures say, if they intermittently suck air and the water. The sump and its pump should be protected by a screen to filter out body hair and other debris, and it should be very easily serviced. I prefer a diaphragm pump such as those made by Par-ITT-Jabasco or Shurflo. These do relatively well when pumping dry, and debris will either pass through or clog a valve, which can be cleared. These pumps also have good lift capability, so you can mount them conveniently.

Of course, we should say something about the head in the head. We have used the Raritan PH II series and its predecessors for almost two decades and have been very happy with them. They work well, parts are readily available, they are easy to repair, and they have improved over the years. The key to any happy use of a marine toilet is regular maintenance. Rebuild yours at least yearly; don't wait for it to break during use.

At this point you may be thinking, "What about all those articles that talk about showering in the sea and all that neat stuff?" We did it for several years and didn't find it so neat. We washed in the ocean (when out in the islands) and rinsed off with our precious fresh water. When it was cold or there were sharks or barracuda about, or for any number of other reasons, we pumped seawater with a Whale foot pump into the shower stall via a separate shower hose. We didn't like it. Sores didn't heal. Our skin often broke out. We found that those who generally spoke so fondly of doing it usually had done it only for a month or so. But if you think you want to shower in seawater, you have all the more need for a shower stall as opposed to a "whole bathroom" shower. The salt water will eat up everything metal. We even found it eats stainless, because most of the "stainless" equipment made for the head and galley is of low grade—manufacturers don't expect it to be frequently exposed to corrosive salt water.

Before we leave the subject of the head and shower, I know you are wondering about all those nice times taking showers in the cockpit. Some boats come with cockpit shower hoses; many are in the recessed "sugar scoop" sterns that serve admirably as a swim platform. Cockpit showers make a lot of sense, and if your boat doesn't have one you should plumb one in. They are great for getting all that salt off after your dive or swim, before you track it below into the place where you live. They are also great for regular hygienic showers, in the right circumstances. They don't add moisture below decks, there is no problem with ventilation, and, let's face it, they are a bit romantic. But everyday? And in marinas and crowded harbors? When it's cold and blowing like stink? As with so many other aspects of living aboard, if you have to do it every day for months or years, you're probably going to find it unappealing. Everybody needs a private hot shower inside where it's warm, at least every once in a while. And, yes, I said "hot," which brings up an entirely new issue.

Although generating hot running water is perhaps more of a systems than a space issue, let's deal with it here, because it isn't much of a systems issue. (For more on water, see chapter 14.) Obviously, we recommend it. Hot-water tanks don't take up much space, they are reliable, and they can be heated by the engine with just a little extra plumbing, as well as by electricity. We used a Raritan for 15 years. We then thought it was leaking and replaced it. When we pulled it out of its corner, we found that it wasn't leaking at all, that it was in great shape. The plumbing behind it had been leaking. Most marine hot-water tanks come with a built-in heat exchanger. You run a hose from the internal freshwater cooling system of your engine through the heat exchanger. Run the engine for an hour, and you have plenty of hot water.

The word "water" keeps popping up here. And by "water" we mean fresh water. For a boat on the hook or at sea this is a precious commodity. We will discuss it in much greater detail in chapter 14.

Yes, indeed, we are spending a lot of time in the bathroom. But this, as unimportant as it may sound, is an important creature-comfort issue for long-term cruising. Before we leave it, let's hit a few more important considerations. Imagine drying off after a shower. Are you looking at one of the heads where you have to glue fluffy towels to the wall and rub against them because there isn't space to get a towel around you and rub? Find out. Is there room to shave your face? Can you look over the mirror and still drip into the sink, or is the mirror off to the side, forcing you to soap your face, turn around, and catch the soap in your hand? Can you shave your legs in the shower space, wherever it is? Is there room to sit and lean over? And look carefully at the ventilation. In any head there should be a very minimum of two opening ports and a Dorade vent. Preferably there will be an opening overhead hatch. You'll want steam and hot air to go up and out, and you'll need cross ventilation so that air moves through. Study the head carefully; it should not rely on an electric blower for ventilation. Wind or natural convection are better options than battery power.

Okay. Let's get out of the head.

LOUNGING AND LIVING AREAS

Sit in each of the seats. Some boats, even expensive ones with fine-looking interiors have really uncomfortable seats. Are the backs high enough? Are they reclined at a comfortable angle from the seat? Remember, these permanent settees in the dining areas are just that. You can't adjust them or move them without spending a lot of money. Don't get the boat if it doesn't have comfortable places to sit.

High fiddles and overhead handrails are necessities of a seaworthy boat. And be sure that the living areas aren't so big that you'll fly through the air as you move about while underway. We like smaller spaces, without the cocktail-lounge dance-floor concept, for these reasons. Smaller spaces can lend a feeling of privacy, even if you aren't isolated from the others.

If you're cruising on a sailboat, try out different boats and settle that age-old sailboat dilemma: Do you want to live like a mole down in a tube and be safer, or do you want a large cabinhouse with big windows and a high floor? Many longtime liveaboards tell us that they wish they had the latter arrangement; they want

Chez Nous has a large cabin house, a comfortable center cockpit, an aft cabin, good deck space, and loads of stowage capacity.

to see out from below when sitting down, or at least when standing up. These boats can be made safer for serious offshore duty by the addition of heavy storm shutters or windows. Most multihulls have a great view from the salon. Many boats with low cabin soles and only portholes are still rather airy because of the number of portholes and because their builders have placed nonopening see-through ports in the hull. Obviously, this must be done with careful attention to strength, but it can be done well. If you have the tunnel-type boat, you may also lighten it up and make it feel larger with light-colored enamel rather than regulation teak. There are many possible compromises. If you misjudge your preference, you may be stuck with it for a long time. Spend some time getting the feel for the overall below-decks complexion of as many boats as possible.

INTERIOR DECORATION, by Mel

Brand-new boats are usually beautifully decorated by professionals, only a few of whom will have considered how the boat will be used. Older boats may have had a quick and inexpensive interior "freshening" in order to help them sell, or they may need to be totally redecorated from top to bottom. Chances are that you will have to make some type of decorating decision whether your boat is fresh from the factory or an older model in need of a remake. You may be one of the fortunate few who can turn it all over to someone else, or you may have the financial need to do everything yourself. Whatever the case, the hints I'm passing on come from many years of hard use on a boat by a growing family and give you some insight into the ever-present fact that things wear—some better than others.

Most new boats and older varnished beauties come with teak and holly floors, some solid wood and some veneer. They are beautiful to look at, but they don't stay that way with a family treading upon them continuously. Keep the wood floor if you don't mind it getting messed up, or if you enjoy sanding and varnishing. Throw rugs help. For us, covering it with carpet helped more. Two layers of foam insulation placed underneath keep down engine-room noise and enable us to have a generator without a hush box. Carpeting has a lot of disadvantages, and sometimes I regret covering our teak and holly—until I think about all the sanding and varnishing. Carpet must be replaced every few years, but that is made easy by using the old one for a pattern. Carpet must be vacuumed, so you'll need a vacuum cleaner and electricity, but many of you would have a vacuum anyway. Carpet thickness calls for possible adjustments in door clearances. Carpet shifts unless it is permanently attached. Carpet feels soft and homey, except when it needs cleaning, and it's harder to keep the boat clean because of the added interior dust. Despite all these problems, I still think laying and maintaining carpeting is better than sanding and varnishing, or looking at and feeling very bad about the banged up teak and holly. Alternatives to the thick carpet and insulation might be a fitted carpet or other heavy covering (I've seen Sunbrella used in this manner) with bound edges. Snaps or fasteners hold it in place, but the carpet can be easily removed to expose the wood underneath. Or you can buy a commercial-grade carpet with the insulation permanently attached (which you might find on remnants from commercial installations).

Unbound carpet unravels, but adding glue (silicone, shoe glue, or Liquid Nails) around the edges on the underside will minimize this problem. Carpets that resist stains and that clean up with water look great, for a while. After the first cleaning, they lose their stain resistance and have to be cleaned more often. To my mind, carpets are disposable items, and I replace them when they are at this point. If you buy well, from a remnant store or one of the many sales, you won't have invested too much to replace carpet as needed. I usually replace carpeting every two to three years; the foam insulation lasts much longer (I bind the edges of the two pieces of foam together with canvas to protect them and so that they move as one piece).

New-boat salespeople will sometimes tell you that the beautiful fabric will not get worn or spotty with your toddlers climbing all over it daily, or your teenagers flopping down on it as they will do. Don't believe it! If anything can be spilled, it will. If anything can be dropped, it will. If you have your choice, choose material that can be wiped off, will resist water and dirt, and that looks like it will. Scotchgard is not permanent unless you reapply it, so don't be taken in by advertisements to the contrary. These reassurances are fine for careful adults who live in houses that don't move, but not for kids and families on boats. My first fabric choice on *Chez Nous* was a good-quality fake leather; I planned to use a nice woven fabric when the kids were older, but I have found that the mess and the spilling do not stop and that I would have been very unhappy without the vinyl. It is sticky in warm weather, but this can be overcome by using temporary elasticized daycovers made from towels, cotton fabric, or canvas, which can be easily removed for laundering or replaced. I have been able to replace the upholstery a piece at a time by buying large quantities. Without kids, I would choose a natural fabric, very closely woven and heavy, probably with a small pattern and medium to dark in color. Even adults will get it dirty, so it's best to minimize what might show. If you sew and if you will have to replace the fabric often, you may want to consider plain covers rather than tufted and buttoned ones. Some of the seats in our salon have to be re-covered every two years; some last four or five, depending on where they are. My industrial sewing machine (Sailrite Sailmaker) paid for itself in the first week I got it, when I made the first set of curtains and replacement seat covers. If you use neutral fabric on your cushions, throw pillows in bright colors can liven up the decor.

Newer boats come with exciting and different window and porthole treatments. If you are replacing either of these, go to boat shows to get ideas for arrangements similar to yours. Boats with large windows usually have miniblinds or curtains. These are similar in cost, depending on how much you can do yourself and whether you choose expensive materials that last or cheap ones that need to be replaced regularly. My advice for curtains is to choose the best fabric you can afford, pick something you can live with a long time, line them with the best, and choose a system for hanging them that will last through several curtain replacements. If you make them yourself, you may not want to go through the process very often; if you have them made, you won't want to pay for the service often either. If you choose blinds, the household ones are much less expensive than boat blinds made with special materials. The household type will not last as long and will have to be replaced, but friends have been pleased with them and have not had to replace them as often as one would expect. The biggest advantage to the blinds made for boat use is that they can be made to fit onto the many curved and slanted surfaces of a variety of boat windows, without rattles, whereas the household ones are made for flat rectangles and no wind.

Fabrics used in sleeping areas on cruising boats vary with the age of children, climate cruised, and personal tastes. *Chez Nous* has the same fake leather fabric on the children's bunks as in the main salon. For little children who occasionally have accidents in bed, this is a wise choice, although plastic sheets could be easily fitted to boat bunks. For children in V-berths or other hard-to-get-to berths, you may not want to have the normal sheet and blanket makeup because of the difficulty for either parent or child to do this every day. Sleeping bags are fine for occasional use in cooler climates, but not for everyday use. Many cruisers have come up with a solution similar to ours. We have removable elasticized covers fitted over the V-berths (ours are a cotton quilted fabric commonly available in fabric stores), acting as a bottom sheet and as a day-cover for the fabric of the bunk. These must be washed and replaced often, but they are easy to make. A nice bright comforter acts as a top cover that is warm in cool weather, but not too warm in the tropics. When the comforter wears out or gets stained, it can easily be recovered for a quick and inexpensive redecoration. Our pillows have shams with easy Velcro closures. We have sleeping bags for sleepovers and occasional guests, as well as extra comforters for cold nights. These extra items are nicely kept at the foot of the bunks in fabric bags made to look like throw pillows. Throughout the years our family has lived aboard, the children have used some variation on this basic decor in the V-berth area they share, although it has been through numerous redecorations. For insulation and protection in rough weather when the kids were very young, I padded the teak hull liner adjacent to each bunk with a layer of 1-inch foam covered with colorful quilted fabric; this has just recently been removed to expose the teak paneling. During those early years we snap-shackled fitted netting over the open area of the bunks to keep them in; there has always been a heavy fabric "wall" between the two berths. Now they each have a privacy curtain that can be used to close off the open part of the berth.

Most cruising boats have a double berth, sometimes even a queen. This berth is usually in a large area and is therefore easier to make up. A sheet and blanket arrangement may be okay here. Some double or queen berths take standard-size sheets, blankets, and spreads or comforters, perhaps with a few adjustments for the corners or pinched ends. If the area is difficult to make up, you may want to use a bottom contour sheet and a comforter for a cover, as in the V-berth area. We use pillow shams, and fabric bags that act as throw pillows to hold extra blankets and covers.

Pillows mildew and need to be replaced frequently. Foam cushions condense under heavier areas of your body and also need replacement when they become uncomfortable or flat. You will quickly develop back problems if you sleep on a cushion that has bottomed out. Special foam that is denser and thicker than that used for seats is available for sleeping cushions. It can be cut to size by most marine upholstery shops and should be at least 6 inches thick and covered with a breathable fabric on top and sides. Waterproof them on the bottom if you will be in cold climates, to keep condensation from penetrating the foam. The last time we replaced our sleeping cushions we went to a mattress company that specializes in bedding for cruise ships. They made a very comfortable, real mattress with extra-dense foam, ticking on the bottom, quilting on the top, and vents sewn into the sides. It was not a budget item, but neither is a bad back.

We all like to have our floating home as "homey" as possible. Attaching mementos, photos, and paintings to the bare walls helps in this respect. I do not like to make permanent holes in the teak because I change and move wall hangings frequently. Foam tape that is sticky on both sides (called *mounting tape;* 3M brand works well) can be used for this purpose and has yet to ruin any of my varnished teak surfaces after years of use (it may have to be removed with Goo-Gone or a similar product). Sticky-backed Velcro can also be used for this purpose. Some paintings last better than others. Photos under glass should have a mat so that the photo is not in contact with the glass surface; acrylic and Plexiglas do not seem to hurt photos in the marine environment. Framed paintings on paper sometimes mold, as do their mats, and I've seen oil paintings on canvas become moldy. Acrylic paintings on hardboard seem to last well if the board is sealed on all sides and at the edges.

In cold weather I became tired of bumping into the cold aluminum mast below decks every time I walked past it. I covered it with the same fabric I use for the cushions, and now it's nice and warm. One lovely treatment I have seen was a spiral "macramé" design, like the one many boaters use on their wheel, made from manila rope with half-hitches that covered the whole mast. Another cruiser we met decorated the mast as a Christmas tree.

SLEEPING AREAS

When checking out boats, don't just stretch out in the bunks—sit up in them. Get up in them. Pretend you are making them. Turn over in them. Sit up suddenly as though you were in a confused panic in a storm. (Did you hit your head?) What happens at the foot end? Some V-berths and after stateroom berths I've seen lately have absurdly cramped V-ends. What will you have to do to make the bed every day? If this is a double sleeping arrangement, what will happen if one person has to get up in the night? In many of these setups, the sleeping partner will be stepped on, kneeled on, or crawled on.

We strongly prefer aft-cabin/center-cockpit boats for families with kids. This gives the parents and the kids their own end of the boat and separates those ends not only with bulkheads but with space. We have repeatedly noticed that families do much better— all members—with an aft-cabin arrangement. Also, the aft cabin allows use of the wide stern found in so many boats for creature comfort and personal storage areas. An after lazarette for storage of large bulky equipment is not necessarily precluded just because you have an aft cabin.

We often hear people say, "Oh, the staterooms on a boat are just where you sleep at night. They don't need much space." For long-term cruising, your stateroom may be the most important part of the boat. It's your refuge. It's your private place. It's where you put personal items that you used to keep on your dresser or in your little middle drawer or special box when you lived in a house. You do much more than just sleep there. You escape there, refresh there, recreate there. You dress and store clothes there. You do a lot of living there. Be sure that your stateroom has the features neces-sary to serve you well. Most of these features are obvious, but some are perhaps not so obvious. For example, if your stateroom has tanks under the bed, be sure that they are exceptionally well baf-fled. If they aren't, the sloshing and banging of the water or fuel against the tank sides and top will keep you up night after night. You won't be able to hear this in the boat show or at the marina. You will hear it remarkably well during your first night at sea or in a rolly anchorage.

Many people also use their stateroom as an office of sorts. In the aft stateroom of *Chez Nous* we set up a desk that stores under the bed. This book was written entirely in our aft stateroom, while we were underway and at anchor. Sometimes the girls use it as a classroom.

Some boats that are designed to emphasize open spaces have completely open staterooms. Curtains provide "privacy," and the rooms are barely separated from the main salon. What a disaster for a cruising boat! Many couples take off with kids whose "stateroom" is an open quarter berth or salon berth. Although circumstances may make this necessary, avoid it if you can. If, for example, your child is to use a quarter berth, try to build a bulkhead around at least part of it. Or close it off with easily worked but heavily insulated curtains. Everyone needs private space. Of course, when adding bulkheading to a quarter berth, you must be sure to do it in a way that will not block quick access to the engine or any other critical spaces.

Thus far, I've emphasized aft staterooms in center-cockpit boats for two reasons. First, most of the older aft-cockpit boats don't come with a true aft cabin. Second, most (not all) of the newer ones that do claim to have an "aft cabin" along with an aft cockpit simply cheat. What they have is nothing more than a quarter berth cramped in where the side-cockpit lazarette locker used to be. These are terrible as liveaboard staterooms. They have very poor ventilation. You can't sit up in the bed. Often you can't even turn over. There is no space to dress or move about when you get out of the bed; you have to step outside into the main salon or the galley. There are few drawers or bins, and there are tiny, or no, hanging lockers. There are no places to put things like glasses, books, watches, and wallets when you go to bed. There are no places to keep little bits of private things. They are just shells coated with teak veneer and carpeting to make buyers think they're getting a 50-foot boat instead of a 35-foot boat. And on top of it all, you would be sleeping right next to the engine (maybe even on top of it), and every time you'd have to get to one side of the engine you'd have to crawl around your bed and bedroom, covered with oil and grease. Many of these aft-cockpit/aft-staterooms virtually preclude any meaningful engine access on that side. I've seen a few good aft cabins in aft-cockpit boats, but these boats are at least 40 feet or more in length. You just can't have everything.

THE COCKPIT

How well does the cockpit work for you? Can you sleep on the seats? This may be very important for night watches during long passages. (You may want to sleep there while your mate is at the wheel.) Are the seats comfortable? Is the back high enough? Is the incline comfortable? Many center-cockpit boats are designed with an uncomfortably low back to avoid too high a profile. I'd much rather be comfortable in this very important space. Can you get around the wheel without getting tangled up with the helmsman or in the wheel itself? When the boat heels, will you slide off the seat, or is the space to the next seat short enough so that you can prop yourself with your legs?

Study the layout of the sail-handling lines. They should be lead so that they don't crisscross the cockpit and interfere with your comfort or your safety. If they are attached to a track just forward of the wheel, for example, you have both a safety and a comfort problem. One good arrangement is to have the main traveler aft or forward of the cockpit with lines leading near the wheel. The jibsheet lines coming in from the side should also lead to a position near the wheel. This arrangement enables you to trim sails from the steering position. Remember that while you may not mind jumping up and down during weekend races, or yelling to the crew to do it for you, this setup will get old quickly when you're making routine sail changes day in and day out on long passages. Some boats have a good arrangement for raising the main from the cockpit. Check all fairleads carefully. As a general rule, the farther the lines are lead, the greater the likelihood of snarls or snags.

Walk around on deck. Do you have to duck and stoop under the stays to go forward? That will be a nuisance, especially when you are tied up (hopefully not too often) bow-in and have to pass fore and aft every time you get off the boat. It is even worse when you are carrying aboard groceries and stores.

PRIVATE SPACES

While you are trying out all these spaces and arrangements, check out the privacy angle. In later chapters, I'll talk about privacy for kids, a factor adults often overlook. You won't be able to overlook your short temper if you find yourself without sufficient private spaces. The opportunity to create these may be scant on your boat, but you should plan for as much private space as possible, as early as possible. Above we noted that the stateroom is the place for designated private space. If you don't provide for it there, do it elsewhere.

WORK AREAS

There is a major difference between fixing and maintaining a cruising boat and fixing and maintaining a weekend boat. This difference is sometimes overlooked by boat designers and builders, and also future cruisers. The failure to recognize the difference can, and often does, ruin a cruise. The typical boat is built with the assumption that when components break or need major maintenance you'll get off the boat, go home with your family, call your friendly neighborhood marina, and have them fix the problem for you. Maybe you can, but maybe you can't. There are many great cruising grounds in the world—actually some of the best—that don't have marinas, repair yards, or parts. There are also a lot of oceans in the world with this deficiency. So, if you're thinking about going cruising, you had better start thinking about this dynamic. If you are the hardy type (or the poor type, like me), you will leave some of your family at home or in the pool next weekend, and tackle it yourself. The only person or people aboard will be those involved in the project. This will not be the case when you are cruising.

When something needs fixing you won't have any place to go. The family will be living on top of, around, over, and/or under whatever needs fixing and whoever is fixing it. This is not fun. And you can pull out scores of pretty magazines that tell you how to fix things yourself, and very few of them will tell you how to handle this problem. While you are doing the job, the family will still need to prepare meals, eat them, do homework, sleep, get some privacy, go to the bathroom, get clean. You may need to do a lot more of some of these things, like cleaning up and sleeping, because of the job in progress. Stress is likely to be at an all-time high. You'll be worried about the broken component and when and whether it will be fixed. Those working on the component will be busting their knuckles, cutting their fingers, battling frustration and sometimes anger—especially at the white-coated office worker who designed the boat or the component. Those not actually doing the job will be doing other jobs related to it. First of all, they'll be putting up with those doing the job. Then, they'll be doing everything else that needs to be done because at least one person is tied up making the repair. As all of you cope with all of this, your living spaces will be disrupted, perhaps totally torn apart. Your life patterns will be disrupted or may be temporarily nonexistent. Everyday habits and customs and movements will be impossible. Everybody on the boat will be in a mood that is not overly conducive to putting up with the crises and with each other. But you will have to deal with it, you will have to deal with it then and there, and you will have to deal with it yourselves.

The place to begin is with the boat you are buying or fitting out. And the good news is, there are many things you can do to lessen the problem. Examine your dream boat closely, *before* you commit to buying it. If it's already yours, start looking at it with an eye toward making cruising-boat changes at least a year or so before you leave. Look at each system and component and determine what you would have to take apart or move if you had to fix or replace it. Think about how normal living routines will be affected. If the answer is "a lot," don't buy the boat. If you already own the boat, begin to do some serious remodeling.

When thinking about workspace, realize that you'll need access space for everything you must service. This sounds absurdly obvious, but it sure doesn't seem to be obvious to many boatbuilders.

I recently inspected a brand-new, expensive boat. It had beautiful joinerwork, a strong hull, and looked very comfortable. But its engine was so low in the bilge that you could get to only the top third. You couldn't get to the starter, the starter solenoid, many fuel-line connections, the injector pump, and the list goes on. This boat had been built specifically for cruising. I was on another boat in which the engine was under the companionway. The hull liner and cabinetry were so tight around part of it that you couldn't even touch the starter and many other components. The builder was aboard, so I asked him about this. He asked, "Why would you need to reach your starter?" He must have assumed that whenever the solenoid hung up or the starter burned up (as they do rather frequently low down in a bilge with salt air and water around), you would just get towed in and call a yard mechanic with a stick of dynamite and a crowbar. As a cost-control measure, things like engines, refrigeration, hot-water tanks, water pumps, and just about everything else are dropped in, and then other structures, such as the deck, are lowered over them. It makes sense until you have to fix something.

And I'm not talking about having just enough space to see the starter. Without powerful mental telepathy, this won't do you much good. Just touching the starter or getting your hands around it won't do either. Healing by the laying on of hands has never worked well on my equipment; it probably won't on yours. Space in which to fix something, be it a starter or anything else, means, at a very minimum, space to see it and get your head and upper body near it without sitting on or lying on and breaking something else, space to get your tools to the object and to use them, and space to disengage the component or its offending part and get it out of the hole in which it resides—again, without breaking it, or something else, in the process. Inevitably, even in the best-designed boat, other equipment, components, or parts will have to be moved to make room. But you should be fanatical about preventing this as much as possible. Remember, many repairs you make yourself will be done in a hurry, with other equipment running. They'll perhaps be done underway, in the ocean. These repairs, then, may be matters not only of convenience but also of immediate safety.

Crawl about and inspect your boat, for hours or days if necessary, to determine what needs to be done to provide good access space for working on its systems and components. The cure will often be easy. (For more on engines, see chapter 12.)

A workshop.   Many projects will desperately require a shop in which you can place parts on a well-lighted work surface and apply force—using drills, Dremel tools, files, wheel presses, and the like. You'll need to be able to leave these parts in the shop and move on to other jobs that come up unexpectedly, or to let the glue dry on one project while you attend to something else.

Unless you have a very big boat, you will not have a "shop." Although this may be asking far too much for the size of your boat, look for some corner, somewhere, that you can use for a small shop space of sorts. It might be a temporary arrangement on one side of the cockpit when you're at anchor. At least it gets the mess out of the below-decks living area, but not out of the salt spray and rain. Boats with engine rooms can often accommodate a shelf that is left open to serve this purpose. Couples cruising without kids sometimes use the forepeak as a shop as well as a storage and hobby area. Some people use the navigation station as a shop, although this is usually in the middle of the living area and interferes with other things, not to mention navigation. If you won't be able to set aside exclusive shop space, you might be able to store large but easily moved items in a space that can be quickly converted for this use.

Our boat came with a second bathroom, so I converted it into a shop of sorts. I don't do any really heavy work there because I don't want to damage the fine teak and cabinetry. I carry a 2-inch-by-10-inch board on deck (more on this in chapter 20) that is secured to the stanchions just inside the toerail. I can set it up in the cockpit, placing one end on each side seat. It is through-drilled to receive the bolts that mount a bench vise, an indispensable tool that is useless without a bench. The piece of timber serves well. It also serves as a gangplank and fulfills other shipboard needs. If the work needs to be covered, I use a heavy-duty garbage bag. This arrangement has been invaluable over the years; it takes up only part of the cockpit, and when the work is done we have that space back again.

The engine and other systems.   One of the first systems people think about is the engine. Some boatbuilders proudly point to a little door you can open to find a dipstick. They think they have solved all the maintenance access problems. Look at where that little door is. Is it under the galley sink? Is it right beside your pillow in your aft stateroom? Is it right beside your only toilet? Do you really think that checking the oil is all you'll have to do? Checking the oil is actually the easiest and least obtrusive thing that you'll do.

Assume that at sometime during your cruise you will perform major surgery on your engine, surgery that will last several days. If the engine is under your kitchen sink or in your galley, you are in for problems. If you can't use the toilet, you're in for problems. Look around and determine who can't do what when major work is required. Make whatever changes you can to remedy this. Often, the engine is so big and consumes so much space that nothing can be done, but perhaps you can change the layout of the systems next to it. Sometimes, just adding hatches—large and easy to remove—around the engine will solve a lot of this difficulty.

A good solution, in boats of 37 feet and longer, is to have an aft cabin arrangement with the engine room under the cockpit. The engine room should contain as many systems as is practical. This setup is an excellent compromise. Some builders don't favor these engine rooms because they supposedly take up too much potential living space. These are the same builders who wedge the engine into a little slot between the galley and a head and an aft passage and whatever else they can think of. A shoehorn is the first tool you'll need with these installations, but there is a wonderful feeling of spaciousness when you go below at the boat show. It is true that a dedicated engine and equipment room takes away from living space, but other arrangements may obliterate most of the living space while you're making repairs.

If you do have a dedicated engine room, be sure it has not become cluttered with additions, such as refrigeration, generators, and air conditioners. The people who install equipment usually haven't a clue about fixing it in the field. They have even less of a clue about fixing it at sea. Therefore, you'll sometimes find a great space that has been rendered almost worthless because component is piled on top of component. The only thing you can get to is the top component. If your engine room is cluttered, you can often unclutter it before you leave by building shelves and moving components onto them. For example, an air conditioner or refrigeration compressor or hot-water heater can live just as well on a shelf glassed to the bulkhead as it can stuffed beside the stringers under the engine. The shelves are relatively easy to build and glass in place, but you'll have to take the components out first. Obviously, doing this after your family has moved aboard would be a nightmare. Remember that many components, such as refrigeration units, won't work as well in a hot engine room.

A refrigeration compressor or extra-duty alternator bolted to the engine can be difficult to access. If it blocks access to anything else on the engine, particularly a high-maintenance item like a water pump, fuel pump, heat exchanger, or bleeding point, move it. Engine-bolted refrigeration compressors are among the most critical sore spots. If you have to move one to fix something on your engine, you may well have to break the refrigerant seal. This can be a major problem and expense, causing loss of the use of your freezer and stored food in the interim. An alternator, which involves only bolts and wiring, is much easier to move.

Access to wiring is another critical problem. If it is crammed in tight between the headliner and the hull, it is likely to fail, possibly causing a fire. It will also be difficult to replace, and you may have a tough time running new wire for new equipment. Check for wire runs that are free and unencumbered, with space to use them. Also be sure that your electrical panel either opens when needed or has enough space behind it so that you can get back there quickly to see what is sizzling and smoking. Be sure, however, that the hot area is properly secured to avoid accidental access by your kids.

Bilge, shower sump, and potable freshwater pumps, with an extra few feet of hose and wiring, can be moved easily. Most can be mounted in any position, including on bulkheads, but you must provide a safe drip path should the pump develop a leak. Don't have the drip path go to any other part or wiring or back into the pump's motor. Hot-water heaters are often in the most remote corner. This, they say, is because you never have to service them. Wrong. You have to replace anodes, heating elements, and plumbing. If the plumbing, or the heater itself, springs a leak, you may have to bypass or fix that leak to avoid continuous loss of fresh water. It is usually easier to move whatever is in front of a water heater than to remove the heater itself, because they do require relatively low maintenance.

The generator.   If your boat has an inboard AC generator, remember that all of its sides and parts must be easy to access. Many boat manufacturers put them in with only one side exposed; the other side is backed up against a bulkhead. Their rationale is that "all serviceable parts are on this side." Indeed, they have the generator manufacturer's brochures that proclaim things like "easy access, regular service areas on one side." Again, these folks have no clue about the cruiser's use of this equipment. Items thought to require regular service include the dipstick, belt, coolant water tank, raw- and freshwater pumps, and fuel pump. These are usually all nicely placed on the "front" side of the unit. But these are not the only regular service items. The starter and its wiring are always on the back of the generator and, on any marine internal combustion engine the starter will fail after a few years, largely because of the corrosive effects of salt air and water. If the starter doesn't fail, its solenoid surely will. When the solenoid fails, the starter either engages and won't release, causing it to burn up, or it doesn't engage at all. This happens as a matter of course, because the solenoid has a metal piston that slides up and down within a metal sleeve with fairly close tolerances. Excess grease inside the sleeve gums it up.

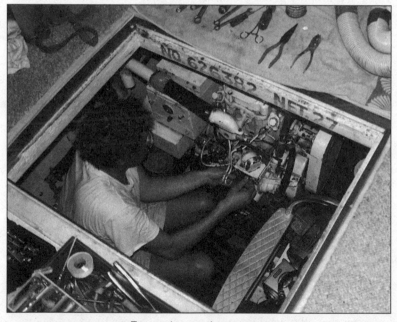

Tom working on the generator.

A little bit of rusty powder stops the sliding action. The piston can sometimes be freed with the tap of a hammer, but not if you can't get back there to do it. The starter has heavy-duty wires that run from the battery to its terminals. When these terminals become corroded, the resultant high resistance causes intense heat; some-times the wires become loose, causing arcing and perhaps a dead short and a fire. These wires and their terminals must be inspected regularly. The exhaust manifold will probably have an injection nipple where seawater is shot into the exhaust for cooling. This is usually cast iron, so it rusts and clogs. If this happens, your exhaust hose could overheat and burn, introducing deadly exhaust gases into the boat, or your generator may just overheat and stop. Obviously, you need to inspect the exhaust manifold and its injection elbow. This is behind the generator.

Interior diesel generators are great if you can afford one and have the space. We love ours. But they are a marriage of an internal combustion engine, seawater, and high-voltage electricity. They are serious business, and potentially dangerous if you don't have good all-around access.

The head. I hate to mention the head again, but access can be a problem here, too. Toilets are commonly stuffed into a tight corner in the bathroom. Gaining access for your tools to turn bolts and screws will be a challenge. The outlet nipple may be jammed into that thick and very rigid outlet hose so that you can't take it off without moving the entire head. And often the outlet hose will be so stuffed into liner and hull stiffeners that you may not be able to see it, much less work on it, except where it interfaces with the head and the through-hull and marine sanitation device (MSD). This hose will require maintenance (see chapter 14). If you don't have the space to get the hose out, you'll be in for a lot of unwanted fun. This space must be more than a spot to put your body and pull. There must be clearance space around the hose to enable you to pull it through the bulkheads and partitions.

Safety. Before leaving the subject of space to fix things, we should emphasize the safety aspect of this subject. We have heard some people say, "Well, if the motor breaks, I'll just sail back. It is a sailboat, you know." This is a good point, and you should always be prepared to sail back. But a working engine can save your boat and your life. You may need to get into a dangerous current-swept cut in order to run from a serious storm. You may need to get out of a congested, foggy shipping lane. You may be in the dark of night, becalmed, and realize that the huge ship bearing down on you does not see you and isn't listening. You may need to reach a doctor on a calm day. There are many instances in which a working motor means safety. Fixing it well does, too. Other components, such as a sump pump or refrigeration, for example, are obviously not so critical, but their failure can result in a chain of events that could lead to safety problems. You don't want to slash open your wrist on that piece of metal nearby while you're pulling out the broken unit.

Adequate workspace is a matter of safety, as well as convenience. And if you think about these issues before you get your boat or, at least, well before you leave, you will have fewer problems.

STORAGE SPACES

The more storage space you have, the better. As you've probably surmised, however, it isn't that simple. Storage space often usurps living space. The comments in the earlier part of this chapter point out the problem with some of the newer boats that have lots of open space but little storage space. This gets us into the question of methods of storage in general.

The main purpose here is to determine the best possible use of the two basic types of storage space: bulk space and special-purpose space. Bulk spaces include the areas under the bunks and cabin soles and in the lazarettes (lockers near the stern). Special-purpose spaces include drawers and hanging lockers. Access to bulk storage is a major concern because it can limit the times when you'll use that space (e.g., not while your kids are sleeping if it's under their bunks) and what you can put in it. No matter what the size of the space, if the equipment won't go into the opening, you can't put it there. And there are other criteria that determine the best use of space. For example, you won't want to store grain or electric motors in a space against the hull that will be sweating and moist all the time. You won't want to store engine parts that are susceptible to rust near the bilge. You won't want to put linen in anything but a very dry space.

Bulk spaces seem to have more value per cubic foot than special-purpose spaces, such as drawers and racks. This is not to say that the latter aren't important, just that these spaces should not eliminate too many bulk spaces. You can put just about anything you want in bulk spaces; they are much more versatile. You may have to segregate items you would normally put together, but that's a small problem if the bulk space accommodates your stuff. You may also want to modify bulk spaces to suit your needs. This takes a only little carpentry skill, unless you also change the visible finished surfaces.

It is easy to keep stored material from becoming a jumbled mass, and to protect it, by using various inexpensive products. We keep a good supply of heavy-duty garbage bags aboard for light, softer items. They're also good for storing our heavy-duty garbage until we can get to a place that will take it. Heavy-duty kitchen storage bags with sealing tops such as the Ziploc brand make great containers, even for small engine parts. You can see what's inside, and you can seal out moisture. They will eventually crack and tear, but you need to inspect all stored items periodically anyway. Plastic bins and boxes, such as Rubbermaid and Tupperware, are good for tougher, heavier items. Various plastic storage systems are available, including stackable boxes. We store grain in collapsible plastic water jugs found in camping supply stores. As a rule, no matter where a storage space is, unless it's in one of those places that you inspect all the time, such as a bedroom drawer, it will get wet or moist. This is particularly true if you take your boat to cooler climates. Normal fall and spring weather can cause condensation inside the hull, particularly on an uninsulated fiberglass or metal boat. If you store items in plastic bags or containers, take care that they aren't flush against a sweating hull. The condensation can transfer to the inside of the bag. Several manufacturers claim that their products soak up moisture in boat storage areas. We haven't tried them all, but our impression is that they really are not able to soak up the volume of moisture found on a boat. There are numerous instances, however, when you may want to include some of these products in a small, sealed container that hold small and particularly vulnerable parts, such as camera equipment. When using ziptop-type bags or other airtight containers, seal them on days of low humidity if possible.

Be alert to possible temperature extremes when you store food and other heat-sensitive items. Obviously the engine spaces will be warm. In the hot sun the areas right under the deck may also be very warm. Items stored on deck within dark containers will get quite warm when the sun shines on them. If, for example, you store diesel fuel out in the sun in red jugs without adding Biobor or a similar product to stop growth of algae, you may quickly get a real mess in the bottom of the jugs. But you can keep them cooler, and make the jugs last longer, by covering them with a light-colored cloth. Except for the section closest to the engine, the bilge is usually the coolest part of a boat.

The worst problem with bulk storage space is remembering what is there and finding it amidst all the other items. Store the heaviest items lowest down and the lightest ones on top. If we have a big hole, we try to put like or related items inside. For example, a big hole forward may have extra rope and ground tackle. Another big and rather dry hole might have grain and food stuffs. A smaller hole, also dry, might contain plastic boxes with delicate engine and sewing machine parts. We label the outsides of all containers, even plastic bags, with indelible marker.

We try to keep a list of stored mechanical items on a simple computer database. This doesn't require a pricey marine program; we use an early version of Microsoft Works. With a program like this, and there are many, you can create a database and tailor it to your needs and your boat. Our database tells us what we have, how much we have, where it is stored, where we last got it, the price and part number, and other information. We devised a list of abbreviations for different storage places; for example, "frd top prt h2o" means "on top of the port water tank, at the forward end." This database will also let you know when to resupply. Many items, such as epoxy, glue, food, batteries—just to name a few—have a short shelf life. Once they have expired, they just take up valuable space and could be harmful or ineffective when you try to use them. This database has been of immense value over the years. No matter how smart you think you are, when you have a crisis you may find it impossible to remember where you put that widget two years ago. Of course, you must discipline yourself to enter the data when you store a part and to change the data when you remove that part, but the effort will save you time in the long run. If you don't have a computer, make a handwritten list and keep it in a safe place known to all crewmembers. Not only could you forget where it is, otherwise, but your crew won't be happy if you're sick or incapacitated or off the boat when they try to guess where you might have squirreled it away.

Yet another aspect of bulk storage is timing. For example, you don't want your hors d'oeuvre bin to be under the locker where your guests sit. You'll want the toilet paper stored within reaching distance of the head (in plastic bags), not in the engine space. Items you use regularly or in emergencies should be stored where they can be easily and quickly obtained. These may include spare anchors and anchor rode, spare fuel and water hoses, fuel pumps, impellers, tools, flashlights (these should be everywhere), duct tape, volt-ohm meter, knives, snacks during passages, and so on. Use the hard-to-reach spaces for items that are seldom used and never needed in a crisis. For us, these items include extra stores of rope and chain, canned and glass-jar goods, wood and metal scraps, extra hoses for water and engine plumbing, and even some durable parts such as a spare heat exchanger.

Again, keep a dated list of items you won't use or see frequently, and inspect them periodically. Date the items as you store them. Some, such as batteries, should already have an expiration date on them. Avoid buying items with a known shelf life unless the expiration date is on them. If you can't find ones with expiration dates, write the date of purchase on the container and use the oldest containers first. Glue, resin, and sealants are examples. Bottled and canned goods will probably lose their labels in the moisture (besides, cockroaches love the glue that's used to stick them on), so it's a good idea to remove the labels anyway and write contents, expiration date, and other relevant information on the container with waterproof ink. Any time you see any breach, bulging, or other even slightly unusual thing about any food product, throw it away. Tomato products should never be kept longer than a year, and most canned fruits have so much acid in them that the cans will disintegrate after a year. Never take chances with this. Food poisoning is bad enough ashore, three blocks from the hospital; you don't even want to think about it at sea.

Treat any engine parts with a liberal coating of rust-preventative oil before storing, and take all parts out occasionally for inspection and re-oiling. Normally, the oil should go inside the part as well as outside. A good spray like WD-40 will usually seep into crevices. I have dipped parts into a bucket of clean lube oil and rotated them when I felt that spray wouldn't permeate well enough. Obviously, mechanical items shouldn't be stored where they will be exposed to salt water or spray, but you should also avoid exposing them to salty air. Any untreated steel or cast iron, especially if it has been machined or has a shiny surface, will rust quickly. Some parts, like spare diesel injectors, should be wrapped in oily cloth or similar material. Injectors are also a good example of mechanical parts that must be serviced occasionally, even when in storage. Sometimes the fuel that has been used to test the injector will turn into a varnishlike substance, as will old gasoline, and plug up the atomizer. You may pull out that unused injector and find that it doesn't work. (Whenever you have your injectors serviced, take them to a reputable shop and be sure that they use the finest oil for testing. This will help to prevent or delay this problem.)

There isn't as much to be said about special storage places. We don't like too many of those pretty drawers, because the framework for them takes up a lot of otherwise useable space. Some of them can make quite an improvement in your quality of life, however. Not only do they generally keep items dry, they are convenient. They are the best answer for folded clothes, which is most of what you will be wearing. What is "enough of them" will depend on the size and type of boat, the size of your family, and your preferences. But each family member should have at least two good-size drawers in or near the sleeping area. It isn't unusual to find pretty bins and drawers that aren't suited for much of anything, so make sure that the things you want to put in them fit. Many boats have hanging lockers that won't take long dresses or suits. We've seen cutlery spaces that won't take normal-size cutlery. We use the space between the drawer framework and the hull for storage of small canned goods and any other appropriate-size, well-protected and well-packaged items.

Bins are a great compromise between bulk space and drawers. They allow easy access without pulling things apart, but they don't require all the framework. They can appear attractive from the outside, with a teak hinged door, but inside they can be as cavernous as the hull allows. Obviously, you don't want a bin that extends beyond your reach. An enclosed bin can accomplish much of the function of a drawer but provide more space. It keeps stored items off the hull or deck.

Records are a very important storage item that is usually overlooked by boatbuilders. Most recreational boatowners keep all their records at home; they need only a small place aboard for a few records, such as the boat registration and title. When you go cruising, you'll need to have many of your records aboard. These will include financial records, warranty papers, manuals and instruction books, receipts, copies of insurance policies, tax records *and forms*, and more. You can and should keep the originals of some of this material at a shore base, in a safety deposit box, for example. Unless you trust someone enough to give them access to that box, you won't be able to get to it without coming back. This could be a very expensive trip. You had better keep aboard at least a copy of whatever you may need. Store all documents in a moisture-resistant box(es) or, at the least, in drawers in a well-ventilated part of the boat. Uncovered envelope seals and any uncovered gummed labels will stick together because of the moisture and heat. To prevent this, insert a sliver of waxed paper between any gummed surface and its mating surface. Store these materials in a sealed ziptop bag. Any airtight container could develop condensation inside as the temperature changes. Check records regularly.

Your boat should have at least one good hanging locker. Hanging lockers are important because you're bound to have some clothing items that have to be hung. In some boats, however, these are worthless. They should have doors big enough to take a full suit of clothes without your having to ball them up, and they should be wide enough at the bottom so that hanging clothes don't get scrunched up. Because the hull curves in at the bottom, this may be nothing more than a pinched slit. Hanging lockers must also have good ventilation.

Many builders try to put one hanging locker in each sleeping area to suit charter-guest requirements and end up having none that are big enough. One good hanging locker for the whole boat is far better than a bunch of tiny fake lockers. When you use these, remember that your clothes will move as the boat moves. You will therefore want to stuff them to some extent to keep them from chafing and fraying. Make sure you have a conveniently located, well-designed wet locker for your foul-weather gear and boots. These items should be stored near the companionway.

It helps to place your best clothes in plastic storage bags, except those that you wear frequently. All hangers should be plastic or wood to avoid rust. You'll typically find unused space behind the clothes rack at the top of the locker. This is a good place to stuff extra paper towels and other lightweight items.

Shoes are always a problem to store, so it's best to limit the number you bring aboard. They are prone to mildew and tend to bring sand or dirt aboard. Our cruising friends have many solutions, from having everyone remove shoes when they come aboard (or even beforehand) to limiting everyone to one pair. We try to be reasonable and limit shoes to one pair of flip-flops, deck shoes, running shoes, and dress shoes per person. Flip-flops are kept on deck in a bin. Everyone's daily shoes go in the cockpit and the remainder are stored in various lockers. Each person will need one pair of good walking shoes for long hikes ashore. Avoid black soles that mar the deck.

Utilize all available storage space. This is how we use the clothes dryer.

▼

Look around your boat carefully for spaces that have been closed in by cabinetry but contain valuable empty space—it might be just the right size for some of the smaller items you need to store. These spaces can be opened by sawing carefully into the cabinet surface, paying attention as you do to any hidden surprises, such as the hull or wiring. We have finished off some of these holes with a fingerhole and battens under the cover or with screw-in deck plates. You will be amazed at how many hidden spaces you'll find.

Another source of storage space may be in designated areas that you are not using. Spare or unused shower stalls and bathtubs make excellent storage spaces. V-berth areas that are unused except for occasional guests can be converted to semipermanent storage by using bins and crates. Our clothes washer and dryer get no use, so we keep them full of various items such as linens and paper products. Be creative in your search for extra space; it's there, you just have to find or convert it. Some cruisers convert the whole second head, which almost no one needs, into a pantry. Some have even gone so far as to use their only head for storage and revert to buckets and water bags heated on deck. This is a drastic solution; we'd rather have the head.

When storing many items, remove excess packaging (remove toothpaste tubes from the boxes, for example) so that you don't have a lot of cardboard around. It gets wet from condensation and takes up space. Some objects may be easier, or more difficult, to store out of their packaging. Ziploc bags are great for bunching together these loose items.

Keep all of this in mind as you buy things. For example, powdered dish soap will harden in the box during storage; liquid soap in plastic bottles won't. Plastic containers store better than glass and tin. Individually wrapped perishable food, while perhaps more expensive, may last much longer.

On-deck storage is especially difficult for cruising sailors. We all know that our decks should be clear in severe weather conditions. We also know that we need extra space to store important things like jerry jugs for gas, diesel, kerosene, and water; we need a place for our toys, like windsurfers, boogie boards, and extra dinghies. All of that stuff that we don't have a place for down below or in lazarettes has to go somewhere. When you determine the type of cruising you wish to do and where and in what conditions, you'll be able to determine how much, if anything, you will be able to safely carry on deck. Most newer boats, in the never-ending quest for larger accommodations below, have eliminated important stowage spaces in cockpits and on deck. Center-cockpit boats with walk-throughs and the new aft-cabin/aft-cockpit models are especially lacking in this type of storage. Whatever is on deck should be securely attached and should not be so valuable that you can't live without it (since you might lose it or have to ditch it). Dinghies, which may have no other place to live, and life rafts, which will probably be on deck, require special mounting considerations. The safety netting we put around for the kids when they were tiny has been replaced many times. It is invaluable for keeping on-deck items in place.

Give special consideration to life raft storage. It must be very secure so that it won't wash off even with seas sweeping the deck. It must be where you can launch it safely, quickly, and easily—without becoming tangled or obstructed. You must then be able to get in it. Extra survival gear should be stored in a place where you can get it instantly as you are leaving, but where it is also safe. This might be just inside the companionway. No one knows what horrors the sea will dish out or what the circumstances will be if they have to abandon ship and use a life raft. I've heard excellent debates between survival experts as to whether the raft should be mounted on the stern. Some say that this makes for easier escape; others say that boarding seas from astern are likely to tear it off. Try to visualize what you would do if your vessel were sinking in a storm at night. Read accounts of others who have abandoned ship and survived. If you are buying a vessel, look for special places that the builder has (or should have) constructed or molded in for this purpose.

We always hear the maxim that space on a cruising boat is at a premium. But if we attack the issue with foresight and planning we can make significant improvements. These improvements will make us more comfortable, will make life more convenient, and will make cruising safer.

Chapter Nine

CHOOSING A BOAT

Chapter 8 covered the basic qualities necessary to make a boat livable, comfortable, and with sufficient space and convenient layout. This chapter continues that discussion by delving further into the process of choosing the boat that's right for you.

To a certain extent, what is livable for one family might not be for another. As a guideline, then, I'll give you our criteria for a cruising boat for two to four people who will do the type of cruising I've discussed in previous chapters. Here's my profile of an "ideal" cruising boat: 30 to 50 feet long—the largest you can afford within that range; a draft of not more than 5.5 feet; a mast no higher than around 60 feet from the water; the ability to sail, motor, and maneuver well; excellent anchoring equipment; a good aft cabin (if the boat is around 40 feet or longer); ample storage space; sufficient private space; a comfortable interior design/layout; wider, modern lines that allow for extra creature comfort; sound construction; good safety features; a solid (not cored) hull with internal lead ballast (many people strongly disagree on the desirability of cored hulls, and new materials and techniques may even change my mind); and good maintenance access throughout.

I explain our reasons for singling out these features below, and in chapter 8.

A BOAT TO SUIT YOUR PLANS AND DREAMS

If you want to cruise up and down the ICW on the U.S. east coast, don't buy a boat designed for round-the-world sailing. Seems obvious? Well, people do get carried away. In this scenario, you'd be spending beaucoup dollars for accoutrements you don't need and giving up creature comforts in favor of design features you don't need. On the other hand, the trend toward building "coastal cruisers" that lack offshore seaworthiness is disturbing. Mother

Nature can dish it out, even on inland waters. If you are sailing around in an unseaworthy piece of junk, you may find to your peril that the dollars saved were dollars lost. Whatever boat you buy, the underlying criteria should be sound construction, safety, and seaworthiness.

FIND QUALITY

If you need help in judging the quality of the boats you're interested in, hire a surveyor who knows his stuff, who is not wired into the local community of boat brokers, who understands that he is working exclusively for you, and who knows how you plan to use the boat. This will be a very rare bird, but there are some around. Ask friends. Ask the marina operator with whom you do business. Ask brokers you know and trust. And interview the prospects before you spend money. If you have a good friend who is qualified, you may be better served at less expense. Look for proven designs and boats. If you are buying new, buy from a reputable company that has been around for a while, one you expect will continue to be around. Look underneath the teak; don't be swayed by how nice she looks on the outside. Remember the ideal boat profile, and the issues covered in chapter 8, such as access to systems, storage space, comfort, and hull construction.

If you choose a so-called coastal cruising boat and later decide that you want to do serious offshore cruising, you may be financially trapped by what you have. Cruisers often take off thinking that to cruise up and down a coast with the seasons would surely be the ultimate dream beyond which no person could thirst. After a few years of this and many nights visiting the cockpits of friends who tell them of far away islands and waters, the coast seems limiting, but they don't have the right boat for safe long-distance passagemaking and perhaps can't afford to upgrade. There are reasonable compromises between the weekend powder puff designed to go to the end of the creek and the ultra-sturdy Niagara Falls barrel. Look for these.

PLAN FOR THE FUTURE

People also miscalculate their future desires. What may be lots of fun the first year, because of novelty and adventure, may get pretty small soon thereafter. It is wise to buy the biggest, most comfortable seaworthy boat you can afford. This acquisition is your home, your estate, and the basis of your new life. In many ways, the decisions you make when buying a full-time cruising boat are far more significant than those for buying a house. Upon this rock you will sink or swim. Again, if you buy too small at first, you might not be able to afford an upgrade later.

You'll also have to determine how hung up you are on the idea of a yachtsman's dream vessel. Many boaters think they must sail about in a teak-covered, bowspritted, curvaceous ship reminiscent of the ones in old movies or books about the South Pacific. If you must have classical beauty, you should know that you're going to sacrifice a lot of creature comfort for it, unless you can afford a huge boat—and know how to sail it. With modern construction techniques and materials, boats can be built by different rules than in the glory days, and you can get a lot more space and comfort for a given length and still have a well-found boat. It may not look traditional, but it will make a good home.

We long ago decided that we were willing to sacrifice the ego trip of traditional lines for the comfort of boats that were, well, maybe just a little fat. Modern designs are so much more comfortable, can have significantly more storage space, and can be a lot easier to work on. Compare, for example, the pinched stern on the classic double-ender with the sugar-scoop stern on a modern yacht. With the former you get looks and maybe (maybe not) better performance in a following sea. With the latter you get a wider, longer cockpit, tons of storage aft, easy access from the water or a dinghy to cockpit, and a swim platform.

SIZE

Earlier I said, somewhat cavalierly, that you should get the biggest boat you can afford—within reason. People always ask us, "How big a boat will we need?" Here are a few guidelines based on what we have seen among people who stick with cruising for more than a year. These observations are not based on formal surveys.

Most couples end up cruising on boats from 35 to 45 feet in length, depending upon their budget and tastes. Families of four seem to need 40 to 45 feet. This gets you easily into many aft-cabin arrangements, the merits of which we discussed in chapter 8. There are many good used boats in this category. Families of four, two of whom are in the "little" stage, and who don't intend to cruise more than a few years, do well in the 35- to 40-foot range, particularly if the boat is of a roomier, modern vintage.

As obvious as it sounds, it is crucial to remember that your kids are going to get bigger. They will need more space in seemingly exponential proportions. They will need space not just to put their bodies but to put their things, to do their schoolwork and hobbies, to have their privacy, and to entertain friends—who also will be getting bigger. Unless you think you'll be able to buy a bigger boat down the road, get one that your family can grow into.

There is more to think about than just living space. It's important to have a deck that provides stable, uncluttered working area for sail handling, anchoring, and docking. It is also critical to avoid buying a boat that is too big for you to handle. Conversely, the larger working platform on a large boat makes it easier to raise and lower the sails, furl, anchor, and do many other jobs on deck. These considerations are affected by your agility, your strength, and perhaps age. Design factors are also important to handling characteristics. For example, a boat with a 7-foot draft, long bowsprit and boomkin, and tall mast is not ideal for most people.

It is also important that your boat be big enough to host the systems you want, and you'll probably want more than you thought you would as time passes. "Hosting" the system means more than a place to put the system itself; you need clearance around the system when doing maintenance.

If the lengths given above are too much for your budget, don't despair; this is all somewhat subjective. What may be too small for one family may be perfect for you.

HOW HARD DO YOU LIKE TO WORK?

I wish my boat had absolutely no teak on the outside. Yes, it looks wonderful and we are proud of it, but on the typical cruising boat there is enough to do without trying to make the boat look Hollywood. If you are a person who must have one of those traditional dream boats we spoke of earlier, you'll be doing a lot of work on things that don't have much to do with anything but aesthetics. For cruising, a well-built fiberglass boat with little or no outside teak, strongly mounted stainless steel rubrails, and an easily maintained interior makes a lot of sense.

And time for the pretty work is not all you might be lacking; you may not have the water or other supplies with which to do it.

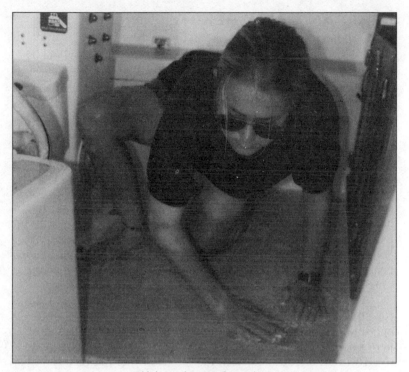

Melanie cleaning the cockpit.

▼

For example, many teak preparations glibly suggest "washing" as a part of the preparation. At this writing, fresh water in some places outside the United States costs as much as 50 cents a gallon and perhaps more. Sometimes you can't get it at all.

Think twice before you get a boat that has been regularly waxed. Some have been waxed and compounded so regularly that a chalky mess will result if you don't keep up the work. Regular waxing may not fit in with your cruising plans. You may need to paint it to keep your sanity. Remember, a cruising boat isn't a marina boat. Cleanliness on deck and outside, however, can affect the way others see you. Avoid the "dog boat" look.

DRAFT AND MAST HEIGHT

When shopping for a cruising boat, your decision about the draft can be a real dilemma. Offshore we like nothing better than a good, solid, deep, internally ballasted keel. When scooting up and down inland waters, we often wish we were very shallow. In storms, we roll at the mercy of wind and waves in open harbors while shallow-draft boats sit peacefully in quiet coves. Our boat's draft is 6 feet; sometimes we hate it, sometimes we love every inch of it.

Of course, a centerboard is a possible compromise, but it requires maintenance and can break. Years ago we were sailing along in our 27-foot sloop and the hinge on the board tore out, leaving it dangling beneath our hull by the pendant. We did not have a pleasant trip back. If this had happened in the ocean in a storm, we might have lost the boat. This board banged as we rolled at anchor, a problem we had with other centerboards. This boat, however, was old and well worn, and thousands of boaters are out there using centerboards successfully. We would never again get a boat with a board unless we could service the hinge and the pendant while at sea.

Another option is a twin-keeled monohull. Built more in Europe than the States, they offer less draft and the capacity to sit aground without damage, although they generally suffer in sailing performance.

The draft of your boat should be a factor that has received the careful attention of its designer. Any general statements I make take second place behind design needs for good sailing performance and seaworthiness.

The type of boat you want and the areas you plan to cruise will affect your decision about draft. If you just cruise the U.S. east coast and the Bahamas, 6 feet is about as deep as you want; 4.5 to 5 feet would be even better. The Caribbean and U.S. west coast have much deeper harbors. If you plan much transoceanic travel, 6 feet probably won't be any bother at all. Like so much else, the draft of your boat may be a compromise.

We would no longer consider a boat with a mast height of more than 60 feet. Although the minimum fixed bridge clearance on the ICW (and in many other areas) is 65 feet, it is lower in some places, such as the 56-foot Julia Tuttle bridge at Miami. On the west coast of Florida, the minimum is only 55 feet. With tides and sloppy construction techniques, clearance is sometimes even less. You'll encounter situations in which it is safer to be inside than making coastal passages outside. If you can't get under the bridges, you'll be more inclined to take chances—especially if a hurricane is on the way and you need to find a hurricane hole to the north or south.

Although we definitely want good sailing performance, we aren't very concerned about loss of sailing characteristics with a mast of this height. We aren't racing, and our boat isn't that big. And when we are at sea, we need to be able to handle our sails easily. We're a family, not a crew of muscle monkeys. While some cruisers think a higher rig results in better sailing, there's much more to think about when it's your home you might tip over. As another matter, we all need to get to the top sometimes. A few extra feet doesn't make a difference, but a lot of extra feet may, especially if the top of the mast is whipping around as you roll over swell.

Often we need to go up as a safety matter. Your mast should be equipped with steps or two free halyards (one to lift you and the other as a safety) and a winch or windlass that enables your mate to pull you up. We wrap our main halyard around our horizontal electric anchor windlass. This enables the girls to get me up quickly and has avoided many problems.

MULTIHULLS

Many cruisers passionately love their multihulls. They often sail well and with good speed (though not all of them), they are spacious and airy, and in most circumstances, roll less than a monohull. It is interesting to see them sitting like platforms in a windy anchorage while the monohulls are yawing about. Some have a rather jerky motion when they do respond to waves.

A major objection to multihulls is that they can't carry large loads without seriously compromising performance. This is certainly true; however, some builders are addressing this concern, knowing that long-term cruising boats simply must carry substantial loads—from gear and systems to water, fuel, and personal belongings. Although you can now find multihulls that are reasonable compromises in this respect, in general they won't be able to take as much weight as monohulls of the same weight. Whatever your choice, don't overload the boat.

Two major pluses of multihulls is their lack of draft and the fact that you can dry them out. The better ones are built so that you can run them ashore, let the tide drop, and paint the bottom with no problem. A monohull grounding at high tide will be likely to roll over on its side as the supporting water ebbs away. You can also seek safer, quieter harbors with a shallow draft, and perhaps feel more comfortable exploring because you don't have to be as fearful of softly going aground—you won't roll over when the tide goes out.

There has been long debate about whether multihulls are more or less safe than monohulls. Some maintain multihulls are more likely to capsize in a serious storm. Multihull proponents argue this. Even if it were so, they say, the multihulls would be far more likely to remain afloat, simply because there are two or three hulls but no ballast to drag them down. The properly built multihull has escape hatches that allow access to the top (formerly bottom) should there be a capsize. In addition, some multihull builders, such as Privilege, are among the current leaders in constructing boats for the pleasure market with watertight and crash bulkheads. To my thinking, it is a scandal that all pleasureboats don't have these. The honest cost of this addition is small. I am not qualified to enter the flipping debate, but I do know that I would seriously consider a multihull, along with the monohulls, if I were in the market.

TRAWLERS

A cruising trawler will normally provide much more space and comfort within a given length. This is simply because they are more boxy. Often they don't cost much more than a sailboat of a similar size. The cost of your mast, rigging, sails, and all that it takes to properly maintain these is very high. Generally, trawlers roll more at anchor and during passages, and they sure don't sail (except sometimes when you don't want them to), but we know many experienced former sailors who now love their trawlers. If you can afford stabilizers, they should do wonders in steadying the boat on passages that would make even a sailboat roll uncomfortably. But stabilizers don't work at anchor. We've seen trawlers with *flopper stoppers* (an arrangement in which weights and/or baffles, such as large buckets or aluminum plates, are hung over each side from the trawler's short mast). But most owners we've seen with these were unhappy with the arrangement. Although the flopper stoppers steady the boat, they are typically noisy and troublesome. Trawlers have shallow drafts for sneaking into anchorages too tight for sailboats; this allows many trawler owners to overlook the fact that their boats may roll more than sailboats do in rougher anchorages. The boatbuilding industry has recognized that many sailors are switching to motorboats, and there are some interesting models out there. When looking at trawlers, be sure that the keel is below the propeller(s) and rudder(s). This gives essential protection in groundings and, for single-screw boats, from debris when running.

Another great feature of trawlers is that, because of the square angles and bigger spaces, it is usually easier to work on systems. Not only is it easier to get to the machinery, the location of the engine room enables you to make repairs out of sight and sound. If you buy a sailboat, you will soon find that this would have been a great advantage.

Fuel consumption is a major drawback, but a well-built trawler with two engines should be able to run and handle well with one. It isn't unusual to see single engines on the ICW and offshore passages. A true displacement trawler with a single engine may burn no more fuel than a similarly sized sailboat. Some builders are now making *planing trawlers.* I wouldn't consider these for cruising unless I really wanted to spend a lot of money for the extra speed. When thinking about fuel consumption, it may be helpful to make the painful admission that an amazing number of sailboat cruisers end up motoring much of the time, anyway. This is because the wind often isn't blowing at all, or is blowing from the wrong direction. If you aren't Sunday sailing, you at least want to make a comfortable harbor or try to complete the passage before you die of old age. Sometimes safety dictates that sailors turn on their motors to complete a passage before a storm rolls in or the light fails. If you choose a trawler with one engine, consider an emergency "come home" auxiliary drive powered by a generator. With a trawler you get a lot of deck space for storing windsurfers, and small sailboats. You can then beat all of us sailboats to the anchorage and be sailing around with a drink in your hand when we get in.

SEA TRIALS

Whatever the type of boat, there are dogs in the lot. Give any boat you may be considering a thorough trial. This is easier said than done, but it is critical unless you are buying a proven boat. Even then, you should insist on some sea experience with your potential purchase. It may require several trips. It may require a deposit subject to satisfactory (in your opinion) sea trials and payments to cover reasonable expenses if a second or third trial is needed, and it may take patience to wait for the right conditions. Your broker might not like it. She or he may say, "No one else does this." Tell him, "That's tough." The broker and seller will have your money; you will have the boat for a long time to come, in all sorts of weather. It's critical that you get what you expect. Take the time here, and spend the money to do it right.

Chapter Ten
SAFETY AND SEAWORTHINESS

I've talked so much about cruising comfort, you may think I'm de-emphasizing safety and seaworthiness. Nothing could be further from the truth; all else pales to insignificance if you don't have a safe and seaworthy boat and practice sound seamanship at all times. Much has been written about this subject. You should read about it voraciously and learn from experience as much as possible before you set off. As I write this, we are anchored in a harbor several hundred miles off the U.S. east coast. Around us are at least three boats whose crew didn't know how to sail before they took off. This arrogant disregard for the safety of those who might be involved in their rescue is inexcusable. They are flirting with death.

Volumes would be required to say all that should be said about safety and the sea. This book is about the cruising lifestyle, and that is our emphasis; so I'll focus on safety issues relevant to cruising. Even though you're probably doing all you can to have an enjoyable, safe cruise, the sea can be relentless and unforgiving. No matter how hard you try to avoid disaster, you and your family will inevitably be tested. You can't travel to all those nice cruising destinations but avoid passages, and even those nice destinations can turn into tumult and terror in bad weather. Design and construction criteria and the desired level of seamanship will vary somewhat according to where you cruise, but some criteria don't change.

LEARN TO BE SAFE

Competence at weekend sailing in your home waters does not equate to competency in seamanship for cruising. Charter, go to school if necessary, but do whatever it takes to learn before you leave. Several years ago, while anchored and awaiting a storm, we saw a large sailing vessel trying to anchor. We commented among ourselves that her crew didn't have the slightest idea about what they were doing. We wondered what great luck had brought them this far from the continent. Others in the anchorage were thinking the same thing. A short time later this boat and its crew were lost at sea in a storm that had been forecast for days as particularly fierce. The boat had left in its face, asking for the worst. News stories indicated that the owner had had experience as a weekend racer and cruiser. We wondered why he didn't know how to anchor. A year or so later I saw the boat's name mentioned in TV hype as another mystery of the Bermuda Triangle. There was no mystery. Those cruisers shouldn't have been there. They were unprepared. The sea is no place to be careless.

Cruisers need to be constantly vigilant against complacency. Having fun isn't incompatible with vigilance, but sometimes we forget this. Some cruisers equate the lifestyle with being laid back, easygoing, and fun-seeking. It's true, these are characteristics of the cruising lifestyle, and when you island hop in protected waters, overnight in sheltered harbors, and enjoy fires on the beach with friends, it's difficult to remember the bad times. When you have been sitting at anchor on even keel for a few weeks, with all of life's little goodies comfortably and conveniently spread around the cabin, it is hard to remember what that little cabin will be like when you set sail. But in a sense, a cruiser is at sea most of the time, and it's wise never to let down your watch.

If you stick to U.S. shores, you'll have a great time, but you'll miss some of the best of cruising waters. Even if you ply only the coasts, as many do, you'll still find yourself in big storms in big waters. Under certain conditions, many bays and sounds can be as ugly as the ocean. Our sailboat is 47.5 feet on deck and weighs around 25 tons. It is sloop-rigged and draws 6 feet. The top of its main cabin is more than 8 feet off the water. We average 5,000 miles (sometimes more) under her keel each year. A large percentage of

▼

this mileage accrues in the ocean, sailing not only up and down the coast but also offshore. *Chez Nous* is a very well-found boat. The closest we ever came to losing her was in a storm in the shallow Albemarle Sound in North Carolina (see "Get Ready").

DESIGN AND CONSTRUCTION

I've been very happy with our solid-glass, heavy boat. She sails well, but she isn't a "spirited weekend performer." She has internal lead ballast, which we like. We don't have to worry about bolts corroding or breaking off. Some boats with bolted-on keels have lost them, and quickly flipped. Some manufacturers tout that even if the keel bolts break, the hull won't be holed. This doesn't matter much when you suddenly drop all your ballast into the deep. You might turn over so quickly, you won't have a chance to look. An internal lead keel should be glassed over, so that there is, in essence, a second bottom above it. If you hole your boat, the ballast and weight stays on, but you won't get water inside. You will have to haul as soon as possible to drain the water out of the keel and fix the hole; however, this beats losing what some glibly call a "sacrificial keel."

The rudder should be strongly mounted. For example, we have a heavy skeg bolted through the hull and through a heavy backing plate. It is also solidly glassed to the hull and has a strong plate underneath that supports the rudder as well as its shaft and load-bearing bushing. You'll want this to face a grounding without damage: it should be well above the level of the keel, to avoid contact with the bottom. But it is asking too much to expect that it never will. For example, it isn't unusual to have to anchor in tight quarters. If you swing, your stern may pass over the shallower bank, snagging that rudder. Obviously, you'll try to avoid this, but it happens. Rudders hanging freely on a shaft (called *balanced spades*) will get you better maneuverability, but they won't maneuver you at all when the shaft bends in the middle of paradise with no haul-out facilities.

If we were to build a boat, we would seriously consider steel. Although a used and improperly built or maintained steel boat can be an absolute disaster, with continuous and daily hard work

(text continued on page 107)

▼

"GET READY!"

I t was a lazy Fourth of July weekend. We had been out to Ocracoke Island and were heading back to the North River, which would take us back up into Currituck Sound and Virginia waters. We were destined for beautiful Chesapeake Bay. In those days we towed a hard 8-foot sailing dinghy astern. Melanie was less than a year old; Carolyn wasn't with us yet.

The air was thick and humid as we left Wanchese, where we had anchored for the night. We had thoughts about staying there but rationalized, "This is summer. It's like this most of the time. If we don't move today, we'll never move." Besides, the trip wasn't long; we could motor and reach North River and the nice anchorage at Broad Creek around noon.

A few hours out we began to get severe thunderstorm alerts on the VHF weather radio. We weren't overly concerned. You hear these alerts all summer along the east coast of the U.S. We kept on plugging. We were in a wide, shallow body of water, with no place to go except back or ahead. Before long, the alerts turned to warnings. High winds and tornado activity were forecast, but it was still flat calm. We were glad for our strong motor as it carried us toward a safe anchorage. We saw other sailboats around us with their sails up, just sitting.

Soon the news on the VHF got worse. The Coast Guard began to broadcast warnings of a strong system sweeping across the inland Piedmont plains, heading eastward. They described storms already forming, with gusts up to 100 miles per hour. Everyone was warned to seek safe harbor immediately. As usual, this was easier said than done. We were going as fast as we could, but shelter was a long way off. We continued to see boats with sails up, drifting about. We didn't know whether they didn't have their VHFs on or whether they assumed their sails could move them faster than their motors. Most of them had auxiliaries. But we knew that the light air wouldn't do us, or any one else, any good. We snugged the sailcover tight, thinking that if the winds hit as forecast we wouldn't want anything up. After all, we were in Albemarle Sound. There was land all around. It was low and distant, not visible in the haze, but we assumed this wouldn't be a place for stormsails or heaving-to.

I was at the wheel. I kept looking for weather, but the leaden western skies revealed nothing. Was it growing darker? Was that a black line within the gray? I couldn't tell, but the sky looked strange. I could almost feel and taste it: a huge, encompassing presence. Ugly and dangerous. We had no radar at that time, but I sensed the sky was closing in. A radar would have warned us.

The water ahead didn't look right. Was it steaming, or had the haze thickened? I looked behind me; the sky was lighter, looked better. I got up from the wheel and peered around the dodger. There was a mist rising in the gray gloom. No, not a mist. Water. How could that be? Water was rising straight up all across the horizon. And that horizon was very close.

"Mel!" I yelled. "Get ready! We're going to get wind, a lot of wind. Get Melanie. Get ready!" I threw two life jackets down below, although Melanie was so little she was still in her basket. The air got so heavy, I couldn't tell whether I was soaked from my own sweat or from the moisture I was trying to breathe. I felt as though I were slowly drowning, clinging to the wheel and watching.

Suddenly, I heard a roar over our engine. I wanted to close my eyes but couldn't. A wall of water hit us in screaming fury. In one instant, there was no difference between the air and the sea. Streaming upward in a wild apocalyptic surge, the sea was on us. *Chez Nous* heeled over almost 45 degrees, even though the 130-hp Perkins was throttling her straight into the force. The storm cast her bow first to one side, then another. A big bully with a toy. As Melanie cooed and slept, Mel wedged the basket tightly between the dinette table and the back of the settee. Mel knelt on the floor beside her, wearing a life jacket, ready to grab our baby. I looked at the dinghy twisting and flying through the air on the end of its tether. I didn't look again.

Then came the waves. They were so high, they battered and swept *Chez Nous,* rolling up over the forward cabin, over the large main cabin, to attack the Bimini. Mel still huddled below and watched as water cascaded through the Dorade vents, 6 feet above the waterline. We could do nothing but hold on and pray. I used every ounce of energy to hold the bow into the waves, hoping the rudder would keep answering. A red light flashed; the bilge alarm sounded. The Dorade vents were often totally submerged. Water poured in, oblivious to the baffles and drains. It was as though we were being held down in the seas, they were so close together. We began to grow numb. I couldn't hear the engine over the fury.

Very suddenly, it stopped, as though Evil itself had come and gone. I looked astern, and watched it—black and strong—receding in the eastern sky. The dinghy was still hanging on but turned over, her painter twisted like a rubber band. Around us the world was quiet, as though it wasn't sure it had survived. We righted the dinghy, cleared the water from the bilge, hugged Melanie, and continued on.

We had forgotten the VHF. We'd heard nothing from it during the storm. Had it been drowned out by other sounds, or had the broadcast ceased? We jumped, startled, and then smiled as we heard the familiar voice of the Coast Guard. It was good to know the world still existed. But the message was solemn. It continued to warn of the storm, advising that many boats had been overturned, some sunk altogether. All mariners were to be alert for survivors. We kept a watch but saw no one. That evening, we gained entrance to the river and found our anchorage. A Coast Guard vessel, heading out from its station in Coinjock, came alongside. We assured the guardsmen that we were fine, and thanked them for stopping. They told us the storm had been one of the worst anyone in the area could remember. They were out in search of missing boats and people. Some they never found.

▼

(text continued from page 104)

required to keep ahead of the rust, a steel boat that is treated properly with one of the currently available coverings can go for many years without any concern for internal rust. You will still have to paint the outside. We have seen some steel boats 15 years old and older with no sign of internal rust. But these were built well. We like the idea of steel because we've seen boats go on the reef numerous times. With any sea, a glass boat will last only a few minutes in these conditions. We've also seen steel boats pounded on rock by heavy seas for days and emerge unscathed. Still, the wonderful ease of maintenance of the glass boat is hard to beat.

Our boat has a big main cabin with large windows. They can be made safer with storm windows or by placing bars inside to prevent inward flexing. But if we were to buy a boat exclusively for round-the-world or transoceanic passages, we would go with a traditional sailboat with small ports and a low profile.

Remember that no matter how comfortable you want to be, you'll encounter terrible weather in which you'll be tossed about and forced to heel. The boat's interior design should enable you to hang on and get about. You will need to have places to sleep while heeling. You'll also need to cook and eat. Many fiddles, a gimbaled stove, and places to safely store things are important.

Lifelines should be at least 30 inches high, preferably higher. Many so-called cruising boats have stanchions and lifelines that are nothing more than trippers—just the right height to hit you on the back of the knees. They should have backup plates, but they should not be bolted through cored portions of the deck. You will need to be and feel safe when getting about the deck in bad weather. You'll need to do this whether it is safe or not. It helps to have a deck wide enough to move fore and aft, a bow with enough room to work your ground tackle, and enough space around the masts to have a good platform for sail handling.

Lazyjacks help to control the mainsail.

You should be able to quickly and easily raise, lower, and reef all sails in bad weather as well as good. The method you choose will depend on the size of your boat, your strength and agility, and the help you get. The number of crew can vary substantially, as may your strength. Fatigue, seasickness and other illness, as well as injury can wipe out you or a crewmember quickly. I've long been happy with our high-quality furling system for the foresail, and have simply used that old standby—a cheap but effective lazy-jack—for our main. Many cruisers prefer a divided rig, such as a ketch, for easier sail handling. We're seeing greater numbers of cutter rigs, for the same reason. Island Packet sailboats are a good example of this.

Your boat should have at least one, better several, good places to board from the water. The popular sugar-scoop sterns of newer boats are good for this; they provide, in essence, a swim platform. Should a cramp hit or shark come along, you'll want to get back aboard quickly. We have a ladder over the stern and a rope ladder over one side; we add trail lines if we're swimming in current. Man-overboard markers (with strobe, flag, whistle, and smoke), flotation systems, and personnel retrieval systems are just as important to the coastal cruiser as they are to the transatlantic voyage. Buy one of each and practice with them.

DINGHY STORAGE

Most cruising boats have a uniquely difficult seaworthiness problem—dinghy storage. Cruisers need large dinghies (dinghies are discussed in detail in chapter 16). At sea, the dinghy should be stored in a place that limits potential harm to boat and crew. Most cruising boats aren't large enough to do this well if the dinghy itself is large enough to suit the cruising crew's needs.

Ideally, you should haul your dinghy aboard and store it on deck when you put to sea, in a manner that will minimize the likelihood of waves tearing it off. Again, many boats are not large enough to safely accommodate a dinghy. If you can store your dinghy on deck, see to it that it doesn't block escape from the hatches. A major benefit of an inflatable is that you can deflate it and store it, and many cruisers use inflatables for this reason. Unfortunately, they often aren't happy with them otherwise. They can "pop," and they don't

last as long as hard dinghies, even though you can patch them well.
The trend favors hard bottoms, which means you get a better ride
but can't fold and store them in a small space.

DAVITS

Because davits are convenient, they are our choice for dinghy
storage. Unless the mother ship is large enough, however, the
dinghy may weigh down the stern. Davits also leave the dinghy
at the mercy of high stern or quarter waves. If you use davits,
mount them so that the dinghy is as high off the water as possible.
Support them so that they will take not only the downward pressure of the dinghy's weight, but also the wrenching side-to-side
pressure as the boat rolls in heavy seas. You can't back your davits
too thoroughly. The dinghy should always be securely tied to the
davits. Many cruising boats with substantial dinghies use davits.

TOWING

Don't plan on towing your dinghy. You will probably lose it if you
do any ocean sailing. We have seen some neat arrangements in
which the dinghy's bow is lifted up on the transom, with only the
stern trailing. Some hardware does this very securely. Following
seas or merely surging quarter seas, however, can make short work
of your dinghy in this position. If you make only short ocean hops,
you may want to take the chance. I wouldn't. Never tow your
dinghy with its motor on, except around the harbor and in very
confined waters.

DINGHIES AS LIFE RAFTS

Chapter 8 discusses storage of life rafts (see under "Storage
Spaces") in some detail.

Some cruisers consider their dinghy their survival raft. Financial and space considerations, coupled with the fact that they don't
spend much time offshore, force these cruisers to make their dinghy
serve double duty. Of course, dinghies are not designed for this and
thus most are ill-suited to this purpose. Obviously, it is best that
we all have a good survival raft, but if we don't, the dinghy should
be mounted so that it can be easily and safely launched in severe
weather. You should have a complete survival pack ready to go, or,
preferably, stored inside the dinghy. Complete treatment of survival

procedures is beyond the scope of this book. Study the experiences of those who have survived severe-weather capsizes. See for example, Steve Callahan's *Adrift*, or Dougal Robertson's *Survive the Savage Sea*.

PROPANE

We use and love propane for cooking. Most cruisers seem to prefer this fuel, and I don't know of anyone who is unhappy with it. It cooks well, it's cheap, and it's easily obtained. In my experience it is more readily available than good-quality kerosene. Unfortunately, it can blow you to Kingdom Come with a moment's carelessness or bad luck. You can make it safe with but a few easy steps. Be sure your tanks are mounted on deck in a compartment(s) dedicated to them. The compartment should have a large drain leading straight down, venting to the air. Escaped propane settles, lies there, and blows at the least spark. The vent hole should be large enough so that it can't accidentally become stopped up with trash. The hole should be protected by screens, particularly if there is any tubing or ducting. I was appalled to see a fancy new catamaran using the same space for propane tanks as sail storage. The drain was in the bottom. A sail or sailbag could easily cover the hole.

The tanks should preferably be situated to minimize damage in the event of an explosion. Although aluminum is costly, it is the material of choice for propane tanks. On a good note, properly cared for aluminum tanks seldom, if ever, need replacing. Steel tanks will rust and eventually leak, sometimes catastrophically. In the States most dealers won't even fill rusty steel tanks. We carry four 10-pound aluminum tanks. Each lasts three to four weeks. The fittings and connections to the stove should be of the finest material and installed according to the latest standards. Consult with your dealer or qualified installer to be sure you have the best available.

A solenoid switch at the tank should be activated by a control at your stove, and a light should warn you when the control is in the open position. Always turn it off as soon as you finish using the stove. If you aren't going to use any fuel for a while, go on deck and also turn off the hand-operated valve (this should be on the top of the tank). There should be a numerical pressure gauge at the end of the hose that connects to your tank. Each time you hook a tank into the system and turn on the valve, the gauge will jump up to the value of pressure in your tank. Note that value, close the tank valve, open the valve, and look at the gauge again a few moments later. It should show the same value. If it doesn't, there is a leak in the system. Find it and get it repaired immediately. This may be a big job, especially if the line from your tank to your stove is buried behind gobs of beautiful teak veneer. But *do it* or stop using propane until you get to a marina with repair facilities. The repair may require new tubing or flair fittings and require a specialist. Note, however, that the pressure will occasionally drop a tiny bit due to line expansion or temperature fluctuation; if it does, run the test again until you are sure that there is no leak. Remember to always close your stove burner valves and the solenoid when you run out of propane. You will always run out in the middle of Thanksgiving dinner preparations—also at Christmas, and any time you have guests aboard. It is easy to rush up to replace the tank, forgetting to turn off those valves below deck. This will flood your boat with propane when you turn on the tank valve. Your gauge will tell you, but it may be too late. Newer stoves usually have devices that will turn off the valve automatically if the flame goes out, but these can fail.

You should also install a good fume alarm, even if you don't use propane for cooking. Mount one sensor just below the stove, and another one in the engine room, as low down as possible— but not where it will be splashed by bilge water. Place additional sensors as appropriate. For example, you may wish to have one in each sleeping area to detect exhaust while its occupant is sleeping. This should not be just a smoke alarm; it should warn you of the presence of carbon monoxide and other dangerous fumes, as well as propane.

LIGHTNING

We all know that lightning happens, very simplistically, when electricity seeks ground due to the imbalance of electrical charges between the atmosphere and the ground. The question of what to do about lightning has prompted many articles and interesting discussions. The various theories all make sense, but many of them overlook one important fact. Lightning doesn't make sense. You may be an electrical engineer and have a Ph.D. in all sorts of esoteric stuff, but if you think lightning makes sense, especially at sea, then you haven't seen much of it. I don't pretend to hold special degrees or to have formal training in the subject, but I'll share the conclusions we've drawn from our own observations. I owned my first boat at age 9. I am now 52. I have seen boats hit by lightning. My boats have been hit several times, my body hairs have literally stood on end from the charge, my stays have glowed and hummed and shocked me, and I've been knocked through the air. I have had all sorts of other fun with lightning. I don't recommend any of it.

Two basic theories have been advanced as to how boaters should deal with the problem:

1. Avoid all ground connections so that the atmospheric charge won't seek ground through the boat.
2. Thoroughly ground the boat so that the lightning will have a quick and easy—maybe even painless—way out.

The first method has been advanced by some rather fancy thinkers, but we think it is seriously flawed. We subscribe to the second method.

The notion that lightning is less likely to strike if you haven't grounded your boat flies in the face of vast experience to the contrary. Occasionally, I'll hear some sage proclaim that he isn't grounded and has never been struck. But we know countless instances in which ungrounded boats have been struck. We also know of countless grounded boats that haven't been struck. Actually, the very notion that a boat isn't grounded if it doesn't employ grounding straps and plates is absurd. In case the Ph.D.s haven't noticed, most boats at sea are wet. In storms, they are generally wet all over. They are actually sitting in water. We have seen ungrounded boats side by side with grounded boats, and only the former were struck. We have also seen the opposite. Fortunately, most yacht-building standards require some degree of grounding, and your boat hopefully is grounded.

The bottom line: you can't really predict which boat lightning will strike. Having observed this repeatedly, we are concerned with what happens if lightning does strike. And when it does, an inconceivably huge amount of energy not only hits your boat, it also has to find a way out. It doesn't dissipate; it seeks ground. If it doesn't have a good way out, it's going to find a way out anyway. Ungrounded boats have had through-hulls blown out as lightning sought its way through them. (I've also observed this in grounded boats, but usually they were not well grounded.) I've known fiberglass hulls of ungrounded boats to be instantly reduced to sieves as the energy made millions of little pinholes as it escaped into the sea. Sections of the hulls of ungrounded boats have been blown off as the energy escaped. Worst of all, people inside boats have been electrocuted as the energy ricocheted, seeking ground. In one of these instances, two people were asleep between two stays. Neither was touching the chainplates, which were bolted into the hull and covered by interior joinerwork. The victims were not in contact with the stays. The energy jumped from one chainplate to the other, killing both people.

So, we ground our boat well. We know that we may be hit whether we are grounded or not, but we want the lightning to have a place to go if it does hit. Grounding is not limited to running little green wires from through-hull to through-hull to engine, although you should do this (use heavy-gauge wires insulated in green cover) to prevent one underwater metal fitting from destroying another through electrolysis. I believe the wires also help dissipate energy when lightning strikes. These wires alone are seldom enough, however. Lightning needs as straight and broad a path as possible; remember, it wants to go straight to ground. We attach heavy battery cable wire to our stays, and trail them in the water whenever we suspect a storm. A cable hangs from each side mainstay, and one from the backstay. At the end of the cable is a plate (copper is probably best) that encourages quick dissipation of energy. We connect the cables to the stays by unsheathing the cables about 1½ inches back from the end and clamping the bare wire to the stays with hose clamps. We watch carefully for any signs of electrolysis at this connection. We squirt it with WD-40 and then cover it well with good-quality 3M electrician's tape. Ideally, we would prefer a rod-type device at the very top of our mast, with heavy strapping running down a stay directly to a heavy plate attached to the hull. This setup would provide a more conductive path. Even boats that have this system still usually lose everything on the top of the mast when hit, and much if not all of their electronics. There are likely to be too many stray currents jumping around looking for an outlet. But this method does provide the best path out. We know of a couple who did this, and they were conscientious about the installation. But there was so much energy in the bolt that hit them that the designated path wasn't enough. Energy went down the forestay, found the chain in the chainlocker, and blew off the door to the locker so that it hurtled back to the main cabin, passing between them as they lay on the V berths on either side of its route. And, it ruined most of their electrical equipment. There is no way to know the size of the bolt that may hit you. Obviously, if you choose to be grounded, as we have, you still can't feel safe in a lightning storm.

We do a few more things. We have recently installed a device that looks like a bottle brush and attaches to the top of the mast. It has tiny metal spikes that, they say, dissipate the charge of your boat so that lightning won't hit in the first place. We haven't been hit since we installed it, but we hadn't been hit in many years before we installed it, either. I wonder about the combined effect of a direct grounding system and the dissipation brush, but have not been able to find any data on it. The manufacturers of my dissipation unit did not recommend against direct grounding.

We also stay away from all large metal objects on the boat when we are in an electrical storm, and when one is building. This includes the mast, the engine, and the galley stove. If practical—never actually during storm activity—we disconnect the antennae and lines running into our SSB, its tuner, radar, and similar equipment. We usually keep the VHF plugged in because we may need it, but we have a spare ready to go, with a spare emergency antenna. We also have the helmsman wear heavy-duty rubber-coated work gloves and rubber-soled shoes. Anyone on deck must wear rubber-soled shoes and remain away from the stays. The area within the stays is relatively protected, theoretically. The stays form a shield of sorts, allowing energy, hopefully, to pass down them to the water and away from the space between. But this doesn't work if you are too close to the stays and they aren't well grounded.

If you have a steel boat, you are completely grounded and probably as safe as you can be on a boat. You should still wear rubber-soled shoes during lightning activity, watch what you touch, and stay away from high points. An aluminum boat is also thoroughly grounded unless some exotic construction technique has been used. For example, some boats have a steel hull and an aluminum superstructure that is, theoretically, separated from the hull by insulation. This is done to avoid electrolysis between the aluminum and the steel. It may also cause unusual reactions with a lightning strike. If you have a boat like this, contact the builder for his comments.

I hope you don't get hit, but if you are out there enough, you're in for some close calls at the least. Just do the best you can, keep up on the latest technology and theory, and when the storms come, enjoy the show.

CHAFE SAFE

Chafe is a major problem for cruisers: we're out for long stretches and spend a lot of time rolling at anchor or moving about. It's always a problem when you think it isn't. Almost everyone has a rag or two aboard to deal with it—but do they?

I venture to say that not one of us who has been at sea for any length of time hasn't experienced this problem. Chafe is typically unexpected and often quite serious—a hidden nemesis. In boating, the possibilities for chafe are staggering, but the remedy isn't a difficult one. Be vigilant and move things so that they don't always rub in the same spot. If you can't move them, use sacrificial cloth or other material as a buffer. Sails, reefing lines, halyards, docklines are all obvious victims. Many experienced offshore sailors keep a spare halyard rigged, anticipating that the one in use will go if they sail long enough.

ANCHOR CHAFE
Anchor chafe is a special concern. A boatowner who is always aboard is able to regularly inspect potential problem areas, but in our years of living aboard we still have experienced our share of problems. We are at anchor much of the time, frequently riding out severe weather—sometimes briefly, sometimes for prolonged periods. We prefer chain, but we also use a nylon snubbing line and sometimes a nylon rode for our second hook. Therefore, anchor-gear chafe is always a concern.

As noted earlier, an effective weapon against chafe is constant vigilance. But chafing gear usually covers the rope it protects, so it's important to remove the gear occasionally to ensure that everything is doing well under all that fine carpeting or whatever. This is

"INTO HARM'S WAY"

The motorsailer lay securely anchored just north of Staniel Cay in the Bahamas. Her owners, experienced cruisers of many years, had taken their normal precautions to see that all was well for the night. It wasn't. When they awoke in the morning, their dinghy was gone. The rope was still securely tied, the chafing gear in place. Their eyes followed the line to where it disappeared between the swim platform and the transom. The end of the nylon told the story. It had been chafed through, probably rather quickly, on the stainless brackets supporting the platform. For countless nights it had remained safely astern, but on that night the current and wind were opposed and the boat hung between them—at a perfect angle to force the rope behind the platform and into harm's way. A call for help on the VHF brought a reply from a gentleman living ashore in the village, who could see the dinghy through his binoculars. It was far away, headed for a cut and the sea, and then perhaps Africa, if it didn't smash on the rocks of Cat Island. The owners filed the supports into smooth round corners, to prevent a recurrence. But like so many, they wonder when chafe will strike again.

▼

often more difficult than you would surmise; by the time you do think of it, the wind is up and the lines are taut.

I have often found anchor and mooring rope chafed under layers of rug or rag. Sometimes this is simply because the sacrificial gear has worn in unnoticed spots. This sometimes happens, even with a buffer, because of constant stretching and rubbing. I have also noticed that some types of chafing gear will themselves abrade rope. Examples include rug with stiff backing, and plastic hose. It seems that over a month or so, good-quality, heavy-duty hose can become brittle and cause chafe, particularly where the rope stretches and contracts past the cut ends of the hose. This is of particular concern in the lower latitudes, perhaps because of the effects of ultraviolet light on plastic.

The type of fairlead through which the anchor line passes is of crucial importance. I've found that chocks just don't work well, particularly if they are off to the side of the bow. We have had the best success with a roller, at the stem. This minimizes sailing around, puts the strain in a straighter direction, and thus decreases windage and, consequently, chafe. The roller should turn freely, causing less abrasion on the line passing over it. It should be wide and heavy enough to take the boat's load, and the line passing down from the roller should not foul on any part of the boat. The design and mounting of the roller should take into consideration the amount of sailing back and forth your boat will do. Some boats behave wildly in heavy wind. You will want the line to stay in place on the roller rather than pop out to the side. A deep V may be needed. If this means that your bow may not be quite as sleek or pretty, consider what it will look like if you break loose in the night.

Another concern whenever we're in strong wind conditions of any duration is the potential need to replace the chafing gear during the blow. Because of the strain on the line, this may be difficult if not impossible. The prudent course is to lay on as much good chafing gear as possible before the blow, but this doesn't avoid the problem of replacement if the winds don't abate, particularly if there is surge or sea, both of which cause the sacrificial material to go quicker.

On *Chez Nous,* I can't lift the line up to wrap new buffer material when the wind is high. I have nearly lost fingers and my hands, even when motoring forward to reduce strain. When at anchor, I keep a box of good chafing material on deck. Whenever we are in a blow, I make regular inspections. When I decide that we need to replace the gear, I wrap and whip new gear on the line between the roller and the windlass, as close as comfortable to the old gear. I then let out the line just enough so that the new gear is in place on the roller. At times I have even whipped two or more sets of gear on the line above the roller, so they would be in place. Then all I had to do was let the line out when first one and then another area of buffer material wore through. This is much safer than trying to set it up during the storm.

And this brings us to the next problem. Any line, particularly nylon, will stretch over the roller or other fairlead as gusts come and go. It is therefore necessary to have enough line covered so that all areas of the line that could move back and forth over the roller are protected. And if the chafing gear isn't securely attached to your pennant or rode, the back-and-forth motion will often cause the material itself to ride along the rope and into a useless position up on deck or down below the roller or chock. Once you get it in place, stay awhile and watch to be sure that it remains in place.

Yet another common area for ground-tackle chafe is under water. If you use rope, innumerable things on the sea floor can snag, cut, or just chafe your line. Even if you use a short length of chain near the anchor and then rope, there will still be times when the line rubs along the bottom. We try to pick anchorages that are less likely to have debris, we dive and check out the bottom if possible, and we regularly check our line down to the chain if we are there for a while. In my experience, 40 feet of chain below the rope is adequate in most areas along the East Coast and in the Bahamas.

If you anchor in strong current, particularly if the wind is blowing, the rope may wrap around your keel, rudder, or prop. Depending on your boat's characteristics, this may happen all the time; with some boats, it almost never happens. A separate rudder, fin keels, wing keels, and trawlers with unprotected running gear and stabilizers all are more likely to catch an anchor line. In these instances, the rope will be chafed through quickly, not to mention the damage to your boat. Know your boat and how it is going to react. Often the correct amount of scope will lessen the likelihood of snagging. And always carefully watch and listen.

We have one friend who uses nylon rope for anchoring. He attaches a short nylon snubbing line to his anchor rode with a rolling hitch. Chafe gear protects the snubbing line, but this is the rope that moves back and forth through the fairlead. If it breaks, the resulting jerk will usually wake crew from their sleep. The main rode holds the boat while he bends on another snubber. As with chain snubbers, the stretch from this line also gives a better ride, produces less chafe, and less jerk on the anchor. One would want to carefully inspect the rode where the rolling hitch is attached to be sure that no damage occurs underneath.

DINGHY CHAFE

Chafe also occurs readily on inflatable dinghies. I thought I had the perfect place to put my windsurfing board overnight—in our spare inflatable. Even though the dinghy was rigidly inflated and the board was carefully stored, the slight flex from moderate wave action during just one night caused the board to chafe a hole through the fabric. Towing lines and just about anything else that constantly rub against the fabric of the inflatable may chafe through. Again, careful attention and soft sacrificial material can save the day. We also glue repair patches over the areas of known chafe, such as the spot where a knot or splice in the towing line will rub on the fabric.

BELOW-DECKS CHAFE

We often forget that everything is moving about below decks, due to the ship's motion in the sea and vibration. I have a pattern of checking my engine each time I start and stop it. I randomly run my eye and hand around various spots. It is amazing how simple vibration can chafe through water hoses, fuel hoses, improper propane lines, and electric wiring. Whether you burn or sink first, or just keep on having fun, may depend on how frequently you check. Plan soon to spend as many hours as needed to find where anything in the engine room (and elsewhere below decks) is rubbing on anything else. Then move the part, and/or buffer it with tape, rubber gasketing material, innertube rubber, or some other appropriate substance. Don't use material that may burn, absorb oil, or be damaged by oil.

We have also experienced what I consider good chafe. When we started cruising, Mel insisted that I bring a suit along, "just in case you die." Being dutiful, I did. We pulled it out not long ago to find that the shoulders were worn through from rubbing against the walls of the hanging locker. Now I can't wear it even if the president visits. Other clothes have suffered the same fate, but bathing suits and diving suits seem to do okay. We use them all the time.

Chapter Eleven
ANCHORING

Suppose you looked out the window of your home one fine day and saw a huge tractor-trailer truck pointing at your house and moving slowly forward, its engine running. The driver had put it in low gear and left. What would you do? Would you sit there idly and watch, hoping something would happen to make it change course or that it would run out of fuel and stop? Not likely. If you don't exercise good seamanship when anchoring, you'll be like the truck driver. If you are near someone who doesn't exercise good seamanship while anchoring, you'll be like the person in the house.

Because the typical cruising boat is at anchor most of the time, good anchoring skills are essential. In general, anchoring is one of the more important seamanship exercises cruisers perform. It's so important that I've devoted an entire chapter to the subject.

As a cruiser, you will probably sail to your destination, anchor, and then stay a while to enjoy it. Or, having reached your cruising area, you might sail from island to island during the day and anchor only at night. When storms come, you'll probably seek out a good anchorage; as I mentioned in other chapters, you probably can't afford to dock at a marina, even if there were a safe one in your area.

Despite the critical role good anchoring skills play in successful cruising, I've encountered much misinformation, misunderstanding, and sheer negligence among new cruisers—and some old ones. And when you don't anchor well, you not only threaten your own safety, you also threaten the well-being of those around you.

ANCHORING GEAR

Good anchoring depends on what you do, how you do it, and having the proper gear. The best tactics may be useless if you don't have appropriate gear.

THE BOW

Proper gear begins with the bowsprit, stemhead rollers, or whatever anchoring platform your boat has. This gear should be extremely strong; that is, strong enough to handle the full weight of your boat as it seesaws in large waves. This won't be a day-to-day occurrence, but your gear should be designed to handle extremes, not average conditions. Our bowsprit has held *Chez Nous* in 100-knot winds; it has held her in high seas and surge. Our gear prevailed in a tornado that lifted *Chez Nous* partly out of the water and spun her around so fast that the wheel spokes were a blur as the rudder tried to resist.

We completely rebuilt our bowsprit. The original was one of those pretty teak platforms with one stainless tube down to the stem, secured by stainless strapping. We left the teak platform as a cosmetic cover-up for a real platform underneath, which we constructed of heavy stainless. We replaced the tube with a V-shaped support of stainless pipe. We ran massive straps well back into the hull and down the sides. Several years later, a boat built by the manufacturer of our boat—with the same bowsprit—was on a mooring near us. The mooring was in the middle of a basin plagued by continuously circulating currents. The boat swung around all night long. As the mooring line twisted, it became shorter. By morning the bowsprit was at a downward 45-degree angle, pulled into that position by the shortening rode.

Our boat was built by a quality builder, and I was present when they built much of it. I know they thought they were doing well when they designed and installed the bowsprit. They just didn't have a clue about the stresses the bowsprit would encounter.

You may well need to get your anchoring platform rebuilt, and this could be a problem. Many yards don't understand storm anchoring requirements. You may have to look at other boats, look at what you have, use common sense, and tell them exactly what you want. Don't accept a yard's assurances that they have built bowsprits for customers with fancy or expensive boats. This may be a self-indictment; these customers probably don't do any serious anchoring.

Some boats have excellent anchor platforms. In the Island Packet design, for example, the bowsprit is an integral part of the hull. The extension is filled with epoxied layers of marine ply and extends back into the hull. It is glassed to the hull and deck, to spread the loading back toward the bow. When shopping for a cruising boat, examine the anchoring platform carefully. You may have to factor a rebuild into the overall cost of the boat.

Many boats don't have an extension from which to anchor. The gear is on the deck, and the line runs out through rollers at the stem. This is a great arrangement as long as there is a fair run and the rollers are heavy enough for the boat, supported through solid deck, and well backed. Often the deck is marine plywood at the stem (and at other places, too). Remember that ply can rot and allow water to leach down the grain. Be sure that the deck fitting is sealed, and coat the bolt and hawse holes with resin to prevent water from entering the end grain.

There should be at least two rollers—both at the stem, or forward of it, and as close to the centerline as possible. Be sure that you can anchor easily with two anchors. Although you might not need two anchors often, when you do, everything must go smoothly. Fouled rode, poor leads, and poor deck equipment can lead to broken lines and broken boats, not to mention broken limbs and crushed hands, fingers, and feet.

Anchoring in heavy weather is dangerous. If your anchor line leads out from bow chocks, your boat won't swing squarely into the wind. Although your boat will sail around a bit no matter what, you'll present more of the boat's side to the wind unless the line(s) comes out from the very tip of the bow. Even if you use two lines, as the wind clocks you will swing on one line or the other. For this reason, you will ride better and safer if these lines run from the foremost point of the boat, near the centerline.

The rollers should be commercially made for anchoring by a reputable company. If they are too soft, they will wear out and tear; if they are too hard, they may damage your line. The fairlead to and from the rollers must be smooth so that it won't cut the line. The rollers must be able to handle both rope and chain; you will assuredly use both at some time or another. You should have spare roller and roller-shaft material aboard and be able to replace the shaft and/or roller quickly.

WINDLASSES

Forget about building muscles on the foredeck. Get a good windlass, preferably electric or hydraulic. I started out with a top-grade manual Plath, the kind they use on fishing vessels in the Pacific Northwest. This is an excellent piece of equipment, but I soon found that for our purposes, anything other than a power windlass was potentially dangerous. Why? Typically, it's getting dark when you're trying to anchor, and you can't sail back out of the cut. So you'll often find yourself anchoring in bad bottom, even if you always do everything you can to avoid it. If it's also very windy and the anchor drags along this poor bottom instead of setting, you must get the anchor up quickly to regain control and then try to reset it. This can happen even in good holding areas. While the anchor is dragging, you probably won't be able to swing the bow around with your engine; you'll continue to be blown sideways, virtually helpless. If there is a boat, a reef, or a shallow area downwind—and there probably will be—you have no time to lose. On several occasions, after quickly cranking the anchor and chain back aboard and trying to reset the anchor, I was exhausted. I couldn't crank it in fast enough when it dragged again, as it so often will on a bad bottom. I've watched many people struggle with a manual windlass in this way, and I've seen quite a few boats dragged ashore or into other boats because the crew couldn't get the chain and anchor in fast enough. Consequently, I went to a good machinist, explained exactly what I wanted and how I wanted it done, and came away with an electric motor nicely mated to the manual windlass. It has worked well for years, it can quickly be converted to manual, and the parts—including switching solenoids—are all easily obtainable from any good autoparts store. The drive from the motor passes through an extra gear box, another off-the-shelf item. This gives even greater power to the windlass, but slows the speed of the retrieve somewhat. The motor is mounted above deck.

On many stylish boats, the windlass motor is mounted below, in the forepeak. But electric motors don't like to live in warm, moist, salty holes where no one looks at them. We can easily inspect and service ours. It is sealed with Rust-O-Leum paint, liberally applied. Although it has been doused numerous times by boarding seas, no water has gotten inside. It is covered by a waterproof cloth, tied tightly at the base of the motor, for additional protection. The wildcat (chain wheel) on the windlass is cast iron and thus very strong. It is easy to paint. The motor casing is plain steel, but the paint has kept it from rusting for years.

We wouldn't have a vertical windlass, and can't imagine why anyone who has done much anchoring would. We prefer one with a horizontal shaft. One side should be able to handle both rope and chain, the other chain only, unless you can afford to have both configurations on both sides. You must be able to progress from rope to chain as your rode changes. This won't be a problem for a good winch manufacturer, but you may have to insist on what you want. This is not a place to scrimp. Newer windlasses offer chain/rope drums for chain/rope splices. We would not use these because we believe that chain/rope splices chafe easily and that the groove in these wheels is too likely to damage rope. We prefer to transfer the rode from gypsy (rope drum) to wildcat, although this too can be difficult and dangerous.

THE RODE

I recommend all-chain anchor rode. The drawback, of course, is its weight, but a cruising boat should be heavy enough to handle this.

(The extra cost of chain is offset by its longevity, if the chain is properly cared for. Care and maintenance are discussed below.) We prefer chain over line because it sometimes requires less scope than does line, it improves holding, and you don't have to worry about little bits of reef or rock or glass or dinghy propellers or anything else cutting it. True, you don't want to anchor in reef or rock, but you never know what little pieces of junk or reef are down there. Chain improves holding because its weight keeps it closer to the bottom, thus pulling the anchor at an angle more conducive to its digging in. Chain also diminishes the tendency of any boat to sail about at anchor. To lessen the strain on the anchor and chain, I attach a nylon snubber to the chain with a chain hook. This line should be undersized yet sufficiently thick to hold your boat in a moderate blow, and it must stretch to provide elasticity and spring to the system so your chain will last longer, hold better, and be less likely to break. The snubber is led back to the post on the windlass, or whatever post is your boat's strongest. I let out enough chain so that the hook is at or just below the water's surface. I then let out more chain, allowing it to loop several feet above the bottom if the water is no more than 10 feet deep. I never put out more than 20 feet total (10 feet down and 10 feet back up). And I never let the loop scrape along the bottom; it would lose much of the catenary effect produced by the chain. The weight of, say, 7 feet of chain down and 7 feet back up to your roller will pull the nylon line down, which adds a lot of give before the line will stretch tight on a sea or in a gust. If the line does stretch tight, there is still give in the line to cushion the shock to the anchor.

I leave the chain in the windlass wildcat but still secure it with a heavier nylon rope (heavy enough to hold the boat) attached to the chain with a chain hook and pulled snug. This is then attached to the post or cleat intended to hold the boat. The windlass wildcat would hold the boat in most instances (many will not), but if the boat were jerked severely, as it might be if the snubber broke, or if there were huge seas, the shaft in the anchor windlass could break if it suddenly became the holding point for the boat. Be sure your primary anchoring cleat or post is solidly attached, with a wide backup plate, and not just bolted through a soft cored deck with washerlike backups. I prefer a windlass with two bollards for securing the rode. With this arrangement, the entire backup of the windlass—which should be very strong and wide—serves as the attachment point for the anchor rode.

If you have to tie off to trees or if your chain breaks, you should have plenty of good-quality nylon anchor line aboard. If you can't handle the weight of two lengths of chain forward, have one all-chain rode and a second rode with around 40 feet of chain next to the anchor and the rest nylon. This combination will hopefully give you sufficient chain for rubbing along the bottom. We almost always anchor out, and on the U.S. east coast we have done very well with no more than 200 feet of working rode on each anchor. In other areas, such as the Pacific Northwest, you will need more. We are able to quickly bend on more line (nylon) if needed. Remember that you should always be able to deploy *at least* 5 to 7 times the distance from your roller to the bottom. This is called a "5 to 1" scope. We often use a 10 to 1 in storms—the more chain, the better holding.

I carry an additional 50 feet of ½-inch chain and 200 feet of 1-inch nylon rode for storm anchoring, in addition to several 200-foot coils of ¾-inch nylon, and various shackles. Old carpeting, stored in a tub, serves as chafing gear. In a storm, you can cut through carpet with amazing speed. If possible, you must keep watch and replace it as soon as needed, if possible (for more on chafe, see chapter 10).

Even if you use chain, be sure to use heavy chafing gear. This will increase the longevity of the roller, the fairlead, and the nylon snubber, and it will make the chain quieter. Because it is undersized to provide stretch, the snubber will break frequently and you'll lose your chain hook. Chain hooks are cheap. Always have several rigged to snubbers and ready to go. When one breaks in a storm, hook on another just below the roller and let out the necessary chain. You'll need to keep the snubber rope taut as you let the chain out, to keep the hook from falling off the chain. As mentioned earlier, this is an excellent system for providing elasticity when using chain.

ANCHORS

Boaters argue incessantly about which is the best anchor. Unfortunately, many seem to judge their gear by the amount of money they have plunked down. They don't like to admit that the thousand-dollar piece of metal hanging on the bow doesn't work well.

I have been anchoring for more than 43 years, not just on an occasional weekend basis, but frequently and seriously. *Chez Nous* is at anchor 90 to 95 percent of the time when we cruise, mostly along the east coast of the United States and in the Bahamas. *Chez Nous* weighs around 25 tons; she is 47.5 feet long on deck, and draws 6 feet. She has a relatively high amount of windage for a sailboat.

My two working anchors are a 45-pound CQR plow and a 35-pound Hi Tensile Danforth. I very much favor the CQR, and I use the Danforth only when the plow won't bite and the Danforth will, and when I deploy two anchors. I use 200 feet of ⅜-inch BBB chain rode on the CQR, and 200 feet of ¾-inch nylon rode on the Danforth, with 40 feet of ⅜-inch BBB chain next to the anchor. I would prefer heavier anchors as my main working pieces, and all chain on my second anchor, but these have served me incredibly well in all kinds of conditions, and I already have a huge amount of weight on the bow in the chain, windlass, and anchors. I also carry a 35-pound CQR on deck at the bow, with around 10 feet of chain, ready to go.

On the stern I carry a 45-pound fisherman's anchor and a 90-pound Hi Tensile Danforth. A fisherman's anchor (also referred to as a yachtsman's anchor) is for emergencies—when I might be forced to anchor in rock or grass, for example. Fortunately, I've have never had to use it. The 90-pound Danforth is our "ultimate storm anchor." I haven't had to use this either, and hope I never will. Once set, it might be impossible to pull up with our boat. With the experience I have had in the 17 years since I bought the 90-pounder, I would seriously consider getting a larger CQR instead.

Overall, the 45-pound CQR has been my most versatile and reliable anchor. It has held in almost anything but hard sand and gravel. (The 35-pound Danforth usually holds in sand and sometimes in gravel.) The CQR will usually reset itself if the boat swings and starts to pull from the opposite direction. This is a normal occurrence, especially in storms. The Danforth and similar anchors will sometimes snag the anchor rode as the boat comes around, rendering the anchor useless until pulled up and unwrapped. You may not have time to do this. This isn't a problem, however, if you are using a Danforth as a second anchor. Because of the instances when a Danforth is the only one that will hold, I don't recommend cruising without one, or a quality anchor of similar shape—many of our friends have been exceptionally happy with the Fortress. Because a Fortress anchor is made with a special alloy, it will be significantly lighter than a Danforth of equal size.

Many people, including experienced cruisers, use and recommend the Bruce anchor. But I've probably seen more boats dragging with a Bruce anchor than with any other single anchor. This may be the result of inexperience, or it may be that the bottom was inappropriate for the anchor. I've seen the Bruce drag the most in grass. Of course, grass doesn't hold any hook well, as I'll discuss later in this chapter. The problems seem to occur after the winds have come up and a few more roots have broken loose.

One advertisement for this anchor shows it wedged into a rock. A cursory examination of the photo suggests that if the current or wind were to reverse, the anchor would pop out. The photo also shows that it could be exceptionally difficult to break the anchor free without diving on it. This, too, can lead to trouble. And one wonders why anyone would anchor in rocks anyway, except in emergencies.

I've used a CQR anchor along the East Coast and in the Bahamas. While this area contains a wide variety of bottoms, I assume it doesn't have them all. In some bottoms, such as mud, the CQR did very well, but so do other anchor types.

Over the years I've seen several new cure-all anchors come and go. They are promoted vigorously, and sometimes a bit of irresponsible journalism from writers with little cruising experience helps to get a bunch out there. The boater, having sunk a small fortune into the anchor, doesn't want to admit it is a disaster as he quietly tries to unload it. I don't mean to disparage research and development and improved products, but I don't like being victimized by boats that bang into mine as their anchors skid across the bottom.

My philosophy is, if you know of a few proven anchors that have made cruisers all over the world happy, stick with them. The CQR and Danforth are two such proven anchors. To those who think otherwise, we say, "Conduct your experiments where no one else will be hurt." If you want to test a new invention, use common sense and test it before you rely on it.

CARING FOR YOUR CHAIN AND ANCHORS

Your anchors and chain will eventually rust. Some people ignore the problem, hoping it will take so long for the process to damage their gear that it won't matter. But it will matter, sooner or later, and you never know when that will be. If you're the carefree type, I hope you won't learn a hard lesson by grinding into a bank or reef on the border of your anchorage in the middle of the night.

Unfortunately, the extent of damage caused by rust is difficult to determine without costly equipment or a survey. It helps to reverse the ends of the chain every year, so that one end is not lying continuously in the forepeak. To be as safe as possible, you can buy new gear; as an alternative, you may wish to periodically hot-dip galvanize your chain and anchor to prolong its life. The American Galvanizer's Association says that this not only provides barrier protection against rust, but also some degree of cathodic protection—the zinc used as a coating is anodic to the steel being protected.

Regalvanizing does not compensate for weakened or lost metal, and it doesn't restore strength that may have been lost. Don't wait until your chain is severely rusted before you explore the possibilities. You may lose more than a chance to save money. You may lose your boat as well.

It is easy enough to determine the cost of new chain, but it may be more difficult to determine the cost and feasibility of galvanizing. Some shops will not accept chain, especially in long sections, because of the difficulty in handling and cleaning it after the process. Shops usually charge by weight and set a minimum weight; some charge by the hundredweight. So, to determine the best course, you need to know the weight of your chain and anchor. The minimum weight typically exceeds that of a cruiser's ground tackle, but by adding all your anchors and other parts, such as chain hooks and oarlocks, you may tip the scales in favor of a regalvanizing job. If you have friends who are willing to share the cost and add their gear to meet the minimum weight, you may find galvanizing cheaper than replacing these parts. Over the last two decades, I've saved considerable money by getting my chain galvanized every three to four years. At this writing, I'm using chain that is 17 years old. I bought it new, and it still looks nearly new. If I purchased a used boat with old chain, however, I would replace it unless I were sure of its integrity.

Some shops charge extra for heavily rusted metal because, they say, it requires extra cleaning. If you have allowed your tackle to rust too heavily, they may not accept it. If this is the case, you should get new gear anyway. Some charge extra if the chain has been painted to mark lengths. They claim their particular cleaning process will not remove the paint.

When calling for prices, ask specifically how they will remove the excess zinc once the coating process is complete. As the hot zinc dries, it will make the links stick together and leave drips of hard zinc unless special steps are taken. Shops may spin it in a basket as it cools, shake it, hang it in loops and move it, or use some other method. You do not want your chain back with the links stuck together and in a condition that requires you to file or break off brittle zinc drips.

Ask about preparation of the metal prior to the dipping, too. The pamphlet "Galvanizing for Corrosion Protection, A Specifier's Guide," published by the American Galvanizers Association, notes that "Surface preparation . . . typically consists of three steps: caustic cleaning, acid pickling, and fluxing."

I've found that different companies use different processes. Many use all three methods. They claim that the combination is very effective, even to the point of removing paint, unless it is particularly thick.

The American Galvanizers Association (1-800-468-7732) can provide information about these processes and their member companies. Because of the difficulty in finding galvanizing companies who accept chain and anchors, we telephoned numerous shops along both coasts and within reasonable shipping distance inland and have listed the ones who provide this service. This is hardly a complete listing, and it is not an endorsement of any company. The omission of a company should not be taken as a negative inference. Check around before deciding. It might be worth your while to borrow a pickup and take a long road trip to get the job done, particularly if you can combine your gear with that of friends. Remember, these shops usually deal in large quantities for an industrial market; volume helps.

Duncan Galvanizing, Everett, MA; 1-800-638-1011
New Jersey Galvanizing, Newark, NJ; 201-242-3200
Virginia Galvanizing Corporation, Richmond, VA; 804-798-3257
Southern States Galvanizing, Aberdeen, NC; 910-944-2171
American Galvanizing Co., Folsom, NJ; 609-567-2090
Metalplate Galvanizing, Jacksonville, FL; 904-768-6330
Hobson Galvanizing, Belle Chase, LA, near New Orleans; 504-394-5700
Galvanizing Services, Inc., Houston, TX; 713-921-5800

▼

Pacific Galvanizing, Oakland, CA; 510-261-7331
Pacific States Galvanizing, Inc., Portland, OR; 503-692-8888
Ace Galvanizing, Inc., Seattle, WA; 800-952-8108

GOOD BOTTOMS

The best anchor in the world won't do you much good unless you find the right bottom. Without a good bottom, a few gusts of wind or even a change of tide may send you drifting onto shoals. In areas of 6- to 8-foot tides, which are not uncommon along the ICW from lower North Carolina to upper Florida, an unexpected nighttime meander could turn a nice trip into a nightmare. A sailboat, after dragging ashore at high tide, may roll over on its side, settle comfortably into the sucking mud, and peacefully stay there as the tide returns. A motorboat can crush its props. I saw a 40-foot trawler that had completely filled with water when the tide returned as it lay canted on the bank.

Even though you may read or hear about a favorite anchorage, don't expect all your cares to be over for the evening when you sight the cove. It may not have been tested in a real blow when your friend or the author of your cruising guide was there; if it was, there may be bad holding just a few yards from where someone else's hook bit. Wrightsville Beach, North Carolina, is a telling example. In that popular anchoring basin one can find bottom that will hold in almost any weather, yet within a few feet there is hard ridge where you will drag all night long (until, of course, you fetch up on the shore or along a former friend's topsides). Any of us can look at a cove or creek and see that it is pretty and protected, and we can all look at a chart to determine depths. But the trick is to find good bottom.

I enjoy diving, and I frequently dive on my anchors to see how well and in what manner they are set. I also watch the hook dig in as I drift over it with mask and snorkel, giving hand signals to my captain. Doing this has taught me some lessons about the types of bottom to seek out, and how to dig in.

MUD

I have learned to rate bottoms, often examining the material on my hook when I pull it up and then making note in my log of the holding it gave me. Gray clay mixed with mud, for example, gets five stars. This mixture may be buried under loose black or reddish mud that will not hold. But once you get either a plow or Danforth into the gray stuff, you've got it made. When the hook comes up in the morning, the flukes will be caked with the gray mud, and you'll probably have to scrape it off in globs. I once read a guide article by a person who complained about having to clean off his hook. I liken this to complaining about having too much money to count.

From this supreme gray clay and mud, the quality of mud generally deteriorates as it thins. In many places, such as Mile Hammock Bay at Camp Lejeune, North Carolina, the mud is so loose that almost nothing will hold even when you back down and use copious amounts of chain. Generally, if the stuff clings to your flukes and has some substance, you can probably get a good bite. If you run your finger through it where it sticks to the anchor, and the mud immediately closes over the cleared spot, plan to be up during the night if the wind blows or the current changes. If the mud runs off the anchor as it clears the water, don't bother putting down the anchor in that spot again.

SAND

Sand can also make a fine bottom, but not always. Some sand, such as that found in the Chesapeake Bay, is too hard even for a Danforth to easily dig in, although this anchor will often work in hard sand when nothing else will. My favorite sand is the soft, fine, white variety found in most of the Exumas. Whether Danforth or plow, simply watch the anchor melt into the bottom and disappear as you back down. Between these two extremes, the best sand to look for is the softer and looser material, as long as it is deep enough. Hills and mounds, such as you see in the Exumas, are a good sign. Small, flat ripples in dark, flat banks often indicate a hard pack. Sometimes, particularly in some areas of the Bahamas, a beautiful layer of sand covers the bottom, but it's only a few inches deep with flat rock hiding underneath. The anchor may look like it is beginning to hold, but when you or Mother Nature put it to the test, it will slide through the sand and across the rock like a brick on a sidewalk. Needless to say, it is best to test the anchor in daylight.

GRASS

Thick grass is seldom good, and it causes especially serious problems for the inexperienced—and everyone else downwind of them. Grass can be very misleading, and this is why you'll sometimes find cruising-guide authors and other writers suggesting that an area with grass has good holding. Any anchor may bite hard in grass at first, but in a blow the roots will often give, a few at a time, until suddenly the last ones break and you are sailing downwind with a clump of weeds clinging to your anchor and crippling your hope of resetting. When encumbered by a clump of grass on their points, or in their joint, even the best-designed anchors will skip over any sort of bottom; the obstruction affects their designed angle of attack. Many cruisers have anchored successfully in thick grass, backed down hard, held fine, and gone on their way the next morning with glowing thoughts of good holding. Maybe a blow even came through but didn't break all the roots. You never know how many roots are broken or pulled up until the last ones go. If you anchor often enough, you will learn to stay awake all night if anyone anchors to weather of you in heavy grass, and you expect a blow.

Sometimes grass is the only thing around. In these cases a kedge (sometimes called a Herreshoff or yachtsman's anchor), which may dig deeply enough through the grass and roots to reach good holding ground below, is most likely to stay. I've seen several new anchors lately that were touted to hold in grass, but the good experiences that led to positive reviews were more likely the result of good luck and the right circumstances than repeated, serious tests of the anchor.

A final point: Anchoring in grass damages the grass bed, and in some areas this practice is illegal. All the more reason to avoid it whenever you can.

ROCK

Rock is extremely poor holding ground, although a rocky shelf, ledge, or even a boulder may grab almost any hook and hold it without a budge, as long as the boat doesn't swing much in wind or current. Like grass, however, rock can be misleading. The anchor may hold, and you may go to bed thinking all is well. During the night, however, a position shift or swing—likely in a storm and in areas of strong reversing current—may result in the hook's pulling free from the overhanging ledge or rock, sending you not-so-merrily on your way. Even if you are fortunate and find in the morning that there was no position change or nocturnal breakout, you may have to dive on the anchor to back it out at the correct angle.

While a morning dive may be okay when the water is warm and clear and shallow, it can be a lousy way to start a day in many other places. For these reasons, if I put down an anchor and achieve a hard and immediate bite that feels like rock, I either pull up the anchor to see if there is anything on the hook (if it's clean, you've probably hit a rocky bottom) or motor around and fall back, feeling the chain to detect vibrations or jerking that may indicate rock.

In my experience, the good old-fashioned kedge is most likely to hook and stay if you really must anchor in rock. These anchors have the disadvantage of easily snagging on your anchor line if the boat swings in the opposite direction, and this typically causes them to pull out. Regardless of the holding you initially achieve in rock, you should be up and on watch whenever any position change may occur.

MIXED BOTTOMS

Mixed bottoms, such as the shell and mud found in the Carolinas and in Georgia, are fairly common. But mixtures can be good and bad; consistency can vary with the same mixture. For example, if the shells are whole and thick along the bottom, they may act like a cement coating, making it difficult for a hook to penetrate. If the shells are whole and deeply mixed in the mud, the hook may hold, but because of the reduced viscosity caused by the shells, it may not hold well. Some areas in the Cumberland Island anchorage, in Georgia, off the main park dock, have this problem. Larger shells will occasionally catch on the point of the anchor, or between the flukes of a Danforth, making it impossible to set. In many areas, however, the shells are finely broken up. When combined with a mud base, they create great holding. On the Indian River, in Florida, for example, tiny shells pack the mud, giving it good holding consistency.

A sand-and-mud mixture is generally a good bottom; a Danforth anchor typically works best when the concentration of sand is high. This mixture will usually be dark when the concentration of mud is high, indicating even better holding, but probably with a CQR. Many areas of the Chesapeake Bay and the ICW have this type of bottom. It often accompanies a gradual slope away from shore; strong current in marshes where the softer mud has been washed away also produces a good sand-mud mixture.

Much is said about not anchoring in coral for environmental

reasons. Anyone who deliberately anchors in coral for any reason is asking for trouble. Not only does it damage coral, you will probably break free unexpectedly, and in some areas, such as Florida, you may be fined.

ASSESSING THE BOTTOM

There are several ways to find out what may be down there when you can't see the bottom. Concave lead weights, used for centuries to sound and take bottom samplings, are not helpful in my experience. They pick up only the surface material, which may bear little resemblance to what is farther down where your anchor needs to hold.

The best way to sample the bottom is to dig it up with your anchor and look at it. However, no one wants to do this on purpose, even though this is what often happens when you drag on the first try. A small dinghy-size plow or similar digging-type anchor can be used to drag up a sample while avoiding the problems of putting out a heavy anchor. You should have a grappling hook aboard anyway. It will save lots of bucks over the years because it enables you to find and retrieve all those items you will drop overboard.

If you don't want to go to this extreme and are searching for general advice, first look at the chart, which sometimes gives cryptic clues such as "stk" or "hrd." I would not depend entirely on these codes; use them as a rough guide. Look along the shore for additional clues. Shells on the bank usually indicate shells below. The entrance banks to Bull Creek opposite Hilton Head are a good example of this. If the banks are marsh held in mud, with a fair current to keep the bottom free of mush, you may find good mud below, or a good mud-sand mixture. The same creek, farther in, is a good example of this. Quiet coves surrounded by beautiful forest tend to have slime bottoms from years of siltation and decay with little cleansing current. The Chesapeake Bay has many such areas. Sandy beaches ashore with a gently sloping bottom indicated on the chart usually have sand bottoms out where you would anchor.

When the hook goes down, it is obviously important to be at the bow to feel and listen to what happens as you fall back. This not only tells you whether you are in for good, but it can also reveal the symptoms of a bad bottom. I like to hang over the rail and put my bare foot on the chain before it contacts the roller (be careful not to hurt your foot). This enables me to feel the bottom more precisely. If the bottom is hard with shells, you can usually hear the chain rattle as it drags across, and feel the vibration with your hand or foot. The ground tackle may lightly vibrate as it slides across hard sand, and it will slide much more rapidly than if it were in soft mud. If the anchor seems to hold but then jerks out, there may be grass, a deep shell mixture, or marginal mud. If the jerking motion is sudden after a seemingly strong bite, the bottom is likely to be grass. If the jerking motion is sluggish, the cause may be loose mud. When the anchor smoothly and quietly slides on back with the boat, it is probably floating through loose, slimy mud.

ANCHORING TECHNIQUES

Always assume that any current will change. Always assume that the wind will change directions and pick up. Always assume that your boat will drag at least somewhat. Always assume that your neighbor's boat will drag also, probably in your direction. Never assume that everything is all right with your anchor. Always assume that the storm will come through, or the boat nearby will drag, at 2 A.M.. Once you've accepted these assumptions, you're off to a good start. Then remember: *Never anchor too close to other boats.*

Inexperienced cruisers tend to have a strong herding instinct. In a harbor 5 miles long, all of it great for anchoring, newcomers will anchor on top of a solitary boat or close to a grouping of boats. This is rude, and it makes people angry. It reflects poor seamanship, and it is often dangerous. Bunching probably leads to more anchoring problems than all other bad anchoring habits combined. After all, if you anchor at a safe distance from other boats, you'll have plenty of room to drag and recover if you do everything else wrong. And besides, if you want to live on top of your neighbor, why did you buy a boat and not a condominium?

Even if the harbor and conditions force you to be somewhat close to other boats, never put your anchor within the scope of another boat's swing, or even near it. This means: Don't drop your anchor between another boat's anchor and a point well off the stern of that boat. The other boat's chain may not have straightened out yet; it may be snaking around on the bottom. When the wind rises, the chain will straighten and the boat will fall back. If you don't know where the other boat's anchor is, ask the owner. If you don't know how much line he has out, ask him. Never drop your anchor in a position that will leave it under another boat after the boats swing. I've seen this frequently in harbors crowded with temporary cruisers. It is a dangerous practice, even if the length of your line puts your boat's bow well aft of the other boat's stern. If you need to retrieve your anchor in an emergency—and emergencies occur often in heavy weather, and heavy weather is common in cruising—you may not be able to if the other boat is over it. And, as both boats sail and swing back and forth, the rudder or prop of the other boat may snarl up your line, leaving both of you helpless and in peril. And if the other boat drags back, your situation will be even worse.

If there isn't room to avoid all of the above, find another harbor if possible. If a storm is coming and there is no other place to anchor, talk to the boaters around you. Explain your concerns about acquiring a safe haven. They may know of another good place nearby. If they don't, it has almost always been my experience that they will try to help you. Everyone will work together to locate a good spot. If you barge into an anchorage when a storm is pending and drop your hook, ignorant of how everyone else has carefully positioned themselves, you'll acquire a harborful of instant enemies (deservedly so). You may end up with damage to your boat and to other boats as well.

SCOPE

Use a reasonable amount of scope. The general rule of thumb is 5 to 7 feet of anchor line per foot of water depth. Of course, this may vary according to the wind, bottom, and waves. I've seen cruisers totally lacking confidence in themselves and their gear put out two, three, four, and more times the amount of scope needed. Thus, an anchorage that normally holds several boats is blocked by one boat. If you do this, other boaters will not respect you. They may anchor within the scope of your swing.

As I mentioned earlier, the safety of your boat depends just as much on the quick retrieval of your anchor as on its quick deployment. Of the many reasons for this, I'll mention the two most important ones: (1) When the boat upwind drags down on you, your only salvation may be a quick escape. If you don't get out of the way, the boat may crash into you, sending both of you downwind. Even if the boater doesn't crash into you, his hook, dragging along the bottom, may snag your anchor or its line, which happens frequently.

Once entangled, neither of you could do much to save yourselves. (2) Your boat may drag, and if you think it never will, you're in for trouble. Until you get all of your hooks clear of the bottom, you will not be in control. You will probably drift downwind and sideways onto whatever is in your path.

TWO ANCHORS

If you anchor well and with good gear, and if you keep a proper watch, you will not need to deploy two anchors often. Two anchors can actually cause problems. When the wind or current changes, the lines can easily become twisted. If a storm is brewing, the winds may clock several times before it sets in, resulting in a tangled mess. And in order to retrieve either anchor, you will have to untwist the lines. In strong wind or current, this can be a difficult, even dangerous, job.

If you plunk down two anchors, you will restrict your swing. If other boats in the anchorage have one anchor down and have carefully positioned themselves, you will be the fly in the ointment and perhaps find yourself dangerously close to another boat when the wind shifts. Tonnage, underbody structure, windage, and other factors can make it dangerous for some boaters to put over two hooks. Don't expect them to sit idly by if you come in and choose to restrict your swing, putting you and them in peril.

Two anchors can also cause a problem when your boat swings around with the wind or a change in the tide. It isn't unusual for the second line to hang up on the keel, rudder, or propeller, and if the current or changing wind picks up strongly, you will be in serious jeopardy. The current will flow against the side of your keel and underbody, and the wind will blow from the side as well. The resistance created by these forces will likely cause you to drag. If you can't get one anchor up because the line is wrapped around the propeller, you'll wish you had bought a condo. Some boats are more susceptible to this problem than others. A deep-keel boat, or one with a fancy, high-tech protrusion such as wings on the keel, a hull with a spade rudder, a poorly protected propeller, or any number of other configurations, may facilitate this sort of foul-up. Different line lengths may cause this problem or help to avoid it. It is unique to the boat and conditions.

If you do have to use two anchors, you can usually make snags and tangles less likely by using two chain rodes with enough length so that the slack of one drops to the bottom and passes under the hull as it swings. If one or both are nylon rodes, and you tighten them so that there is little slack in either one, you'll be much more likely to have one of them snag your bottom as it swings.

There are some instances in which two anchors may be necessary, such as when you are in an anchorage that has sharply reversing, strong current and a questionable bottom, or when there just isn't any room to swing. For example, if in swinging on one line you're apt to foul the rudder on a nearby reef or shoal, you would want to limit your swinging room by setting two anchors. Although it's best to avoid such restricted areas, sometimes they're all you've got.

You might need two anchors if you expect a sharp reversal of wind and you are unsure of the bottom or there simply isn't room to reset. If a storm is approaching and there isn't room in the harbor to swing on one line because everyone else has set out two anchors to minimize swing, you will have to set out two as well.

If circumstances force you to use two anchors, just remember that you could be trapped from quick escape. Do what you can to minimize tangling as mentioned above.

There are several different ways to set out two anchors. One is to put both out in a V from the bow so that the bow points into the wind with the anchors to either side. This setting gives you double security in strong winds (gale force or higher) that blow from one direction for some time. It may also reduce sailing about. If the wind reverses suddenly, you may have to change settings quickly. By deploying one anchor upcurrent and one downcurrent, you can somewhat hold your boat in place as the current reverses. This prevents the direction of pull from popping the anchors loose. It also reduces your swinging radius. This method is called the *Bahamian moor;* when folks come to the Bahamas for the first time, many think they must use it everywhere. We use it wherever circumstances dictate, but only when circumstances dictate.

Some anchors, such as Danforths, Fortress anchors, and yachtsman's, have long stocks. The rode can foul on these and trip the anchor. The rode may also ensnare the flukes on these types of anchors. If the rode remains entangled, you will not be able to reset the anchor. Because of this, I don't use our Danforth in reversing currents unless I put out a second anchor. I typically use the CQR alone, except in hard bottoms. The CQR resets readily, although it usually doesn't pull out once set.

I've too often seen panicked skippers (some are perpetually panicked) create a spiderweb around the boat with three, four, five, and even more anchors set out in all directions. If you have good gear and good bottom, and if you set your anchor well, you don't need to do this. Perhaps these skippers think they are staking a territorial claim. It seldom works.

SETTING THE ANCHOR

As I mentioned above, you want to feel for the bottom as you back down. The main purpose of backing down is to set the anchor so that it digs in. If the anchor holds after you've backed down, don't stop there, particularly if you expect bad weather (and you should *always* expect bad weather). Continue backing down while slowly increasing the rpm until you are sure the anchor has firmly dug in and your boat is no longer moving back. The rpm will vary with the type of boat, engine, and propeller, so I can't give you a magic number. You'll get the hang of it as you gain experience.

I've watched boaters trying to set an anchor by tugging with their hands. If your boat is under 12 feet long, this method may be adequate; otherwise, it's completely useless. Use the motor to be sure the anchor has set.

To be extra certain, use the motor to give the anchor a few jerks. Do this by allowing the chain or rope to slacken. If there is wind or current keeping it taut, you may need to motor forward a bit to slacken it. Back down using fairly high rpm until just before the chain pulls tight, then put the engine in neutral to avoid jerking the drive train. If you are well dug in, the stern should swing around smartly, and the bow will jerk when the line tightens. Before you do this, however, be sure you've secured the rode to the mooring post or a cleat that is designed to take maximum strain. Anything less, including your windlass gypsy or wildcat, may break loose. And stand clear in case something breaks. Don't put any undue strain on your equipment; only you can judge what is safe for your boat.

Repeated jerks will really dig her in. I've tested this technique by diving on the anchor and watching the anchor bury itself after a gradual backing down failed to set it well. If the jerking motion pops the anchor out, just be glad it released in daylight, with your knowledge, and not at night. Be careful. Failure of rode or gear could cause injury or death. Also, take a bearing as you back. Sight a tree or structure on shore, and line it up against another tree or structure behind it. If the two stay in line as you reverse, you are not dragging.

As I mentioned earlier, it is good practice to dive on your anchor to be sure it has set. I realize that there are many places where the water is too deep, too muddy, too cold, or the current too swift to do this, but do it when you safely can. If you can't dive but the water is clear, view the anchor with a look bucket (a bucket with a glass or plastic bottom). Try to establish that it has buried itself in the bottom, the deeper the better. Also check for coral heads or debris in the water nearby that could foul your rode, or the anchor should it drag.

A CQR may begin to set on its side. While I prefer mine to set straight in, I've found that this side-setting will normally straighten out as the anchor is buried deeper. If feasible, continue to dive on your anchor every day or so. This is particularly important if there has been a blow or sudden reversals of pull.

ANCHOR BUOYS

Anchor buoys are jugs or other floats attached to the anchor. Theoretically, they mark the position of your anchor and enable you to trip the anchor and pull it up if you can't otherwise. They let other boats know where your anchor is.

In my opinion, anchor buoys are seldom a good idea, for several reasons: First, you should know where your anchor is without a buoy, and you can advise someone else who may not know. Second, you should be able to get your anchor out of the bottom with your foredeck equipment. Third, when the boat swings, the buoy may catch on the propeller or rudder, and your own boat could trip the anchor, and then be helpless with its fouled propeller. I've seen this happen. Fourth, boaters traveling in dinghies at night can't see these buoys. If a dinghy or larger boat snags your anchor buoy, it will probably trip your anchor.

I've heard boaters say, "That's what insurance is for." Well, as I mentioned in an earlier chapter that covered insurance, taking advantage of your insurance policy may not be as easy as you think. If you are in an out-of-the-way cruising area, you might not be able to locate a boatyard to repair the damage, even if you had an insurance check in hand. If you had a check, you'd probably have trouble finding a place to cash it. You might be forced to stop cruising and limp back to civilization—if possible—where you could find surveyors, yards, fax machines, and telephones. By that time, any witnesses would be scattered to the winds.

FOULED ANCHORS

We all spend a lot of time talking and worrying about getting our anchors to hold. We spend a lot of money buying the best equipment to securely hook us to the bottom. But what happens if you can't get the anchor to come up? Facing the loss of perhaps well over a thousand dollars' worth of rode and anchor is not an ideal way to start a cruising day.

As I mentioned earlier, if the water clarity allows, you can study the problem through a glass-bottom bucket, or you can dive on the anchor using a mask and snorkel. But who has such luck? When the line doesn't come in, it is usually receding into murky depths, leaving no clue as to what is holding it.

The next time you experience this cruising delight, some of the following tips may help.

Assuming that diving is out of the question, try to figure out what has happened. A successful resolution often results from a series of educated guesses and a lot of luck. First, determine whether it is your line or the anchor that is fouled. Check to see which way your line is running, and make sure it isn't caught on your keel, rudder, or propeller. If it is, you will probably be able to clear it relatively easily if there isn't any current. You may be able to unwrap the line in the direction opposite that in which it wound on. If there is current, the strain may be more than you can pull against; you may need to either wait until the flow slackens or set out another anchor to take the strain. Using a boathook might help. Try sliding the hook down the rope to push or pull the line out from under the keel or rudder.

If the line is fouled around the prop, the boathook may free it; if it has taken several turns, you may need to do more. Sometimes, you can unwind anchor line that is wrapped around a prop by grabbing the shaft from inside the boat and turning it. Have someone hold the line, pulling just a bit, to be sure that you are unwinding rather than winding it in. If you get slack by turning the shaft, you are probably making progress. Have your helper take in the slack and maintain a slight pressure. (This tactic may also free a jibsheet or dockline fouled in the propeller.)

(text continued on page 144)

"WE THREW HER INTO REVERSE"

In the fall of 1995 we were anchored on a stormy night in the wilds of Georgia, far up a lonely creek surrounded by marsh and clumps of trees. We knew the bottom was good, and indeed, the anchor snugged quickly. The next morning a mild northeaster was blowing; the current was ripping at around 3 knots as the 8-foot tide rushed past us to the sea. We had 125 feet of chain looped between our bow and the bottom. The wind, blowing from our stern quarter, sailed *Chez Nous* against the current. The creek banks sloped steeply, not far from us on either side.

We knew it was important to get the anchor aboard immediately after it broke free. With the gear dragging bottom, it would be impossible to bring the bow around quickly given the wind and current. We would soon be aground.

The electric windlass strained unusually hard. Thinking it was struggling against the force of the wind blowing us against the current, I continued to crank in the chain. Suddenly, the circuit breaker popped. Time to stop. I looked up and saw that the bow was moving with the current as the wind pushed us toward shore. I had almost no control. No time to play. I flipped the breaker on and tried again. The anchor stock finally breached the surface, but the boat continued to act as though the gear were dragging. Then I saw it: A huge coil of heavy steel cable hooked and tangled around our plow. The spirals, like a giant metal monster, hung down into the muddy water as we continued to drag toward the shore. I knelt down on the bow pulpit and tried to lift off the coils, but the anchor was dangling too far below me. Mel ran forward with two boathooks in hand. Each of us grabbed a section of coil with a hook and lifted—just enough to clear the point of the plow. The snarled cable sank to the bottom, one of our boathooks tightly clamped between its loops. We shuddered, just thinking about the hand or leg that so easily could have been caught instead.

We didn't have time to ponder. The boat was sailing freely toward the shoal. So, we threw her into reverse, backed against the wind, and headed south.

▼

(text continued from page 142)

Sometimes the anchor rode has wrapped around a protrusion such as a rock or stump. If you take bearings when you put down your anchor (always a good idea) but the line later tugs tight vertically at a different bearing, you know that something other than the anchor is holding the line. If your line is much shorter than it should be when it snugs tight, you have a further clue that this is your problem. If, for example, you are in 20 feet of water and you put out 100 feet of rode when you anchored, you know there is a problem with the line if later on you can pull in only 30 feet.

When you're sure that your line is snagged on the bottom, first try a few judicious tugs, as much for the purpose of fact-gathering as for retrieval. Vibrations or sounds may offer clues. For example, if you experience short, sharp releases, the line may be snarled in a tree trunk, with branches clutching the line. If the line vibrates or jerks as the boat swings, or as you pull it across the bottom, this may indicate rocks. If the current allows you to get straight over the point of the snag, so that the line is vertical, you may find more play from one particular angle, indicating that you may be wrapped around something from which you can unwind. If your boat is being held strongly by the tide or wind, you may need to set another anchor and pull the boat up so that the fouled line loosens. Then get into the dinghy and tug and pull on the line. You might obtain information about what's going on below, or the line might unwind. Sometimes, without applying tension, you can unwrap the line or pull it out backward by carefully working from directly over the site.

If this doesn't work, try dragging a grappling hook. We keep a small one aboard for this and similar purposes. Carefully drag it across the bottom between the snag point and the anchor. If you hook the line between the snag and the anchor, you may be able to pull the line out backward, or at least get some line up above the surface so that you can pull up your anchor and, if necessary, cut and lose only the portion of line or chain that remains caught. Or, you may be able to free it by sliding a loop of chain down the anchor rode until it reaches the anchor and then pulling it out backward.

If the anchor itself is snagged, try to get the boat directly over the anchor and negate the effect of tide and wind by setting a second anchor. Then work the rode back and forth and around, tugging as you do.

Another tactic is to explore the spot where the anchor lies with

"THE WAY IT CAN BE"

You've had a long passage and a tiring day. A beautiful cove opens up. You look at the chart and see that it is deep enough. Trees surround the far reaches of the cove, marsh grasses wave near the entrance. A white heron arches its neck as it carefully explores the edge of the grasses. You head in and carefully circle around, watching the depthfinder to learn the contours of the bottom. When you have found a pretty area near the middle of a circle of water you know will be deep enough at low tide, you stop the boat and lower the anchor. As it hits bottom, you fall back, paying out chain until there is around 5-to-1 scope. You secure the chain, then slowly back down, gradually increasing the rpm, and feel the anchor resting firmly. The stern swings around, and you know that it is holding. You put on a snubber, cut off the engine, and return to the cockpit.

It is quiet except for the evening noises of birds, the wind in the trees, and the occasional plop of a fish breaking the surface. The water around your home reflects the colors still haunting the sky from the setting sun. Despite the heat of the day, a slight chill steals over the water with the coming dark. A few stars emerge through the pale last light of day; they remind you to turn on your anchor light. The night breeze builds and you feel your boat turn into the wind and settle down. Perhaps you sip a glass of wine, perhaps nothing at all—you are thinking that you don't need more in life than what is around you. This is what cruising is all about.

▼

a grappling hook. If you lower it alongside your anchor chain and pull up some chunks of wood, you can probably conclude that a tree or log is holding your main gear. You'll then feel more confident about using a strong pull with the motor. Obviously, you may snag this equipment and lose it too, but you will be less likely to do so if you tie a second, smaller trip line to the hook end. This will enable you to pull it backward.

If the current allows you to lower the grappling hook directly down the rode, you may be able to feel your anchor, perhaps snag it, and pull it out backward. This is all hit and miss, blind groping, and guessing, but that's often the best you can do.

When all else fails, brute force might break your gear free. But it may also break something else free. If you use brute force, be sure the chain or rope is secured to something strong enough to take the strain, and use the engine rather than the windlass to apply the force. Be careful. Tug only as is safe under the circumstances, keeping in mind the integrity and strength of all your anchoring gear. I have seen boaters collapse their boat's anchor platform by pulling too hard (perhaps a fortuitous warning). Only you can be the judge of your equipment's strength.

It will probably be best to pull from more than one direction. When doing this, have someone stationed on the bow to listen for sounds that may give clues. As when testing holding ground, I place a bare foot on the chain to feel for vibrations or small jerks that may hint at what is going on below. But do this very cautiously. Should your gear suddenly break loose from below, or on deck, you could suffer serious injury or death. Be careful not to stand in a loop or coil of chain or line.

If all fails, you will have to leave your anchor and chain with a buoy marking its presence. With help from a bigger boat and a heavier windlass, you may be able to retrieve it later.

Once you find good bottom and the anchor is well set, you can relax and enjoy the anchorage—and hope that your neighbor upwind has done as well. I hope my admonitions have not discouraged you. I've been on anchor most of the time for the last 17 years, and I love it. It's nice and it's fun. Like anything else, however, you must learn to do it well.

Chapter Twelve
THE ENGINE

The cruising sailboat's auxiliary engine is one of the most important and critical pieces of equipment. Unfortunately, it has been a tradition for noble sailors sitting on the bar stools of their favorite yacht clubs, and for cult cruisers writing from

their homes ashore, to disparage the engine, to claim that the
true sailor hardly needs it, and to imply that to give it credence
is to show a lack of toughness and seamanship. At this writing, the
truth is that cruising without a reliable, well-found, and well-in-
stalled diesel engine is like going to New York City on I-95 via
horse and buggy.

Some of the best cruising areas in the United States require
an engine, not all the time, but much of the time. This includes
the Intracoastal Waterway, many coastal rivers, parts of the
Pacific Northwest, and wherever you travel on canals. In many
inlets, the current is too swift and the traffic far too heavy for
anyone to prudently sail in or out—unless their engine has failed.
Captains of cruise ships, freighters, and tankers don't have to give
a sailboat right of way in these channels if they would be forced
aground. In the Bahamas, with its wide-open waters and beautiful sailing destinations, many cuts and anchorages between small
cays are dangerous to traverse without an engine because of swift
currents, meandering channels, and sharp rock and reef. Many of
the most perfect anchorages can be accessed only in good light
because there are no aids to navigation, and you can clear the
reefs only by seeing them through the clear water. Thus, in many
instances, you would have to stand offshore all night long in order to make safe harbor—unless you turn on the engine to ensure
your arrival in good light. The prospect of standing off a rocky
shore all night may sound romantic, but it isn't at all if you are
fatigued or if a storm is developing. Although these examples
pertain to the States and Caribbean, conditions are similar
around the world.

Having a good engine is not only a matter of sound seamanship and safety, it is a matter of fun and creature comfort. Let's
say you've been sailing for days (or even for hours), you are becalmed, and a great storm is building. Wouldn't it be infinitely
nicer to turn on the engine and motor into that beckoning safe
harbor rather than stay out, playing it tough—and stupid?
Today's cruising sailboat engines can interface with a lot of
other equipment and avail you of many features you might
not otherwise be able to afford. These include watermakers,
refrigeration, and high-output alternators and 110-volt
generators.

THE DIESEL AUXILIARY

Of the many types of diesel engines available, we prefer the old-fashioned, slow-turning, naturally aspirated (no turbocharging) heavy-block engines. They are heavy and take up a lot of room, but they are usually reliable and fixable.

Contemporary engineering has given us lighter block engines that run at higher rpm. These engines are also smaller and they develop more horsepower for their size (often relying on turbo-charging). These features make them ideal for many lighter sailboats. The old-timers say these just don't last as long as the old-time heavy diesels. The new-timers say they will.

Whereas a naturally aspirated diesel relies on the natural suction created as the pistons travel downward, the turbocharged diesel forces in extra air with turbo blades. I don't like them because they require extra maintenance. I look at this advancement as just an additional system that can run amok. Besides, they are usually expensive to replace. Most of the newer, smaller diesels are turbocharged, and many cruisers live with them very happily. You may have little choice given the configuration of your boat. Whatever engine you have, make sure it is a reliable brand with readily available parts and made by a well-known manufacturer.

KNOW YOUR ENGINE

Whatever engine you have, go to a good diesel school that offers specific hands-on instruction about your engine. Also get a shop manual and any special tools you may need. These include at least some offset wrenches and deep-socket wrenches. The shop manual will probably list special tools needed to work on your engine, but these are usually obtainable only from the manufacturer and are specific to total overhaul jobs that you will probably not be doing yourself. Talk to a mechanic who has done a lot of work on your engine for specific suggestions. Explain why you need to know; you'll probably get better help if he understands that you aren't just somebody in the neighborhood who is trying to cut in on his business. And since it is his business, you might want to consider paying him to talk with and work with you for a few hours.

"THE BOAT SURGED FORWARD"

We were tied up at a marina in a North Carolina seaport following an offshore passage up from Florida. Another boat approached, advising the marina of a much longer passage. The owner and crew of three had been at sea for over a week, having left from the lower Caribbean to bring the boat back to the owner's home. The trip had been blessed with good weather. The sailing had been great. All aboard were very tired, ready to tie her up, take hot showers, and treat themselves to restaurant meals.

The current runs strong and parallel to the shore in this spot, so docking is usually a bit tricky. The owner knew this, however, and was prepared. Lines were out and the crew were well placed around the deck to handle them. The approach was critical, and it was executed well. Because the current was running into the slip, some speed was necessary to effect good steerage; he used just the right amount and the boat slid gracefully in. The helmsman put her in reverse at exactly the right moment. Nothing happened. He throttled up. It didn't sound right. The boat surged forward. A second later it hit the main pier, going full speed, assisted by the current. The bow first cut through the water main. Then it cut through the power line. Next, it plowed partly through the dock, which yielded a bit and then flexed ahead, crumpling as it did. The owner of the yacht on the opposite side, secure in his slip and confidently enjoying the evening, watched in horror as the entire mess crashed into his bow.

It wasn't a good cruise after all. The transmission linkage had come loose sometime during the voyage.

▼

MAINTENANCE

When I say "maintenance," I don't mean simply changing the oil, filters, and belts. Anyone should be able to do those things, although it is frightening to think of the number of cruisers I've seen at sea, away from the U.S. coast, and in the islands, who don't know how to change the oil. The following maintenance and repair procedures are the *minimum* you should be able to do on your engine. The more you know, the better. In some instances, my specific

▼

suggestions may be inappropriate to your particular engine and installation, but I hope they will serve as a guide to the types of maintenance procedures you should routinely perform.

OIL

Let's begin with the lube oil. You should know what mixed oil and water look like so you'll recognize this problem immediately. It basically looks like chocolate milk. Getting water in the oil can totally ruin the engine if you don't deal with it properly and quickly. And, surprisingly, it isn't an unusual problem. A bad head gasket, for example, can allow freshwater coolant to leak into the oil. Below, I discuss several scenarios that allow raw water in. If this happens, pull the injectors, turn over the engine—preferably by hand—and pump all the water off the top of the piston heads. Then pour diesel fuel into the injector holes. Pump out all the oil in the sump and refill the sump with new oil or diesel oil and pump it out again. Do this at least three times if your store of oil or diesel allows. Then pour a little low-viscosity oil (regular is okay if it's the only thing you have) into the cylinders. Find and fix the cause of your water leak (more on this later). The leak is most likely to be on the saltwater side unless the water level in your expansion tank is low; and you will readily know this because you will have inspected it every day. Then, with new oil, replace the injectors, bleed, and start (you hope). Run 15 minutes or so, stop, remove the oil, fill again (put in a new oil filter with each change), and start again. Do this several times until you feel sure there is no longer any water in the lubrication system. As you will have surmised, always carry a plentiful supply of spare oil and filters.

If there is water in the engine oil, trying to start the engine could cause serious internal damage, namely, hydraulic lock. Water on top of your pistons won't compress like air. Because of this I always check the oil before I start the engine. If it is high on the dipstick after several dips, I check it out. If water has gotten in during the night, it may be down at the bottom of the oil pan because water is heavier than oil. The chocolate milk color won't be noticeable because the engine hasn't run and mixed the solution. Removing the liquid from the bottom of the oil pan will usually tell the tale.

VALVES AND HEAD GASKET

Know how to remove the valve cover and adjust the valves. Learn how to find top dead-center on your engine. Keep several valve-cover gaskets among your spares, and at least one spare head gasket. You will not want to pull the head gasket unless you're sure it's necessary and you have competent help nearby if needed. But if you do have to pull it, you can be sure that there won't be a head gasket readily available unless you've brought a spare.

WATER PUMPS

Be able to replace and rebuild your raw-water pump, not just the impeller. You'll have to do this regularly. The bearings and seal often go in these pumps, sometimes even the shafts. Carry a rebuild kit and know how to use it. It's best to have a completely new pump in addition to a rebuild kit.

FUEL SYSTEMS

Be able to service your fuel system. Have a spare fuel lift pump. I also carry a spare injector pump, because these are difficult to find away from population centers and they must be rebuilt in special injector shops. Know how to quickly bleed the engine. Practice doing it. Reading a book and trying to do this for the first time while heeled at 45 degrees and pitching and rolling along a rocky shore is not what I recommend.

Know how to pull and replace injectors. This may be easy, depending on the engine, but you need to know how to handle the high-pressure lines. These can be troublesome to hook up again, and if you crimp them or strip or crack a union nut, you have a big problem. Nothing works like practice, but in general you'll do well to remember not to tighten down on any high-pressure line until all the fittings have been hand-threaded. Never force anything.

Be sure that changing fuel filters is a snap for you. Ideally, you want to have a dual set of filters. We prefer the Racor type so that we can see when they are dirty, a pressure gauge to indicate when they are getting dirty, and a Y valve to switch to another set, giving us time to change the filters in the dirty unit. An electric feed pump just above the fuel tank will help with filling changed filters and bleeding the system, but remember that the more joints you put into the fuel line, the more likely you are to develop an air leak (often hard to find). Air leaks cause erratic performance or shutdown. Also be familiar with how to retrieve and clean the pickup tube that goes down into the tank. Particularly in older tanks, these may get clogged with debris or algae that actually grows in the tanks. Rolling around at sea can shake this stuff loose and allow it to stop up your intake. Have your tanks cleaned occasionally by a professional.

PLUMBING

Be familiar with your engine's plumbing on the raw- and internal freshwater sides. In chapter 8 I gave an example of replacing our freshwater pump. This part often fails quickly and with little warning. Know where the thermostat is and how to change or remove it. (Carry a spare, but it is possible to run without one for awhile. Your motor may simply run too cool. Over a period of time, this could cause increased carbon buildup and poor firing.)

Be able to diagnose causes of overheating. An oven thermometer placed in the expansion tank (you will have to run the engine with the pressure cap off—be careful) may tell you whether it is just the gauge or the sending unit that is malfunctioning. Never remove the cap when there is pressure.

Know how to inspect and clean your heat exchanger, as well as how to replace it. If it leaks, it will introduce salt water into the freshwater cooling system. You will probably see the water level in the expansion tank rise, even overflow. If this happens, you must know how to drain your fresh water system. You will have to flush it several times with fresh water before refilling. Of course this will come after you replace the defective heat exchanger with your spare. If you don't have a spare, a temporary repair can be made. In most units, you remove the end cap, and plug the freshwater outlets at the other end. Add fresh water into the freshwater side. The seawater usually runs inside the tubes from one end to the other. If you see water rising in one of the tubes, that's the one that's leaking. Clean it to facilitate adherence and plug it off with J-B Weld or a similar product.

Know how to bleed your freshwater system. This coolant flows through many small passageways around the block. Once you drain it, there may be air blocks in some of these areas after you fill it again. This could cause rapid and serious overheating. Some engines have a bleeding vent on the highest part of the block that you open as you fill. In others you may have to fill the engine and then run it for several hours with the top off the expansion tank. (Watch the temperature gauge.) Bubbles occasionally bursting at the surface of the water in the tank indicate that the trapped air is escaping.

The raw-water side of the cooling water will probably pass into your exhaust at or near its exit from the exhaust manifold. Usually this is done with an injection fitting in a riser or other cast-iron extension of the manifold. If this part rusts you could get salt water down into your block, reduce water flow into the exhaust, or get a leakage of carbon monoxide. Reduced water flow can cause overheating of the engine and exhaust hose, causing the line to burn, which also introduces carbon monoxide below. Leaking carbon monoxide could easily cause fatalities. Know how to inspect and replace the injection fitting. Be able to follow your exhaust line throughout its course and to its exit. Leaks in this line, for any reason, must be detected and fixed quickly. The fume sensor we recommended in chapter 10 will help here.

Your raw-water cooling flow, particularly if you have a sailboat, must pass well above the waterline and through an antisiphon loop before it goes into the exhaust. The high loop keeps seawater from siphoning into the exhaust system and backing up through the exhaust manifold and down through the valves into the cylinders—a very nasty deal. The antisiphon device introduces air into the high part of the loop, breaking the siphon when the engine is off. These devices are valves of one sort or another, and they all fail eventually if you leave them in. I removed mine so this wouldn't happen, letting a small stream of water flow from the top of the loop overboard via a tube. This way I can look at the stream just before I cut off the engine to be sure that the passage that will then introduce air is not obstructed, and we have a rough flow meter that lets us know if the impeller in the raw-water pump is losing its blades.

Learn whether your exhaust manifold is cooled with seawater or internal fresh water. Seawater-cooled manifolds eventually rust out. This can dump salt water into the engine. If yours is so designed, replace it periodically. Learn also if your lube-oil and transmission-oil heat exchanger is cooled with internal fresh water or seawater. Replace this unit about every three years, especially if it uses seawater. Be sure it is protected with sacrificial zincs, which must be checked periodically. Any breach inside introduces water into the engine and, if applicable, the transmission.

TRANSMISSIONS

Know how to check your transmission fluid. Check it before each start-up. If it begins to look or smell burnt, you have a problem. Changing it as the manufacturer recommends will help, and will also warn you of impending problems. For example, grit or pieces of metal draining out are a very bad sign.

THE STUFFING BOX

The stuffing box or dripless shaft seal, which is located where your shaft exits the hull, will require regular maintenance. You may have hardly ever needed to look at one when you were running your boat only every weekend or so, but now things are different. Have plenty of stuffing twine, or O-rings, or whatever your system requires, and be able to install them in the water using the proper tools. Also, check your shaft alignment periodically. If it is bad you are not only giving your engine and Cutless bearing a hard time, you will also find yourself working on that always hard-to-reach stuffing box more often than you should.

THE CUTLESS BEARING

Your cutless bearing is the rubber-surfaced insert through which your shaft runs. If your boat's shaft doesn't run through a strut, the bearing may be in the hull where the shaft exits. Wherever yours is, be warned that these eventually wear, especially with a lot of use. Wear can cause vibration severe enough to do damage. We usually check ours by diving, grabbing the shaft, and shaking it to see if there is any play. There shouldn't be any lateral movement at all. If there is, you will probably have to get hauled to replace it. A spare should be part of your inventory. If you keep the old one, you can use it as a tool to help force the bad one out the next time you need to.

OTHER SKILLS

Many skills are indispensable as you perform these and other repair jobs. For example, you need to know how to remove a seized bolt or nut. If you break off a manifold, or worse, a head bolt, you have real problems. Learn the skill of judicious tapping. Creating vibrations, while introducing WD-40, Liquid Wrench, or a similar penetrant may save you thousands of dollars, but it takes skill and knowledge.

Know when to use grease products that prevent seizing. Sometimes they can be a lifesaver down the road. But in some places, as on the head bolts, you should not use them. Know how to use tools that extract broken bolts, and try to develop skill at drilling them out, inserting new threads, or cutting new thread with your tap and die set. The list goes on forever, and learning these skills takes time and training. Start the learning process well before you begin cruising.

Inspect the engine regularly. I try to check mine every time I start it and every time I shut it down. This inspection includes oil and water, transmission fluid, transmission linkage, throttle linkage, electrical connections, belts, plumbing, and chafe areas. I tighten up on the set screws holding the shaft in the coupling. I also touch different engine parts such as the cooler, the header tank, the cooled area of the exhaust manifold, and the valve cover. Any of these areas may be too hot to touch; you will have to learn. Practiced touching helps you pick up and identify potential over-heating problems and unusual vibrations.

Listening is very important. You are more likely to hear things beginning to go wrong as the engine starts and stops. A mechanic's stethoscope is handy for this. I usually use a long screwdriver with a plastic handle. Touch the blade to the part and put your ear against the end of the handle. Don't get hurt: Your head and hands will be close to moving machinery. As you become familiar with the sounds from different parts of the engine, you'll be able to diagnose developing problems. Key areas include different parts of the block (particularly fore and aft—but be careful of the spinning parts), the freshwater pump, the raw-water pump, the injection pump, and the transmission.

There are many more aspects of engine work with which you should become familiar. Remember that it is quite hard to learn during emergencies, and if you are learning where there are no parts or mechanics around to help you if you make a mistake, you probably will.

Chapter Thirteen

POWER TO THE PEOPLE

Like so many cruising traditions, the notion that electricity doesn't belong on a cruising boat faded long ago. It is still true, however, that the less electricity you use, the more money you'll have in your pocket. You would have a little less to worry about, too. But you'd miss out on the added safety electricity provides if you hardly used it all: significant repairs can be made quickly and well with power tools. You'd miss the advantages of many navigational tools as well. True, the skippers of clipper ships in bygone days didn't have them, but they didn't have a lot of other things—Dacron sails and nylon ropes, for example. And you would miss the ability to do many things that add to a productive life, like using a computer. And, perhaps most important, you would be giving up an array of creature comforts that make all the difference between a cruising camping trip and a viable cruising lifestyle.

THE 12-VOLT SYSTEM

With today's technology you can choose to cruise with either no electric equipment at all, exclusively 12-volt, exclusively AC current, or a mixture. If your choice is the first, all I can say is that I hope you have fun. I have done it myself, but it's not my cup of tea as a lifestyle. If you have any electricity at all, you will have to deal with 12-volt issues and storage batteries. Even an AC system will rely on 12-volt batteries, unless you want to run a generator all the time; but take my word for it, you don't. The two major concerns with a 12-volt system are the batteries and the means to charge them.

Let's digress a moment to acknowledge that there are DC systems other than 12-volt; these are used particularly in boats built for use outside North America. These systems are similar to 12-volt because they all involve direct current, but there are differences. For example, a 24- or 32-volt electric motor will probably need fewer windings to do the work of a 12-volt motor. A 24- or 32-volt system might use thinner wires than a 12-volt system. Nevertheless, your boat probably has a 12-volt system, so that's what I'll focus on.

BATTERIES

Battery technology is developing rapidly. Necessity being the mother of invention, I expect the technology to continue to improve, particularly because of the emphasis on alternative energy sources and the interest in electric cars. This will directly benefit the cruising sailor. We should all keep up with these changes.

The two most common types of batteries used on cruising boats are so-called *gel cell batteries* and *lead-acid deep-cycle batteries*. Some batteries supposedly have characteristics of both, and other variations, but I'll concentrate on these two types because they are, at this writing, so common.

Lead-acid batteries are less expensive than gel cells and, based on my experience, will do just as well if serviced properly. Proper servicing, however, can be a problem on cruising boats because access is often poor. If access is poor enough, cruisers dread the job and put it off too long. In some cases, accessing the batteries is a dangerous undertaking. For example, if there is little clearance between the overhead and the top of the batteries, you could get acid in your eyes when adding water. But lead-acid batteries must be inspected regularly for leaks and terminal corrosion, and also for water level. If the level gets too low, the battery's life will be substantially shortened. Lead-acid batteries must be seated in a fiberglass or strong plastic container that will not leak acid should it bubble out of the battery. This container must be strong enough that it will not break when the battery moves. Theoretically, the battery shouldn't move, but it will, especially when your hernia pops out as you gently lower the battery. Good ventilation is essential to prevent the accumulation of explosive hydrogen gas during charging.

If your boat has good access, you can save a lot of money over gel cells by getting heavy-duty, 6-volt, "golf cart" industrial batteries; wiring them in parallel for 12 volts; and taking good care of them. But remember, taking good care of them also includes proper charging, which is discussed in more detail later.

If you don't have good battery access, a gel cell may be the best answer. I've used gel cells for around 12 years with no real complaints except that they have never lasted longer than five years. This isn't long when one considers the extra cost (and lead-acid batteries may last almost as long). But I use them because my boat's battery access is poor, and I really can't do much about this without making sacrifices I've chosen not to make. I do charge them properly, which involves different techniques than those required by lead-acid batteries.

Whatever you choose, remember that any battery has a finite number of discharges. The more you discharge it, which you do to some extent every time you use it, the closer it is to death. Even when it sits unused, a battery is slowly discharging—especially if it's lead-acid. A complete discharge will shorten its life considerably, so it's better not to let the banks run all the way down. There are times, however, with both types, when you may want to discharge them and give them a strong boost charge to try to revive them or clean up their plates. When performed on lead-acid batteries, this procedure is called *equalizing;* it is supposed to remove sulfur buildup on the plates, making them do a better job. With gel cells, the acid isn't entirely liquid. It is suspended in a gel, and the plates are thinner. Equalizing these plates could cause them to explode or boil over. Gels cells can be helped after a few years by a boost charge, properly administered according to the instructions of both the battery and the battery charger's manufacturer. Both types need to be charged in different stages using different amperage and voltage levels.

BATTERY CHARGING

A good battery charger is a must with either type of battery. It will charge in the right sequence for the type of battery, it will equalize a lead-acid battery, it will maintain the battery at a proper floating level once it has been charged and while in use, and it can be adjusted for different battery types and varying circumstances. For example, batteries are temperature-sensitive, and your battery charger should be adjusted for this as it charges. Failure to do so can shorten the battery's life.

An AC-driven battery charger must, of course, have an AC source of power. On most boats and for most practical purposes, this can come only from shore power, which is becoming an increasingly expensive proposition, or an AC generator powered by an internal-combustion engine. Although I have the latter and am happy with it, you can get by just fine without an AC generator.

You should, however, always have a good AC battery charger for occasions when you will plug into the dock. Sometimes your batteries will need a little pampering; they might need to be charged really well, equalized, or whatever. Most "at sea" methods of battery charging, such as the three discussed below, don't charge the battery as ideally as will a battery charger with AC input. So, when you do tie up, you'll get much more for your dockage money if you have a good AC charger and can do your batteries a favor. Besides, you may find it either inconvenient or impossible to use an "at sea" method at the dock.

Most cruisers who don't use an AC generator use either solar panels, a wind generator, a high-powered alternator bolted to the engine, or a combination thereof. Those of us with generators will sometimes use one or more of the above as well. I've always loved wind generators; they have saved us much diesel generator running time. Your decision about what to use will depend on your anticipated consumption. Many books tell you to add up all the amp requirements of your consuming equipment and to multiply this figure by the hours you anticipate using each piece to arrive at a total consumption figure. In practice, this is almost impossible. You don't know how often things will run (consider your freshwater pump, for example). Amp usage will vary according to the status of the battery, wiring runs, connections, condition of the equipment and other factors. And what happens when you add more equipment, which you're bound to do? Go ahead and come up with an estimate, but then get a lot more than the estimate suggests.

WIND GENERATORS

Most serious longtime cruisers who don't use a generator will probably have a high-output engine alternator that charges the batteries with 12-volt DC. They also have a wind generator. Most large wind generators claim to put out around 15 amps in 25 knots of wind. Of course they have to be mounted properly, and the wind needs to be steady—but the wind seldom blows at 25 knots all the time. I've found that nothing less than a 15-amp output (theoretical) wind generator suffices. It seldom yields this much output anyway. If you anticipate very low electricity consumption, you might be able to get by with less, but you're likely to find that your electricity consumption will grow much more than expected. I decided to buy the highest output because the price isn't that much higher.

Some wind generators have a considerably smaller blade length and more blades than the two to three blades of the 15-amp units. These put out less amperage. Many cruisers claim these units can sustain higher gusts of wind without needing to be shut down and are sometimes quieter. Users say they feel more comfortable leaving the boat unattended with the units up and running. In my experience, boaters should never leave any wind generator running unattended unless they can return quickly should storms or high winds come. I won't rely on claims that some units can take high winds; Mother nature isn't so easily anticipated by technicians and machinists. I, and many friends who have smaller units, wouldn't feel comfortable leaving any unit up in more than 25 knots of wind (perhaps 30 to 35 knots with the small-blade, lower-output, higher-wind-tolerance models, if the specifications warrant it). This isn't to say that these shouldn't be considered. If the output of such a unit is going to be enough for you (consider wind variation and usage variation), they certainly make good sense because of the qualities noted in this discussion.

Whatever wind generator you get, buy experience and quality. If the blade or hub or blade mounting breaks as the unit spins, any part could be a lethal weapon. I've heard of blades breaking off and making a hole in the deck, or flying out to sea, or just missing the crew. Some folks build their own wind generators. The basics include an electric motor, blades, and mounting. This seems simple enough, but when you consider the stresses on this equipment and the damp, salty environment, you must agree that this is a job for someone who knows what he or she is doing and can do it well. Wind generators made by reputable companies incorporate many safety features such as balancing of the blades, locktight screws, and specially designed blades and hubs.

A wind generator must have a means to shut down in high winds. I've never been comfortable with ours running in winds over 25 knots, regardless of the manufacturer's claims. Not only can you possibly burn up the motor, the likelihood of mechanical failure—such as a blade separation—is higher at these speeds. There are several basic ways to shut down these units. Some use a switch to reverse the current, which causes a temporary shutdown so that you can tie them down. If a blow comes and you aren't aboard, this obviously won't work at all. Some use a clutch operated by centrifugal force. As a certain speed of revolutions is reached, the clutch pads are slung out, overcoming their retaining springs, and the unit grinds to a halt. Be sure that the clutch or brake pads are not asbestos, particularly if you catch water on the deck underneath the unit. Others use foils on the blades. As the rpm increases, the foils open and interfere with the air stream, slowing down the blades. This type has many more parts spinning around that could fly off at high speeds.

My favorite design was on two of my early units. The tail rotated on a strong ball-bearing swivel and was held in place fore and aft by a spring. Attached to the tail was a vane that stuck out at a 90-degree angle to the tail. When the force of the wind became great enough to overcome the pull of the spring, the tail turned like a rudder and steered the unit out of the wind, thus slowing it down. The spring tension could be easily adjusted by hooking it into different holes, thus allowing the owner to set the shutdown wind speed. There were no extraneous nuts and bolts or other pieces of metal on the spinning blades.

Whatever unit you buy, make sure you have a thorough understanding of how it shuts down. Never leave a unit up in winds higher than the manufacturer recommends or you feel comfortable with, whichever is less. And regular maintenance is imperative.

A wind generator has special mounting problems. If you hang it from a rope in the foretriangle (between the forestay and the main) or between the main and mizzen, the rope will absorb most of the vibration. As long as you tie it so that it is upright and therefore squarely facing the wind, it will work well. You must take it down whenever you sail and whenever you want to tie off the blades—usually in severe weather, regardless of what kind of speed dampener it may have.

A permanent mount requires that it be out of reach and thus out of danger. The least collision of a hand or head with a spinning blade could be disastrous. The mount must be strong and securely fastened. Typically, the best place is on the transom. Often the same bracketing can be used for davits, radar mounts, and other equipment. With a permanently mounted unit, you can tie off the blades without lowering the whole thing as it swings wildly on a rope. On the other hand, permanently mounted units transmit vibrations to the hull more so than a rope-mounted unit will. The mounting must be solid and tight to limit noise. Ask the manufacturer for advice about mounting. Smaller lower-output, shorter-blade models do better on a permanent mount than do larger units because they are quieter and vibrate less, they require less clearance (which means they are easier to mount out of harm's way), and they can take higher winds without attention. Some manufacturers of larger-output units, such as Windbugger, use three blades on their permanent-mount units because this configuration produces much less vibration. They use two blades for rope-hung units because two blades pick up speed faster and, being in a straight line, are more easily stored. None of these units, if well built and properly mounted, should produce a lot of noise. There will be the constant swish of the blades, but this is not unpleasant.

From time to time we see sailboats with a wind generator permanently mounted high on the mizzen. This is not a good idea. You must be able to regularly maintain your unit and carefully inspect the blades and hub at least every few days, and certainly after any blow. You should also be able to tie down the blades manually if necessary, no matter what kind of braking system it has. You can't do that up there. You'll often be anchored in current, not facing squarely into the wind. Even when you are not in current, the boat will sail from side to side. Some boats are notorious for this. Your wind generator must face directly into the wind to produce maximum power. It must swivel or turn as the boat turns. I've occasionally seen wind generators mounted on the bow pulpit. When I question the owners, they usually say that this position gives them cleaner wind. I don't want to imagine what it must be like to run up to the bow in the dark to deal with an anchor emergency only to face a lethal windmill.

Any wind generator must feed its electricity to the batteries via a diode. The diode acts as a gate that lets electric current flow in only one direction. Without a diode, on calm days the battery current will flow back through the wire and merrily turn the motor until the batteries have been depleted. Most manufacturers sell a large enough diode and the heat sink necessary to prevent the battery from overheating. If your electricity consumption is low and your batteries are small enough so that the wind generator could overcharge them, you must monitor the batteries closely. On many boats this is seldom a problem; consumption is typically greater than the capacity of the battery banks. Nevertheless, it will cost you in the long run if you don't install and use an adequate battery monitoring system.

▼

HIGH-OUTPUT ALTERNATORS

A high-output alternator allows your engine to serve a dual purpose. It enables you to keep your batteries well charged without an expensive, separate, self-powered generator set. As I've said numerous times by now, buy this unit from a good manufacturer. Don't just get an alternator with larger diodes.

To withstand extra heat and running time, these alternators need to be built with many extras, such as extra-heavy windings, bearings, heat sinks, terminals and terminal wiring, and diodes. Don't be misled into simply getting the biggest. An alternator's output is affected in part by its running temperature and rpm. If you will be charging with your engine running at 1,800 rpm, your alternator will put out according to that speed. Of course, you can vary the speed of the alternator with different-size pulleys, but with many configurations, this is true only to a certain extent. Consult the manufacturer of the alternator to determine the size that is right for your engine.

When setting up my system, I planned to use at least a 150-amp alternator, but I later realized that my customary engine usage would not require the full capacity of that large an alternator. A 120-amp alternator was all I needed. I saved quite a few bucks.

Sometimes a high-output alternator can be mounted in the existing brackets for your old unit; sometimes special bracketing is required. It takes extra power to turn the bigger unit. If the bracket isn't strong enough, it could break at the worst possible time and cause a necessary engine shutdown, damage to other engine components, and arcing and fire. Again, you may need to consult with the manufacturer or his retailer about this. Don't let anyone talk you into mounting an alternator on a base independent of the engine, such as the fiberglass engine bed. I've often seen this in installations for both alternators and refrigeration compressors. This setup allows the auxiliary component to vibrate separately from the engine, causing almost sure failure eventually, sometimes at the engine's front bearings. I've heard many boatyard mechanics swear that this doesn't cause a problem. Well, it doesn't—at first. Eventually, however, it will, and the mechanics won't be there when it does. They'll be back in the yard, thousands of miles away, imparting their wisdom to someone just like you. Bracket the alternator to the engine itself. If you opt for a particularly heavy-duty rig, you may need two belts and double pulleys on both the alternator and the engine. This adds a lot of expense, which may not be worth it depending on how much output you require.

You must also consider the loading the alternator places on the engine. On the one hand, you don't want to use your diesel engine at anchor for long hours on a light load. It won't be running at normal temperature, and excess carbon deposits will result. If you also use the engine to run a mechanically coupled refrigerator compressor at the same time, there may be adequate load, depending on your engine. On the other hand, if the alternator takes too much engine power, it may interfere with engine performance while underway.

Finally, you can waste a lot of money and effort if you don't purchase a modern, three-stage voltage regulator to control your new alternator. If you don't, it will never charge and maintain your batteries as well as it should. A surprising number of boats were and still are built with automotive alternators that have automotive voltage regulators. Automotive alternators and regulators are designed to charge a lot for just a few minutes and then put out just a little for the rest of the run. This is because car batteries usually don't get discharged very deeply, and most battery usage occurs when the motor is running. Your boat is different. While anchored overnight, at least the house bank of your batteries will normally receive a substantial discharge. These may also be deep-cycle with thick plates for high reserve capacity, unlike the thin-plate car batteries designed for cold cranking power. Therefore, in order to catch up, the alternator has to put out a heavy load when you start up. On a normal cruise, your boat's batteries will probably use a lot more current than would your car batteries. The car doesn't have a water pump to give you fresh water, a bilge pump to keep you out of salt water, radar, and many other things that may be drawing down the boat's batteries. The three-stage regulator will not only improve your batteries' life but also your life.

Mounting is not the only important installation issue facing the new owner of a high-output alternator and regulator. The wiring from the alternator output to the batteries will need to be very heavy, as will the alternator's terminals and anything else in line. Your battery-blocking diodes (if you have them) may need to be larger, and you may wish to shorten wire runs. Carefully read and follow all literature that accompanies the alternator and/or regulator.

Several good alternators are designed to put out high amperage over long hours; they have state-of-the-art, three-stage voltage regulators. Powerline is one popular manufacturer. Balmar also sells a good line of alternators and auxiliary equipment and has knowledgeable staff. I visited the Balmar plant in Seattle, Washington, and was very impressed with their products. Heart Interface, in conjunction with Cruising Equipment, sells well-designed voltage regulators that you can plug into most high-output alternators and adjust to suit your charging needs. They also sell a battery monitoring system that not only enables you to determine exactly what is going on, but also to control the Heart inverter/battery charger and the alternator. I toured the Heart plant in Seattle and was exceptionally impressed with their operation. (I stress again that the mention of a product does not imply that there are not other good products out there; I generally talk of those products with which I've had some experience.)

As you can see, there are many variables to finding the right alternator and regulator; it is seldom wise to go to the store and get a bigger alternator without doing research and obtaining advice about your anticipated usage, your existing system, including wiring, and your engine. You may wish to spend the extra bucks and buy the systems offered by specialists in the field such as Heart, Balmar, and Cruising Equipment. Obviously, it is important to consult with the experts when buying an alternator, and the manufacturer should be a prime source of specific information. If I couldn't talk to the manufacturer about his product and my particular use of it as a cruiser, I probably wouldn't buy it.

SOLAR PANELS

The solar panel is a great concept, and one that we would like to be using exclusively some day. But today's units are hardly adequate to make up for the electricity consumption of the average cruising boat. If you're sure you'll consume little, if you have space to spread a lot of panels, and if you cruise where there is a lot of sun a lot of the time, you may be able to use them exclusively. Because most cruising doesn't fit these constraints, most cruisers use solar panels only for supplementary charging—rather expensive supplementary charging. There are many days of heavy cloud cover that tend to be windy. A wind generator is a better option in this case. Even on clear days, particularly along coasts and in the islands, there's often enough wind to rely on the wind generator.

One great advantage of solar panels, however, is that they may allow you to leave your boat unattended for long periods without discharging your batteries. Another is that after the initial purchase, and if properly installed, they are usually trouble- and maintenance-free for years. If you don't use electricity for refrigeration (more detail on this in chapter 15), solar panels, coupled with another source such as an alternator, will probably suffice, particularly if your consumption is low otherwise. I realize that enormous amounts of money are being invested to make this a more efficient technology, and I hope that time will soon come.

AC POWER

We use an unusually large amount of electricity for a cruising vessel because I frequently write with the computer, Mel paints and often uses extra lighting, the girls use lights and a computer for school, our refrigeration unit runs on electricity, and we always have a repair project underway that requires power tools. The longer you intend to cruise, the more useful you will find a diesel generator. If you plan only a year's trip, for example, you're less likely to need one.

GENERATORS

Although we put around 5,000 miles under our keel each year, as I've mentioned, we are at anchor in one spot or another most of the time. The generator helps us to do this. We're able to make our refrigerator/freezer extra cold, we heat water for great showers, we make water at the rate of 15 gallons an hour, we do heavy repair and rebuilding work that requires AC electricity, we do chores such as vacuuming, running the grain grinder and food processor (perhaps for conch fritters), and we charge the batteries quickly and well with a Heart Interface Freedom inverter/charger (more on inverters later). While doing all this, the generator consumes less than a half-gallon of fuel per hour. Depending on what we are doing, four hours of generator time per day (two each, morning and evening) usually more than suffices. This includes maybe eight hours of desktop computer use, some laser-printer usage, and all-electric refrigeration.

If we didn't use the computer so much (or used a laptop) and if we had cold plates with an engine-driven refrigeration compressor, we would be able to get by with probably an hour's genset time. With an engine-driven compressor we would also probably be charging the batteries from an alternator. But this would involve using the engine for charging, and running it without adequate load. I prefer not to do this. I want to save my engine for propulsion, and I don't want carbon deposits to build up inside. A wind generator, coupled perhaps with solar cells, could possibly keep electric refrigeration going most of the time and give you enough electricity to power a laptop and do whatever else you wish; it really comes down to preferences. I've owned two portable gasoline generators; the best thing they were good for was chasing away people who anchored too close. They didn't charge the batteries well and did not perform well; they were cantankerous and very noisy, and I feel that they were unsafe for us on a boat. The customer support was worthless. Both were made by a well-known company.

Because of noise and exhaust fumes generators emit, some cruisers don't like them. Those of us who use generators should always be mindful of the preferences of others. This includes not running them at the dock. A properly working and installed diesel generator won't make much exhaust or noise; some make almost none. And wind generators and auxiliary engines with alternators also make noise. The latter can make a lot of exhaust, too, while sitting at anchor charging batteries and refrigeration units. The fuel doesn't burn thoroughly when they aren't being run at load. Many long-term cruising boats have to use an independent generator, because they aren't just sitting around on a quiet vacation—they need the power. The bottom line is that we all need to respect each other's needs and likes.

ALTERNATIVES TO THE GENERATOR

There are some interesting alternatives to the traditional diesel generator. Some companies produce generators that you bolt onto the main engine. One manufactures a large alternator that bolts to the engine. Its power is rectified, controlled and inverted by sophisticated electronics in a black box so that it produces 20 amps and more (depending on the size) of AC power while you are running your main engine at various rpm settings. Obviously, with any unit like this, you'll have to plan on serious bracketing and dual or triple belting to mate the generator to the engine. Also, some require that you run at 1,800 rpm to get 110 volts at 60 cycles, the standard current required by typical U.S. products.

Balmar has its new VST (variable speed technology) units. Most standard diesel generators run at a constant rpm of 1,800 all the time. Some, such as certain Onan units, use fewer windings in the generator end of the unit and turn at 3,200 rpm. These speeds are maintained whether or not you use any electricity. The Balmar VST units have diesel generators that run at a slow speed when there is no electricity demand, but which speed up to meet demand as it occurs. Again, this is controlled by sophisticated electronics that come with the unit. Since it isn't running at a high speed all the time, the diesel is smaller and quieter. As an option, Balmar couples a water-maker to the unit so that the diesel is directly driving the pump and making water at the same time. The small size of this unit, as well as its exceptionally low fuel consumption, make it a serious contender for the cruising boat.

INVERTERS

The combination of the alternator, diesel generator, and wind generator has served us well over the years. It has given us redundancy and a lot of power for the dollar. What really made it work well was an electronic wizard that improved our life quality more than I would have ever imagined—an inverter.

I used to be a 12-volt man. It was simple. It was inexpensive. It was pure. It was the thing to do. There was even a song about it. And no one except those rare birds who didn't have any electricity aboard at all (along with a lot of other things they didn't have aboard—like family, probably) could question my hoary seamanship credentials.

But you know how it is when you have a little. You want more. And they don't make all appliances for 12-volt electricity. When they do, they think they have done something really wonderful, and they make you pay for it to prove it. After years with only 12-volt electricity, I began to use a generator and turned it on whenever I wanted to be like everyone else ashore. This was noisy, expensive, and inconvenient. I did have a small old-fashioned inverter that would run even smaller old-fashioned things. I tried never to use it except in winter when we needed heat. It made a great furnace. I didn't buy one of those newfangled inverters, because they cost so much. That was a mistake. I recently corrected my error and can't believe it took me so long to see the light.

A modern, top-of-the-line marine inverter will improve your life aboard immensely, charge your batteries probably better than anything you have now, and may quickly pay for itself by extending battery life. Unlike the older types, the new ones are extremely efficient, losing little in the process of inverting DC to AC. They will power computers and other sensitive equipment with better quality electricity than what you would get from a generator. An inverter can charge power tools that will make better repairs at sea, and it will make lighting your boat for the Christmas parade a snap. And once you install a quality inverter, it should work for you without bother, silently regulating current and switching on and off when you add or cut external AC power.

We chose a Heart Interface and are happy with the product and the service. I certainly haven't tried all the various brands, and I don't mean to imply that there aren't other good ones on the market.

QUALITY AC CURRENT

A persistent problem with generating AC current on cruising boats has been voltage and cycle fluctuation. A good modern inverter solves these problems with its internal regulating devices. Even with a large generator and a sophisticated voltage regulator, the addition or removal of loads can cause the generator to operate at different speeds. Even slight variations in speed can cause the voltage and/or cycles to change. With some AC equipment this is unimportant as long as the fluctuations are not large, but with other equipment this can cause immediate problems or early demise. Computers quickly come to mind; they're nice to have aboard but can react disastrously to these fluctuations. A good inverter will keep the voltage within its stated range of 110 volts and the cycles very close to the 60 cycles per second that most equipment loves. Of course, it draws its power from your batteries, but it will maintain these values within a fairly wide range of battery voltage. When the batteries get too low for the inverter to perform properly, the better units have an indicator and will warn you.

Another problem that has long haunted cruising AC users is the sine wave. The wave pattern produced by electricity can be recorded on an electronic measuring instrument, which registers the pattern as a line, or *sine wave*. While some appliances don't care what kind of wave they get, many do, and the number that do is growing steadily. Even a good generator will not always give you a pure sine wave. Until recently, most inverters produced a very impure wave, frequently referred to as a *square wave*. At this writing, a high-quality marine inverter will produce a sine wave close enough to perfect that even computers seem to be happy with it (more on this below). It is often called a *modified sine wave*.

Inverters designed to produce a pure sine wave (Heart makes a few models) are more expensive and, at this writing, do not have battery-charging capability. I've listened to the debate over whether the life span of finicky appliances such as computers and laser printers is adversely affected by a modified sine wave. Heart advises that their products do well with computers, and I have used a Heart Freedom with a desktop computer (running around eight hours a day) and laser printer for about five years without a problem. They also say that if a modified sine wave doesn't affect the picture on a monitor or TV set, it will not adversely affect a computer. A manufacturer of pure sine wave inverters told me that only the pure sine wave won't harm the power supply of computers and other sophisticated equipment and that this fact—coupled with the other characteristics of these inverters—makes them cost-effective.

He may be right, but my experience indicates otherwise. I'm not an expert, though, so I can only tell you that there is a pure sine wave alternative, albeit expensive, if you are concerned. Make sure that the inverter you purchase produces either a pure or a modified sine wave. Get a commitment from the dealer or manufacturer that the unit will properly power a standard desktop, AC-powered computer. If it won't, don't buy it. Even if you have no intention of using a computer aboard, you'll probably use other equipment that is sensitive to this problem.

Before I leave this discussion, there is another angle to consider if you use a desktop computer with AC current. Using a desktop will save you considerable bucks because desktops are so much less expensive than laptops. And an inverter will enable you to do this as long as the inverter is in control of making the AC current from your batteries. In this case, you should be assured of good, steady current. There is a wrinkle, however. If the inverter is designed to automatically convert inverted AC power derived from the batteries to external AC power when it is available (and a good,

Tom at work on his standard desktop computer.

▼

large inverter should be designed to make this transfer), but the external power comes from an onboard generator, this could damage your computer. As noted earlier, surges and other irregularities are not uncommon in a typical generator's output. This is especially true of small, gasoline deck generators. The best solution I've come up with is to purchase an inverter (perhaps a pure sine wave unit in this case) just large enough to handle your computer and perhaps printer, and dedicate it to this use. Do not wire for incoming AC power to the inverter; only wire for DC power to be inverted for your computer's consumption. It will not be charging batteries, and it will never be transferring through unreliable external current. Also, because of the inherent qualities of your batteries, if you follow the directions closely when wiring, this setup can probably serve as the surge protector you'll want to have anyway.

I have done this with a second Freedom (10-amp), and I have been very happy with the results. Power can fail on the dock or with the generator, but the computer never knows it. If the other inverter fails, I can wire this for incoming AC and use it as a charger as well as an inverter. I should note that if you use a laptop computer powered from your battery bank, you will also have this inherent

▼

buffer and surge protection without using an inverter. I opted for a desktop not only because they are so much cheaper but also because they are easier to fix (some new laptops are modular with easily replaced components).

COST AND CHARGING

You may need a new battery charger, so you may as well get an inverter/charger because it doesn't cost that much more. "Why should I get another battery charger?" you may be asking. Most earlier-generation chargers, even if rated at high capacity, cut back and taper down quickly as the battery voltage increases, resulting in slow and incomplete charging. A good modern charger like the Heart Interface Freedom has three phases of charging that enable it to charge a battery much quicker and better than older, conventional chargers. If you've been charging your batteries at sea from a generator (many cruisers use small deck generators for this purpose), using a top-quality battery charger will significantly shorten generator running time. If you only use an alternator or wind generator, the inverter's superior battery-charging capability can result in quicker charging and better results from that expensive "plugged in" time at marinas.

The Heart Interface Freedom (and other good inverter/chargers) allows you to modify some of its charging characteristics to suit your particular batteries and circumstances. As mentioned earlier, if you have traditional deep-cycle lead-acid cells, it's helpful to give an equalizing charge to these batteries periodically to remove residual lead sulfate from the plates. The Freedom has a special setting that enables you to boost charging voltages to remove the lead sulfates from the plates, mix the electrolyte, and equalize the cell voltage. For everyday charging, the Freedom switches easily from lead-acid batteries to gel cells; you can select a warm or cold ambient temperature for each type. Tailored service that accommodates different charging circumstances will increase the longevity of your batteries and improve their day-to-day performance. The bottom line is that for a few more dollars you'll have a state-of-the-art battery charger that will probably save you money in shorter generator running time and healthier battery charging. If you need a good battery charger anyway, this is a great deal.

Before leaving the subject of charging, I should mention an important consideration if you plan to use an onboard generator to

▼

recharge your batteries through an inverter/battery charger at sea. Although many cruisers prefer this method, it can be frustrating under certain circumstances. If your generator puts out the proper voltage and cycle range, the charger will work well and will charge your batteries relatively quickly, enabling you to shut down the genset within a reasonable amount of time. But a well-designed, phase-controlled inverter/charger, to protect itself and its load from excessive current fluctuations, may have safeguards that with other characteristics will diminish its battery-charging capacity. This reduction in capacity can be considerable if the generator varies its output due to load or other factors, such as poor fuel. In other words, if your generator is not running well or is not evenly maintaining its rated output, your fancy charger will not work well and you will wish you had a fancy high-output alternator on your auxiliary instead. My gasoline deck generator had a rated output at just under 20 amps. It never powered my inverter properly. Its rpm, voltage, and cycles per second decreased significantly when I gave it load. My Onan diesel generator, specifically designed for onboard use, powered the same inverter/charger well. Heart Interface has recognized this problem, and its Freedom series has been designed with a much wider window of tolerance for AC input. They do point out, however, that many generator manufacturers recommend that a phase-controlled charger not exceed 40 percent of the generator's rating. Before you buy an inverter, check its specifications to determine its tolerance for incoming AC power in voltage and cycles, and obtain a written commitment from the generator manufacturer.

CAPACITY

What capacity should your inverter have? My bias reflects my lifestyle. I live aboard permanently with a family of four, so I purchased the biggest one I could fit on my boat and still afford. I wish I had a bigger one. The larger they are, the more AC current they give you and the greater the margin for those unexpected needs. And the larger the capacity of the inverter, the quicker it will charge your batteries if you have enough current from the generator.

Some small inverters that do not have battery chargers have standard AC plugs on the face of the unit into which you simply plug your appliance directly. Some of these are not much larger than a handheld VHF radio, and of course they have less complicated installation. But you always have to run a cord to the unit

when you need AC. And there are other drawbacks. First, their
capacity is limited, usually to not much more than running a TV or
video. Many cruisers buy them thinking that they will just plug the
inverter into DC wiring wherever they want to use an AC appliance, moving it about as needed. But even small inverters require
fairly heavy cables running to the batteries, and these may not be
readily available throughout your boat. The thickness of the cable
that powers your lights, radios, and similar equipment probably
would not be enough, and you would probably have to run special
cable. Another drawback, which I mentioned earlier, is that these
small inverters don't charge batteries.

If you are still convinced that you will always be satisfied with
just powering a small TV or VCR, and only one thing at a time, and
if you already have ample battery charging equipment, a small unit
may be what you need. I've talked with many people who have installed small inverters, and almost every one of them wishes they
had gotten a larger model. Once you are accustomed to living normally with electrical appliances, you will want to use more. And
remember, repairs that require heavier power tools are not feasible
with the smaller units.

With my inverter, I have AC whenever and wherever I need
it, just as though I were plugged into the dock. When I start the
generator or plug into the dock, the unit switches automatically
to draw power from the external source. It also automatically begins
to charge my battery. This happens so quietly and precisely that
neither I, nor my computer, know that the switching has occurred.
I think having this capability is worth spending the extra dollars and
working a few hours to complete the initial setup. I shudder at the
thought, but it is almost as convenient as living in a house.

INSTALLATION

The installation of my Heart was simple, and I received good factory support. The best advice I can offer is to follow the owner's
manual carefully and to call the manufacturer if you have any
questions. The suggestions that follow are not intended to replace
the manufacturer's instructions; they're intended to give a general
idea of what one can expect during installation.

As you probably imagined, there is an AC connection and a
DC connection on the inverter. Connecting the inverter to the batteries is not much more than that: you connect two heavy-duty

lines from the batteries to the inverter. These get the DC into the inverter when you are making AC, and they serve as the charging lines when you are in that mode. The connection between the inverter and the AC panel can be more complicated, depending on how your system is set up and how you wish to use the inverter. It is still far simpler than what I had anticipated. Very basically, the three wires for the AC side (white, black, and green) must be connected to the proper corresponding wiring in your system. This run gets the AC power from the inverter into your panel, and it gets the AC power from shoreside or the generator into the inverter for battery charging. It sounds simple enough, but you have to remember that there may be circuits on your AC electrical panel that you don't want to power. Be sure to follow ABYC (American Boat and Yacht Council) and UL (Underwriters Laboratories) standards. For example, ground fault interrupters that are compatible with your inverter (check with inverter manufaturers) should be properly installed. Signs should warn that your boat may have AC power in its circuitry even if unplugged from the dock.

When you unplug from shore power or turn off a generator, the Heart inverter will, if you have it set to do so, automatically shift from that AC source to inverter-produced AC from the battery source so that you will experience no loss of AC. With the Freedom, you will not even notice the switch. But if, for example, your hot-water heater is turned on and is part of the circuitry that is powered by the inverter, you will quickly and completely deplete your batteries as they heat water through the inverter (assuming it has a high enough capacity). Because of potential problems such as this, some cruisers might prefer to divide their existing AC panel. One side will never be powered by the inverter (this would probably include the water-heater circuit and any other battery charger you may already have in line), and the other side would be items such as wall outlets. Others may wish to wire the inverter into the undivided panel and remember to turn off the circuit breakers for the circuits they don't want powered by the inverter. This is simpler and creates more options, but you have to pay attention when shutting down a generator or unplugging shore power. The Heart Freedom enables you to activate a switch that shuts off the inverter side automatically should you lose external AC power from the dock or generator. Depending on your use and customs, this could be an invaluable feature.

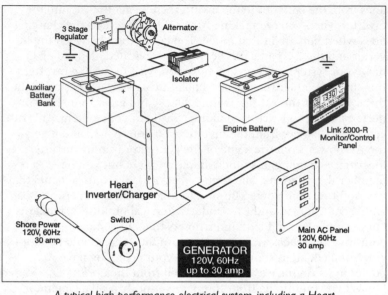

A typical high-performance electrical system, including a Heart inverter/charger. (Courtesy Heart)

The inverter should always be installed fairly close to the batteries to avoid long runs of cable. The instructions will tell you the size cable you need, and they aren't kidding about thickness or maximum length. Even though you may not intend to use heavy loads on an inverter, start-up loads can take quite a bit of power from the battery momentarily. Also, using wiring that is too small will lessen the capacity of the internal battery charger.

The fact that you should have short runs to your batteries probably means that the inverter will not be where you can easily see it. You should be able to see the inverter control panel and monitor its signals. For this reason, it is helpful to have a remote-control panel so you can readily receive messages from the inverter. For example, you'll want to know if your batteries are getting too low, or if the charging is almost complete, or if there is too much heat. An inverter that must be kept out of easy sight and that cannot give you this information readily is not a good idea. Whenever I see a recommendation for remote panels, I immediately wince at the thought of extra installation troubles. This is not the case with the Heart Freedom. You just plug the wire from the panel into the plug on the inverter and mount the panel. That's all there is to it. Then you not only have an excellent indicator of how your inverter and new battery charger are doing, but also of other factors such as battery voltage displayed in an LED bar graph and DC amperage going through the inverter or charger. Heart also offers the more complex Link 2000, which has a digital display that tells you everything you ever wanted to know about the state of your batteries. It even indicates amps consumed since the last charge and efficiency of charging, both of which are a good indication of battery life. It also controls the Freedom inverter/ charger, allowing much fine-tuning. The Link 2000R contains a voltage regulator that controls your alternator, or you can buy a separate voltage regulator. The accompanying diagram shows a typical inverter wiring arrangement.

USING AN INVERTER UNDERWAY

There is yet another aspect of inverter use that could mean savings as well as convenience. In order to have AC current, many well-to-do folks cruise regularly in motorboats with their generators going and their propulsion engines running at the same time. As they roar by on the waterway in conspicuous AC consumption, you can smell the croissants and bacon cooking. If you have a high-output alternator, as mentioned above—and you probably should—you can cruise along with AC power all day long just like the fancy motorboats running their generators, but you'll be using only your propulsion engine. The alternator will be pumping all the electricity you can use into your batteries, and the inverter will turn it handily into AC power. Of course you won't have enough to run air conditioners and keep your sauna heated, but it'll be enough for most purposes. It's almost free decadence. Even if you don't do this, a good inverter coupled with a high-output alternator enables you to get more use from the propulsion engine and the diesel fuel it burns by harnessing some of its power to make AC electricity.

The ramifications of this in convenience and cost savings are obvious. For example, if you have refrigeration, you won't need to pay the extra cost of 12-volt systems. A standard, off-the-shelf AC compressor will do fine with a good inverter. (Refrigeration is covered in detail in chapter 15.)

The bottom line: If you have an inverter and a sufficient at-sea charging system, the cost may be offset by the benefits.

Chapter Fourteen
WATER AND WATER SYSTEMS

The question of water supply generally doesn't even arise in the minds of those who are shorebound. Boaters who stay in the States don't have to give their water supply a second thought either; they just go to a marina or fuel dock and fill up. Once you're at sea, however, water supply can be a critical problem. Figures vary, but conservative reports indicate that the average American household uses 300 to 350 gallons of water per day. In our early days of cruising, our family of four normally cruised more than a month on this amount, and we weren't atypical.

Once you leave the U.S coast, the availability and quality of water vary considerably. Let's consider the Bahamas. In the hub of the Abacos you can get fairly good water from the docks at a price ranging from nothing to around 10 cents a gallon. In Nassau you have to pay at least 10 cents a gallon for water I wouldn't even put in my tank to wash the decks with, let alone drink. Most of it is shipped over from Andros via the tanker *Mini Lillie*. In the Exumas, only 40-odd miles away, you pay a minimum of 50 cents a gallon for reverse-osmosis water (more on this shortly) and cistern water. The quality of this water is sometimes questionable; it depends on the maintenance done by those in charge. You can go down to George Town at the lower end of the Exuma chain and pay 10 cents a gallon again, but for water similar to what you choked on in Nassau. There are abandoned cisterns here and there in the Exumas, but there is absolutely no assurance that a fellow cruiser didn't bathe in it, or wash clothes directly over it. Also, cistern water can be contaminated by spraying for pests and from water running off asbestos-tile roofs. On the larger islands in the Caribbean, there is generally a better supply, but one never knows.

If you cruise beyond the States, you must be prepared to get by on exceptionally small amounts of water, take health risks, or make your own water.

COLLECTING WATER

During our first several years out we filled our tanks when we could get good and affordable water, and relied on collecting rain the rest of the time. To do this we would remove any gas or oil jugs or similar material from our decks upstream of the fill pipes, let the rain wash the decks thoroughly, plug the scuppers with clay, and let water pour into the tanks. Often, however, by the time the decks were clean, the shower had stopped. If we expected rain, we would wash the decks with Joy and seawater. Then the rain would have to wash off only salt before we could open the tanks. The rains came mostly at night, so we had to get out of our warm, snug berths and go through this regimen on deck, getting wet and cold in the process. Other folks catch water with their Bimini tops by running hose from drain holes in the corners to the tanks. Others use awnings. These types of catchments, as neat as they might look in a book, seldom work well because when it's raining, it's usually blowing; they dump the water no matter how hard you try to tie them down. Biminis with lips around the edges work better because they are already up and are more stable. Hard-topped covers over cockpits do even better. I've noticed, however, that most cruisers who are serious about catching water keep their deck clean when they expect rain and use that method. You can very quickly construct temporary dams with sticks of wood and modeling clay to funnel the water to a fill hole.

TANKAGE

Our tanks hold 300 gallons of water, and we carry at least 25 more gallons on deck in 5-gallon jugs. Your boat should carry as much water as possible. If your tankage is sparse, add more before you go. Yes, carry jugs on deck. Sometimes you'll need them in order to ferry water from shore. Also, if you sink you can throw them in your survival raft to supplement the emergency water supply and survival watermaker that should already be there. But jugs are easily punctured, and too many affect weight and stability of the boat, so you can't rely too heavily on them. It is easy to add tanks. You can glass-in areas under bunks or settees, or just add bladders sold for the purpose in marine-supply stores. Consider the effect of the weight on your boat when you add tankage. Normally, it is better to add this weight near the middle and as low as possible. Anytime you add a hard tank, be sure to build in strong and numerous baffles, and coat the interior with epoxy—or some other material designed for the purpose—not polyester resin. Let it cure well and wash it thoroughly before using it to hold water you will consume. Water from a new tank will often have a taste and an odor. Add baking soda in liberal doses when you put the water in, let it sit, then slosh around and pump it out or drain it.

WATERMAKERS

While in clean ocean water, we used seawater for such things as bathing, dishwashing, and boiling eggs and potatoes. But rain can be scarce at times, and our skin didn't like constant saltwater bathing, even with a freshwater rinse. We had frequent sores that were slow to heal. Our stainless steel galley utensils rusted, and the salt on them transferred to other things. Besides, we never felt clean; even in the tropics there are times when you would give anything for a hot shower. There are some tough and admirable people who do well with this regimen, but not us. We began to look for alternatives. As alien as it seemed and as expensive as it was, we decided that the only viable alternative for our lifestyle, especially when we factored safety into the equation, was a good reverse-osmosis watermaker. It turned out to be one of the nicest things we could have done for ourselves.

Not everyone wants a watermaker, however, and you should consider your needs before you plunge. If you hang around the States, or any area where good water can be easily obtained, you will have little need for one. And you can always purchase one if you extend your cruising range. If you think you can get by on the rain-catching routine, by all means do it. It's probably safe to say that most people who cruise for only a year or two do this. Many take their hot-water showers in the cockpit using dark bags or jugs heated by the sun. These use very little water. Although we found rainwater we caught in the States to be dirty and poor tasting (which probably means unsafe) on average, offshore rainwater was great.

One issue in particular has made the watermaker almost indispensable—independence. With the watermaker, we can find a perfect spot in an unpopulated island chain, set the hooks in tight, and stay for as long as we like in perfect comfort. When we need more diesel, we just jug it in with the dinghy. With our generator, a gallon of diesel will make around 30 gallons of water, and do a lot of other things for us.

Many cruisers shy away from watermakers because of their cost and the general conception that they perform alchemy and require the constant attention of wizards in the bilge. Actually, the basics are simple. If you are skillful and have a good bit of mechanical, electrical, and plumbing experience, you can probably assemble one yourself from readily available parts. I don't recommend doing this, however, because a poor job could cause big trouble. For example, the unit operates with seawater under 800 pounds of pressure per square inch (psi). This much pressure can be dangerous at worst, very damaging at best, if it leaks. There are many hidden pitfalls in putting one together that could escape the casual mechanic. Besides, the prices seem to be on a downward trend, and manufacturers are becoming more realistic with the options they offer. For example, Village makes a unit without many of the bells and whistles that can be such headaches with other brands. I purchased a Village unit when I made the plunge years ago, and in the ensuing years removed many of the extras. I'm much happier with it now, although it's not as automatic. I have to turn a valve to direct product water into the tank when I start up. Although the original unit did

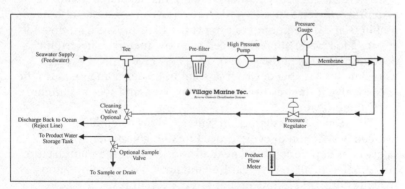

Flow diagram of Village Marine Tec's "No Frills" watermaker.
(Courtesy Village Marine Tec.)

this for me, it relied on electric probes in salt water and a stainless solenoid valve that, although it was of excellent quality, would stick because of the salt water. With my renovations, I have to check the water quality to be sure it is good, but I used to do this anyway. If a membrane or O-ring blows, I could end up dumping bad water into my tank, but this hasn't happened in around nine years of operation. Now Village's simple unit is similar to what mine has evolved into, it makes just as much water that is just as good, and its cost is comparable to what I would probably spend if I made it myself. The manufacturer's unit comes with a warranty and maintenance help, big pluses over building one yourself.

The following discussion describes how a typical reverse-osmosis watermaker works. From this, perhaps you can better judge whether you want one and, if you do, what to look for. The accompanying diagram is a basic flow chart of a typical system.

DESIGN

To extract good fresh water from the sea, one simply runs the sea-water through a special membrane at high pressure, usually 800 psi. The basic components for a watermaker are a pump capable of producing that amount pressure with seawater, a membrane, a pressure vessel to contain the membrane, an adequate pressure valve, and the plumbing.

There are, of course, other components needed to make the system work well and safely. Most reverse-osmosis units also have prefilters and a feed pump to protect the high-pressure pump and ensure good water supply, gauges and flow meters to determine operational status of the system, a bypass valve for bad water, a water-quality sensing device that sounds an alarm and operates the bypass valve if the freshwater quality is poor, and special plumbing to facilitate cleaning.

The scope of this discussion will not allow a complete and detailed description of every procedure and component or of all safety considerations. You'll need to consult with the manufacturer and supplier of all items regarding intended use, warnings, and specifications; and follow proper safety procedures.

Although "survival" watermakers are available that produce, sometimes with just muscle power, a small amount of water strictly for survival purposes, this discussion is not geared to those units. The units practical for boating use are large watermakers that can supply all the water you need, within reason, to cruise and live comfortably every day. These units should put out at least 7 gallons an hour (gph), preferably more. The same pump will push raw water through one 7-gph membrane, or two, or three. Thus, for not that much more money and no additional power consumption, you can have a comfortable output once you decide to go with a watermaker.

PUMPS

The heart of the system will be the high-pressure pump. Most manufacturers agree that a low-pressure feed pump with a magnetically coupled hard impeller is important to ensure a good supply of water to the larger high-pressure pump. Cavitation in the high-pressure pump will quickly cause damage. It is best to install these two pumps below the waterline. Doing so ensures adequate pressure to both pumps and avoids wear that can occur with priming. Of course, any potential breach below the waterline presents additional risk, and proper precautions should be taken. These include using equipment designed and built for the purpose, double hose clamps, and bilge alarms.

The high-pressure pump must be able to safely maintain the required pressure when using seawater. CAT pumps, which use ceramic pistons, are a common brand; other pumps pulsate instead. In my opinion, the preferred method for powering these pumps is an AC motor, which requires a generator capable of providing enough power to handle the starting surge. Many cruisers use DC motors, but these require a fairly large DC alternator or DC generator and good batteries. Running your main engine long enough to keep charging the batteries may not be a good idea; your diesel would be pulling a very light load and would thus be likely to build up carbon. There are several low-output, 12-volt models that are intended to run many hours, and they make a few gallons per hour. In my opinion, these don't serve as well because they don't put out sufficient water to warrant the battery drain. But many people are happy with them. The units that produce 7 gph and up don't cost significantly more than the low-output units, but you get much more water with less running time. If you are strongly committed to a 12-volt watermaker, it helps to know that reputable companies have been working on these systems for some time, and you should feel safer in getting a DC unit than in years past. Obviously the motors require proper and safe wiring.

PRESSURE VESSELS AND MEMBRANES

The next major component is the pressure vessel and membrane. The vessel is simply a stainless or fiberglass container that houses the membrane, enables water to flow in the correct directions with special O-rings, and can withstand the pressure. Various companies produce these pressure vessels, and there are numerous opinions as to whether fiberglass or stainless is best. To my mind, either will do well if manufactured by a reliable company and given proper care.

The pressurized seawater flows past the membrane, which allows relatively pure water to seep through and flow out of the pressure vessel in a low-pressure, product water line. When functioning properly, these membranes will not let something as big as a salt molecule pass through, but they will let the much smaller water molecule pass through. Since bacteria are much larger than salt molecules, we are told, they too are filtered out. The volume of seawater that passes by the membrane is much greater than the volume of freshwater produced. This unused water runs out of the pressure vessel, via a high-pressure line, to a valve that enables you to regulate the pressure and then flows overboard through a reject-water, low-pressure discharge hose.

The size and number of membranes are determined by your water and space requirements. For example, to make 15 gallons per hour you can use either two-membrane/container units that are approximately 20 inches long, or one unit that is 40 inches long. Before ordering, decide where you will mount them. Membranes are sensitive to excessive heat and should not be mounted close to the engine or generator. The pressure vessels are not unattractive; one boater mounted them in the head and used them as towel racks. You do need to be careful with such arrangements to protect the high- and low-pressure lines running to and from the vessel.

When deciding on the size membrane you need, think of output in gallons per hour. You'll need to run an engine or generator for whatever time it takes to make the water you need, unless you have a low-output, 12-volt unit that runs on batteries for a long time. It's nice to be able to make 15 gallons by running your unit for one hour rather than two. The generator or engine you use will appreciate the difference even if you don't.

When estimating water requirements, remember that there is not much point in all this if you can't make enough water to substantially improve your shipboard life.

▼

PLUMBING

The plumbing up to the membranes is simple. It begins with the through-hull intake, which should be at least ¾-inch diameter to supply sufficient water for most requirements. A large seawater strainer is important. I use one inside and a wide clam-shell-type strainer over the through-hull hole outside. If the intake becomes clogged while the unit is in use, the pump(s) can quickly burn out. Some people install low-pressure shutoff switches in the line after the small pump. All runs should be reinforced hose that will not collapse and that is suitable for underwater use. The usual rules about double hose clamping with quality, all stainless clamps apply. Rust, oil, chlorine, excess air, and many other things can seriously damage the membranes. The inlet should be well below the waterline, and any material that will rust should not be used.

Most factory units come with two particle filters; some come with an air and oil separator. I, and other cruisers I know, use only one filter with a 5-micron element, available in most hardware stores. If your filter(s) will be installed below the waterline, be sure it is suitable for underwater use. The air and oil separators are usually nothing more than small filter bodies with a pipe fixed inside that theoretically enables the oil and air to float to the top and flow off via the raw-water discharge. If the intake is well below the surface and the plumbing is snug, you probably won't need this separator. Some quality manufacturers don't use separators. The feed line goes to the feed pump, through the 5-micron filter, and then to the large pump. To indicate whether there is a positive head of pressure, there should be a pressure gauge where the low-pressure water enters the head of the high-pressure pump. If the high-pressure pump tries to pump from a vacuum, it will be damaged. A prime cause of reduced pressure or a vacuum is often a dirty prefilter(s), so this gauge acts as a good indicator of when to change your prefilter.

The plumbing must be able to withstand 800 psi from the high-pressure pump with an adequate safety margin. My preference is to use Aeroquip or similar hose and fittings for this purpose. Manufacturers also often use this. You can cut and fit it yourself. A spare length of hose with a few fittings will enable you to make repairs at sea if a rupture occurs. As always, consult the manufacturer or his representative regarding the best brand and type of hose and the best installation procedure for your product. Take care in routing and protecting these high-pressure hoses. At this pressure, even a small leak can be dangerous.

The high-pressure hose that runs from the high-pressure pump to the pressure vessel introduces the pressurized water at one end of the vessel. Additional high-pressure hose exits this vessel and goes to the pressure valve. This should be a high-quality, stainless valve assembly that enables you to maintain the correct pressure by regulating the flow of seawater exiting the vessel(s). Factors such as water temperature and salinity sometimes require adjustment of pressure to ensure proper operation. For example, if you are making water using low salinity seawater, you probably won't need 800 psi to get your rated flow of water. Actually, too much pressure under such circumstances could damage the membranes. A high-pressure gauge just before this adjustable pressure valve is necessary to set proper operating pressure. From the high-pressure valve, plumbing should conduct the seawater overboard, well above the waterline. Some cruisers prefer a saltwater flow meter here, which indicates whether the pumps are performing normally.

The pressure vessel will have a small-diameter outlet from which product water will flow. There is very little pressure here, but the tubing for this should meet FDA standards for drinking water. There should be a flow meter in this line to help determine the status of the membranes. Decreasing flow can indicate dirty or damaged membranes. The size of the meter is determined by the capacity of the system. Systems producing around 400 gallons of water per day yield only 15 gallons per hour and would not need a meter measuring more than 20 gallons.

This product water run should also have a valve downstream of the meter to divert the watermaker's output from the tank. The first water produced at any start-up will be below standard and should not be consumed. It often takes at least several minutes to produce good water. The minimum acceptable quality is 500 parts per million (ppm) of total dissolved solids (TDS). The expensive units have an electric sensor that operates a three-way solenoid valve to divert poor water overboard. The advantage is that it serves as a safety should something happen to water quality during operation. It also requires less attention at start-up. However, these sensors need frequent cleaning, the valves stick with use and require replacement or rebuilding, and the package requires additional wiring and, usually, a printed circuit board with all of its frailties.

A simple way to avoid sensors and solenoid valves is to install a manual three-way valve, buy a water-testing meter, test it yourself, and divert the good water to the tank and the poor water to a bucket for washing clothes, the deck, or your salty feet before you go below decks. This requires more attention at start-up but less time overall because there is less to maintain. If you had the fancy bells and whistles, you would eventually need a testing meter anyway to determine whether the sensors or membranes were faulty.

The gauges should be mounted where they can be seen together and where the on-off switch and three-way diverting valve are located. You should be able to access these quickly and easily without disruption of the rest of the boat. This will allow simple operation and control and merely involves running a suitable length and type of tubing from the take-off point to the control area.

Operating properly, these units will provide you with much better water than you would probably get in most cities. The membranes, functioning at top performance, should reject approximately 99 percent of the TDS contained in the seawater. If desired, you can purchase a gadget that allows the product water to pass through an ultraviolet light that kills viruses. Most cruisers we've talked to don't do this, but it is a good idea.

OPERATION

Although the length of the above discussion may have made you feel otherwise, the daily operation and care of a reverse-osmosis watermaker is not difficult. You turn it on, test it manually if yours isn't automatic, and turn it off when through. Be sure that the high-pressure valve is open all the way when you turn on the unit; a sudden hydraulic shock could damage the components. Then gradually turn up the pressure. Look at the high-pressure valve and product flow gauge. If you get the rated flow well before the normal 800 psi, you are probably in water fresher than normal and should stop increasing pressure. Water temperature and salinity both affect membrane performance and the amount of pressure required. As a general rule, 800 psi suffices for all ocean use in the Bahamas and off the U.S. east coast. I don't run my unit in rivers and bays out of extra caution and concern about pollutants that could damage the membranes or us. I will, on occasion, run it just inside inlets when a clean tide is flooding in.

It will be necessary to clean the membranes periodically. If you notice decreased product water flow and greater parts per million of total dissolved solids when you test the freshwater, it's time for a cleaning. Chemicals are available for this procedure. The simplest units are cleaned by mixing these chemicals in a bucket with water, placing the intake hose in the bucket, and sucking the solution through. When not in use for more than a week, the membranes should be preserved (pickled) with another solution. Again, with the simplest systems, this involves mixing the solution in a bucket, sucking it in, and shutting down. For my unit, I mix the chemicals in the empty canister of the 5-micron prefilter and let the water recirculate with special valving supplied by Village. Membranes must be pickled again after a few months, because the preservative solution loses its potency. Instructions should be obtained when purchasing the chemicals and carefully followed. Many experts are now recommending that you just pump product water or, better, distilled water through the system instead of pickling with a chemical.

THE HEAD

Your marine toilet will fail at the very worst of times. When you consider that any time is the very worst of times for this lovely machine, you'll understand what I mean. Eventually the hoses will get old, crack, and need to be replaced. But long before that, the inside walls will narrow with a buildup of calcium deposits. Some cruisers treat this with a regular flushing of muriatic acid, in anywhere from 10–90 to 50–50 (the first figure being that of the acid and the second, water—preferably fresh) percent solution. Those I spoke with suggest using only 10 percent acid. (Acid is dangerous. Be sure to comply with all warnings and instructions. Carefully add acid to water, not the reverse.) But this doesn't always dissolve all the deposits. Also, bits of calcium can break off and lodge in a turn, firmly catching the next wad of toilet paper that flows down the line. And here we have what is known as the "clogged head," one of the less popular aspects of boating. The trick to fixing this is to either cut the hose where you think (hope) the restriction may be or to take the whole thing out and flog it against a piling (or your neighbor's boat if he has anchored too close) until all the calcium breaks up and, along with various and sundry other matter, falls out the ends. This is a regular and almost inevitable part of boat maintenance if you are cruising long-term. You will probably need to do it every one to three years, depending on the waters where you cruise. If your boat is already more than several years old, it may be very close to needing a treatment.

Maintaining the head also means maintaining the approved marine sanitation device. We have a very large holding tank, but we find tanks impractical for serious cruising boats because most places outside the United States don't have pumpout stations (this includes the ocean), and even within the States availability varies. Often pumpout stations have difficult access, even if you find one. We prefer to use an approved flow-through treatment device; ours is a Lectra/San by Raritan. It doesn't add chemicals to the water and probably does a far better job than the land-based septic tanks and leaking, overflowing sewage treatment centers into which holding tanks are pumped. And we can use it anywhere except in the few areas where the government requires holding tanks only. These areas we avoid.

Chapter Fifteen
REFRIGERATION

I have two reasons for wanting refrigeration aboard my boat: to fulfill a social need and to keep fish. The social need takes the form of ice for my bourbon. I have to have it; I don't care what the hoary seamen say. As far as the fish goes, I don't always get fish; when I get more than one, I want it to keep so we can eat it for several days. My family has another reason: it's the only way to live.

There are lots of things you can do to avoid having a refrigerator, but we don't want to do them. A lot has been said about drying fish. Well, dried fish tastes good, and in principle it's a great idea. But I don't want dried fish hanging around on my boat. And you always read in the how-to cruising guides about getting unwashed eggs straight from the farm, smearing them with Vaseline, and storing them in the cool bilge. We don't want dirty, greasy eggs in our bilge either. Have you looked under a chicken lately?

Another way to avoid refrigeration is to eat like a cave dweller or a yuppie (I'm not sure which is worse). For example, you can eat only beans and rice and grow sprouts. We do a lot of this anyway, but what happens when the beans and rice grow all that fuzzy stuff as they get too old? For these reasons and more, we need refrigeration, and we'll pay—which is exactly what one does—in various ways in order to have refrigeration aboard a boat.

COMPRESSORS

The best refrigerator we ever had was on a previous boat. It was a system specifically designed for boats by a company that specialized in making equipment for boats. I installed it myself. This unit had two compressors that cooled a holding plate that had dual refrigerant tubes inside, one for each compressor output. One was a Tecumseh compressor mounted to the engine and driven by a belt. Its pulley wheel had a clutch so that I—or the thermostat—could turn it off and on as needed. This was a readily available, standard, automotive-type compressor. The other compressor was a standard off-the-shelf AC-powered refrigeration compressor of the type you might find in your refrigerator or freezer ashore. This rig allowed me to cool down the holding plates while running the engine at sea, or by plugging in at a dock. Back then, I didn't have an inverter or AC generator. These days, I would be able to power the second compressor from either of those sources. If one of the compressors broke, or its refrigerant circuitry developed a leak, I could always use the other one—an important added benefit. The cold plate was in one end of the box with a partition near the middle that had a window through which cold air spilled. I thus had a good freezer and a refrigerator, with separate access. Dual function is important in all aspects of cruising gear, but it is especially important when you stand to lose several months' worth of fish. There are many good units out today, including ones run on 12 volts.

You'll have to decide how you want to cool the refrigerant, and your choice will depend on your boat's layout and the compressor configuration you use. Seawater cooling is generally most efficient, but this requires an extra raw-water pump and plumbing and maybe even an extra through-hull. Depending on where you cruise and whether your boat has room to cool the units by air, this may be an option. Typically, however, engine-mounted compressors need raw-water cooling. I mention this subject because it deserves the same attention that you give the rest of the system.

Experience and overhearing many calls for help during the years suggest that certain spare parts are important to have aboard. Clearly, a spare engine-driven compressor and clutch would be great if you can afford them. You might be able to afford at least a rebuilt spare from an old automobile. It is also important to carry a spare thermal expansion valve and several spare dryers. I don't intend to delve into all aspects of how to build refrigeration systems, but if you get this system the supplier will know exactly what you are talking about when you ask for these spares.

You must also know how to change the spare parts, and this will probably involve compression fittings or soldering. These and other refrigeration repairs require spare refrigerant, of whatever kind is legal and environmentally in vogue at the time you do this. You will need to be able to add the refrigerant or its substitute. This can be done without pressure gauges if you have a bit of luck, but you can also get into trouble doing it without the gauges. They are expensive. Ask your supplier about all of these items when you install your system. Most people, including us, prefer to invest what bucks we have in more critical areas such as spare parts for the engine, but sudden loss of refrigeration that results in loss of a lot of frozen food can be a substantial financial loss; it is a decision you must make. Refrigeration work is one of those areas of specialty listed in chapter 5 that may help you to earn some income along the way. If you don't get into this, you will have a reasonable chance of finding a good refrigeration specialist in most popular cruising harbors, but do what you can to keep from losing all your frozen foods when the thing goes out in the cruising boondocks. *Note:* Depending on when and where you are, it may be illegal for you to do any refrigeration work unless you are licensed and certified, and fully blessed by the government of the country in which you are located.

THE BOX

Whatever refrigeration system you use, it will not work well unless you have a good box. And, believe it or not, I have almost never seen a good box on a production boat unless it was specifically ordered with full specifications given and enforced. No matter what the salesperson said, your boat probably doesn't have good box. Before you spend money on compressors and holding plates, spend the money and time to fix the box. If you don't, you'll throw anything else you've spent on the system to the winds. A good box should have a minimum (more is better) of 4 inches of good closed-cell insulation all around, including the top. The insulation should have an outer seal to prevent moisture from wicking through and eventually impairing the insulation. The box should have a drain that does not go into the bilge, unless you want a really stinky bilge. It should drain overboard or into a sump, but it should be looped at least once so that there is always a barrier of water standing in the drain tube. You don't want to constantly drain cold air out of that tube, just water. And by the way, it is best that the box not be up against the engine, as I have seen from time to time. This can have a devastating effect on the cold stuff. Further, if it is against the hull, as is often the case simply because of spatial necessity, remember that if your goal is to be sailing in warm waters—add extra insulation here. Complying with all of this may require that you completely remove the cabinetry around your refrigeration box and start again. It may also result in a lower capacity because the extra insulation will take up space, but if you want refrigeration, especially in the tropics, you had better do it.

The opening should seal well. I prefer a top-opening unit. Yes, it can be a real pain in the neck to reach down there and find the good stuff on the bottom, but refrigeration is a real pain in the neck anyway, and there is no point in dumping all that cold air on your feet every time you open a side door. If you must have a side door, hang clear heavy plastic curtain strips just inside the door. These will help some in keeping cold air in the box as you reach through. We have noticed that some are installing both top and side hatches, and that they use the side hatches only when in port at a marina where there is plenty of electricity.

OTHER SYSTEMS

Our old system would keep ice cream hard as a brick in 100°F heat. It required some attention, but we could easily fix it with readily obtainable parts and it served us well. Various manufacturers put together this and other types of systems, and most will send you detailed information about their products. You can also build one yourself, but you'll need a lot of knowledge about refrigeration to make it work. It isn't just a matter of running refrigerant through tubes; there are numerous pitfalls, some of which I mentioned above.

There are also self-contained units; The Cold Machine is one that we often see on cruising boats. It runs on 12-volt power, and you can easily install it yourself. It isn't as powerful as the system I described above, but it has made many people happy. Raw-water cooling, a well-insulated box, and good battery-charging systems help a lot. I've seen some systems that have 12-volt compressors that suffer substantially in performance as the battery voltage lowers. And, of course, the voltage drops rapidly when the compressor is eating up the battery. One friend of ours had an expensive unit installed, found that it just didn't cool well when the boat was disconnected from shore power, and was eventually told by the retailer that he should run the compressor only with the motor going to maintain the battery voltage. He would have been better off with a mechanically driven compressor, with all of its simplicity and power, bolted to the engine. With any 12-volt system, battery voltage will be a critical factor. It's easy to have it creep down unnoticed with the ensuing loss of effectiveness of the compressor and increased rate of discharge. And remember that the compressor motor doesn't care about what the voltage reads at the battery terminals. This is probably what your panel sensor is reading. The voltage that counts is at the end of the wire going into the compressor. And the longer and thinner that wire is, the more of a voltage drop will occur between the battery terminal and the compressor. This isn't to say that 12-volt compressors aren't good. Just buy a proven product and obtain specific guarantees about performance. Use wire of the proper gauge or better. Also ask about repairs in the field; see what kind of instructions and parts are available for this purpose. Remember, "send it back postage prepaid" doesn't work from paradise.

Unfortunately—very unfortunately—I now have one of those stand-up fridges you see in houses and RVs. (Don't ask me why I have one. Okay. Ask me. It came with the boat and we couldn't afford anything else. Now that I have been cruising 17 years, I really can't afford anything else.) Stand-up refrigerators do two things: they make people at boat shows say in admiration, "Oh, it looks just like the one that we have at home; how convenient . . . we'll take this one." They also keep your feet cold. Every time you open the door, they dump all the cold air out on the deck. It's a wonderful feeling, especially when you think about what you will have to do to your batteries to get that cold air back again in time for your next forage. And there's an extra convenience: when any sea is running, you have to stuff towels around the food to keep it from sliding around. Cold towels have lots of uses at sea; I just can't think of any right now. I don't recommend this type of refrigerator unless you're going to do all your cruising from marina to marina.

Several years ago our refrigerator broke far out in the islands. We had to throw lots of food overboard because nobody else was around to eat it. I guess that would be considered polluting today. From this I learned two important lessons about refrigeration: (1) Don't let your refrigerator break unless other people are around to eat the food. You don't want trouble with the law. (2) If you're out cruising and hear of a friend who is having trouble with his fridge, hang around. There may be some good food coming your way.

When your fridge breaks while cruising, look for friends who will loan space in their units. Local stores in island communities may agree to keep some frozen food for a short while, especially if you have been a customer. If you have a top-loading box and you can conveniently buy ice, turn it into an ice box. We carry a cooler on deck so that we can transport food and store it when needed. Coolers make good bins for other stuff in the meantime. If all else fails, have a big cookout on the beach and make some new friends.

For more detail than I can give here, see Nigel Calder's *Refrigeration for Pleasureboats* (International Marine, 1990).

Chapter Sixteen
DINGHIES

Tell them to bring a good dinghy. We have really missed out because we had no idea how important our dinghy would be and we had no idea we would use it for so many things." This is the message innumerable cruisers relayed to me when I asked them what advice I should give readers of this book.

It's understandable that this comes as a surprise to cruisers new to long-term cruising. Just think about how you use the dinghy for weekend cruising: You get in your boat and sail to a favorite harbor, usually a marina where you don't use a dinghy. If your favorite spot is an anchorage, one of the reasons you go there is because it's snug, it doesn't have large waves, and it has little or no current. You use the dinghy to visit the boat anchored next to you; you use it to go ashore and explore, or to go to a restaurant in the evening. You can probably row to all of these places. You have chosen this harbor because the odds are good that you will have a favorable sail getting to and from it. You don't want your dinghy tailing along behind you. So it's probably a deflated inflatable rolled up on deck. You don't particularly like to huff and puff, especially when you want to row to cocktails, so your dinghy isn't too big. Besides, it really doesn't need to be. You brought all your groceries aboard while you were at the dock, and you pulled up to the fuel dock for diesel. Your dinghy is just an extra toy, handy to have, but not a big deal.

For long-term cruising to far-off areas, your dinghy is one of the most important pieces of equipment you have. It is the family car, the family pickup truck, the fuel tanker and water barge; it will probably be your towboat or tugboat, your fishing boat, and your reef-diving boat; it will be your far-off and rough-terrain exploration four-wheeler. And that's just the beginning. It will have to do these jobs in rough water, in current, in wind, and over distances of at least a mile and at times much more. All of these capabilities must be contained in one dinghy that can be easily and safely stored aboard during long ocean passages.

THE EVERYDAY DINGHY

As you have probably surmised, we have the makings of a problem here. The small, classic rowing or sailing dinghy isn't going to work for cruising purposes. It will be great to play around with, but you can't play around all the time. The little 45-minute dinghy won't work well either. You know the ones: you're sitting in your cockpit reading or working, and the faint sound of an outboard drones into audible range. It comes and it comes and it comes. Finally, it passes. You look up and see that it is a little rubber ducky or a toy classic, with a small outboard and a bored and probably very wet driver. It goes by, and then it goes and it goes and it goes. About 45 minutes after you first heard it, the drone fades.

When you reach a place you like, you want to hang out for a while, on the hook. Unless you like crowds and wakes from speeding motorboats and noise and pollution and clamor, the spot you pick will probably be comfortably far away from the town dock. Once you've dropped anchor, you'll want to get on with everyday enjoyment of your new harbor and your daily chores. You'll probably unrig from sea status—you'll untie all the things you plan to use daily, and you'll set out the little comfort items or work items that you stuffed into some corner to keep them safe during the passage.

You won't wish to move to a dock or close enough to a dock to enable you to row in or putt-putt in with that 2-horsepower motor every time you need groceries or supplies. That would be a real pain in the neck. You won't want to explore reefs or go spearfishing in the mother ship. You pursue these activities near reefs, probably heading out into the ocean, that is, out the cut and into the swell. When you go out for dinner or cocktails on another boat, you may want to wear clothes that aren't caked in salt spray. Fortunately, cocktail parties aren't limited to times of no wind and no waves.

If you found a really nice spot, it may well be a mile or more from civilization—our favorite anchorages are. If you leave to take on water or fuel, someone else may find your spot while you're gone. When you get back, there may not be enough swinging room. If you use a dinghy to get the fuel and water in jerry jugs and supplies, you could save your spot, save a trip through difficult reef or channels, and save some rolling around.

When you do these errands and explorations in the dinghy, you may go through or pass just inside of ocean cuts or inlets where strong current flows. In some of these, the current can easily get up to 3 knots, maybe more, at times of peak flow. The seas may be rough. A small boat without much power will have a difficult time traversing these areas in these conditions.

Often you'll want the entire family along, particularly for snorkeling, fishing, exploring, or picnics on deserted beaches. When in the islands, we get most of our fresh fish by spearfishing. The whole family likes to go, and everyone contributes. Anchorages tend to be overfished, so we usually go out some distance, often at least several miles, to find good fishing. A dinghy that isn't fast and tough enough to do this will limit your success at fishing and limit other enjoyable dinghy excursions.

There isn't a grocery store on every island, so when you find one you may want to stock up. Diesel fuel and water are heavy. Groceries can be heavy. Traveling some distance in rough waters, you'll want the boat to plane. A well-built dinghy will normally be drier if it planes on top of the waves instead of wallowing in the troughs. And planing will give you much greater speed and range. If you can't plane with a load—at the least with your entire family—you won't be able to reach many places without moving the mother ship. A good cruising dinghy is tough, reliable, and able to

Your dinghy will be the family car, pickup truck, and delivery van. (Julie Culver photo)

▼

▼

carry large loads while planing, and it gives as comfortable and dry a ride as possible.

The size dinghy you can accommodate is limited by your on-board storage space (see also "Dinghy Storage" in chapter 10); you simply cannot successfully tow a dinghy on ocean passages of any distance. You may be able to get by with towing for awhile; eventually, however, the weather will catch you and you'll lose the thing, or worse. In my experience, it isn't practical to tow a dinghy even in sheltered water. For example, if you have to come alongside a dock for fuel, or back and fill waiting for a bridge to open, the dinghy can get in the way. When you do tow it, take care at all times to prevent the line from becoming fouled in the prop. This can disable you at the worst of times. With a floating line, tangling is seldom a problem unless your prop sucks the line down. Floating lines don't wear well, however, and are quickly weakened by ultraviolet light.

INFLATABLES

I said the dinghy should be tough. Does this mean no inflatables? Hardly. Inflatables can be durable if made by a reputable company. Some look good but don't last. One well-known inflatable manufacturer received numerous customer complaints that their boats were coming unglued. The company determined that it was due to a large batch of faulty glue and made repairs. A fly-by-night company might not have responded to the problem or offered any recourse.

Punctures are much more likely to occur in inflatables than in hard dinghies. The fins and spines of fish and lobster used to puncture our Avon inflatable when the catch would jump out of our tub. Even conch, if not carefully placed in the dinghy, can puncture it. Many people dive regularly with inflatables; they're very careful and carry a lot of glue and patches. We have known Avons to last longer than 10 years with almost daily use, although they were heavily patched toward the end.

Hard-bottom inflatables ride better, plane better, and are far less likely to be punctured on a rocky beach. Our chief complaint is that the hard bottom defeats one of the best reasons to own an inflatable: the ability to deflate it and store it easily on deck. You can't roll up hard-bottom inflatables, and they're heavier than standard inflatables. If you don't want to deflate the dinghy, it should be light

Carolyn lowers the outboard to Melanie in the inflatable.

enough so that you can hoist it with a halyard for storage, and it should be soft enough to store well without banging into things.

Inflatables are the most popular type of cruising dinghy, so don't be disillusioned by the few drawbacks. Be extra careful, carry repair material, and accept that it won't last forever. (For more information on the selection, maintenance, and repair of these boats, read *Inflatable Boats*, by Jim Trefethen; International Marine, 1996.)

HARD DINGHIES

After owning three inflatables, I long ago purchased a hard dinghy. I couldn't continue to replace inflatables that invariably became punctured or chafed from the hard and continuous use we subjected them to. If we had intended to cruise only a few years, we might not have made this switch.

I first got an old Boston Whaler fiberglass dinghy about 11 feet long. I didn't like its ride or its weight. It pounded without mercy in waves, and it wasn't dry enough. I finally decided to build my own.

I gave detailed ideas to a friend who had experience in metal-working and aluminum-boat building. The result, after a lot of mussing and fussing and several changes and returns for extra stiffening, is an aluminum dinghy that comes close to doing it all—for us.

The first design criteria was to make it so ugly that nobody would want to steal it. We succeeded. It is unpainted, looks mean as a mad dog, is a bit squat, and has split toilet hose around its gunnels for a rubrail. I wanted it to be stable enough so that all four of us could climb in quickly while being chased by a shark. This has happened when we were diving. We also wanted the boat to plane quickly, carry a large load, and be relatively dry. She is wide aft and fine enough forward to have a comfortable entry. As is true of the rest of the boat's lines, this had to be done carefully to obtain the desired effect without creating a bow so fine that it would plow into the water while going down a wave. Going into the waves with her bow up, just prior to planing, she is very dry; coming back, she still is. Going across the sea can be wet if a stiff beam wind is picking up spray, but this is true of any boat. She has three flotation tanks filled with closed-cell foam. One is in the forepeak, the second under the midships seat, and the third under the broad stern seat. Ports with gasketed screw-on lids access an open area in each tank with enough room for storage of a VHF radio and other essentials. A small keel gives the directional stability so important in towing and rowing. Two sets of oarlocks enable two to row. She is about 12 feet long and weighs around 215 pounds empty.

I carry her on davits and keep two 6-gallon fuel tanks and the 25-horsepower outboard on the dinghy when we lift her up. The davits are mounted on the transom at each corner where the fiberglass is solid and thick. They are backed with stainless plates. The winches are manual and simple. The davits are strong enough so that one or two of us can get out in the dinghy while she is hanging on the stern. This gives us an extra length of stern to do hot work such as soldering, or perhaps messy work like cleaning fish and conch. Yes, we have reservations about seas grabbing her during passages; but it is the best compromise we could come up with. We have been out in exceptionally high seas and done okay. Once during a particularly rough passage out of Nassau, the captain of a large ship told us that the ground swell was 20 feet with 6 feet of wind-driven wave on top. We didn't have any problem then, nor

Chez Nous' *custom hard dinghy*

▼

have we in other bad weather. Perhaps we have just been lucky over the years.

With davits, you must always be on the alert, especially for quartering or following or rogue seas. Note that *Chez Nous* is 47.5 LOA with a high and buoyant stern. Our dinghy storage arrangement would be too heavy for many smaller boats.

MOTORS

Unless your family is unusually slight of build, you'll want a dinghy that will take at least a 15-horsepower motor. With two people and a good load aboard, this much power will be necessary to get up on a plane and cover distances at a reasonable speed. By the time the girls reached the age of 10, our family of four did much better with a 25-horsepower motor. Remember that we love faraway anchorages and travel great distances to fish or to carry fuel, water, and other heavy loads.

The horsepower required depends in large part on the design

of the dinghy itself. You have probably seen the planing tabs sold in boating stores; they attach to the lower unit of the outboard and supposedly make your dinghy plane better. If the largest motor you can afford and/or store can just barely plane your dinghy, you may wish to experiment with planing tabs. First try to find other boaters with a comparable rig and ask them if the fins worked.

A dinghy should not be towed with its motor, except for short distances under predictable circumstances of wind, sea, and maneuverability. The motor's weight adds significant drag to the dinghy and its towing rings. It will also greatly increase your losses should the motor be lost in a capsize. Every boat should have a place to store the outboard and a way of getting it aboard and back on the dinghy. We have seen many methods, from muscle power to elaborate rigs. It depends on you, your boat, and the size of the outboard. Most people make a harness with ropes around the power head, and attach a halyard. This setup enables them to haul it up using a halyard winch, with one person in the dinghy to steady the operation. Don't let the lower unit get above the power head during this operation, or at any other time. This could allow water in the lower unit to get up into the cylinders. Even if you just muscle it up, it's wise to attach a rope. I'd love to know the number of outboards (and/or boaters) that have gone in the drink during this operation. It can easily happen. Once aboard, the motor needs a place to live. One option is to bolt a mounting board to a stern pulpit or between stays. This arrangement will vary from boat to boat, but wherever it is, it should be a place where lines are not likely to tangle in the motor.

DINGHY SEAMANSHIP

One of the more neglected aspects of seamanship is safety equipment in the dinghy. If you are just cruising close to home in protected inland waters, and if you use the dinghy only as a weekend toy, then there is some argument (although I fervently disagree) for carrying only the legally required safety equipment. When you leave populated areas, however, you also leave areas of quick rescue. Many people leave the United States and still expect U.S. Coast Guard protection. It isn't there. If your motor fails in a cut and you are sucked out to sea with no means of signaling, you may be lost. It happens.

Your dinghy should have all the equipment required by U.S. laws and then some. It should include a handheld VHF, flares, a good waterproof flashlight in which you keep fresh batteries, a jug of water and emergency rations, basic tools, a set of oars or paddles, a knife, and a good anchor with at least 10 feet of chain next to the anchor and then at least 50 feet (the more the better, depending on where you sail) of nylon rode. Obviously, you need a watertight storage area or box. The best we have seen are those made by Pelican. All of these can be expensive, but they may save your life.

You should also have and use permanent or removable running lights. Most dinghies are too small and wet to have permanently mounted lights that will last long. I use portable lights, but most portables I've seen are inappropriate for the job. They make no pretense of being water resistant, and they can't take any shock. Much of the section on flashlights in chapter 20 pertains to portable running lights because they are essentially slightly modified double C- or double D-cell flashlights. One company, Recmar, seems to do a good job with this type of light. There may be others. Recmar advertises removable running lights that are submersible to 200 feet. Instead of a switch, Recmar uses a system in which you screw in the head over a lubricated O-ring to make on/off contact. The batteries are held by a coil spring at the bottom. A thin strip rubbing against the bulb holder completes the negative (–) circuit, but it is protected within a raised part of the interior of the casing. They use two C cells and come with a krypton bulb. These can be mounted to inflatables with a glue-on fixture that allows the light's quick removal when not in use. The stern-pole mount can also be used as a flagpole. The approximate retail price for a set of bow and stern lights is around $19. A set of bow and stern brackets with pole and glue is around $15. They can be ordered directly from Recmar at 9222 Easthaven Blvd., Houston, Texas 77075.

Small-boat handling skills are extremely important with dinghies. These skills don't come with the boat; you have to acquire them. Every year I see or hear of people being seriously injured by propellers when the dinghy is driven carelessly. Waves in cuts or even in some harbors can cause broaches or capsizes if the operator doesn't have sufficient skill. High winds will try to pick up the bow of lighter dinghies, particularly smaller inflatables, and flip them. Kids are often given the use of a dinghy and a high-powered motor with no thought of training in small-boat handling. Many

U.S. states have laws prohibiting or curtailing use of small boats by younger kids; other countries are enacting similar laws. This is partly because boaters have been irresponsible. If your family isn't already skilled in this area, get some training before you use the dinghy.

THEFT PREVENTION

Dinghy theft is yet another problem confronting cruisers. In many places, it is a serious dilemma. These include almost any urban waterfront area, and particularly areas in the warmer latitudes. It is easy for thieves to swim out, cut the line, and drift away in the night with the dinghy and its motor. Often, the motor is what the thief really wanted. It isn't unusual to find the dinghy without the motor shortly after the theft. Some people deliberately junk up the cover on their motor to make it look old, abused, and unattractive. The best solution is to get the dinghy up on deck or on davits at night.

Getting the boat off the water without davits can be a real hassle. Many cruisers rig a sling and lift the dinghy and motor a few feet out of the water with a halyard, letting the dinghy lay along the side of the mother ship overnight. This is quick and easy, and it seems to work.

If you leave the tender in the water in risky areas, use a stainless cable or chain. It may not stop thieves if they are determined, but it may discourage them enough so that they will look elsewhere for easier pickings. The same is true of securing your dinghy when you go ashore. Use a stainless cable or chain and lock it to something solid. In many areas theft is not a problem, but you never know.

I can tell you from unpleasant experience that dinghy theft is a bigger headache than you might expect. It leaves you totally helpless. If your car is stolen ashore, you can get on the phone and call the police. If your dinghy is stolen, you can't get ashore unless someone gives you a ride, or you take your boat to a marina and start shelling out a fortune. But you have to contact the police, call your insurance company if you were lucky enough to have insurance, and get another dinghy so you can stop paying marina bills. Because of this, we've carried a spare, rolled-up Avon for years. These days it makes a great car for the girls, as well as a spare dinghy.

Chapter Seventeen

CATALOG CATASTROPHE

There are many pieces of equipment you may want or need that weren't covered in earlier chapters, so I'll discuss them here. Before I begin, however, let me say that it's important to get a grip on yourself in this department: avoid catalog catastrophe.

If you're like us, you hungrily read every new boating catalog. A trip to a marine-supply store is like a trip to wonderland. Now that you are casting off and adopting a new lifestyle, you have the perfect excuse to buy up all sorts of toys and gadgets and really have some fun. But don't do it. Make your purchases slowly, after deliberation and study. Avoid ending up with useless stuff you don't want. Avoid going broke.

Some pieces of equipment should be purchased as you prepare to leave and some just before you leave. Some can wait until you're sure you want them and can fit them in.

WHEN TO WAIT

Electronics is an obvious category of equipment that's best bought shortly before departure (by shortly, I mean roughly six months; see below). The technology changes rapidly; prices change drastically— usually downward. An early purchase may be obsolete long before you leave and worth perhaps a quarter of what you paid for it by the time you leave. For example, my GPS unit cost around $1,000 almost five years ago. I needed it when I bought it, and it has served me well. But a new, similar unit that may work better costs only $250 or so at this writing.

Communications equipment is particularly volatile at this time. The price of VHF radios has been stable for years, but that is changing. By 1999, I was told, the Coast Guard will not accept distress calls on VHF 16. They'll ask you to call them on a Digital Selective Calling set only. This could render obsolete most VHF radios in use today. Stay tuned.

While you wait to make these purchases, study the market and read up on anticipated developments. Visit friends' boats and see what they have and how they like it. But don't wait until immediately before you leave; electronics are most likely to fail early in their life. Purchase your equipment so that it gets at least six months of heavy use before you head out to an area where it will be difficult to replace it. If you don't have this option because you are about to leave your familiar shopping and shipping area, just leave the equipment on for extended periods while the boat is at the marina. Any other sophisticated equipment that is likely to continue to develop or to receive increased competition should be put on the late list.

Also check the shelf life of equipment. The membranes in a reverse-osmosis watermaker, for example, have a short shelf life. An industry representative told me that at this writing these membranes last only six months to a year while stored on the shelf. Obviously, you don't want to get a deal on one a year or so before you leave and then find you have to replace this expensive component before using it.

WHERE TO BUY

When you start buying, shop around carefully. Many so-called discount houses don't really give that much of a discount. And don't look only for the best prices. It isn't unusual for some outfits to buy up odd lots or troublesome lots and sell them cheaply. This may be exactly what you want, but maybe not. If it is a VHF radio that has had a lot of warranty claims, your deal may be hollow.

It helps to shop in areas where there is a lot of competition. Ft. Lauderdale calls itself the yachting capital of the world. It supports a large community of marine retailers, suppliers, and service people. Many boaters make their purchases there because the competition has kept prices down. The Ft. Lauderdale marine industry represents a good deal of collective knowledge as well; it's a good place to find out about things. If you saw that VHF radio priced mysteriously low in one shop, you may find people in several other shops who know exactly why. Ft. Lauderdale is but one example of many—there are boating centers all over the country that give you opportunity to shop around for good information and prices.

WHAT TO BUY

Many items are durable, won't deteriorate or undergo technological changes, and are ideal for selecting early if you find a good buy. Chain and anchors come to mind first. A hard dinghy is a good item to purchase well in advance. The windlass and winches, and hardware such as boathooks, boarding ladders, cabin heaters, and dinghy motor mounts are among the myriad items that fit this category. Of course, if you buy new a year or more in advance of your departure, you may lose the warranty before you get a chance to use the item. Still, the price may be so good that it's still worthwhile to purchase it early. Garage sales can be a great source of low-price items that are in good shape.

Comfort items can be a real snare to the new cruising shopper. There are so many neat things in the stores that it may be hard to resist spending a fortune on goodies like nautical cocktail napkins. As important as creature comforts are, they should not take precedence over safety and basic survival equipment. You may want to give yourselves comfort items for birthdays and other special occasions. This spreads the damage out over the year. But don't spend heavily in the nautical doodad category until you are actually aboard and have a realistic idea about what you need, want, have room for, and can afford. Many of those pretty doodads are useless aboard a real cruising boat.

Do the best you can to buy equipment that will match your anticipated cruising goals. I realize that you may not yet know how far you want to go, but you should have some idea of what you will be doing in the next year or two. For example, it may be easy to find a good deal on a set of charts for the South Pacific, and you always wanted these anyway. But you will probably also find good deals two years down the road when you're sure you will be going.

Much equipment made exclusively for offshore work can also be obtained later, with little change in price and quality. The offshore survival raft immediately comes to mind. Anyone going offshore should have one, but these rafts—and their supplies—deteriorate with age. The manufacturers advise that you have them serviced frequently—usually at least every two years—for a large sum (at this writing, at least $500). If you are just going to cruise the inland waters of a coast for a year or so, you may not want to get one of these yet. Coastal survival rafts are available as a compromise. You can also rent both kinds. There are other examples. If you are cruising close, you may want to get only a single-sideband receiver now. It will cost $200 to $300, but will bring you offshore weather, let you listen to other cruisers chatting far away, and allow you to receive weather-faxes and other fax transmissions on your computer. Get the transmitter/receiver later. This will cost around $2,000, but you can talk on it and call friends thousands of miles away. A GPS is a must these days. Get one now, and get a spare later. (But know how to find your way without it, or don't go.)

As a final thought on all that neat stuff, always ask yourself: "Can I fix this?" Check the manual to see if the manufacturer wants you to fix it and whether they will help you with instructions and readily available parts. Then get the parts while it is easy, and be sure you have the tools needed. If the manufacturer isn't going to be helpful, leave the thing on the shelf unless it is so important to you that you feel you can afford to throw away its remains and get another one when the time comes. A small microwave may fit into this category. Obviously, some items such as electronics aren't going to be fixable by most of us anyway.

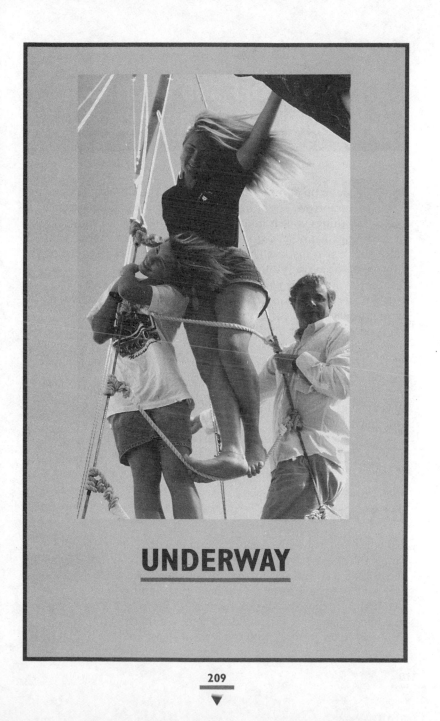

UNDERWAY

Chapter Eighteen

TAKING OFF AND GETTING INTO THE GROOVE

You wake up at night in a cold sweat. The things you have to do tomorrow. The things you should be doing right now. The things you should have done yesterday. All those years of dreaming, planning, working, scrimping to save money. Am I ready for this? Is my family ready? Will this be a terrible mistake? How will we get everything done? It's impossible.

Stop worrying. If you have planned well, it'll be great. The world won't come to an end when you take off. Many new long-term cruisers pressure themselves needlessly by thinking that everything they ever thought of and everything they should have thought of but didn't must get done before they leave. They work themselves into a frenzy that often results in a lousy beginning. Do the best you can, make lists, divide labor, prioritize. But relax. You can still accomplish things after you leave. You'll still be able to get things. You'll still be able to talk to shoreside denizens. Life will go on. As a matter of fact, it will be great.

If your communications systems are in place (see chapter 6) and you're otherwise ready to go, let's move on to a few suggestions for making the transition as smooth as possible.

GET ABOARD

Early in this book, I talked about taking practice cruises with the family long before you begin cruising. If possible, you should actually move aboard at least several months, preferably longer, before you take off. Try to have most of your boat spaces and systems in order before this, so there will be no major work projects. Everyday repair and maintenance projects should be a part of this trial run. Because you're in home territory, you can always go ashore for a brief time if a major problem does come up. Living aboard at the marina or on a mooring will ease your adjustment to life aboard. You'll discover hidden problems and learn about storage, groceries, refrigeration, privacy, and all of the other things I mentioned early on. And when it comes time to go, you will already be somewhat in the groove. You won't have the added stress of moving aboard. During this trial period, continue to take weekend and/or vacation cruises.

YOUR BOAT ISN'T A BUS

Many first-time liveaboards take the "taking off" part too seriously. They dash off down the coast, or out the cut, or across the ocean as if they were on a 9-to-5 job assignment in the "real" world. It's as though they were driving a tour bus. They try to tick off destinations without regard to the weather, waves, currents, and the need for repairs and rest. Tour-bus cruising is not only dangerous, it deprives you of the time you need to adjust. It will ruin your experience.

"THEY BARELY SURVIVED"

One family we met was heading down the East Coast in the fall. They had serious plans. They had figured exact mileages between points of interest where they had made marina reservations. They planned to be in Ft. Lauderdale by late November so they could fly back to their former home for Thanksgiving. Then they planned to tour the Bahamas—with several days' layover at Freeport and Nassau—and other islands enroute to Venezuela, which they hoped to reach by spring. They didn't worry about meeting their schedule, because they knew how fast their boat was supposed to go.

Halfway down the East Coast, they barely survived a gale off Georgia as they came into an inlet with huge and dangerous breakers on both sides. The tension in their voices was audible on the VHF. But they'd had to keep going because they were determined to meet friends at a marina in north Florida. When they reached Ft. Lauderdale, the children were near revolt and the parents were spending long evenings in expensive restaurants. At Nassau, the husband decided he needed to fly home to investigate a business opportunity. That's as far as they got.

▼

This lifestyle is supposed to be fun (even though it's work). Enjoy the nice spots as you go, and allow quiet time for yourself and your family. Begin with easy cruising. Hang out in familiar territory at first, or at least easy territory. Many cruisers leave as winter is rushing down from the north, chasing them before its cold gales. It is much better to leave in summer or early fall, so you can take your time and get used to your new life.

Don't leave the mainland at first. Once you do, it will be much more difficult to get parts and equipment, and more difficult to make unexpected adjustments. We have actually seen families hop onto their boats and head off around the world with little or no cruising experience. It works sometimes, but often it doesn't. Even when it does work, the experience may be unpleasant. Give yourself time to get used to what you're doing, to get over the first phase of breakdowns, and to learn about your boat and yourselves. In chapter 23, I discuss our neighborhood and why we like it. It's a large area, but it includes great places for beginners.

In case all else fails, leave room in your schedule and budget so you can leave the boat in an inexpensive location and take an inexpensive trip (via bus, for example) back to friends or family if you feel the need after a month or two. In some areas, such as south Florida, rental cars are inexpensive. At this writing, you may be able to rent a car for a week, off season, with unlimited mileage for a base rate of around $130 for in-state use.

Taking a short break can quell separation anxiety and reinforce your decision to go. Your parents may be complaining that you have abandoned them and stepped off the edge of the world. If your kids are old enough to have begun social bonding (it happens early), they may need to see their friends again. If you don't return to your former home, you could make a vacation excursion to a resort close by or to an inexpensive marina. You won't be able to afford to continue this sort of high living; this is just a way to leave room for a temporary escape. But you may find that you don't need it because everyone is excited about the cruising adventure you've planned.

Chapter Nineteen
WHAT ON EARTH DO YOU DO ALL DAY?

The question "What do you do out there all day?" vividly illustrates what a poor understanding most folks have of the cruising lifestyle. Our shoreside friends ask this question more than any other. To answer briefly, we say: "We work, play, eat and LIVE out here all day and all night." And unlike so many people who live ashore, we enjoy our life. But, as I said in the first few chapters, there is a lot of work to do on a cruising boat. Unless you're ready for it, your venture may turn out to be not much more than a tediously long weekend cruise.

WORK

There's always plenty of regular maintenance and repair—of pumps, engines, electrical motors, wiring, sails, rigging, line. The list never stops. Remember, there is no one else around to do it, you probably wouldn't be able to afford to hire someone anyway, and things will be wearing out and breaking much more often simply because you are using them more often. I have long believed that some boating component manufacturers deliberately make their parts for occasional weekend use only, knowing that by the time a few weekends of hard wear go by, the year's warranty will be have long expired. The bright side of all this labor is that you'll know, as you deal with the daily breakdowns, that your boat is in constant good shape because you are there and on top of things. You'll also learn more about your boat and its systems; as you do so, most of the jobs will become easier. But you don't want problem solving to be your sole source of entertainment. That isn't what cruising is all about.

PLAY

Planning pleasurable and constructive things to do while at anchor and at sea help immensely as you adjust to life aboard. They are a necessary part of your daily routine. But you will have to rely on your own devices to create diversions and entertainment. Watching TV and going to the mall won't be among your options. Many new cruisers don't realize this until after they are well on their way and it's either inconvenient or too costly to buy what they need to create diversion. They become bored and tend to dwell on the unpleasant aspects of cruising.

Before leaving, think about things that you, as a family and as individuals, might like to do, and can do, on the boat for entertainment. Drawing, reading, computer work, and educational pursuits are good because they take up little space but consume a lot of time and interest. Other hobbies that may not have occurred to you to try when you lived ashore may intrigue you on the boat. Check them out, and if they seem interesting, take along what you need to explore them. The examples I list below are but a few of many possible cruising pursuits.

TAKE ADVANTAGE OF NATURE

One of the main reasons most of us go cruising is our love of the outdoors, yet few cruisers use their appreciation of the natural environment as a way to entertain and educate. I know of a family who took off from the upper East Coast and made it all the way to George Town, Exuma. But they didn't even understand the effect a rising and falling tide would have on a dinghy pulled up on the beach but not anchored. They constantly complained of being bored, and the cruise ended quickly. You can do so much more than exclaim over cocktails about the beautiful sunset. Nature study takes on a whole new meaning when you are in the midst of manatees, alligators, dolphins, exotic fish, reef life, deer on the shore of an anchorage, pelicans and osprey, to mention just a few. With a little preparation and thought, cruising can be a link to the natural world.

WEATHER

Meteorology is one of the most important and exciting things you can get into while cruising. Weather isn't just a life-and-death issue at sea, it's a great and entertaining pastime. Your understanding of and respect for the weather will go a long way toward helping you develop a mind-set that results in enjoyable cruising.

On shore, the weather forecast may only help you determine whether the air conditioning will be running at work the next day. As we travel up and down the East Coast, we're often amused by the different TV weather forecasters on the six o'clock news. Physical attractiveness, a chic hair style, and the ability to read quizzes obviously helped them get the job. Detailed weather maps with intelligent discussion are becoming increasingly rare. Arrogant indifference to nature is not a luxury cruisers can afford. Shore people can't afford it either; they just may not realize it. Weather can affect electric plants, hydraulic drives in dams, power lines, fuel supplies, transportation in general, food supplies, and just about everything else that shoresiders take for granted.

Before you take off, learn as much as you can about meteorology. Bring along at least one good book on the subject, and equipment such as a barometer, hygrometer, thermometer, anemometer. Often you will be out of range of VHF weather transmissions, unless you limit your cruising to the U.S. coasts. Buy at least a single-sideband receiver ($200 to $300) so you can listen to offshore forecasts of direct significance to you. At this time these are broadcast by the U.S. Coast Guard and Navy, the AT&T High Seas radio-telephone service, and private groups such as ham (Licensed Amateur Radio Operators) nets. Many cruisers record the voice transmissions on a small cassette tape player because they may not be easy to understand the first time around. It also helps to plot the weather features on a chart to understand the more complex forecasts. You can interface your computer with most receivers and receive weather-faxes, but you'll need a modem and the program. (I've used those by Software Systems Consulting of San Clemente, CA 92672.)

Start listening to high seas weather before you leave. Compare it with TV weather. You'll soon notice that television stations report as though weather stops at the coast (except during hurricane season). Observe the weather systems that are likely to cause high winds and big waves in the offshore areas where you expect to travel. Offshore broadcasts are given for large sections of ocean

215

▼

described by boundaries of latitude and longitude. Cold fronts will run from points of latitude and longitude, not from states or cities. It takes a bit of getting used to, but you'll need to learn to decipher all of this before you leave the coast. When you do, you'll find weather broadcasts exciting.

It's interesting to watch huge weather systems move across the globe and to feel their intimate effects on your life. Talk about feeling plugged in—this is it! But you feel plugged into the universe— not the wall. It is fascinating to look out the hatch, watch the wind, barometer, and hygrometer and then figure out what is going to happen right where you are. Who cares what that computer says back on the coast?

As you may be realizing, appreciation of the weather has a lot to do with attitude. While cruising you will be almost totally at the mercy of the weather. It will control you every day; almost all plans will be made contingent on it, your thoughts and conversations will be permeated by it. You do what it lets you do. If it rains, you don't have a picnic. If it's cloudy, you don't go diving. If it's blowing from the wrong direction, you stay put or go somewhere else. If a storm is building, you move to a safe anchorage.

The realization that you can't control nature and that you must go along with it and respect it will be one of the greatest attitude adjustments you will make. And when you do, life will be much easier. You'll stop worrying about what you can't do anything about and start doing what you can. You'll begin to feel yourself in tune with nature, not the Channel 10 TV news. And it will make you feel very, very good.

You'll also find that weather brings cruisers together. We're all affected by it daily, we all need to know the latest information, and we like to share our information and interpretations. In harbors, people who are well versed in meteorology (and some who are obviously not) and who have the equipment will volunteer to pass on weather information at certain times via the VHF radio. At gatherings on the beach, during cockpit cocktail parties, and in banter on the radio, weather will be a major subject of conversation. Knowing and caring about what is going on will even help you win friends.

REFERENCE MATERIAL

Bring along reference books about the waters, fish, birds, plant life, and land creatures where you expect to travel. You'll be amazed at

(text continued on page 218)

"GO LOOK OUTSIDE"

Once we were heading northward up the East Coast around 50 miles off South Carolina. Around two o'clock, in the dark morning hours, we began to experience severe squalls. From the lightning, we could see that the storm wasn't local; more were ahead. The wind was erratic but often to the north. The air was moist and heavy. The official forecast assured us of easy southeastern winds and clear skies all the way to Beaufort, North Carolina. But we knew we were approaching that vast region south of Cape Hatteras where weather is born. And we saw what we saw.

We raised the Coast Guard station at the entrance to the Cape Fear River on the radio. By this time it was 2:30 A.M., and he answered quickly, probably surprised to hear someone out there in the night. I asked him for the weather. With no hesitation, he read the official forecast—the same one we had been listening to on the VHF weather channel. When he finally finished, I patiently explained that something else was happening where we were. I had to find out what was going on so I could make a decision about putting in at Cape Fear.

"Sir, I can only read you the weather. That's what it says, and that's all the information that we have."

"Well, have you been outside lately?"

"No sir, I have been on duty."

"Well, will you please go look outside and tell me what it is doing." Long pause.

"Sir, I don't think I can do that."

"Yes, you can. It isn't hard. Just go to the door, open it, and look out."

There were a few moments of silence on the wire as thunder crashed around us.

"Uh, sir? It's blowing and raining like. . . .Well, uh, it's blowing and raining very hard here. The wind is around 25 knots out of the north. It must be a squall. Sure doesn't look like what they're talking about."

There was a subtropical low forming, even as we were speaking, and no one seemed to know about it except those of us who dared to be— or to look—outside.

▼

▼

(text continued from page 216)
the educational amusement this provides younger children whose curiosity provides the key to hours of fun for all of you. Our girls, at a very young age, could readily identify and talk about fish, sharks, whales, and other creatures as if they were professional naturalists. At an early age they had stroked dolphins in the wild, and had communicated with them.

Although we see dolphins regularly, they always impress us with their grace and sense of understanding. Once, several were diving and playing in our bow wave. When this happens, we always go forward to join them in whatever way we can. On this occasion we noticed that one seemed to move his head from side to side as he surfaced. At first we thought this was a coincidence or a peculiarity of his swimming motion. We began to reconsider this as he continued to do so, intermittently. The girls began nodding their heads in an affirmative motion. The dolphin did the same, not negatively as before but affirmatively. Then we began to nod negatively. The dolphin did the same as he arched over the wave. Each time we changed our nod, the dolphin followed suit. This went on for a long time, all of us thrilled in this sharing. It prompted an earnest desire to learn all we could about these creatures. It was great to have the right books aboard.

Identification books such as those by the Audubon Society are invaluable. These field guides are soft but sturdily bound, and of ideal size for storage on a boat or carrying ashore. They cover many subjects, ranging from seashells to mammals and more. The first part of these books contains color photographs for identification, the second part contains written descriptions and other information. We have particularly enjoyed *The Audubon Society Field Guide to North American Fishes, Whales, & Dolphins* (Alfred A. Knopf, Inc.). We also carry other fish identification books. Be sure the books you pick have good pictures of the fish, and comments on edibility. We also use *Guide to Corals & Fishes of Florida, the Bahamas, and the Caribbean,* by Idaz and Jerry Greenberg (Seahawk Press), which is water-resistant. *Fishes of the Atlantic Coast,* by Gar Goodson (Stanford University Press), has helped us to identify sea life and to gain insight into these creatures. The whole idea is that it isn't enough to just say "Look at the fish." If you can find out all the neat things about the fish, it will be a hundredfold more interesting. Broader reference matter is found in *A Field Guide to the Stars and Planets,* by

Donald Menzel and Jay Pasachoff (Houghton Mifflin), *North American Wildlife*, by the editors of Reader's Digest, and *Oceanography, A View of the Earth*, by Grant Gross (Prentice-Hall). Of course, no boating library is complete without *Chapman Piloting, Seamanship, & Small Boat Handling*, by Elbert S. Maloney (Hearst). A knot book such as *Ashley Book of Knots*, by Clifford Ashley (Doubleday), or *The Art of Knotting and Splicing*, by Lee Hoffman and Ray Beard (Naval Institute Press), is helpful for adults and kids and is a good teaching tool. Kids catch on a lot easier than most adults to things like Turk's heads and splicing.

Reference books provide both entertainment and enlightenment.

STOP AND LEARN

Stop at places that have special significance for learning about nature. You will find these everywhere. Along the East Coast our favorite is Cumberland Island, Georgia, a national wildlife preserve. You can anchor and land by dinghy, walk quiet paths among lush foliage, and see wild animals such as deer, armadillo, wild horses, wild turkeys, sea turtles, and more.

In places such as Annapolis on the Chesapeake Bay, ecological boat tours can acquaint you with bay life. Several seaquariums along the East Coast are within easy reach of the anchored cruiser. When anchored in Baltimore's Inner Harbor, you're literally in the shadow of one of the nicest.

If you tie up at the relatively inexpensive city docks of Ft. Lauderdale, you can easily get to the Everglades and take instructional tours. In the Bahamas, the Exumas Cay Land and Sea Park will teach you about the life of the underwater reefs and the islands above them. Visit places like these. It will make your cruising three-dimensional, and will make it very difficult not to develop a more fitting attitude about what you are really doing. The daily problems of water pumps and motors will take a back seat in your psyche.

Discussing Chesapeake Bay fishing with 84-year old Wilson Rowe aboard the Linda R.

EXCITEMENT IN THE SKY

We are in the lower Exumas as I write this. Each night for several nights we have stood on our bow and watched the comet Hyakutake. It leaps out of the familiar sky, reminding us of our insignificance—and at the same time of our importance.

If you live in or near a city, once you start cruising you'll see a night sky you never knew existed. When we return to the U.S. coast from the islands, we almost always see the smog first if we make landfall in daylight. It hovers like a dirty cloud over the horizon. But even when we are cruising the coast we find distinct differences in the clarity of the night sky in different areas. For example, we see many more stars from an anchorage in the marshes of Georgia than we do from an anchorage on the western shore of the northern Chesapeake Bay. A clear night in Maine can be spectacular. And you'll see a different night sky as you head farther south. But you won't know what the Southern Cross is unless you can find and identify it. Even if the subject has bored you in the past, take along at least one good book to identify stars, constellations, and planets. Sit on deck at night talking about what's out there, how far away it is, and what the ancients thought of these constellations. See what it does for your kids. Listen for news of meteor showers. If you have a ham radio or receiver, listen to the ham net on 7268 lower sideband. They often announce meteor showers and space launches and similar occurrences. There can be few things more exciting than a show of shooting stars over an ocean sky, and you never know what else you might see. If you pass down the Chesapeake Bay, stop and learn at Davis Planetarium in the Maryland Science Center in Baltimore. You can anchor within sight or tie up. All this could be a prelude to learning celestial navigation, which is a fascinating marriage of the beauty of the skies to practical application. If you have the time, you should learn it. If you intend to travel far offshore, make the time to learn it.

DIVING FOR FUN AND FOOD

The sea can provide some of the best amusement the earth has to offer. Snorkeling is one of the greatest things you can do as a family. Just drifting along and looking down at the reefs or ocean bottom can amaze, amuse, and thrill for hours. We also free-dive and hunt fish as a family.

Free-diving is what porpoises and whales do. We do it too, just

"THAT GAS TANK BURNING UP IN THE SKY"

Once, while anchored in the Bahamas, we noticed a strange glow through the hatch as we were eating dinner. It looked like a kerosene lantern flickering out on the deck. We quickly went up and saw that the glow was coming from the sky. It pulsated and moved with unearthly colors, like nothing we had ever seen before. It was beautiful, but also a little frightening because we couldn't imagine what was causing it. We thought of the northern lights. We had seen pictures of this phenomenon, but this didn't look like any of those pictures. And besides, we were around 23.5 degrees north latitude.

The girls, very young at the time, spontaneously and naturally sat down before the mast and began singing "Amazing Grace" as they looked up. I'll never forget the moment.

The VHF was alive with comments and thoughts. The Bahamians were concerned, as were cruisers. The oldest islander had never seen anything like this before. One well-known and respected Bahamian (also a good friend) soothed the local island populace by explaining on channel 16 that "the Americans shot up one of those space rockets today, and you know they always drop off the gas tank after they get way up into the sky . . . and that's what you are seeing . . . it's that gas tank burning up in the sky."

Finally, consumed by curiosity and growing concern, I tried to raise the Coast Guard on the single-sideband. We had been experiencing much interference that day, and I was unable to raise them either in Miami or Norfolk, on any frequencies. Finally I got a voice from New Orleans. I told him where we were and what we were seeing. Puzzled, he asked me to stand by. A short time later he came back and said, with some surprise, that we were watching an extremely rare occurrence of the northern lights, visible even at that latitude.

▼

not as well. Like them, we hold our breath underwater, swim for a while, and surface for air—only much more often. Over the ages human beings have surrendered most of their freedoms, some forever. But with a little practice and a little help, we can link to a part of us that still knows primordial sensations, and find that we remember and enjoy it beyond imagination.

▼

Snorkeling doesn't require much equipment. A diving mask and flippers are needed to replace our lost fins and some of our lost perception. A snorkel compensates for the fact that our noses have drifted to the wrong side of our heads over the millennia. A wetsuit protects our skin from the cold water and sharp-edged reefs. And weights adjust our buoyancy so that we can still float, but also effortlessly glide down. If we want to fish, a Hawaiian sling is our sting. We are woefully unprepared by our former standards and no match for those who still live below the surface, but with a little luck our family can bring home dinner after an afternoon's dive.

For the past 12 winters my family has enjoyed snorkeling and diving in the clear and beautiful waters of the Bahamas. We seldom go down more than 20 feet, although just a few feet is often enough. The equipment is not expensive and will pay for itself every day in fun alone. It is readily available in most dive shops in the States and also in many areas of the Bahamas such as Nassau, Marsh

Melanie and Carolyn dive up some conch in the Exumas.

▼

223

Harbor, and George Town. The prices are competitive or lower in the Bahamas, and there is often a greater availability of spears and slings.

A good mask is important. It should fit your face well; try it on to be sure before you buy it. Look for masks with molded slots on either side of the nose; you may need to hold your nostrils to equalize pressure when diving. If buying for a child, don't skimp just because the child will soon outgrow the mask. A poorly fitting mask will leak and can even come off while swimming. This is not fun for anyone, and can scare a younger person who is just learning. You'll have no problem selling this to another family when it is outgrown.

Snorkels can be pretty exotic these days, but we use the straightforward, no-frills version. It's important to have a bright, colorful tip so that you will be easily seen when you are swimming on the surface. While it isn't necessary to buy the fanciest version in the shop, you should buy from a reputable company and select a snorkel designed and manufactured for this use. An inexpensive swimming pool version, while fine for a pool or playing at the beach, could collapse or distort under the rigors of ocean diving.

Well-designed flippers are also important. If they don't fit well, they can chafe and even cut your feet. I prefer flippers with straps rather than the type that fit over the entire foot like a shoe. Straps can be adjusted, and they are cheaply replaced when they wear. When shoe-type flippers tear, usually around the ankle, the entire flipper must be replaced. I use diving boots inside the flippers. These cushion my feet and protect them if something goes wrong and I have to walk on a rocky surface. My wife and daughters prefer shoe-type flippers because they come in small sizes; they wear socks underneath to prevent abrasion.

We don't use scuba tanks. It is illegal to use them while fishing in the Bahamas and various other places, and even though we have them aboard, we prefer to not have their encumbrance even when sightseeing. There is so much beauty within 20 feet of the surface that we have never felt a need for them except when working on the bottom of *Chez Nous*.

Wetsuits add safety and pleasure in the winter months. Usually a lightweight "shortie" suit, with short pants and long sleeves, is all you need in the Bahamas. Wetsuits keep you warm in cool waters, give extra buoyancy, and protect from cuts and abrasions. They also protect you from the sun, which can cook your back without warning as you glide along the surface. When the waters are warm, we still wear heavy, long-sleeved T-shirts.

Weights are helpful for most people. They are worn around the waist and come in different types and shapes. The most important consideration is that you use the right amount for your body. Never overload. The idea is to remain buoyant, but only enough to be safe. Most people have sufficient natural buoyancy; they have to work hard to get down and stay down. This is great for surface swimming, but when diving, this makes it difficult to see the sights or to hang motionless in front of a cave so you can shoot a grouper.

Use the manufacturer's guide to get an idea of how many weights you might need, and then take the time to experiment in shallow seawater. Learn just what amount works best for you. If you buy these weights in small increments, you can achieve perfect buoyancy. Never use too much. When you wear a wetsuit, you'll need extra weights to compensate for the buoyancy of the suit. Buy a belt designed for the purpose. Distribute the weights evenly around your waist; make sure it has a buckle that unsnaps quickly and easily. Always wear the belt over all other clothing so you can quickly drop it from your body if necessary.

A look bucket, preferably with a broad mouth, is a great tool if you're searching for a place to dive. It's also great for those who prefer to stay in the dinghy and watch from above. You can buy them readily in the Bahamas, at prices competitive with and sometimes lower than stateside. They are also easy to make by cutting out the bottom of a bucket, then bolting and gluing a piece of Plexiglas in its place.

If you will be spearfishing, wearing a glove on your left hand (if right-handed) will protect you from fins and spines. It will also help you to hold on to sharp rocks as you look under ledges and into holes. (Take care not to damage coral in the exuberance of the hunt.) Most people find that a glove on their right hand impairs shooting. We use inexpensive rubber work gloves or garden gloves; others go the full mile and buy diving gloves made for the purpose.

We feel it's important to carry a good diving knife at all times. It serves many purposes, most safety related. People have become entangled in monofilament fishing line. This line can get caught on a reef and be difficult to see and almost impossible to break without cutting. We have also been approached by aggressive sharks. Some say that they are merely curious, but we don't want to test their disposition. The shark may want to nudge you to see what you are like. If it nudges soft skin, we feel it is more likely to return. If it nudges a hard knife or similarly unattractive surface, it probably won't be hurt, but it will be less likely to stay interested. We don't wait around for a nudge, but we carry a knife just in case.

If you wish to hunt for fish, you will need at least one spear. Spear guns are not allowed in the Bahamas; they allow hand-propelled spears such as the Hawaiian sling, which is essentially a slingshot. It's nothing more than a rounded block of wood or other material, just big enough to hold in your hand, with a hole cut in the middle. A length of surgical tubing is attached to the block, one end on each side. The spear is inserted through the hole, with its flat end resting in a metal cup in the middle of the loop of tubing. You pull it back to stretch the tubing, aim, and let it fly. The spear is a stainless shaft, 5 or 6 feet long, with a barb on the pointed end. We prefer spring stainless steel because it is less likely to become permanently bent.

Some people prefer a different arrangement called a pole spear, which is also acceptable under Bahamian law. The surgical tubing is attached to the end of the shaft. To shoot, you pull the spear back against the tubing held in your other hand. A benefit is that the spear never gets away and is less likely to be lost in a hole or deep water. These don't have the range of free spears, but for most of us this is unimportant.

As clumsy as they seem, both types of spears are potentially lethal and should be used with great care. Practice not only brings in more fish, but more safety. Start by shooting on a deserted beach at mounds of sand. Then move to the water where you can practice on ripples or lumps of sand on the bottom. Never carry a spear cocked in the sling. In the excitement of looking, someone may swim within your range as you prepare to shoot. Be careful.

Our dinghy is also our dive boat. It helps to have one that is stable enough, and with low enough sides, so that you can climb into it easily in a hurry. Before you start diving, practice getting into yours with your gear and weights. It also helps to have a dinghy with enough speed and range to enable you to scout around and safely handle the current in cuts. (See chapter 16 for more on dinghies.)

Some people leave a crewmember in the dinghy. That person

follows the divers, enabling them to roam freely. This should be a mature, experienced small-boat handler. Spinning propellers, breaking seas, and divers clambering over the side can be a challenge. Others anchor their dinghy in the diving area, moving it when needed. Beware the current. Dive on the anchor and be sure it is planted firmly in sand, not coral; the anchor can damage the reef and also may not hold well. There should be a length of chain next to the anchor to prevent coral from cutting the line if it does get close. Some divers drift with the dinghy, swimming with the anchor so they can drop it when they see a good spot. Extreme care should always be taken to keep the dinghy in close range of the divers. Even if there is no current, some tenders, particularly inflatables, rapidly sail away on the wind if given the chance. You may be diving in an area where no other boats will happen along and pick you up.

Among the best places to learn about and enjoy reefs are the land and sea parks prevalent in the Florida Keys and in the Caribbean. These areas are carefully protected from fishing of any sort to preserve the sea floor from human encroachment. This encourages safe spawning and the spread of sea creatures to other areas. Our favorite is the Exuma Cay Land and Sea Park. The small headquarters building is located at the north end of Warderick Wells. From its harbor and moorings you can easily visit reefs teeming with life, as well as walk nature trails on the island. A park warden is usually available to answer questions and show good spots for sightseeing. Classes are sometimes conducted for visitors by study groups from universities and other educational centers. This park, administered by the Bahamas Land and Sea Trust in Nassau, depends on our support.

If you are not interested in fishing, the parks may be the best place to snorkel and dive. Not only is there information available, you will have the camaraderie of other cruisers doing the same thing. If you wish to fish, take care to be well beyond the park boundaries. The laws against taking things from the parks are strict.

Among the many wonderful things about the Bahamas is that it is possible to enjoy the reefs, get exercise, and fish at the same time—as long as you follow the rules. We prefer this type of fishing to hanging a baited line from a boat. In spearfishing, you only shoot at the fish you want. When hanging a line over from the boat, you have relatively little control over what will innocently take the bait. If it is too small or inedible, you must throw it back, probably injured. Spearfishing is not only selective, it is more sporting. To spearfish, you have to swim after the fish or find it in its carefully selected hideout, out-think it in its own environs, and then hit it with a spear propelled by rubber tubing and your muscles, all while holding your breath.

Finding fish is never a problem; finding the right fish often is. Each coral reef is an ecosystem of indescribable beauty with thousands of life-forms. Exotic fish dart in and out of holes, nibbling on the coral or snapping up smaller fish. Some don't swim away when you approach. Some are altogether inedible, but a few are quite good. While learning, we followed a general rule: colorful fish are not good to eat. Grouper, for example, are drab yet beautiful. You'll quickly learn what to look for. It helps to buy and study a good fish book before you begin; I mentioned several earlier in this chapter. There are many others. It also helps to go out with an experienced friend. *(Always dive with at least one partner and keep track of each other.)*

It is not only important to avoid fish that are too small; you may also wish to avoid many that are too big because of the ever-present threat of ciguatera poisoning. Of course, some fish should be avoided altogether for this reason (see "Ciguatera Poisoning" on page 231).

We have many favorite fishing spots. To find yours, begin searching for likely areas with your look bucket. After finding a good location, get into the water and spend some time observing from the surface through your mask. Then begin diving down and looking into the holes. As I mentioned, we seldom dive in more than 20 feet of water, and there are many good areas at less depth. Sometimes a deeper dive will bring in a better catch, but not always. Again, diving with experienced friends certainly helps, if you can talk them into sharing their secrets.

Fish like to hang out in and around holes in rocks and reefs. A plain-looking bottom can be riddled with holes and tunnels. Grouper, lobster, and other fish often dwell here. Perhaps they prefer the country life over the spectacular hustle and bustle of coral condos. Grouper can often be found motionless outside a cave or hollow brain coral, where they are likely to catch an occasional snack. A grouper may watch you approach, as though trying to decide whether you see through its camouflage. (Grouper subtly change color to match the background, disappearing like magic before your eyes.) As soon as it knows that you know, it will be gone. If it takes off into the open, forget it. If it goes inside the hole, you may still be able to see it. Don't shoot unless you have a good shot and can get the fish out. Often a grouper will turn around once it has entered the cave, and look for a moment to see if you are still there and interested. Sometimes it will scoot into a hole in the flat rocky sea floor and speed through the mazes of tunnel to emerge far away. I wonder if I hear it laugh as it glides out of reach.

If you approach noisily, everybody down there may have disappeared except the small ones, who linger around enjoying their immunity. These pretty little fish must know the law. But if you peer into the holes, you may see something large slowly materialize as your eyes adjust to the darkness of the cave. By the time you realize that it's a grouper, you will probably have to surface for air. Do it easily and come back to look again. It will probably still be there.

Never put your hand or any other part of your body into a hole. They frequently are guarded by moray eels that can give a nasty bite at best. It's not unusual to find nurse sharks basking in the larger cavities. While reputed to be docile, they can be dangerous under certain circumstances.

The citizens of the reef will become familiar friends, so much so that you cannot bear to shoot one. Queen trigger fish have beautiful, innocent faces. They almost seem to bat their eye lashes. These fish may present an easy target if you can bring yourself to shoot one. Once frightened, however, they move away rapidly. Then they stop and look back, as if to be sure you understand you've offended them. Despite their delicate beauty, their skin is so tough that the islanders formerly used them as sandpaper for scrubbing decks. They are excellent eating, although some people say they can carry ciguatera.

Yellowtail snapper school in and out. They seldom sit still for a shot. Occasionally a grunt will peep at you from just within a hole, the fine blue and yellow lines of his face blending with the indigo shadows inside the reef. If one stops long enough, it may make a good meal.

Lobsters like narrow ledges. On rare occasions you may see them walking along the bottom, but you usually won't find them unless you get down and look up under ledges. Sometimes a telltale feeler protrudes, barely recognizable in the seaweed and reef. As you dive more, your eye will readily pick out the feelers from the surroundings. If you see a lobster, be sure it is not carrying orange eggs on the underside of its tail. Generally this will not happen during the lobster season (August 1 through March 31), but as the off-season approaches, particularly if it is a warm spring, be careful. Often a lobster will be hunched deep within a cave, just far enough so that you will probably lose your spear if you shoot. They seem to know about those things. But not other things. If you tickle the sand near the mouth of the hole and back off a little, it may come curiously creeping to the mouth to see what's going on. Dinner!

With all the beauty and excitement, it is sometimes difficult to remember that you are diving in a world with many dangers (see "Perils of Paradise," in chapter 21). Don't be discouraged, just be careful and observant while you are having fun.

Many cruisers brag about swimming with shark and barracuda. We get out when they come. We've heard of attacks by both and feel uncomfortable around either, especially the shark. Both are incredibly swift. Because of this we never swim far from our dinghy, and as mentioned earlier, we have one that is designed for easy and quick reentry.

Sharks are attracted by blood, smell, and excitement. Anytime we shoot something we are extra vigilant to see whether it has attracted attention. Our standard procedure is to look around every few minutes. Sharks often swim in the twilight of your underwater vision, barely noticeable as shadows. While sighting a shark should cause you to leave, it should not cause panic. This is where they live. A few years ago a hammerhead more than 12 feet long swam between us and our dinghy, gliding in from nowhere. He passed on. We did too.

If you spear a fish, immediately take it to the dinghy and get it inside. While swimming back, keep the fish on the end of the spear, holding it away from you, so that a hungry predator swooping in will not aim directly toward your hand. If you see a shark or a barracuda, drop your catch and leave. A long swim back to the dinghy with a fish trailing blood and sending other signals can be a bit spooky. (This is another good reason to dive close to the dinghy.) In 12 years we have seldom known a shark or barracuda to hit our catch, but it does happen. If the fish has struggled or bled much (something to avoid), or if we have hunted the area for awhile, we usually leave the vicinity and dive elsewhere.

If a shark approaches when we are away from the dinghy, we swim backward while facing the shark, shoulder to shoulder with our partner and spear or knife ready should he come in for an inquisitive nudge. Don't unnecessarily stab or shoot the shark; this could be unsuccessful and dangerous. As mentioned above, that first encounter with a hard inedible object will sometimes cause the fellow to lose interest.

Currents, particularly around cuts, can be very swift. It is nice to be swept along, watching the sea floor below. But don't get lost in the thrill of the ride. Stay with your partner and stay close to the dinghy. Even if you feel confident about swimming against the current, you are no match for a shark. It is best to dive only at slack tide in areas with strong current.

CIGUATERA POISONING

Ciguatera is a toxin found in fish that inhabit coral reefs. Not all fish are affected, and it is not unusual for the same species to be toxic in one area but not in a nearby location. Humans are poisoned by the toxin when they eat fish that have ciguatoxin in their system.

The toxin comes from the dinoflagellate *Gambierdiscus toxicus*, which is found in coral reef beds and is apparently related to outbreaks of red tide. Many fish eat from the reef and ingest the toxin. Ciguatoxin accumulates and remains in the flesh. Larger fish that feed on the smaller ones may thus ingest and retain even larger amounts of the poison. The toxin is also cumulative in humans; over a period of time, one can eat many fish containing small amounts of the poison but remain unaffected. At some point, however, enough toxin will accumulate to trigger a reaction.

It's difficult to draw clear lines between safe and potentially unsafe fish. Donald P. de Sylva, Ph.D., Professor of Marine Science in the Division of Biology and Living Resources at the Rosenstiel School of Marine and Atmospheric Science, University of Miami, has specialized in the cause of this disease for many years and has published many papers on the subject. Dr. de Sylva and Mark Poli wrote a paper titled, "Ciguatera—Tropical Fish Poisoning," which was published in *World Record Game Fishes*, 1982 edition (later reprinted by the International Game Fish Association). It suggests avoidance of the barracuda, certain groupers, certain snappers, jacks, tropical mackerels, morays, parrot fish, amberjack, large king mackerel, and hogfish. It notes that the black grouper and yellowfin grouper are much more likely to be toxic than the Nassau and red grouper, which are normally fairly safe. The silk snapper, dog snapper, and some of the fish sold as red snapper are more likely to contain the toxin, it said, but the vermilion snapper and the yellowtail snapper are relatively safe. The paper further states that fish not associated with the coral reefs, such as tuna, wahoo, swordfish, marlin, Spanish mackerel, small king mackerel, and dolphin, should be safe.

Many fish, of course, are not suspect, and no one suggests that we stop eating fish. Freshwater fish, of course, are considered safe. The paper notes that the simple avoidance of large predatory fish from coral reefs in the tropics should alleviate anxiety over the subject. All experts caution, however, that much has yet to be learned. Acquaint yourself with the latest information on this problem before you leave.

The fish-eater's dilemma is complicated by the fact that any one of the unsafe fish may actually be quite safe, depending on the amount of toxin the fish has consumed. Dr. de Sylva's paper notes that it is wise to ask local people whether there has been any significant outbreak of the disease. The paper also advises not to eat fish you cannot identify. Restaurants sometimes purchase fish that is not what it was purported to be. One of the few times we ate out while cruising, my wife and oldest daughter both suffered from this poisoning after eating small portions of a large unidentifiable fish (supposedly a grouper) in a restaurant. Eat only the smaller of the species. We never eat a restaurant fish unless we can see the whole fish and/or know for sure what it is. In a conversation with me, Dr. de Sylva cautioned strongly against eating any barracuda, and said that large older conch were also suspect. He cautioned that what is safe in one area may not be safe in another.

There is now no way to know in advance whether a fish contains ciguatoxin. Caribbean lore suggests interesting but unlikely possible tests. These include the theory that flies, ants, and cats will not eat an affected fish; a silver coin will turn black if cooked with the toxic fish; and toxic barracuda teeth are dark instead of white. Several studies are in progress to develop a "stick test" that will be inexpensive and easy to administer. This would involve a simple procedure to determine whether a particular fish is toxic. As of now, according to Dr. de Sylva and colleague Dr. Donna G. Blythe, none has yet been developed, although this may change any day.

Dr. Blythe practices internal medicine in Miami and specializes in this field. Along with Dr. de Sylva and Susanne Cramer-Castro, she published a paper titled "Ciguatera" in *Miami Medicine* (August 1992). The paper describes symptoms including nausea, vomiting, cramping, abdominal pain, diarrhea, intense itching, joint and muscle pain, tingling of the lips, and burning or pain from cold liquids. Often the sensations of hot and cold will be reversed, and the consumption of alcohol can seriously intensify symptoms. Usually, the first symptoms are noticed within several hours of ingestion, and they can last in one form or another for months to a year or more. A serious case can be debilitating for at least a few months. The paper reports no instances of fatality.

There are no known cures, but Dr. Blythe asserts that the intravenous administration of mannitol, a type of sugar, significantly relieves the symptoms in many cases. This has been substantiated in various studies, she notes. Early treatment is much more likely to be successful.

WHEN NATURE DOESN'T COOPERATE

There will be days when you can't do much except stay below decks and hope the anchor doesn't drag and the sail doesn't blow out. There will be long ocean passages during which all is going well, and simple diversions will make it go even better. And, I have to admit, there are some pretty nifty gadgets that can make cruising better. We might as well take advantage of them.

BOOKS

Books are a main source of entertainment in the cruising community. Take along a good selection of paperbacks, both for you and your children. In most anchorages you'll meet people who are anxious to swap, and many marinas have paperback swap libraries. I suggest paperbacks because humidity can destroy most books eventually. Paperbacks have their problems, but they seem to survive better than hardcover and are much cheaper to replace. And paperbacks are much easier to store. We do have a few hardcover classics as well as the softcover versions. Many cruising kids enjoy classic tales; be sure to bring some along. Take turns reading passages aloud. This is entertaining, helps the child to read and learn, and is a great family experience.

In addition to the highbrow educational and enrichment material, be sure to take books that provide simple entertainment and escapism. Even if you want to watch TV, you hopefully will be too far away for good reception and everyone will need to curl up, from time to time, into a world of fun fantasy. So many cruising children realize for the first time how fun reading is when they are bored. (What, no TV?) Go to a good, well-stocked bookstore and see what is available for kids in your children's age group.

STORYTELLING

And don't forget storytelling. It can be better than the best books. I told a bedtime story almost every night for years, making them up as we went along. They usually related to what we were doing or to past experiences. You can also tell them to each other on long passages and night watches, or simply for evening entertainment.

TOYS

Although space will be limited, a few well-chosen toys are essential for younger kids. Without the constant sensory barrage of TV, your children will probably develop an active imagination. And the right kind of toys can fit right in. In choosing, you must consider your child's interests and aptitude, and this will require some thought. For example, we have seen small children have great fun on the boat and the beaches with earth-moving toys. Shovels and buckets do for most small kids. Floating beach toys like volleyballs and cheap boogie boards provide hours of fun. One doll can be dressed a million different ways. Our dolls were carefully bathed in precious fresh water until we found out and pronounced them forever clean. Our girls, when small, had fun roller-skating around the decks. The wheels were hard rubber and didn't scratch at all. They had to make quite a few detours, but it was fun anyway. With Legos we created fascinating castles and mazes and animals and everything else. This, too, filled hours and hours. It was interesting to see what could withstand rolling. We did have trouble with the small pieces getting lost in small places, and you have to watch anything tiny with small children who may want to put them in their mouth.

MUSICAL INSTRUMENTS

Musical instruments are an obvious help. Teenagers particularly enjoy guitars; social gatherings on the beach provide ample

The music room.

▼

opportunity to play them. The humid and salty environment is not particularly good for guitars and many other instruments, so you may wish to get a low-end instrument. If it is too inexpensive, however, it may not last.

Instructional books take almost no room and can translate into hours of constructive fun. Harmonicas take almost no space and are great for campfires. This may be the opportunity for you to learn to play an instrument you never had time for. Keyboards are great fun on rainy days and in the cockpit. As I'll discuss later, you can interface these with a computer and learn to play the piano while you cruise.

Although it's not a musical instrument, a good AM/FM radio and CD player is indispensable. If you equip your boat with a high-quality inverter (see chapter 13), you'll be able to buy quality AC units at reasonable prices from discount stores. I've had consistent trouble with tape decks, including the best-quality cassette tapes. But our CD players have done well. A hidden benefit of the AM/FM radio is that it enables you to listen to local stations wherever you travel. Not only can this add to your understanding of the society hosting you, it may help you with a foreign language.

(text continued on page 238)

▼

"STAYING IN SHAPE" by Melanie

Pursuing fitness aboard may seem frivolous when you look at the reasons for abandoning life ashore. After all, aren't we trying to get away from the stateside icons who grace the covers of rip-off magazines with their perfect bodies? Yes. But it's important to be in good shape, especially when your physical condition affects how well you can perform various jobs that add to the well-being of your family.

Most of the time, you'll be far away from the convenience of gyms and health clubs. Most exercise machines are out of the question. Also, most boats are too small for popular video workouts that many people do in their living room. Besides, you may not have a TV. This may sound like bad news to the health nut, but in truth it leaves us with more options than it seems. The best part of it is that the options are cheap, relatively easy, a lot more realistic than TV workouts, and, best of all, they are natural things you can do in a natural environment. That's something you just don't get in a house.

First of all, you get exercise just doing things like handling sails and keeping your balance in rough water. But that's not all—look at your boat. There are a million things from which you can hang and swing. And there are things to climb. For example, Dad does pull-ups from our ratlines all the time. I won't get into detail about all the things you can do on deck—just use your imagination. We've seen people do everything from stomach crunches while hanging from the boom of a smaller boat to yoga on the bow pulpit.

Another point to remember is that there is water all around you, and swimming is one of the best exercises you can do. You can combine it with practical jobs like checking the anchor or diving for fish, or you can swim laps around the boat.

Exercising off the boat can be even better. I love to jog on beaches when I get the chance. It's a great way to see the scenery. Frequently, someone will have organized a beach walk at a crowded harbor. The social aspect of this is great; you meet new people and exercise at the same time. But there is something to be said for the serenity of jogging or walking alone on a Bahamian beach in the early morning when nobody else is up. It gives you a chance to reflect, think deep thoughts, and enjoy nature. Also, it may be the only time during the day that you are completely alone.

I know cruisers who join health clubs because they plan to be in one port for a long time. They say they want the professional help of a trainer. This may be good for people with special needs, but often there are experienced trainers, aerobics instructors, physical education teachers, and doctors out cruising. These folks sometimes get together and have aerobics classes on the beach. This is also a good social and physical activity, but I never participate because other people tend to exercise during my school hours. That's why I get up early.

I have an easy daily routine that I do before everyone else gets up. I have a set of 8-pound dumbbells plus smaller ankle weights, which hardly take up any space, and I work out with them for about 15 minutes (as a warm-up and for muscle tone). Then, in about 4 square feet of deck space, I run in place for an hour. I've been doing that for more than two years.

There are plenty of opportunities to exercise onboard.

It's an easy schedule for me to keep because I can do it regardless of the weather and regardless of where we are. I admit, it gets a little boring, but listening to music helps.

Like everything else, safety is a factor. You don't want to jog in a new place early in the morning with no one to hear you if you get in trouble, and you should avoid going out alone in places with the possibility of high crime. Also, most of the time you will be far from doctors, so it's important to take your body into consideration when you plan a workout schedule. Don't engage in any program before reading thoroughly about it, and *don't* push your body beyond its limits.

Good physical condition directly affects your performance in daily jobs around the boat. It can also make you more reliable in a crisis, and of course it improves your appearance. But the most important thing is that the better your health, the longer you will be able to live and keep cruising.

▼

(text continued from page 235)

COMPUTERS

Many cruisers take along a computer. At this point you might be throwing up your hands and saying, "I thought it was supposed to be simple." Well, it is. But a computer can be beneficial to cruising in many ways. Computers can provide creative, constructive playtime. Some of these pursuits can add to cruising safety and convenience.

A computer can entertain kids and grownups for hours. It can play cards with you, play hundreds of other games, help you to write letters to friends, assist in the education of your children, and help you to do shipboard tasks more efficiently and with more pleasure.

Our computer and a program called Miracle taught the girls piano keys and notes. We plugged the included keyboard into the computer, and the instructional feedback actually worked. Our computer also taught our children how to touch-type with the program Type to Learn. It's all fun, and the educational possibilities are endless.

A computer is becoming increasingly useful as a navigational tool, even on small cruising sailboats. Many programs are available, and more are being developed. These range from complete and sophisticated programs, such as The Cap'n, to simple ones that provide tide tables. You can buy programs that have built-in maintenance logs and storage record features, celestial navigation tables and formulas, and interface capability with GPS and loran. Soon we may be getting all of our charts on disks or CD-ROM. Most of these applications are far too expensive for the typical cruiser at this writing. But as time goes on, the cost will come down and you may actually save money using these programs.

It is possible to interface a powerful personal computer (PC) with sensors and have the computer do all the calculations—you can dispense with individual black boxes for each application, including the radar, depthfinder, and GPS. Sonar and sounder manufacturers are developing a concept for interfacing a PC with a sonar-sounder so you can see underwater as you travel. You buy the program and the sounder, but your PC includes most of the hardware you'll need. At this writing, dedicated units already do this, but without the performance that we will soon enjoy with the capabilities of a PC.

As mentioned in chapter 6, a modem and special computer programs can bring in weatherfaxes and other shoreside transmissions via a single-sideband receiver. At present, you can use your computer to communicate to shoreside bases via SSB, satellites, and cellular phone. Prices are high at this writing, but the technology is booming. Services will expand and the cost will deflate within a few years. I have little difficulty faxing via cellular phone when I am in range of towers along the East Coast.

Any thorough discussion of programs would be outdated before this book leaves my computer. Suffice it to say that a program with general word-processing and database applications is a must. After 17 years (and counting) of living aboard and storing parts and odds and ends, I can't begin to remember everything. But I can ask the computer where the shaft keys for the RPBC Sherwood brass pumps are located and it will tell me, as well as the number that I have remaining, the part number, and a source and price should I need more. My computer has saved me untold grief. As I mentioned in earlier discussions, you have to remember to tell the computer every time you add or delete a part in some musty corner of the bilge, but that isn't hard to do.

On-line Internet programs and capabilities may be irrelevant to you as a cruiser—you need to be plugged into telephone lines to use them. CD-ROM disks are self-contained and include large amounts of data; there's no need to plug in.

The type of computer you bring along will depend on your budget, your electrical system, and the space aboard your boat. I bought a relatively inexpensive desktop PC built for use in a house. We run it with an inverter (for power issues, see chapter 13). If you have the space, buy a desktop rather than a more expensive laptop. You'll probably save enough bucks over a comparable laptop to pay for the inverter.

When I first purchased a computer, I was told that I should not take it anywhere near the sea. If I lived close to the ocean, I should expect early and serious problems. I smiled and took it home to the boat. Over the years I haven't noticed many difficulties with computers and my salty environment. In my experience, standard laptops and desktops survive if treated reasonably well. Besides, computers designed specifically for use aboard boats are extremely expensive. As I mentioned above, there's no need to spend megabucks on a water-resistant or marine grade computer.

Motion as well as dampness can cause problems, however. Be sure to strap them in and cover them when not in use.

I strongly recommend that you bring along a good computer diagnostic and repair program like Norton Utilities. You usually can't send the computer back to the manufacturer or dealer, and you certainly can't "take it in" when problems arise. Our Norton program has paid for itself many times over. Incidentally, my computer is an IBM clone, and I have therefore been able to readily find and replace components. Keep this in mind when you shop.

TELEVISIONS AND VIDEO PLAYERS

Heresy though it may seem to some, the videotape is very popular in the cruising community. TV sets and video players, either 12-volt or AC-powered, come in sizes that will accommodate most space restrictions on a cruising boat. If you have a quality inverter aboard, you can buy AC units at discount stores for much less than the 12-volt types available in automotive and boating stores. Movie swapping is common in many popular anchorages, and limited movie rentals can be found in the most out-of-the-way places. Having your own video library enables you to determine what your kids watch and what they learn. It beats unlimited TV and cable options shoreside. We sometimes have movie nights, with pizza and popcorn. You can use this medium to support your parenting, not to replace it. Some of our kids' favorite videos were taken with our camcorder. Unfortunately, camcorders don't do well in a salty environment unless they are water-resistant.

Of course, you are stuck with that TV when you aren't watching a video. TV actually serves our cruising lifestyle well in two ways: First, it's our poor man's weatherfax. Whenever we are within range of a coast, we can get weather forecasts (hopefully with maps that at least show systems moving up the beaches) that give us an idea of what's ahead (occasionally we find a good weatherman). Second, whenever we sail back into the States from the islands, we need only watch a bit of TV to become more convinced than ever that it's a place to visit—and for a short time.

TAKE ADVANTAGE OF WHAT'S AROUND YOU

Be prepared to take advantage of things around you. Use your imagination. Once our kids built a snowman from heavy frost on the deck after a cold night anchored in the Little River in South Carolina. When we used an inflatable as our main dinghy and stored it upside down on the bow, I would scoop up buckets of water while we were at sea, pour them onto the sloping bottom of the inflatable, and give the girls a squealingly delightful time on a water slide. We also purchased an inexpensive, small, inflatable backyard wading pool. We blew it up on the bow. It didn't fit well, but it held a little water and made a great splashing pool for our toddlers as we sailed along. Let your kids try to open a coconut some time, if you really want to keep them amused for awhile. Open one first so they know how good it will be if they are successful. (Be careful that they don't use any dangerous tools—you may need to help with that part.) You'll be amazed at the fun you can have with what nature and your new environment has to offer.

BOATS AND BOOZE

Unfortunately, a negative note is necessary in this discussion of cruising pastimes. We have noticed that many people have come

(text continued on page 244)

"NOTHING TO DO?" by Carolyn

I was once talking with a kid who had crossed the Atlantic Ocean a few times. He had spent many days with only himself, his parents, and a blue expanse of water for company. He was extremely creative, and I don't think he ever ran out of things to do. When he ran out of the standard distractions, he created a few of his own. One time in the short period I knew him, he was bending the points on a plastic fork. Curious, I asked him what on earth was he doing. He explained that if you were to put this fork on the ground, no matter how it was lying, at least one of the four points would stick up in the air—just waiting to be stepped on. I'm pretty sure he came up with this out on the Atlantic, somewhere between England and the Bahamas. He was joking, of course, and no, he wasn't an antisocial person and never did anything like this; but I thought it was sort of neat as an example of what you can do with your surroundings, no matter how boring it may seem to some people.

Cruising is all about traveling around with fellow boaters and seeing new and exciting places, and meeting all sorts of people. But there are times when you have to enjoy your own company, and you have to be creative.

Let me just say that you don't have to turn forks into cactuses to entertain yourself on a boat. There are, of course, many other alternatives to explore. To start with, probably the most convenient, and in my opinion the most enjoyable, pastime is reading. I've always loved to read, and I think it's because I was turned on to reading at an early age. The good thing about books is that they don't take up much space, which is one thing that, as we all know, can be scarce. Books are easy to find even if there's no store nearby; they're a common trade item among cruisers.

Another thing I enjoy is music. I play the guitar. It's something that I just recently picked up, and I'm finding that it provides me with many enjoyable challenges when I might otherwise be bored. Obviously, it's nearly impossible to bring a piano along on a cruise, but a keyboard is another matter. A keyboard may not quite live up to a real piano, but keyboards are portable and take up a relatively small amount of space. If you play the piano, I would recommend having a keyboard on the boat. I've run into more than one pianist who didn't bring one along, and they've really regretted it. As for listening to music, it's a good idea to have a high-quality sound system and lots of CDs.

Artistic people have an advantage on boats, I think, because hobbies such as painting, drawing, and jewelry making are all things that are easy to

▼

take with you almost anywhere. I'm artistic, and my sister is too. I've noticed that many of our fellow cruising friends are artistic as well, simply because living the lifestyle encourages creativity. I'm sure it has something to do with the fact that you get to see so many down-to-earth places and meet all sorts of unique people. Also, it seems that being out on the ocean makes us feel closer to life, possibly because we all originated here. Maybe we are all destined to go back one of these days.

Sports can be a problem on boats. You can't exactly play something like football or soccer on deck. That might be just a bit inconvenient. Actually, though, when my sister and I were a lot younger we used to roller-skate all around the deck. Anyway, even though sports are a problem, if you get to places with a lot of other boats you can usually find enough people to get a game going. For all you volleyball players, this seems to be a really popular choice among cruisers. I play it a lot. Obviously, we really love watersports. Kneeboarding behind a dinghy, boogie boarding on the beach, surfing, windsurfing, snorkeling, diving for fish and conch, and just plain swimming are all easy to do. Just jump in!

Of course, when all else fails there are responsibilities such as keeping the boat functioning and looking nice. My sister is passionate about keeping *Chez Nous* clean, and I work at it a lot myself, too. For all you people out there who are worried about keeping fit while on board, I've heard that scrubbing algae off the bottom of boats and polishing stainless steel and brass can burn a huge amount of calories. . . .

You might be wondering by now how on earth school fits into such a busy lifestyle. For me school is the first priority. It's easy to slack off on it because you don't usually have somebody hovering over you insisting that you get it done. That's where self-discipline comes in. If you put your schoolwork off because you don't really feel like doing it at the moment, you're forming a bad habit that will catch up with you. Setting a schedule and keeping up with it is a necessity. However, there are going to be times, such as on rough traveling days, where it's impossible to do schoolwork. Because of this, it's a good idea to get ahead if you can and have the time.

My advice for being on a boat is this: Don't let yourself get bored. It just isn't necessary. I've talked to some people who say that the only thing to do other than schoolwork is eat. Hey, it's not that bad! You just have to accept the fact that there are going to be times when you need to make the best of being yourself. Whatever you do, be creative.

▼

(text continued from page 241)
to associate boating with extra drinking because their boating occurs on the weekend or at vacation time. It's far from my intention to imply that the judiciously used cocktail hour is anything but great. But it needs to be said that those who maintain a weekend level of drinking on a daily basis while cruising generally find that they have the same problems (often much worse) that they would have with everyday party drinking ashore. And we have seen more than one cruise come tragically to an end because of this pattern. It just doesn't work.

A cruiser is never really off duty. When you're in a house, you can usually go to sleep at night unconcerned about whether a squall will blow through, whether the tide change will pull out your anchor or your neighbor's, or whether something odd will happen in the bilge. And in the home, if something bad like a plumbing leak occurs, you can call a plumber. A million things can happen any time that may demand your careful attention. If your brain is polluted, a simple problem may become a very serious— even fatal—problem.

We were once anchored near remote islands with an acquaintance who was new to cruising and a little bored. He and a friend got into a dinghy one fine day and headed to a nearby settlement to get some fuel and groceries. They also got a bottle of rum and celebrated all the way back. By late afternoon they had passed out aboard their boats. Should one of them have fallen overboard on their wild dinghy ride, there would have been no Coast Guard or anyone else nearby to help them. After they passed out, I noticed water in my aft stateroom. A coupling for the exhaust hose for my generator had begun to leak. The problem had to be fixed immediately as a matter of safety. I wondered what would have happened if this had occurred on one of the boats with unconscious skippers aboard.

They say, "God looks after fools and drunks." But He doesn't always. During one party in the islands, a couple had far too much to drink. They dinghied back to their boat, and the husband climbed aboard. His wife had passed out. He couldn't get her out of the dinghy and into the boat by himself, so he left her to sleep it off. Later in the night she awoke and tried to get aboard. She rolled into the sea and drowned. End of the party; end of the cruise.

On a similar occasion, a different couple both made it back

aboard. He had to relieve himself over the side after she went to sleep. He didn't hang on. She found him in the morning, his body entangled in the line to the tender peacefully bobbing astern.

We have seen tenders flip in high seas, pile up on rocks at high speeds, crash into anchored boats, catch under stretched anchor lines injuring and ejecting occupants, and much more—all because the occupants thought that drunken driving didn't matter at sea. Being on a boat is not an excuse for more drinking; it is a reason for less.

Chapter Twenty
SELF-RELIANCE: YOUR GREATEST ASSET

Once you begin cruising, you have to forget your daily walk through the Yellow Pages and trips to town. Unless you are wealthy, extreme self-reliance is your only hope of financial survival. It may be your only hope of survival in every sense, because things tend to break when there is no one else around to fix them, even if you do have the dollars to burn. Self-reliance can save you considerable money.

Our shorebound friends think they are self-reliant when they replace a washer in a leaky faucet after a quick trip to the hardware store. As a cruiser, you'll not only need to have the washer aboard, you'll need a spare screw to replace the one that you discover has disintegrated as you replace the washer. If the faucet handle is stuck on the valve stem (a common occurrence in a saltwater environment), you'll need another handle when the old one breaks as you try to wrestle it off. If the valve stem is corroded within its seat, you'll need to know how to coax it out. And if the whole job turns into a disaster, there won't be a hotel to stay at or a relative to spend the night with until a plumber arrives. And that leaky faucet will pale to insignificance if you can't fix the pump that gets the water from the tank up to the sink. I've met "cruisers" who didn't know that this pump is turned on and off automatically by an in-line pressure switch. These switches frequently fail because they are designed for weekend use. I know people who have spent hours trying to fix the pump and then spent hundreds of dollars to have a new one shipped in; all they had to do was replace the pressure switch—a 15-minute job. A spare pressure switch costs a few bucks in the States. The Saturday-morning Mr. Home Fix-it Show on TV has little to do with self-reliance on a cruising boat.

FIX IT YOURSELF

When your diesel breaks, you can respond to it one of two ways. The weekend boater's way is to take the boat to a marina repair yard. The mechanic will cost a fortune. To pay him, you'll have to go out and earn what he charges per hour, plus roughly one-third more, depending on your tax rate. While the mechanic is fixing your engine, he's probably sitting on your alternator, stepping on the exhaust manifold, and kneeling on the remote voltage regulator. You'll figure out that he did this soon in some cases, months or years down the line in others. When the alternator rattles off as you start the engine, he will tell you that he noticed that the bracket had a stress crack in it and that you are very lucky that the problem occurred while you were still in the marina. And, of course, he can take care of it for you. When the exhaust manifold begins to leak coolant into the exhaust ports, you will marvel at your bad luck.

Or . . . you can fix it yourself. You won't have to earn enough to pay the mechanic's wage plus taxes. You'll be familiar with the layout of your engine space and will have intense interest in doing the job well. Before we go further, let me stress, as you probably already know, that there are many good and caring diesel mechanics out there, and many good yards. The trick is to find them and to use them only when you really need to. If you're well prepared, you won't need to very often.

PRACTICE FIXING THINGS BEFORE YOU TAKE OFF

Long before you take off, begin making all the repairs you possibly can. Don't call a mechanic or yard for anything if you can help it. If

"THE DIAGNOSIS WAS EASY"

We were motoring along a beautiful section of the Georgia ICW route. One of the things we like most about this area is its seclusion. Its marsh grass, clumps of trees, and salt air are aspects we're particularly fond of.

I opened the engine hatch, as is my custom, for a regular inspection. It was covered with a reddish black stain, and water was slinging upward and around from the front end of the engine.

The diagnosis was easy. The freshwater-coolant recirculating pump was leaking. When this happens, I know that a worn bearing has probably caused a seal to fail. It is an inevitable breakdown from extended wear on the pump—whether on a gas or diesel engine. To fix it, you can remove the old one and install a new or rebuilt one. The alternative, pressing out the bearings and seal, typically requires special shop tools and is impractical on a typical cruising boat. I had a spare pump. We anchored just out of the channel. In about an hour and a half we were on our way. We did have to shave off the side of one bolt head because of an unusual clearance problem, but this was a piece of cake with our Dremel tool. Later, while waiting out weather in Florida, I got another spare water pump for $90.

A year or so later, I learned of a boat that had a similar engine and had experienced the same problem, also in a remote area. The owner had no spare pump, no Dremel tool, and little understanding of the problem. He had to call for a tow to a marina, pay the marina, pay a mechanic, and have the pump shipped in from Savannah for an exorbitant price. His total cost: $850 and four cruising days lost.

▼

you mess up, you'll have access to professionals to straighten you out. If you mess up at sea, the situation will be different. While you're fixing things, you'll have the secondary benefit of learning what other special tools your boat or systems may need.

Let me repeat some of what I said early in this book: try to donate one or more cruising vacations to repairing major systems and doing maintenance work. But don't just do it at the yard. Be a masochist. Do it out at anchor with the entire family aboard and involved. It is important that all of you have some idea of what this is like before you leave, because it will happen to you after you leave.

Prior to taking off, you'll have time to make systems changes, move systems, or even build cabinetry—changes that will make life aboard much better for you once you're underway. For example, if your engine is under the galley sink, as some are, you may wish to rearrange things in the galley so that food can be prepared while you are pulling the exhaust manifold. This is much easier and cheaper to do before you leave.

If, as is quite likely, you are installing new equipment, try to do it yourself. This will teach you a lot about how to fix it when it breaks. Talk to the manufacturer about the installation and start-up as you go. If the manufacturer doesn't offer this opportunity, buy another brand. Always remember that you *will* have to fix it and you *will* have to fix everything around it. Don't install any new system in a manner that unduly interferes with access to any other system. I had a friend who did a beautiful job mounting a refrigeration compressor over his raw-water cooling pump. When he eventually needed to change the impeller in that pump, he had to bleed the Freon, remove the compressor, and recharge the refrigeration (a job that now requires an EPA-certified technician).

If you do have to call someone in, insist that you be present to watch to learn. Some yards have cute signs saying that they charge extra if the owner helps. Often these people have no idea what it is like to be at sea with no help. Perhaps they've had bad experiences with know-it-all owners who caused innumerable problems. But you can watch without getting in their way. If you ask around, you can usually find a good yard with good people who do understand.

PREPARE FOR YOUR NEW JOB

Start out by getting complete rebuild manuals for all mechanical parts on your boat. Before you buy something, check to be sure that a shop manual is available, and perhaps insist that it comes as part of the deal. If the manufacturer is not helpful, and some are not, don't buy the product. Many manufacturers offer complete rebuild instructions. For example, most good freshwater-system pumps and marine heads come with these. Before you buy, study the manual and the component to determine whether field repairs

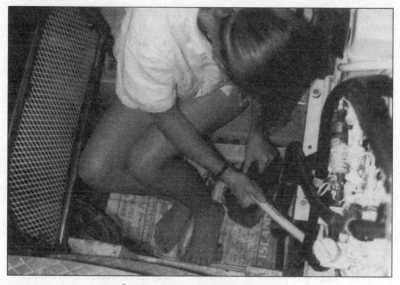

Carolyn changing the generator's oil.

▼

will be reasonably feasible. What do you have to do to get to the innards of the component? I have seen boxed watermakers that require an hour or more of work to tighten a few hose clamps.

Consider getting training in diesel mechanics and possibly other fields such as refrigeration. This training could be invaluable when your diesel breaks, and may enable you to earn some money along the way. Be aware that many diesel courses are so basic that they're of no help unless you know nothing about diesels at all. If you have a general understanding of diesel operation and are already changing your raw-water impellers and bleeding your engine, you may need an advanced course. Some courses offer lectures and diagrams only; look for ones that offer hands-on experience. Investigate the course thoroughly before you invest the time and money.

Canvas and sail repair are particularly expensive, yet it is easy to do yourself if you spend a little time learning and have the right equipment. Dodgers and Biminis can be repaired or replaced without assistance, especially once you have the original pattern made.

▼

We purchased a large Brother industrial sewing machine, available through Sailrite, and it has paid for itself many times over.

Interior decorating and cabinetry are popular do-it-yourself items. The job may not look as professional as you would wish, but the savings can be huge. Besides, a few crooked seams or rough edges won't impair the integrity of your boat.

INVEST IN TOOLS

Invest wisely in good tools and learn how to use them. I've always felt that good tools are worth more than money in the bank. Attractively packaged kits may offer some value, but study them carefully before you sink a fortune into them. Often, they are overpriced and understocked. I make my own selection of tools I know I need.

Some tools are indispensable, and here's what I recommend, as a bare minimum:

- As large a bench vise as you can accommodate. I don't have room to permanently mount mine, but I keep it stored and then bolt it to a 2-by-10 board that I place across the cockpit when I need it. (This board also makes a good gangplank.)
- A good Dremel tool with a flexible shaft and many cutters. I've repeatedly made repairs I could not have made without mine.
- A large selection of wrenches and socket wrenches, including metric ones. Get whatever size is needed to fit the main wheel bolt on the front side of the engine and the two parts of your stuffing box.
- Several very long screwdrivers, both Phillips head and straightedge. Also get an impact screwdriver with both Phillips and straightedge points.
- A magnet on a collapsible wand. Keep this near the engine. Place another heavy-duty magnet elsewhere (not near the compass).
- A set of tools to extract bolts that have broken off is a must, although these often don't do the job. When they do, though, they are worth it. They are called by different names, such as EZ Out, and are found in most good hardware stores.
- A heavy-duty hammer or maul, and a soft hammer. These will serve different purposes.

- A good crowbar. I once moved a 15 kW diesel generator, single-handed, across a deck with nothing but a maul and a crowbar and patient tapping.
- Heavy-duty wire cutters for your rigging, and smaller wire cutters and crimpers for electrical work.
- A mirror that swivels on the end of a collapsible wand is indispensable for looking under or around the engine to see what is going on or what the job will be like.
- Two of those grabbers with claws on the end for retrieving small parts dropped into the bilge and other impossible crevices. The first grabber is to go after the part, the second is to retrieve the first grabber after you drop it in the crevice.
- A heat gun. This speeds drying (don't overdo it or some resin and glues will dry brittle), helps to loosen some sealants, helps to loosen hose ends for tight installations or removals, and much more. A hair dryer will perform some tasks like these, but not nearly as well. You'll need a generator or shore power to run a heat gun. Inverters, as a rule, don't do well with that much load.
- Gasket-making material in tubes. Any good autoparts store, such as Pep Boys or NAPA, will have a wide selection. Get several tubes for different applications. Buy good brands, but not too many—their shelf life is limited. Be sure to have liquid gasket material for extra-high heat and for use in gasoline and lube oil.
- Solvent. You'll need this to clean the carburetors (as in your outboard). I prefer Gunk, which comes in a can with a parts basket. This is becoming hard to find in small quantities, but is better, I believe, than spray-on solvents when you really need to dissolve varnish and gum deposits in the carburetor jets.
- Thread-repair material. This epoxy-like product isn't as good as coil inserts (get these if you have the equipment to use them), but can get you through in a pinch when you strip out a bolt hole.
- Specialty tools such as C-clip pliers.
- At least two ice picks for innumerable jobs.
- A portable drill press for your electric drill.
- A large tap and die set (expensive, but it will probably pay for itself the first time you use it out in the boondocks).

- A set of metal punches.
- Extensions and adapters for your socket wrenches.
- A large assortment of stainless nuts, bolts, washers, and screws.
- An assortment of stainless cotter pins.
- An oil-filter wrench.
- A cooking thermometer to check the coolant temperature if your gauge is failing.
- A good-quality digital multimeter.
- A flashlight with a long, flexible fiber-optic extension. The usual assortment of pliers, screwdrivers, Vice-grips, and adjustable wrenches.

If you do all your own maintenance, you'll acquire all sorts of specialty tools that you wouldn't be without. For example, two small shark hooks—one slightly straightened—are among my most used tools; they come in handy for lots of things.

FLASHLIGHTS

Flashlights are invaluable on a boat. Without good flashlights you won't be able to make most of the repairs you need to make, because things love to break at night. The things that break in daylight are usually the ones that live in dark corners where the light never shines—except the flashlight. When you need to fix something, you want to see it clearly, not with a flickering beam.

You'll use flashlights regularly to find things, even in daylight, because most of your stuff will be stored in dark holes and corners.

Flashlights are emergency equipment. On *Chez Nous* we keep them everywhere so we don't have to rummage when something important happens. And don't waste money on cheap lights. I have been let down by so many flashlights that I've begun to believe that candlepower ratings refer to the number of times I will need to light a candle when the thing doesn't work.

I prefer sealed underwater lights not only because I may need to use them underwater, but because I know they will probably last much longer. Pelican makes these to such high standards that their lights include special catalyst pellets. According to Pelican, these "help absorb hydrogen gas that could possibly be emitted by defective, leaking, reversed polarity, or heavily discharged batteries." Pelican warns that, particularly with any sealed light, it is extremely important to always check batteries to ensure that they are properly installed and in good condition.

I buy flashlights that cushion and securely anchor batteries in place, that can be serviced in the field, that have as few circuit breaks as possible, and that allow little or no movement at make/break contact points. I avoid side slide switches and prefer lights in which you turn the head to make contact—these have no switches to go bad. I also like the ones with a separate switch that clicks on and off. I've given them the generic name click switches, although there are many types, some good and some bad. I get flashlights that are shaped so that they won't roll. I look for lifetime guarantees, although these are worthless at sea.

Good flashlights usually cost more, but the expense is worth it when you need to see in the dark. My overall favorites among double D/C-cell flashlights and 6-volt handheld spotlights are Pelican lights. They are expensive but reliable. My second choice among double D/C-cell flashlights is the far less expensive Ray-O-Vac Roughneck. I use these in my engine space and drop them repeatedly, mostly in the bilge (as I do everything else), and they keep on working. My second choice among handheld 6-volt spotlights is the Garrity Tuff Lite, which uses four D cells (easy to obtain and store) and is well anchored in a removable battery tray. It also is much less expensive than the Pelican.

I also find a trouble, or drop, light indispensable. Get a good-quality set with wire that won't easily kink and that has an AC plug inlet. (We recommend AC power, as discussed in chapter 13.) It should be rated to take at least a 75-watt bulb. You will need a lot of light. Be sure to buy the extra-tough lightbulbs made for these lights. These can be found at most good hardware stores. They are expensive, but regular bulbs simply won't take the shock of typical engine-space use.

INVEST IN PARTS

There is an old saying that the parts for which you buy spares will be the least likely to break. That isn't a reason not to buy spares; it's a reason to buy as many as possible. A list of spares could go on forever, limited only by storage space and money with which to buy them. I can only scratch the surface, but here are a few scratches chosen according to the likelihood of failure and the amount of warning you are likely to get.

For your diesel have at least several spare belts, a spare oil cooler (change it at least every three years if it is raw-water cooled), spare injectors, either a set of injector high-pressure pipes or one pipe that is long enough and can be bent to replace any pipe (and a pipe-bending tool to bend it without any crimps), a fuel lift pump, a raw-water pump with at least three additional impellers, a freshwater circulating pump, an alternator, alternator adjusting brackets (get some from any old junkyard), a starter or starter solenoid with spare brushes and bearings, hose-mending material and a set of spare hose lengths, Aeroquip or similar pressure hose with an assortment of fittings and the tools necessary to install them on the hose (the hose would normally be used for lubricating-oil or transmission-oil runs but should be rated for the highest pressure used in your boat so that you can make up whatever you need), a shaft-key stock, and anything else you can afford.

Talk to a good mechanic who specializes in your type of engine and let him or her give you advice about what you might need. Bring at least six elements for each of your fuel filters. If you take on bad fuel you may have to change these every hour or so before getting to shore. Also bring many oil filters and enough oil for several changes. The cost of these items can be double or more in the islands than stateside. Although you won't wish to pull the head gasket unless it's really necessary, have a spare head and the entire "top end" set. Bring lots of gaskets for your raw-water pump. You'll need one every time you change the impeller. If you have to make gaskets from liquid gasket material, you may need to let it harden before starting the engine again. Preformed gaskets are cheap and easier and quicker to use.

Have a spare pump to supply water from your freshwater tank, as well as parts kits for this item. Carry a spare automatic bilge pump and be able to rebuild all of your bilge pumps. You should have at least three—all heavy-duty—and at least one run by electricity so that it can keep up with a serious leak for awhile should you be off the boat.

Have sufficient parts to completely rebuild your head at least twice. Parts that break most on the typical cylinder pump head are the yoke—which connects the handle to the pump piston—valves, the connection between the piston shaft and the piston, and seals for the piston shaft. If yours is a diaphragm head, carry a spare diaphragm and valves. If you have an electric head, be ready for more trouble. Whatever head you have, consult the manufacturer about the parts you're most likely to need. Anything that takes stress or a lot of wear is suspect.

Be prepared to fix your steering cable and steering system. The same goes for the anchor windlass. Extra pulleys and blocks can save the day not only in engine-room matters but also with the sailing rig. Sailcloth and sail tape are indispensable for sails repair and other uses. Carry at least three rolls of good-quality duct tape. This is probably used for more emergency repairs than you could possibly imagine. Have a spool of waxed twine to fit your stuffing box. If you hit something in the water and bend a blade on your prop, or if your engine becomes misaligned and you are unable to fix it right away, or if your stuffing box or shaft wears, you may need to restuff it a lot until you can make a repair. These can normally be stuffed rather easily with the boat in the water. Learn how to do this on your boat. We carry a spare propeller (and prop puller), shaft, and cutless bearing. Spare lightbulbs for all applications, especially the anchor light and running lights, will be needed sooner than you think.

BRING RAW MATERIALS

Often the part that breaks is something for which you did not or could not bring a spare. When this occurs, the ability to make do with some sort of fabrication may save the day. I keep on hand several pieces of mild and stainless steel bolt stock, flat pieces of mild steel that I buy from the hardware store as large hinges, assorted pieces of aluminum flat stock, and whatever pieces of wood I can fit into whatever corners I can find. Bring along an old inner tube. They are free in just about any tire-changing shop. With them you can cut gaskets and repair valves (as in water pumps) and leaking hoses. You can work aluminum almost as easily as wood, and make all sorts of brackets, covers, etc., from it. We also bring a large supply of J-B Weld, which makes great repairs to metal and wood. You can find it in most autoparts stores. It claims to consist of metal and epoxy. Whatever it is, it works so well that we now often use it instead of the old reliable Marine-Tex that we have loved for so long. Remember, however, that anything not specifically designed for the job may not work well for long. Always watch any jury-rigged repair and fix it with the right parts as soon as possible.

I carry lots of epoxy and fiberglass. Be sure that any epoxy or similar material you use has not exceeded its shelf life. If it has been opened and is old, you will probably need to replace it. I regularly renew our supply of underwater epoxy and hull-repair kits. These can save your cruise, not to mention your boat. They may also prove helpful in other repairs, to water and fuel tanks (temporary only), for example. I also carry a sheet of thin scrap plywood (⅛ inch) and a large supply of sealant that will cure underwater. I use Life Calk for this. If your boat is seriously holed, you may be able to effect a relatively secure temporary repair by cutting the plywood to form, smearing it with sealant where it will mate with the good part of the hull, and screwing it on underwater or with the boat healed or temporarily dried. We have seen this done underwater simply with mask, flippers, and snorkel. Thread the screws through the plywood before you take it underwater. Have a helper hold it in place until you get enough screws in. The Life Calk should hold it fairly well against the hull if the hole isn't in an area of great curvature, but align the sheet carefully before you press it against the hull. Resetting the sealant doesn't work well. Obviously, the hard part is to get the screws going into the glass. Tapping them with a hammer helps, as does just plain muscle. Use a lot.

FOOD AND PROVISIONING,
by Tom and Mel

Self-reliance with respect to food supply adds immeasurably to your range of travel and freedom. It also saves a lot of dollars. Becoming self-reliant may involve changing your eating habits. You will be somewhat limited to foods that you can store, catch, or grow and that are, incidentally, probably much more healthy than what you ate in the past. If you plan to continue your stateside custom of visiting a grocery mart at least several times a week, you'll find yourself on a short and expensive leash when outside the United States.

Obviously, food provisioning and preparation are more difficult and time-consuming, and far more important, aboard than they were when you lived shoreside. Ashore, people seldom stock up for more than a week, often relying on nearby shops for daily needs. And prepared food items, even entire meals, are a frequent and easy answer. None of this works while cruising. Food preparation is done mostly from scratch, and if you don't have that ingredient you need for the soup, you do without. With the blandness inherent in most readily stored stock, pleasing a family with variety is more difficult when cruising, even if the family has sublimated its fancy cravings. Skillful use of spices, which are easily stored for long periods of time, can spruce up many meals.

You may wish to buy a few cruising cookbooks for ideas about dishes prepared from very basic foods that are nutritional and provide variety. Beware that some of these books are geared to the

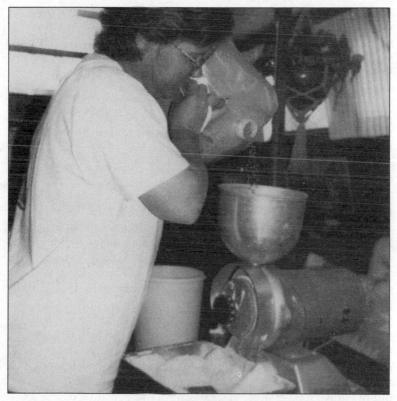

Mel grinding wheat into flour.

charter cruiser who is only out for a week and who has a huge supply of grocery-store specialties aboard. Mel has compiled a few of our *Chez Nous* cruising recipes in Appendix A.

We grow whatever we can aboard, including sprouts and herbs. We also have a grain grinder that works either with muscle power or with an electric motor. It grinds the grain between two stones. We carry approximately 100 pounds of wheat and large amounts of beans and other grains such as sesame and sunflower seeds, rye, corn, and rolled oats (for oatmeal). Wheat will keep much longer than flour. We make our bread from the grain we grind; this not only saves money, but it also means we often have bread when no one else can get any. We make granola from our store of grains and dried fruits. This provides a great breakfast cereal very inexpensively. We use only powdered milk. It is fat free, keeps for a long time, and is inexpensive. We make yogurt regularly (see "Yogurt" among the recipes in Appendix A).

Our primary meat is fish caught either by diving or trolling. We buy fresh, locally grown vegetables inexpensively whenever possible. This may mean a salad of cabbage instead of lettuce, but consider the view. And we usually have around nine to 12 months basic food supply aboard. This gives us freedom and cuts costs.

PRACTICE

The key to learning how to provision your cruising boat for a long trip is to practice before you take off. You cannot know how much flour to stock unless you have been using it to bake bread for your family; you cannot know how much powdered milk to get if you buy fresh milk at your corner convenience store daily.

If you study the guides to the area you will be cruising, you should get some idea about the types of foods available locally and their cost. Try to feed your family for a while using only those items that will be available once you're cruising, and those that you can stock in cans or bottles, dried, vacuum-packed, or however you will be able to store them on the boat. With some practice cooking this way, you should be able to determine which foods your family likes and which it doesn't. Then start to keep a record of how much food (staples and favorites) you consume over a set period of time, say, two weeks. Then multiply these figures by the amount of time that will lapse before you can conveniently reprovision. The result will provide you with the amounts you need

(text continued on page 264)

"SAMPLE PROVISIONING LIST"
by Mel

The amounts listed here will vary according to storage space, length and geographical area of your cruise, number of crew, and personal tastes.

I usually stock up in major grocery stores on the East Coast, supplementing with items from health food stores and catalogs. If you buy from any of the large wholesale chain stores, make sure that the size of the packaging is appropriate for your storage space and that you are buying name brands your crew likes.

I stock for a long cruise in the general order given below.

CANNED GOODS

Meals in a can (for emergencies only, not as a steady diet)
Stew
Prepared spaghetti sauce
Prepared chili
Chow mein and noodles
Full-bodied soups (or dried Ramen with a can of meat added)

Beans
Whole beans (black turtle, small red, kidney, pinto, chickpeas) cooked
    without spices for adding to recipes
Prepared beans for special purposes (refried beans, baked beans)

Tomato products
Paste
Stewed slices
Whole
Sauce (or crushed or pureed)

Vegetables (some bottled products are good)
Mixed (for quick soups, stews, and pies)
Mushrooms
Ripe olives
Special items (Chinese vegetables, three-bean salad, etc.)
The usual that your family likes (peas, corn, spinach, green beans,
    asparagus, potatoes); check salt content

Fruit (unsweetened; some bottled types are good)
Apple (sauce and slices)
Pineapple (crushed, tidbits, and slices)
Mandarin oranges
Pears, peaches, mixed
Pie fillings

Dairy
Evaporated milk (to supplement powdered milk, not to replace it)
Sweetened condensed
Long-life milk in cartons (if space allows)
Canned cream (not usually available in the States)
Canned butter (not usually available in the States)

Meats (check salt and fat content and buy name brands; some people
  can meat before long cruises)
Tuna fish and salmon
Chicken and turkey
Ham and beef
Tinned meats (sardines, smoked oysters and clams, kippered snacks,
  spreads, sausage); these are not for a steady diet
Special seafood (shrimp, crabmeat, minced clams)

DRIED FOODS
Prepared cereal (as concentrated as possible; only a few boxes for
  passages that are too rough for cooking)
Powdered milk, non-fat (1-quart envelopes packed in Ziploc bags are
  easier to store than large boxes)
Egg substitute
Yogurt culture (try to keep it going so you don't have to rely on
  buying this expensive item repeatedly)
Yeast, baking powder, baking soda
Dried vegetables (mushrooms, peppers, tomatoes, onions, mixed,
  etc.); try them out first
Dried fruits (pineapple, apple, peaches and apricots, banana, prunes,
  raisins, dates, etc.)
Dry soup mixes (Ramen, noodle, starters, onion)
Dry beans (split peas, lentils, black turtle, kidney, pinto, garbanzo, navy,
  soup mixtures, etc.)
Pasta (spaghetti, lasagna, elbows and twists, linguine and fettuccine)

Special mixes
Pancake (complete)
Bisquick
Cornbread and muffin
Rice and bean mixtures
Veggie burger
Others (tabouli, falafel, pilaf, macaroni and cheese—the universal kids'
  favorite "prepare it yourself" meal)
Prepared special sauce mixes (lemon dill for seafood, Hollandaise,
  chili, dips, prepared salad dressing mixes)
Sweeteners (white sugar, brown sugar, artificial, confectioners' sugar)
Dessert mixes (cakes, brownies, icing mixes)
Nuts (walnut, pecans, peanuts, raw shelled sunflower, sesame seeds,
  etc.)
Snacks and treats (popcorn, granola bars, candy bars, trail mix, gum,
  candy)
Sprouting seeds (alfalfa, mung beans, salad mixtures)

Grains (check for any signs of insect or rodent infestation and do
  not purchase it if there is any)
Rice (long-grain brown rice for basic cooking, specialty rices)
Oats (flaked or rolled for cooking for breakfast and for granola)
Wheat (whole berries for grinding into flour for bread and other
  baked products—I usually get spring wheat, 100 lbs. at a time,
  cracked or flaked for breakfast cereal, flaked for granola mix)
Others (try them in small amounts first)
Flour (unbleached white, cornmeal, rye, whole wheat—if you do not
  grind it)

SEASONINGS
Salt and pepper
Seafood seasoning (Old Bay)
Vanilla and other extracts
Special sauces (Crystal or other hot sauce, soy, steak, marinades)
Bouillon cubes and vegetable seasonings
Herbs and spices (make your own list; this is a partial list of mine—
  cinnamon, nutmeg, pumpkin pie spice, chili powder, basil, oregano,
  sage, parsley, cilantro, rosemary, thyme, dill, marjoram, coriander,
  cumin, paprika, cayenne pepper)

CONDIMENTS
Mustard, ketchup, relish
Mayonnaise
Salsa
Salad dressings
Olives (green and ripe), capers, pickles
Preserves and jellies
Syrup and honey

BOTTLED ITEMS
Cooking oil
Olive oil
Vinegars
Spaghetti sauce
Honey
Corn syrup
Peanut butter

DRINKS
Coffee and tea
Instant drinks (Kool-aid, Gatorade, Crystal Light, Tang)
Mixers
Soda siphon with CO_2 cartridges
Cocoa and cider mixes
Soft drinks
Juices

PLASTIC AND PAPER
Paper towels (Bounty)
Toilet paper
Paper napkins (one large package; use cloth except for emergencies
    and lots of company)
Ziploc bags (all sizes and all types)
Plastic wrap
Food storage bags (with wire closures)
Heavy-duty aluminum foil
Waxed paper
Garbage bags (large heavy-duty ones for double-bagging trash when
    you have to keep it for a while on deck and for keeping water off

your gear; get an assortment of sizes that fit your cans and that will
fit over items you store)
Paper cups and paper plates (for emergencies only)
Unwaxed paper cups (hot-drink type for mixing resin)
Tissues

PERSONAL HYGIENE
(each crewmember will have special needs; request a list)
Toothpaste, floss, toothbrushes, mouthwash
Shampoo, conditioner, hair spray
Soap, lotions
Deodorant
Sunscreen
Shaving cream, razors, and blades
Feminine hygiene items

CLEANING PRODUCTS
Detergent, bleach, fabric softeners
Dishwashing liquid
Special cleaning products for head, galley, wood, carpets and upholstery, mirrors (these depend on your preferences and your boat;
all-purpose cleaners like Simple Green will simplify your choices
and storage of cleaning products)
3M pads (green mesh scouring pads)

FRESH FOODS
(not requiring refrigeration, long-lasting)
Onions, garlic, potatoes, sweet potatoes, winter squash
Citrus fruit (grapefruit, lemons, limes)
Apples (Granny Smith keep best)
Cabbage

FROZEN FOODS
Meat, poultry, seafood
Herbs (frozen in plastic bags)
Concentrated juice

FRESH FOODS
(not requiring refrigeration, not long-lasting, may be kept in baskets
or netting)

Tomatoes, green peppers, carrots, squash (summer)
Bananas and plantains
Peaches, pears, grapes, oranges, melons
Eggs (keep in carton in cool place)

REFRIGERATED FOODS
Cheese, cream cheese, yogurt
Butter and margarine
Perishable fresh fruits and vegetables (lettuce, celery, cucumbers,
  radishes, broccoli, cauliflower)
Horseradish

▼

(text continued from page 258)
to stock. (See the accompanying sidebar for our list of staples and
stocked items.)

SAVE WEIGHT AND SPACE
After determining amounts of common foods, try to search out
ways to save weight and space. For example, soft drinks are heavy,
take up excessive space, and make for a lot of unnecessary trash,
whereas powdered drinks like Kool-aid, Crystal Light, and others
occupy very little space; you add the water and there is no trash
until the whole package has been used. We like soda water for
mixed drinks; Mel has used a soda siphon and CO_2 cartridges to
make my own soda for many years, thus saving the weight and
space bottled soda would consume. Soda water can be mixed with
powdered drinks for a fake soft drink or mixer. We know cruisers
who couldn't do without Coca-Cola, so they purchased the syrup
to make it with soda water as needed. Powdered instant milk is a
great space and weight saver compared to long-life milk; it tastes
just like real skim milk when refrigerated. Some fruit juices are
now available in concentrated form that does not need refrigeration or freezing. Look out for short shelf lives on these and especially on boxed juices.

Look for alternatives to canned foods. Canned foods are heavy
and have a limited life in the marine environment. Dried vegetables
and fruits are tasty and can be reconstituted quickly and as needed.

Dry soup mixes are good and easy to prepare, as are pasta mixes and beans and rice mixtures. Investigate in the larger supermarkets, health food stores, and catalogs. Don't stock up on something new, however, until you have taste-tested it on your family more than just once. You may want to try one of the vacuum-packaging systems to save space and to preserve them longer.

When we do purchase cans for long-term storage, we remove the label and put the date and contents on each with an indelible marker. We try to store them where they will not be exposed to heavy moisture, and we put the newest ones in the back or bottom of the stowage area so the oldest ones will get used first. We plan to use all tomato products within a year of purchase because they go bad; the acid in canned fruit will start to destroy the can seams if kept longer than a year. Even aluminum cans will disintegrate quickly if they are exposed to salt water.

Wine drinkers should try boxed wines to save on the space and weight that bottles take up. To avoid breakage when stowed, bottles of wine and other alcoholic beverages can be placed in old socks. Beer drinkers should attempt to limit their consumption to conserve space and weight (their own too); beer and soft drink cans are thin and puncture easily, and beer bottles are heavy space consumers.

Snack foods such as chips will probably have to be minimized as they take up huge amounts of space, being packaged in bags of mostly air. If you must have chips, consider Pringles, popcorn (pop it yourself), and buying them as needed. Your pocketbook may soon tell you that you really don't need all this snack food anyway.

PRACTICE SHOPPING

Before you take off on the boat, try shopping as you would for a long trip. This is a good exercise even if you are still living in a house. See what it is like to buy, carry, load, and stow perhaps a month's worth of food. Then don't let yourself shop again except for a few fresh vegetables or whatever you think will be available in your chosen cruising area. This will not be easy, but it is great practice in organization and self-control.

STORAGE

Another major consideration in your provisioning routine will be the type of storage spaces available and what shape and size containers will fit into these spaces. We have some unusually shaped small

Carolyn retrieves some rice from the dry storage area under the settee.

spaces next to the hull in *Chez Nous* that we fill only with certain cans or jars. There is a tuna fish compartment, a canned chicken space, a special little place that holds only the mustard, and so on. After you have carefully studied your spaces, you should be able to come up with unique ideas about what will work best where, although some can sizes change when you buy outside the States.

Make sure that the items you use most often are easily accessible and that your food will not be subjected to excess moisture in out-of-the-way places. Also make sure that it is not so well hidden that you'll never get it out.

The amount of money you have to provision is important in your planning. It is expensive to purchase a lot at once, and it may not be cost-effective to overstock on some things, especially if food goes bad from being stored too long. Some cruisers are on a fixed monthly income and may not be able to spend large amounts at the grocery store at any given time. They may have to stock up at whatever port they happen to be in when money is available. These folks will be able to sample a much more interesting variety

Small bottled items are stored under the floor.

▼

of food than those still eating from hometown groceries, but they may also be spending a lot more money in the long run. The best advice we can give is to stock up on foods you eat often, foods that are heavy (like canned goods) and that you won't want to carry any distance, things you know will be expensive or unavailable in your cruising area (like paper products, personal hygiene items, baby foods, diapers, feminine hygiene items, spices, certain condiments, plastic bags), and treats (like good candy bars or whatever you would like to have once in a while that is special and often not available elsewhere).

We try to store enough basic food staples to last us at least six months to a year. As we mentioned, we shop for fresh vegetables and fruit in local markets. The more equipment and living and work items that come aboard, the fewer food spaces available.

PRESERVATION

Your refrigeration system or lack of one will have a tremendous effect on your method of provisioning, the types of foods you stock, and obviously the way you cook. We don't pretend to be an expert on this subject because we've always had some type of refrigeration or ice box. Obtaining ice in secluded cruising destinations, as you might imagine, can be difficult or impossible. Still, many cruisers opt for ice boxes, getting it when they can and doing without otherwise.

Even if you have refrigeration, have a contingency plan—refrigeration systems break down, usually when they are full and usually when there are no mechanics or parts available. The closest we have been to having no refrigeration was in the Bahamas many years ago when our unit died about a month before we planned to return to the States. We had a choice of leaving immediately or doing without—it was unrepairable. We chose to do without for the month and get a new one when we returned. Once the initial shock of losing all that food had worn off, we became excited by the challenge of figuring out how to do without it. The thing we missed the most, in addition to the convenience, was ice in our evening cocktail and, far more important, the ability to store fish when we were lucky enough to spear more than what we needed for the night's dinner. This is a serious consideration for us, because fish is an important part of our diet. Sometimes you get no fish; sometimes you get a lot.

Without refrigeration, we did have to shop more frequently because we like to cook with fresh ingredients (luckily we were staying in an area with several small markets). We planned for no leftovers, and we went diving more often and only speared enough to make one meal. The ordinary long-term provisions in my galley were sufficient to round out our diet. Eggs kept for at least a week, and we always tested them by cracking them in a separate bowl (this is a good idea anyway when cruising in remote areas; now we also keep a supply of powdered egg substitute). Canned butter was available, and margarine could be kept unrefrigerated. Cheese kept for a short period, so we bought it more often. Fresh fruit and veggies lasted almost as long as they did in the refrigerator (except lettuce, which was not affordable anyway) and maintain their fresh taste. Even now we don't refrigerate vegetables and fruit we know have not yet been refrigerated. We did without mayonnaise, although people told us it could be used unrefrigerated as long as it had never been kept cold and a very clean utensil was used each time we dipped. We just did not want to take a chance. Friends of ours keep a supply of the mayonnaise packets from fast food restaurants for this contingency. These are the only items I usually refrigerate; obviously frozen foods cannot be kept any other way. Other condiments (mustard, ketchup, relish, hot sauce) do not need refrigeration. I make salad dressing from scratch or use powdered packets as needed.

Even if you plan never to have your refrigerator break, it's a good idea to try to figure out how you would continue a cruise without it, because it will happen. A week or two living without it at the dock or before you leave civilization would be rewarding practice. There have been many excellent articles on the subject in cruising and boating magazines. If your refrigeration space won't hold ice you can buy ashore, you'll want a cooler. You can use it to store other things until the compressor stops.

LONG-TERM STORES

We have seen many lists of provisions for long-term cruising, and I feel that they can be helpful as general guides. However, no one family cooks or eats the same way; different boats have different storage capacities; budgets vary. It will be best for any couple or family planning a long cruise to carefully study their own habits and preferences to determine what is best in their particular circumstances. You will be doing a lot of cooking from scratch that you might not be accustomed to, and keeping the raw materials for this type of cooking may be difficult if you do not practice first. Once you get the hang of it, you will find that all those cake, bread, cookie, brownie, and pancake mixes aren't necessary and are easy to make if you have the accessible raw ingredients. Most are made from flour, sweetener, leavening (yeast, baking powder, or baking soda), eggs, salt, oil, and liquid. A varied supply of nuts, raisins, dates, cocoa or bar chocolate, chocolate chips, honey, brown sugar, and various herbs, spices, and seasonings will go a long way toward making many exciting baked goods. If you want a real taste treat and healthy food for your family, try freshly ground wheat flour in bread and pizza dough recipes. The grinders and bulk wheat berries are available in most health food stores as well as by mail from catalogs (try Walnut Acres Organic Farms, 1-800-433-3998; there are many others).

Some bulk food, packaged grains (even vacuum-packaged), cereals, and pasta can come to you with bugs, or eggs that might hatch months later in the middle of a tropical paradise. They are usually some form of weevil that can quickly infest your entire supply of grains and beans and begin to migrate into other foods for something else good to eat. It helps to put all your food that might be susceptible to weevils into a freezer overnight as soon as you purchase it (if you are lucky enough to have a friend ashore with a large freezer). Everything should be packaged as airtight as possible and in as heavy a container as you can find. Good choices include Tupperware, reclosable 2- to 5-gallon buckets, plastic restaurant supply containers, collapsible water jugs (these take almost no space once empty), or even glass (if you have a secure place to put it). The larger your container, the more food that will go bad at one time, so you may be better off with several small containers spread out around your boat rather than one large one for important staples like rice. Weevils excel at eating through plastic bags and cardboard containers. If you detect an infestation, it is best to discard all suspect food and repackage whatever you can. Clean out your storage lockers and spray with insect spray if you have a way to protect your food from the poisons (do this only if you have really heavy storage containers). Some cruisers swear by putting bay leaves into bulk storage containers to fight off weevils; in my only experience with this, we must have been too late with the leaves. Don't make the mistake of leaving a weevil infestation to take care of later; you may have no food left. Have you ever seen a rice recipe that said to wash the rice in a pan of cold water before you start to cook it? This is to drown the bugs that will float to the top of the water where you can skim them off before you cook. You will then have no black specks or crunchy surprises in the finished product. We don't like to think about what is left in your rice and empty rice grains when you cook it.

LAUNDRY, by Mel

As we've repeatedly emphasized, many things you take for granted ashore are quite different and difficult at sea. You will have to adopt and learn to handle these things in an affordable manner that still gets the job done. Laundry is a good example.

A daily laundry routine is usually impossible once you have moved aboard. Most cruisers have no washer, no dryer, and no place to put all the clothes that keep piling up, especially with active kids. An obvious solution is to sail in the tropics so that you wear bathing suits most of the time and therefore have little to launder; but we are not always lucky to be in warm climates, and some of us don't like to be hot all the time anyway.

WASHER/DRYERS
When we were planning our cruising life and choosing optional equipment for *Chez Nous,* we thought that, with a baby on the way and another in our plans, surely one of the best pieces of machinery we could squeeze into the budget was a washer/dryer that fit neatly into the main cabin living space. Surely it would save time and quarters and headaches. But once we began to use it, it became obvious that this was not the solution either. While it got the clothes clean and dry, the capacity was only half that of a household washing machine. Each load consumed 14 gallons of water and quickly drained all that was hot, and each dryer load took at least an hour (longer for towels) to dry and vented hot air directly into the main living space, raising the temperature by at least 10°F unless we also ran the air-conditioning. Needless to say, this was not acceptable. In defense of onboard laundry systems, in a pinch and when you have adequate water and electricity (when the boat's plugged into a marina with no laundromat) they can be great. With only two people aboard it might also suffice at other times, assuming you have the necessary water and electricity.

LAUNDROMATS
Over the years we have determined that the best solution is to find a nice, clean, empty, cheap laundromat around once a week. Lacking this ideal, we have found that laundry, like everything about the cruising life, must be treated with flexibility and faced with a positive attitude. Laundromats are a gathering place, so they provide a good opportunity to get to know different folks as you discuss detergent, lint traps, and underwear. You also get to study a lot of different personality types when you share a crowded laundromat. Some people take out your clothes and dump them in a pile on the floor; others remove them and place them in the dryer for you, and use their own quarters. Others will let you go first if you have a small amount; some have to grab everything first. My advice: be polite and treat everybody's laundry just like you'd like yours treated, have plenty of quarters (usually you can get them from an attendant), do not leave your

laundry unattended, don't get in a panic if you have to wait a bit, and try to make a few new friends. Since you all must wait a fair amount of time, you might as well have fun doing it. Separate your laundry ahead of time. If you must transport your laundry in the dinghy, some type of waterproof bag is helpful for keeping out salt spray.

We keep our dirty laundry in net bags on the boat until we find a suitable laundromat or other laundry solution. I usually transport the clothes in these bags and in Rubbermaid Roughneck 10-gallon tubs covered with garbage bags. The tubs are easier to carry than bags. The concentrated liquid detergent I use takes less space on the boat than powders, but it does add weight. You should also stock whatever else you would ordinarily use in your home laundry—bleach (go for the nonchlorine type as chlorine kills reefs and watermakers), spot remover, and softeners. Just remember that some clothes will get dirtier than you might ever have imagined, you won't be doing "real" laundry as often, and you may actually have fewer clothes to wash because everyone on the boat will help you conserve on laundry items.

MINIMIZING LAUNDRY

Since you will not find a good laundromat every time you might need one, everyone can do a few things to help get through the long spells. Towels are a big problem because they take so long to dry. If you buy ones that are less plush than what you might be used to, you'll find that they dry faster and don't become as musty. We try to put them outside to dry each day in the fresh air, and this goes a long way to avoid mustiness. Bedding can also be aired on the lifelines and rigging on a blustery day at anchor for a freshening between washes. Undergarments can be washed daily by hand in your leftover shower or other water using a clean rinse if you are recycling washwater. We often use this method (except for the really grubby workclothes, towels, and bedding) when we know it will be a long stretch to the next laundry spot.

HAVING IT DONE

There are several other ways to get the job done, depending on where you are and how much time, energy, and money you have. In many areas outside the States, local women take in laundry and do a wonderful job either by hand, wringer washer, or in their own washing machines and dryers. They pay dearly for the equipment, the electricity to operate them, and the water, which is scarce in many places. Consequently, this laundry solution usually comes with a high price tag. Some areas have laundry services that will do yours for a set price per pound. This is also expensive, especially if you have a family.

The out-island solution we use, as do most of the cruisers we know, is the "do-it-by-hand" method. Children, and grownups too, who suddenly have to wash the clothes they wear develop a new respect for the whole process.

BY HAND

Washing your clothes by hand can be a good family project on a beautiful sunny day. We usually do it after there has been sufficient rain to collect 30 gallons or more from the deck (we close off the drains with children's modeling clay or towels and scoop it up as it collects in the lowest spot, after the tanks are full). We fill the 10-gallon Rubbermaid Roughneck tubs mentioned earlier and as many other buckets as we have on deck. One tub is used for washwater and one for rinsing. Because rainwater is so soft, you should use about half or even less (you may have to experiment with your brand) of the detergent than you would normally use. Even so, it takes a lot of rinsing to get the suds out, so we sometimes use a third 10-gallon tub for a second rinse. On some islands you may find abandoned cisterns. Here, also, you must use less detergent. Be sure to transport the water a good distance from the cistern before doing your wash, so that it does not contaminate the clean water in the cistern. Also, as I learned from some experienced cruisers, flowers and shrubs do not mind a little detergent, so be sure to use the leftover washwater to water some thirsty plants. After the water is collected and detergent put in, the fun begins. I use an old-fashioned wooden and galvanized washboard, although I've seen some nicer newer ones with molded plastic and fiberglass-reinforced scrubbing surfaces. (Some people use a plumber's helper plunger in buckets as an agitator. I haven't tried this because my system works fine.) Place your least dirty and lightest colored clothes in the washtub and let them soak for a while, after which you should begin scrubbing them on the washboard, which fits nicely onto the tub. They should be agitated again in the washwater to remove the soil that you have loosened with the washboard. Wring the clothes as dry as possible before placing them in the rinse water. This is a good job for energetic kids; sometimes it takes two of them to do towels and sheets, each holding an end and turning in opposite directions. Be sure to let the wrung-out water drip back into the washtub. Clothes should then be placed in the rinse water and agitated for a while, wrung out in the same manner, and placed in a third rinse (if you are using one), and then wrung as dry as possible. Continue in this manner with progressively dirtier and darker clothes. Hang clothes in the rigging and on lifelines to dry. Wooden clothespins work better than plastic ones. They are stronger, and the sun's ultraviolet rays don't disintegrate them as quickly. (They can also be separated and used as a finger splint when first aid requires it.) Discard rusty clothespins—they leave spots on your clothes. Be sure to take in your clothes before the sun goes down; evening dew will wet them again. If you have a lot to wash and it has rained heavily, discard the washwater after a few loads, use the first rinse water as washwater, and use clean water for the final rinse.

Some of my most memorable cruising experiences are associated with laundry. During our first year in the Bahamas I had my first experience doing it by hand, with water from one of the "wells" ashore. It was muddy water that had collected in a deep hole in the rock. I collected the water and took it to a nice spot in a meadow and proceeded to wash our clothes in peace and harmony with nature and life. A mockingbird joined me and watched and sang beautiful songs; we talked and had a wonderful time. Whenever I start to think of doing laundry as drudgery, I try to remember that moment. The second best laundry experience occurred in New York City. We had filled our watertanks and all our empty tubs and buckets at a marina. Nobody felt like hiking the five blocks uphill to the laundromat, so we all did it by hand on deck, just the way we do it in the islands. This was different, though, because we were moored in the Hudson River, surrounded by Manhattan and watching the traffic whiz by and the city churn. We hung out our laundry just long enough to dry it— the air pollution might have ruined our hard work. I don't know if anyone shoreside observed us; I think they were too busy to notice and would not have known what primitive thing we were doing anyway.

HEALTH

A medical emergency can be the most serious problem you encounter while cruising. It could threaten your survival and/or your financial security. In remote areas, the prospects can be truly frightening.

The best approach is to be careful, avoid unnecessary and foolish risks, and take care of yourself. This sounds obvious, but the number of cruisers who miss this point and end up in serious but avoidable trouble is relatively high. It is difficult to think of disaster in paradise and hard to remember that an easily solved medical emergency stateside can be almost insurmountable where you are cruising. For example, be careful about what you eat, especially in countries with low health and inspection standards. Listen to your body. If it hurts, it's probably telling you something. A common example of the trouble that can result from failure to heed your own warnings is the frequency of ear damage caused by diving too deep. Another frequent injury results from lifting heavy objects and exercising. Use common sense.

Many cruisers are injured while cleaning fish. Filleting knives are (and should be) very sharp. Clean fish on a stable platform and don't let other people, especially small children, get too close. And don't clean fish on your boat in a crowded harbor or on beaches where people swim. Fish blood and meat attract sharks and barracudas. They come in ready to eat. Take your catch to a beach or rock or someplace else far away from areas where people may be swimming from boats, dinghies, or the shore.

FIRST AID

Before I begin, let me say that you should consult your doctor before leaving, and at any other time appropriate and possible. The advice I offer here is just that; I am not a medical doctor. These are our regimens that we have tried numerous times with good success.

Carry complete first aid supplies, tailored to your family's needs and your anticipated lifestyle. Usually, if your doctor and pharmacist understand your plans, you can put together—with their advice—a set of supplies superior to the various commercially available kits, and at substantial savings. Do this just before you leave, so that the doctor knows everyone's current medical condition. All supplies should have current dates to ensure the longest expiration dates possible.

These supplies should include items you may not have thought of. For example, dental supplies are important. Drugstores sell over-the-counter temporary filling material and related supplies. Ear wax removal kits, such as those sold by Murine, may save the day when diving or snorkeling compresses formerly unnoticed wax and causes pressure and pain. Bring eyedrops to wash out debris.

One friend purchased a beautiful wool watch cap in Spain, and set sail for the Caribbean shortly afterward. About a week later he realized that the cap had lice in it. Now he and the boat were full of them. He had no treatment aboard. He was a doctor, but with the supplies available (including lots of seawater) there was nothing he could do but scratch for two weeks. The lice had a great cruise. Talk about these things with health-care specialists. Infestation by unwanted pests can cause serious health problems on a cruise, in addition to other problems. Several large bottles of delousing shampoo and soap are indispensable. You never know when you might pick up these things, especially if you ride buses and cabs in Third World countries. Bring treatment for fleas if you have any pets, and even if you don't.

Before you take off, learn as much as you can about medical care and the use of the various medicines you are taking along.Obtain good reference books, including the *Physician's Desk Reference*. For general medical information, we like the American Medical Association's *Family Medical Guide* and the *Mayo Clinic Family Health Book*. Take CPR and other emergency medical courses before you leave.

Take these books along for your kids, even if not for yourself. As you know, kids, particularly the younger ones, have a propensity for coming up with medical emergencies. Breaking arms, stepping on a nail, getting hit by a baseball, getting cuts and scratches— all have new significance if they occur somewhere out in the islands away from stateside medical assistance.

When we return to the States, we take our kids to the same doctor who has treated them for years. He knows what we're doing and will talk to us over the phone if we need him. We learned early on to take any injury as a potentially serious problem. Cuts and abrasions are perhaps among the most common, and they are also a prime cause of infection. Did you ever hear that soaking an infection in salt water is good for it? Sure you have. It is, too—but not tropical, salty ocean water. This stuff is full of organisms that thrive in infections and skin breaches. If your kids (or you) have a cut or abrasion, keep them out of seawater until it has healed. If you want to soak it in salty water, get clean fresh water from your tanks, heat it, and then add salt from your galley store. If your kids play around the water and getting the cut wet is inevitable, cover it well with Neosporin or Polysporin and a good bandage. This will help to heal the wound, and the greasy coating may keep seawater out of the wound.

We keep a large stock of good bandages that stay on, even when wet. In our experience, the best way to treat cuts and abrasions is to clean them with fresh water and antibacterial soap (Dial and Phisoderm are good brands). Then bubble the wound liberally with hydrogen peroxide. It is particularly useful for removing foreign particles, which may include little pieces of reef or bacteria-rich shell that will continue to grow, even thrive, in the body. Then we treat the wound with Polysporin or Neosporin and keep it covered, if needed, with a Band-Aid. Watch for allergies such as those associated with neomycin.

We also keep at least one aloe plant alive and healthy. These are nice plants, and grow easily. If one of us has a minor cut, abrasion, or burn, we cut the tip of a stalk, squeeze out the slimy juice, and spread it on. It works very well. Try it on a mild burn and see. Don't buy the expensive drugstore junk that has little aloe and a lot of chemical. You can find the plants in greenhouses; in many of the Caribbean islands it grows wild.

Discuss your plans and all medical concerns with your doctor. Be sure that he or she understands that you may have to deal with medical emergencies on your own. We have noticed that some doctors are incapable of imagining a world where there isn't a clinic with an attached drugstore around every corner; others are really helpful. Your doctor must understand that you may need to call from the high seas and that he or she won't be able to examine the patient. Explain to the doctor, and insist that the doctor explain to his personnel, that you may be calling with an emergency from the middle of the ocean or a Third World country, that the phone and/or radio connection may be tenuous and delays could be dangerous, and that you may have absolutely no other viable recourse but to ask him for medical advice. He or she will have to respond based solely on your description of symptoms and other observations, and on your file. If your physician can't handle this, and some of them can't, find another physician. Rest assured that understanding doctors and other medical professionals do exist. You will be able to find someone.

From time to time we see advertisements for medical services offered to cruisers. Some of these have come and gone; a big problem is that the doctor can do no more than what I have described above, and he or she may not have the benefit of your medical file. These physicians may have had special training in treating unusual boating-related maladies. Examples are coral infections, ciguatera poisoning (see the detailed dicussion on this illness in chapter 19, page 231), and tropical infections. Before you go, check out the advertisements in cruising magazines to see what is available, but interview and investigate thoroughly before totally relying on any service. We have also seen many instances when doctors and nurses, who happened to be cruising nearby, helped when an injured party put out a call on VHF.

If you have insurance, find out whether it will cover you where you will be cruising. If you have children, insurance coverage is critical. Some cruisers limit the boundaries of their wandering during their children's early years. The simplest injuries can have life-threatening consequences in Third World countries and at sea.

On a hopeful note, in our experience most long-term live-aboard cruisers do relatively well in the health department.

PESTS

Cockroaches come aboard in cardboard boxes and in just about anything you may get from grocery stores. They also fly. They board indiscriminately. They don't care if you are dirty or clean. Where you see one, there are usually many more. Their droppings may be large enough for you to think they came from rodents. Carefully inspect all groceries before loading them aboard your boat. Never bring paper or corrugated cardboard boxes and bags aboard; roaches even like the glue that holds labels on cans in place. Some cruisers remove these labels on cans (they will probably come off in the moisture anyway) and mark the containers with indelible marker. Bring plenty of cockroach traps. In southern latitudes, they come extra big; these bugs won't begin to fit in the dainty little northern cockroach hotels. Powdered boric acid judiciously and carefully laid out also has been reported to kill them, although I'm not sure what else this may kill. They like dark and moist places. Your boat has plenty of these. They also like to eat hoses (as in below the waterline) and electrical insulation, making them a super health hazard.

Mice and rats come aboard in groceries, from other boats, and docks. Rats will swim and climb aboard; I've heard that mice do also. Like roaches, they eat hoses and insulation and can carry serious illnesses. Bring plenty of rat and mousetraps. Forget the poison; you don't want a dead rat in the bilge.

Have screens for all of your portholes and hatches, as well as for Dorade vents and any other vents or holes from the outside to the inside. We put stiff aluminum screen in engine-room vents and Dorade vents to keep out rodents should they come aboard. These have to be replaced frequently because they disintegrate in the salt environment. If you plan to anchor in marshy areas, along the ICW in the Carolinas and Georgia for example, or in mangroves farther south, bring no-see-um netting. These bugs will drive you mad. The worst mosquitoes pale to insignificance. This superfine netting is the only thing that keeps no-see-ums out. It is so fine, it also keeps most breezes out. We put it up only when needed, and then do so by stuffing it around our porthole and hatch screens. This material usually must be ordered from suppliers of outdoor sports equipment.

EQUIP TO SAVE MONEY

Some equipment actually saves money while making life better.

On *Chez Nous* we use diving gear regularly to install zincs, check the prop, change it if necessary, clean out through-hulls, and clean the bottom. This way, we haul out only every three years. This is a savings of at least $2,500 per three-year period over what it would cost us if we hauled and painted each year. We also use the gear to catch fish in winter. Our "gear" consists of wetsuits for each member of the family, weights, good-quality masks, snorkels, and flippers. I also have a heavy-duty winter wetsuit with long sleeves, feet, gloves, and a hood. This paid for itself the first year I had it, when we snagged a large tarpaulin with our prop. Years ago, we purchased a compressor and tanks, but we hardly ever use them.

Let's now move from simple to much more complicated equipment. The inverter immediately comes to mind as an all-time winner

(text continued on page 281)

"THE BOAT BEGAN TO VIBRATE"

On the sloop *Green Waters*, Ed and Judy had been waiting three weeks for a comfortable weather window to cross from Ft. Lauderdale to the Bahamas. This wait had lasted through Christmas, with front after front slamming down from the north during an unusually brutal winter. Two weeks after Christmas, the break came. By this time hundreds of boats had piled up in south Florida, also waiting. *Green Waters* cautiously found her way out of the tricky channel from Lake Sylvia, where she had been anchored the last few days of her watch. Once out into the ICW channel just south of Bahia Mar marina, all would be go. The channel was deep, with only one bridge, an easy one, before the easy inlet.

Halfway between Bahia Mar and the bridge, however, something happened. A loud thumping noise suddenly came from under the stern. The boat began to vibrate badly. Ed ran below and opened the engine space. He could almost see the propeller shaft whipping around. He put his hand on the stuffing box and felt it moving. The boat began to lose power and was swept by the strong current. Ft. Lauderdale Marina lay ahead to starboard, and there they headed, more under control of the current than their own power. The long fuel dock running parallel to the channel made an excellent place for a near crash landing.

The course was obvious. The water was frigid from days of record low temperatures. Ed, who was retired, knew that it would be dangerous for him to attempt to dive under his boat to look. Besides, there'd be no way to fix whatever had happened. They began to arrange for a tow to a yard. The cost of the tow was estimated at more than $250. The cost of hauling would be at least another $200. From there, the figures could only go up. The Bahamas, the dream of a lifetime, had suddenly become a remote and seemingly unachievable goal.

Ed decided on a towing company, and, VHF microphone in hand, took a deep breath and started to call. "Wait a minute, wait a minute," Judy urgently interrupted. "Don't you remember? I gave you a new wetsuit for Christmas—and all that diving gear. You can stand the cold water with that. Why don't you go over and look first?—before we tell them to come." Ed stopped, chagrined that he hadn't remembered. He had been delighted to get the suit because it meant hours of diving over beautiful reef, unhampered by winter's cool waters, an inconvenience even in the Bahamas.

Splendidly clad in his Christmas gift, he disappeared under the stern, a long rope trailing out in the current in case he needed to grab hold.

Thirty seconds later he came up, spit out his snorkel, and grinned. "A palm frond. A bloody big palm frond; that's all it is. It's huge, but I can cut it off easily." He unsheathed his diving knife and, feeling a bit like Tarzan, headed under again.

Half an hour later they had cast off and were steaming around in circles in the wide basin off the marina. No vibration. No noise. Full power and control. That night they drank a grateful toast on the Bahamas Banks. The diving gear had cost about $225, and it had just paid for itself at least two or three times over. It had paid for itself in enjoyment, too.

▼

(text continued from page 279)

in the category of cruising equipment dollars well invested. I mentioned inverters in chapter 13 with respect to electrical power, but let's talk about them now as something that will not only make your life better but also save money.

A good inverter will save money in the following ways: First, you don't have to keep paying a premium for 12-volt gear. Compare the prices of a 110-volt AC television and a 12-volt unit. Do the same for music systems, video players, refrigeration units, and power tools. The difference is significant. And even if you don't want any of the above now, you probably will as time goes on. Try just finding some of the things you may need in the 12-volt mode. The only place you can find them is typically in marine discount stores. Their prices start well above what you would pay for the standard 110-volt item in a hardware or electronics store that doesn't have "marine" in its name.

Many other AC items make life easier and nicer. These are especially conspicuous in the galley. They include a blender, a food processor, a mixer, and a microwave. Are you aghast? Throwing up your hands? Well, after some time at sea, your family may be happy to have the benefit of some of these conveniences. The food processor is particularly useful in preparing certain types of seafood, baby food, and breads, for example. The microwave saves propane and enables you to prepare quick, hot meals when you really need them. An inverter opens the door for all these items. The extra cost for DC units would be very high, if you could find them in the first place.

Power tools are indispensable for making proper and quick repairs, and AC power tools are much cheaper and usually more

▼

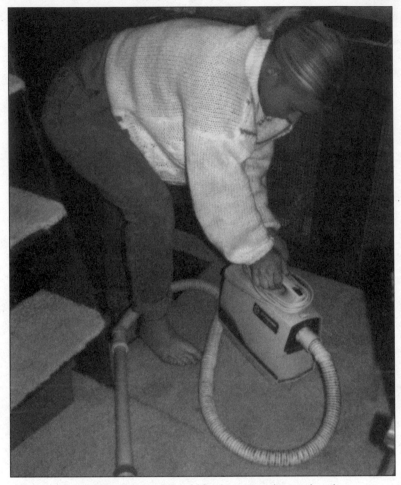

Melanie using a standard 110-volt vacuum cleaner aboard.

▼

effective than DC tools. Often, many tools simply aren't available in DC, such as Dremel tools and electric soldering tools. (I have been happy with battery-operated Makita drills for such places as the mast top, but I use a standard AC household drill whenever possible.) I long ago concluded that having AC power tools aboard translates directly into saved money and quicker, easier, and better

▼

repairs. This means added safety. If you have an inverter, you can buy and regularly use these tools.

Our industrial sewing machine has paid for itself over and over again because it has enabled us to repair sails, make covers to protect things stored on deck (such as plastic fuel jugs) from UV deterioration, and make our dodger and Bimini. (You need AC power for a good industrial sewing machine; hand or foot cranks aren't adequate for large jobs if speed is a factor).

Our fast, large planing dinghy has saved us big bucks by enabling us to leave *Chez Nous* in one place and make fuel and supply runs. This enables us to can anchor in cheaper areas and avoid marinas. Our dinghy also helps us to fish and can be used as a tow boat. Our heavy-duty anchor gear and ground tackle let us anchor safely and further avoid dock fees.

I could expand this list for several pages, but you get the point. Think of gear as a way to save money and get tough jobs done.

Chapter Twenty-One

KIDS ABOARD

If you take even a year or two from your shoreside lives to go cruising as a family, and if you do it well, years from now I think you'll have to say that the cruising years were the very best. Doing it well is critical to this outcome, however, because it isn't unusual for parents to get so wrapped up in their great adventure, so immersed in the change of life stresses, and so ecstatic to finally be free that they assume their children are as excited as they are. With cocktails in the cockpit, potlucks on the beach, new cruising friends, and the incredible beauty all around, a pervasive vacation lifestyle can develop that will overwhelm even the role of parenting. As I said in the early chapters, cruising should not be a vacation from parenting; it should provide an opportunity for the very finest parenting. And it begins with a dream.

START EARLY

Talk with your kids about your cruising plans as you begin to
envision them. Make the topic part of family conversations. Talk
about why you want to do it, what you expect it to be like, what
problems you might have, how you might solve them, and when
it would be good to go. Involve them in buying or refitting the
boat. If you are buying a boat, take them along and ask their opinion. Explain what you are looking for and why one factor or another may be positive or negative. From the start, talk to them
about where they will sleep, do schoolwork, and keep their stuff.
If you're refitting a boat, show them the plans and discuss the
same subjects.

Involve them in equipment purchases. Most kids like to shop,
and everybody likes new and neat things. If you can't take them
shopping, at least show them what you bought and explain what
each item does and how it works. Have them aboard when you install equipment, and when you first try it out.

As the countdown draws nearer, get equipment that will be
helpful to your children, and let them help choose it. For example,
get good snorkeling and spearfishing equipment for them. Even in
the Bahamas, the water is cold enough in winter to warrant a wetsuit. Children generally have less body fat than adults, so they chill
quickly. Without a wetsuit, what might have developed into a lifelong passion for diving in the earth's last frontier could become
something they dread and avoid. A sailboard, surfboard, knee-
board, or boogie board are great fun, build skills, promote group
recognition, and provide good exercise. If you can store and afford
it, a sailing dinghy, or some other small dinghy for their own use,
is a great idea. It fosters independence by giving them a sense of
control. Be sure they know how to use it. Cards and board games
provide hours of entertainment on rainy and windy days. Good old
Monopoly (there's a computer version now) is a favorite among
many cruising kids. When they help you select these items, they
begin to anticipate the fun and look forward to getting out there.

Consider letting them participate in special courses before you
go and when you anchor in one place for a while. These might include instruction in boardsailing, wavesurfing, scuba diving, sailing,
small-boat handling, seamanship, and meteorology. When kids

have to leave their friends and everything they have known, it helps them immensely to know that they can do something they enjoy and that also helps the family. It's also neat for kids to know all about something their parents don't know. For example, if you want to learn sailboarding, perhaps your child could learn before you take off and then teach you once you're underway.

Whenever you can, however, try to teach your children yourself. This helps all of you prepare for home schooling and hopefully will give you a closer family life. An example would be navigating and steering the boat. You must be pretty good at this before you leave. Have the kids stand watch; explain navigation on weekend cruises.

As you may be thinking, the age of the child will make a difference in how you involve them, but it should not make much difference in the extent to which you involve them. The extent is simple: the more, the better. As soon as a child starts communicating and understanding, she or he should be included. Younger kids (and the younger they are, the easier this is) are quicker to accept their parents' excitement about a new adventure. Older kids are likely to be skeptical.

Whatever the situation, be sure to listen to, watch for, and respond to the voiced and unvoiced concerns of your kids. For example, one of the most frequent questions I hear from kids whose parents are considering cruising is, "Aren't you scared in storms?" This can be a real dream killer. Think about it. Were you exceptionally frightened of storms when you were little? Many of us were, even more so than we are now. If your kid is concerned or fearful, explain what causes them. Encourage the family to watch a good evening weather forecast with frontal maps and systems explanation (try the Weather Channel on cable TV). Familiarity helps to take the bite from a strong fear. Explain how people ashore cope with storms; then explain how cruisers handle bad weather and their methods of avoiding it. Talk about safe harbors, anchoring techniques, lightning protection, heaving-to, and storm drogues. Soon they'll understand that cruisers aren't helpless in a storm and that other people deal with them all the time. And when a storm comes, try to sit on your own anxieties a bit. Kids can read you like a book. "If there's nothing to be scared about, why are mom and dad so uptight?"

(text continued on page 287)

▼

"WE COULDN'T BELIEVE IT"

We were in that unfriendly little section of ocean between Eleuthera and the Abacos. To the west was a lee shore covered with rocks and reefs. To the south, a long reef reached out into the ocean, ready to ground any unwary cruiser. The landfall to the north was unmarked and meandered through reef that could be cleared only if you could see it. Landfall had to be made in daylight, with the sun overhead or behind, free of dense clouds or storms. To the east was ocean—the only safe route.

We had left harbor in Royal Island at first light, making our way carefully around the reef. At 7:45 we were well out to sea, far beyond what we considered the point of no return in the prevailing winds. We have always disliked this little stretch, and we listened to the weather on the ham band.

For the first time in years of Bahamas cruising, we heard a strong thunderstorm warning from the Nassau meteorological office. We couldn't believe it. At that time, "forecast" was a misnomer for this station's reports; they told you what had happened the night before and what the weather was doing at the moment, with about 270 degrees of possibilities. That day, the sky was leaden and the air close. But we kept on.

Around 10:30 A.M., a solid wall of strange weather overwhelmed the ocean. We had been through many storms at sea, but this one was particularly fierce. Fits of high wind shrieked and tore at the sails. Between gusts, the air was silent. Dense, unremitting rain made vision and radar useless. Occasionally the deluge softened to a smoky, hazy downfall, and in the near distance we saw dark swaths of heavy rain. Ragged clouds appeared to brush the cresting waves.

Never knowing from which direction and with what force the winds would hit us next, we doused sail. Left at the mercy of the waves, we kept lookout not only for seas and other vessels, but also for the waterspouts we knew must be there. Melanie and Carolyn looked up and around at every chance.

Around midafternoon the system passed, heading uncharacteristically northeast. The seas became more orderly, and we began to discern the rocky shore we had known would be west of us. Melanie, 12 years old at the time, leaned back in the cockpit and said, calmly and matter of factly, "Well, I guess we all were pretty close to dying that time." Both girls had gained enough experience and maturity to perform without a hitch, and their help had been vital. They had learned to overcome their fear enough to accept the storm as a natural, if unwelcome, aspect of their cruising life.

(text continued from page 285)

PRACTICE

I've said this earlier, but I'll stress it again: to convey your cruising dream to those you would have share it with you, plan family vacation cruises before setting off for good. Try to arrange something you are reasonably confident of making a success. If you don't have a boat, chartering may be a good primer. Take the kids along and plan the trip around their interests as well as yours.

Avoid long, rough beats to windward; open anchorages in bad storms; and similar bad cruising experiences. All too often, kids experience sailing and cruising during tough-guy racing weekends, with dad screaming at everyone and the lee rail in the water as much as possible. This isn't what cruising is about, and your family should know it. In other chapters I suggested taking practice cruises that include hard times, like putting up with maintenance chores with everyone aboard. This is indeed important, but at first you want to enthuse your kids and inspire them to share your dream.

Your kids can dream with you more easily if they know that other kids are cruising too. Take them to boat shows, especially those that feature seminars on kids and cruising. They'll meet other kids who are already enjoying the cruising life. Look for articles in boating magazines about kids afloat. Your kids may want to write to the kids featured in the article; they will probably write back. Mine have over the years. It will help your kids to know that there is a peer group of sorts afloat as well as ashore.

It may also help your kids to know that cruising peer groups don't necessarily have the same rigid requirements with respect to being "cool." Cruising kids tend to get to know one another quickly. They are sensible enough to leave behind facades and social ploys. There isn't time to get past false fronts. You want to know quickly whether someone is a potential friend. You don't need purple hair or the right clothes. It's easier to make friends and easier to be accepted for what you are. You start off with cruising as an obvious common experience, and that makes starting a conversation a snap.

If your kids are reluctant to leave their friends, reassure them that you will help them find more—and keep the promise. (See more under "Finding Friends" later in this chapter.)

As I mentioned in an earlier chapter, Carolyn has developed

(text continued on page 290)

"WHAT IT'S LIKE" by Melanie

Wow, that boat's so big you could almost live on it." I heard this when *Chez Nous* was tied up at the public dock in Wilmington, North Carolina. I guess this person had no idea I was within earshot—right down the forward hatch. But they were right: We're full-time liveaboard cruisers, and four of us live on *Chez Nous,* a Gulfstar Sailmaster 47. On that day, we were on our yearly migration northward after another great winter in the Bahamas.

I'm Melanie Neale, age 16, and I've spent all my life on the boat with my parents and my 14-year-old sister, Carolyn. We have very basic living quarters—two staterooms, a galley, two heads, and a living/navigation/dining room. It's a little space in which to grow up, especially when you have to share a room with your sister. However, I've been to so many neat places and met so many interesting people that every day I've spent cramped up on the boat has been worth it. Actually, I feel really lucky.

Chez Nous isn't that small; she's a great boat, and I'm very attached to her. We sometimes motor, but she sails unusually well. Nothing can describe the feeling I get when she's heeled over and cutting through the dark ocean, a thousand stars overhead, taking me to someplace new.

It's all a part of the liveaboard lifestyle, which has its good sides and

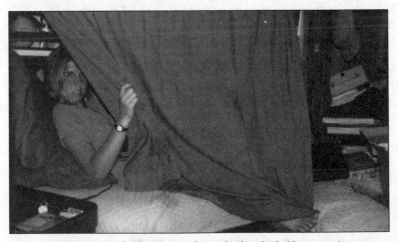

Melanie and Carolyn share a forward cabin divided by a curtain.

▼

its bad sides. Cruising can be harder for the kids than the parents, because, let's face it, cruising kids are not quite "normal." I don't go to a
regular school for eight hours a day, and I don't know what happened on
the last episode of *Friends,* but I do get to spend hours on Bahamian
beaches and I could probably sail from Norfolk to Miami without charts
(even though that wouldn't be the most intelligent move on my part!).
Anyway, I think it's a great life, and I'm excited to be writing about it.

People often ask us what we do all day. I was talking to one of my
friends, who has been cruising for three years. She lives aboard full-time,
too, and she finally thinks of the boat as "home," even though it took three
years. It's natural for me to think of *Chez Nous* as home because I haven't
ever had another home. It would probably take me three years to adjust to
a house. Even though the idea of being stuck with your family for weeks at
a time in two or three rooms may sound scary, you can do a lot of the
things on a boat that you can do in a house. So, just think of it as home.

School can take up a lot of time. I've been enrolled in Brigham Young
University's independent study high school program for two years. So far,
it's been really good. All the courses are written for the students, so I
don't need my parents' help very often. If I'm in an unexciting anchorage
or the weather is bad, I try to do as much schoolwork as I can. I even get
ahead in my studies. This way, I can take time off when we're out in the
ocean or there's something I'd rather be doing than studying (like diving,
kneeboarding, sailing, going to a beach, being with my friends, scrubbing
the decks, you name it). So it's a good idea to get schoolwork out of the
way when you can.

What is the worst possible situation on a boat? Surprise . . . bad
weather. Imagine a black sky, rain, thunder and lightning, wind, and too
many waves to even try and get into your dinghy. The good news is that
days like this are pretty rare; the bad news is that it's clouding up right
now. There's a thunderstorm closing in from the northwest. At times
like these a little bit of extra schoolwork doesn't sound so bad.

My sister and I usually read, write letters, or practice our hobbies.
Carolyn has a guitar, which is a great way to pass time. If I'm lucky I can
even sing with her! I paint and sell T-shirts, mostly underwater scenes. A
lot of cruisers I know make jewelry out of beads, shells, and other things,
which they give away and sell. These things don't take up much space and
are a lot of fun. Most boats have TVs and VCRs, and you can usually find
someplace to rent or borrow movies. A good stereo is also a must (don't
expect to get full musical enjoyment out of your Walkman), and you can
swap tapes and CDs with other cruisers.

I live for sunny, hot, gorgeous weather when you don't have to do anything I talked about in the last paragraph. I can simply jump over the side and go swimming, and Carolyn can play her guitar outside. There's always cosmetic work to be done on the boat; I just finished a seven-hour project: polishing our stainless steel. Honestly, this kind of work is fun!

I have to admit that the best part of cruising is when you finally reach a harbor and can get off the boat and explore a new place and meet new people. There are a lot of things to do on a boat, and even more in all the harbors.

▼

(text continued from page 287)

a fine talent for guitar playing, reading music, and employing sophisticated picks and rhythms. Unfortunately we can't share this in a book. I have included two poems by Melanie, one on page xi and the other on page 351.

SHARE THE LOAD

We can't think of any one concept more important to kids, parents, the boat, and the overall cruise than involving the kids on a daily basis in jobs, chores, and activities that contribute to the seaworthiness of the boat, the progress of the cruise, and the well-being of the family.

When kids pitch in, they develop a commitment to the boat and pride in what they do. Most important, they learn and grow into responsible people you can be proud of.

Kids of any age can share the load, and the more they do, the better. Melanie and Carolyn admitted that they would have liked more jobs and involvement in the past, even though they understand more and handle more responsibility than most adult cruisers. I did hesitate to involve them in some chores because of safety concerns, but they tell me I could have let them do more.

I generally kept them away from moving machinery, and they didn't handle the anchor and chain rode on the bow (although I did let them pitch in; more on this later). You don't want really young kids in the engine spaces with machinery running—certainly not when you aren't there. But they can still help you and learn. For example, they can be the mechanic's helper, bringing you tools that are out of the way. You might have to take the time to explain, once, what the open-end wrench is, but they will remember and probably have it out and waiting the next time you need it. They'll watch to see what you do with it. You may well have a better mechanic aboard than yourself. Make sure you don't exclude girls from the mechanical work. They do as well or better than guys.

There are many jobs that kids, of both sexes, can do aboard. Below, I'll just scratch the surface with a few examples. It's important that they all be real jobs, not busywork. For the younger kids, it will help if they can see the results of a job well done right after it is completed. For all, it is important that they realize that what they are doing contributes, and that if they fail or do a job poorly there will be discernible negative consequences.

One of the two most commonly heard compliments about cruising kids is that they are responsible people on whom you can depend. This shouldn't be surprising. It is one of the clear results of the cruising lifestyle. If your job is to pump out the bilge and you forget, the alarm comes on in the middle of the night and everybody is up rushing around wondering if the boat is sinking. If your job is to keep a lookout for markers and you start daydreaming, the boat goes aground and everyone aboard knows why. If your job is to tie on the sailcover and a little squall sends it billowing downwind, you and everyone else knows how well you tied the knots. At sea, it just doesn't do to say, "It's not my fault" or "Someone else should have done it." The cruising life teaches important lessons about life that people ashore don't seem to learn.

Our girls have also helped to clean the deck, hull, and teak. (Actually, they have taken over those three chores with a lot of pride. The boat looks much better now that they have.) When we are hauled, they help to paint the bottom, sand the shaft for zincs, and do other work. When they were smaller, we gave them the job of painting the rudder. They felt an immediate sense of accomplishment when they saw "their" part newly painted. Now they help us with the entire bottom. This makes them familiar with all that's below the waterline and gives them a better appreciation of what their home is all about. In all these jobs, it's important to be sure that they are not exposed to harmful chemicals or dust. We don't allow our children anywhere nearby when the hull is being sanded unless they are well protected. All of us protect ourselves from the paint.

I used to have them watch me and help in whatever way possible when I was working on the engine and other mechanical equipment. When I pulled apart a pump or motor, I would try to show them what it looked like inside and how it did its job for us. As they've grown older they've been able to do many jobs themselves. For example, they can change the engine oil when I don't have time. When they got their own "car," a 12-foot inflatable with a 15-horsepower outboard, they had to rebuild the carburetor and learn about troubleshooting and other aspects of outboard maintenance.

Kids should be asked to stand watch and steer the boat as soon

Carolyn at the helm.

as they are able. Some states don't allow this without some kind of licensing, but kids can sure steer at sea. We were always with them and watching in the early days, but now that's no longer necessary. This is a great opportunity to help kids learn about handling waves, wind, and other dynamics.

When the girls were small, before the family's curse of near-sightedness set in, they made incredible lookouts. They could pick out aids to navigation, landmarks, landfalls, and other boats incredibly well. Even if you can see well, this is a great job for a younger child. The sighting of the lighthouse is an immediate reward, and everyone knows how important it is.

Although there are only four of us, I try to have two people in the cockpit on watch at all times when we are at sea at night: one child and one parent. This creates some great moments of sharing. It also allows you the benefit of younger eyes in picking out a boat off in the dark. Now, we feel comfortable dozing in the cockpit while either of the girls is at the wheel. They know to alert us instantly if they have any questions or if there is any possibility that another boat may be nearby.

Younger members of the family should be involved in sail handling, anchoring, docking, and every other aspect of the operation of the boat. Some jobs, such as anchor handling at the bow, can be potentially dangerous. But they may be forced to do it at some point if you aren't there. It's better to teach them at leisure in ideal circumstances, pointing out and watching for the dangers. The more kids do these jobs, the less dangerous the tasks will be. And even if they don't regularly do them, occasional practice keeps them ready for when they must.

Melanie and Carolyn, even when tiny, would help me get the anchor up. They would stand on the bow, leaning out to look for mud on the chain, which I would clean off. This had the immediate and obvious benefit of keeping the boat clean. It also had the long-term benefit of showing them how I raised the hook and judged different types of bottom.

We raise our main dinghy on davits. At first, either Melanie or Carolyn would help me by cranking the easier winch for the dinghy bow while I cranked up the heavier stern. Now they can do it all without me.

It helps to teach them in stages. For example, when the girls were small they couldn't furl and tie the sailcover because they

"WHAT WERE HIS PARENTS THINKING?"

I was in my dinghy, crossing a crowded harbor in the islands after dark. A bonfire on the beach attracted many cruisers, who had gathered around to sing and play. About 200 yards from the beach, a black shape loomed in front of me. I turned on my spotlight, and the beam settled on an inflatable floating free. The outboard was in the down position. No anchor or line hung over the side, so it didn't appear to have come untied. Someone could have fallen out in the dark, though, so I called out and searched around. Finally, I towed the boat in to the beach, where I saw the name of its mother ship on its side. In the light of the bonfire I called out again, asking if anyone from that boat was around. A teenager stepped from the crowd. He had come ashore in the dinghy and had just pulled it up on the beach, neither tied nor anchored. The tide had come in and floated it off. He had had no idea that this could happen, although he had been cruising with his parents for several months, down the East Coast and out to the Bahamas.

We had to wonder what life aboard was like for this kid. What were his parents thinking? Had he been sitting below all the way down the coast and through the islands?

▼

couldn't reach up high enough or around the bundled sail even if they climbed on the boom. But they did stand on deck with the sail ties, handing them to me when I needed them. They didn't have the strength to pull up the main, but they could pull on the halyard with me, and watch it go up. They couldn't handle the jib winches, but they could tail the rope. Then they could crank the winches once set up. Now, they can do it all.

The more cruising kids participate in running and maintaining the boat, the more they appreciate and enjoy the cruising life. It's impossible to be bored when you're involved, but it's easy to be bored and frustrated if adults think you can't do things.

And all this doesn't just benefit the kids. Recently I injured both my back and right arm. I was unable to do most of what I was accustomed to doing daily while underway. It was time to

▼

leave shore and head across the Gulf Stream for the Bahamas. We had been stuck in the States far beyond our normal departure time. Knowing the competence of my family, I was able to let them do it all. And they did it very well. An added benefit: I was able to type part of the manuscript for this book while sailing south down Exuma Sound. No convalescing in some stateside city for this live-aboard cruiser.

HELP YOUR KIDS ADJUST

Any effort you put into helping your kid adjust to cruising will be worth more than you could imagine, but it may take a little under-standing and time. Your dream won't work if you have sullen fam-ily members who feel they are being dragged along for the ride. This is perhaps most likely to happen with kids in their early and midteens who are leaving behind their Oh-So-Important social norms, their sports or school activities, and their friends. In most cases, the unfolding excitement that is inherent in each passing shoreline, each new place, and each new day at sea can transform the worst skeptic into an aficionado. But if your child has lived confined to pavement and malls and planned communities, if there has been little stimulus beyond TV and popular music and politi-cally correct public pabulum, he or she may need to be guided to-ward accepting the cruising lifestyle as a better way to live.

If you observe other cruising kids, I think you'll find that they generally have strong values. They don't grow up in a world that leaves the teaching of values to surrogate parents and governmen-tal agencies. They are aware, however, of what happens shoreside when children are raised with poor values and allowed to be irre-sponsible. Cruising kids are special because they develop great imaginations and entertain themselves with their own creative ideas; their minds are unfettered from the effects of TV. They find neat, interesting, and fun things to do in the world around them.

TURN ON TO THE NEW WORLD AROUND YOU

Earlier in this chapter, I mentioned buying special equipment for your kids. When you leave, don't let these sit in the lockers. As soon as possible, encourage use of the equipment. If they took lessons prior to the cruise, encourage them to practice what they learned. If they don't, it may not have anything to do with their resourcefulness. You have to ensure that they have the opportunity. For example, if you spent money on boardsailing lessons and a board but rush right on through and don't lay over in any good boardsailing areas, what can they do? If you taught your kids about the constellations but don't involve them in celestial navigation, you've wasted an opportunity. If you don't stop at interesting historical sites, they'll flash by like pictures in a textbook. If you don't go ashore and explore, they might as well watch a movie about someone else's cruise. They need direct experiences. In chapter 23, I list waters and landscapes we are particularly fond of and know well. Take time to see these, and more.

Conduct frequent family outings or projects that strengthen family ties. This is one of the nicest parts about cruising with a family. Outings with other families and their children will help your kids meet new friends. Hiking on deserted islands, exploring caves, snorkeling over reefs or wrecks, diving or spearfishing, sightseeing in foreign lands, shopping and bartering in island markets—these are but a few of the things you can do and enjoy as a family.

As I mentioned in chapter 19, bring resource books to answer questions about stars, fish, reefs, the sea, weather, seamanship. New experiences are more interesting when you already know a little (or a lot) about a subject or region through reading. Make sure books are accessible, and take them out yourself from time to time. Be a role model. See chapter 19 (pages 218–219) for a list of resource books we like to have aboard. There are many others. Shop for the latest before you go.

You'll also be able to pick up books relevant to particular regions as you pass through them. For example, in St. Michaels, Maryland, the Chesapeake Bay Maritime Museum has a bookstore full of material about that area. In Beaufort, North Carolina, the North Carolina Maritime Museum also has regional books, including a good selection dealing with the Outer Banks of North Carolina and the shipwrecks and ghosts of the graveyard of the Atlantic.

FINDING FRIENDS

We've noticed that cruising kids make friends easily. The experienced ones are usually sensitive to the plight of the new kid in the harbor, so they don't make it tough on newcomers. The cruising community, however, doesn't have as many kids as the public school community, so it will take some effort to find other kids.

You can help. First, simply look for other cruising boats with kids on them. They will be looking too. We sometimes hear first contacts being made on the VHF. Boat shows, such as the annual sailboat show in Annapolis, Maryland, in October, is a favorite place for cruising kids to gather and hang out. October is just the time when many cruising families are passing through the area on their way south. This event seems to bring cruisers in from far reaches, by boat, in a sort of temporary community. For some, it offers the chance for a big reunion. The Newport, Rhode Island, boat show also attracts families beginning the trek south. The special stops discussed in chapter 23 are additional places where you might find other cruising kids.

Exchanging kids for the day.

▼

Any harbor that lures cruising boats for longer visits attracts families with kids. George Town, Exumas, is such a place, although this harbor can get too crowded. Other good spots are Beaufort, North Carolina; Vero Beach, Florida; Marathon in the Florida Keys; and Marsh Harbour in Abaco, Bahamas. In the ICW, where the channels are narrow, you can easily spot a boat with kids on it.

Once you begin to find other kids, get to know their families. Try to cruise together for a while, sharing anchorages at night. The trip down the ICW is particularly conducive to this; many families new to cruising travel the waterway at about the same time. They're probably looking for "kid boats" as well. Often we have shared kids for alternating days while traveling with other kid boats along the ICW. If you're traveling about the same speed and sharing anchorages, it isn't difficult to take other kids aboard to spend the day (including school) with yours. This gives the parents an occasional, well-deserved break.

Depending on the age of your kids and your location, you and other parents can help by organizing kids' cruising events. If you share a harbor with a bunch of other kid boats for a while, plan things such as sailing dinghy races, sailboarding races, beach scavenger hunts, and sand sculpture contests. And there's nothing like a bonfire to get people involved. Obviously, many of these activities need the organization, and sometimes close supervision, of parents. For years, in early to mid-March there has been a formal regatta full of kid's events in Elizabeth Harbour, George Town. Families flock to this, and it isn't unusual to see 400 to 500 boats in attendance. But this is just for one week. Don't limit your imagination and activities to special events.

Many cruisers try to zip around the world, or run a straight line, checking off destinations. In our experience, successful long-term cruising families develop cruising patterns; you might even call it migration. They visit favored harbors and cruising grounds every year or every several years. This pattern creates a feeling of continuity and permanency, the chance to make shoreside friends in different places, and the opportunity to learn more about different cultures and geographical features. The kids can look forward to annual events like the Cruising Regatta in George Town, Fourth of July fireworks in special places, and favorite harbors to spend Christmas in.

NEW FAMILY RELATIONSHIPS

The physical closeness of cruising families and the inability to escape siblings will impact your kids' life, as it will yours. Be aware of
the dynamics and be prepared to deal with them, or at least understand what's going on. This can be a very positive development
(see sidebar, page 300).

HOLIDAYS

Don't omit holidays and seasonal celebrations because you are
cruising. To the kids this could be devastating in many ways (to
most adults as well). We celebrate each holiday wherever we are,
and we often try to observe and practice local customs. For Hal-
loween, if appropriate, many kids play trick or treat in dinghies.
(Always set this up with the recipients before doing it.)

(text continued on page 302)

Christmas aboard Chez Nous.

"SMALL SHIPS, CLOSE FAMILIES"
by Carolyn

I've shared the same bedroom, the forward cabin, with my sister ever since I was brought home to the boat as a baby. Together, the two small beds form a V. Some people (usually the ones living in spacious houses) are amazed that we don't hate each other by now. I guess when people live in a house with what I would call too much space, they don't find themselves having to put up with other family members unless they want to. On a boat, of course, this is all much different because the living quarters are smaller than what most people are used to. Our boat is considered large by many of our cruising friends, but the fact is that there's no way to avoid other family members unless you jump ship (that is, of course, not recommended). Somehow, though, my family and I all get along fine.

When we were younger, my parents were concerned that we would fall off the beds because of the motion of the boat, so they enclosed both of them in netting. Needless to say, the netting is gone now, but we do have curtains my mom made that we can close if we want privacy. From our forward cabin it's less than a 50-foot walk to our parent's bedroom, so we're pretty close.

My family and I have shared some unforgettable times together. One of the most memorable times for me was at Compass Cay in the Exumas. We started going there when I was around five years old, because we had some very dear friends who lived in a house on one of the island's hills. We would tie up our boat at their dock, which was located in a snug, protected harbor, and find ourselves within a short walking distance to an oceanside beach where we would go swimming or body surfing. We would also run along the water's edge under the bright sun. We sometimes spent all day exploring trails that wind through the tropical undergrowth. When a trail led to the water, my sister and I would climb along the high sandstone shoreline until we found hollows in the rocks that were comfortable for us to sit in and watch the ocean. This and experiences like it have made me consider it a good thing that we've all lived so close to one another. We are able to learn together and from each other in a way that would not be possible otherwise.

As much as I might say about how nice it is to live so close together, I have to admit that, like everything else, it has its down sides. It's certainly natural for any human being to want to be alone at times, and when this happens you do the obvious—make some room for them to be by themselves. On our boat, this usually involves either my sister or me leaving our bedroom for a while, but somehow it all works out.

There's one other thing I'd like to mention about living in close quarters, and I've observed this not only in my family but in others as well: the roles of the younger and older siblings seem to be more defined. There are, of course, some exceptions, but it seems that the older siblings are very noticeably the ones who like to be in control, and in many cases are more outgoing, while the younger ones tend to be just the opposite. Also, I think that cruising siblings, since they live side by side and share all their experiences, have a strong influence over each other. They try to do everything alike, and usually it's the younger who follows the older's actions. For example, it's a tradition on *Chez Nous* to have a live Christmas tree, complete with elaborate decorations and candy canes. These candy canes were objects of tremendous value to my sister and me. They were a rare treat because our parents didn't allow us to have too many too often. So every now and then when my sister was feeling extra adventurous, she would secretly converse with me in our bedroom. A few minutes later I would come toddling through the galley and up the two steps to our main salon where the tree was located. I would then stand on tiptoes to sneak or, as my sister and I pronounced it back in those early days, "neak," a candy cane from its branches and toddle on back to my sister. It was a long time ago, so I may not remember correctly, but I'm pretty sure that I was *not* the one who ate the stolen treasure. I think it's pretty obvious who did, though!

Needless to say, my sister doesn't have that much power over me these days, but even though we have our disagreements at times, we are pretty much open toward each other about our feelings. When you're living aboard with your family, you have to remember that not just you, but everybody, has to be understanding of each other's needs. Even though it might seem unavoidable at times, arguing with people because you are temporarily sick of living so close to them isn't the answer. What's important is to have a good attitude and to appreciate the unique experience you are sharing with the people you live with.

▼

(text continued from page 299)

We have spent our last 17 Christmases aboard and have always had a live tree, usually cedar or pine. We carry the tree in a bucket down the ICW, and sometimes we even cross the Gulf Stream with it wrapped in a bag to keep off the salt spray. We keep the tree on deck until a week or so before Christmas. Tugboat and megayacht captains, and even bridge tenders, hail us with a special greeting when they see it.

Melanie and Carolyn never worried about Santa Claus finding us, but we have always worried about finding a good harbor in which to greet him. For us, Christmas in a deserted place, no matter how beautiful, just isn't Christmas. Sharing the season with other cruising families is one of the many highlights of this lifestyle, regardless of religious beliefs. We love to get into the dinghy and go from boat to boat singing carols. Many bustling anchorages become lonely and empty around this time, as cruisers seem to congregate in certain spots where they don't have to worry much about the weather, where it is easy to get about in the dinghy, where the people ashore are friendly, and where there are sure to be other cruisers.

We plan to arrive well before Christmas. This lifestyle is full of unsettled weather and unmet schedules, and it's easy to get caught by bad weather and spend the time hanging on for dear life behind some rock. We have friends with kids who spent Christmas Day and night crashing across the Great Bahama Banks because of a surprise front. That isn't the way it's supposed to be. Plenty of lead time not only ensures that you'll be there, it also gives you the chance to relax and get into the mood. In chapter 23 I'll talk about our cruising neighborhood and the places that make great Christmas stops.

CONTINUED CONTACT FROM "HOME"

It might also help reluctant new cruising kids to adjust if they begin a newsletter to their friends. You can do it as a family, or help your kids to set up their own. Work on this before you leave. Talk with a favorite teacher. She or he may be interested in a newsletter addressed to the class. This is but one of many worthwhile projects your cruising budget should underwrite. It costs only the paper and postage. Sometimes recipients are so interested, they will pay the postage. You'll also need a computer aboard.

Talk to your kids about writing to their friends. Bring along plenty of paper (let them pick out or decorate their own stationary, if they wish) and stamps. This ancient and important art is now all but dead, except in the cruising community. Our kids sometimes mail and receive two to three dozen letters a month.

Also consider inviting that best friend from your old hometown for a visit. It shouldn't be too difficult while you're still in the States. Interestingly, even though the visit is eagerly anticipated when it is planned, both kids often find that they've moved on and a bit apart. The separation anxiety tends to melt away as they realize they are each enjoying new things unfamiliar to the other. Some parents have reported to us that they've sent their homesick/old-friend-sick kids back home for a weekend or more to visit and that this quickly cures the blues. The child returns with a better appreciation of how neat the new life is and a bit skeptical about how limiting the old mall mentality is. This may not be a cure-all, but keep it in mind if you're having a problem.

OTHER THINGS TO DO

I've mentioned books a few times, and that the video player has found its way firmly into the cruising world. Watching videos can be immensely entertaining for kids (as well as the adults) and they give you control over and awareness of what your kid is watching. In almost any cruising anchorage you'll find rentals ashore, and other cruisers are often willing to trade. The supply is almost limitless.

Diaries or journals are popular with many cruising kids. The vessel keeps a log; the kids keep a diary. New places and the new things they are experiencing—from storms and groundings to breakdowns and new acquaintances—make interesting and unusual diary material. Many cruising kids, girls especially, have friendship books, sometimes one for each year, in which their newfound friends write something memorable. Photo albums and photography are both fun and particularly relevant to the cruising life.

Games can be a help, although you need to watch their space consumption. Computer games can be educational and fun but take up little space. The Carmen San Diego series entertained our kids for years. Me too. The computer itself opens untold entertainment and educational opportunities for kids. They can learn to touch-type with it. They can learn music on it, such as playing the

(text continued on page 306)

"WRITING LETTERS" by Melanie

L etters are great to receive, but if you're a kid and you live on land, it isn't likely that you get very many. Most people on shore think of the Postal Service as a way to pay bills and receive catalogs. In the land of phones and the ever-present and ominous Internet, who needs letters anyway? We do—"we" being the population of cruising kids.

I have pen pals all over the place. One is going to college in California; I met her years ago when she was visiting her grandparents in the Bahamas. Another is eight years old and cruised for a year before moving back to Massachusetts. Yet another lives on a farm in Virginia. How I met each of these people is a story in itself, but when we met I can tell you one thing for sure—we had no idea that years later we'd still be writing. A friend who takes the time to write is special, and, more often than not, whether a person writes can be a fair gauge as to whether or not they are worth your friendship.

One of the most interesting letter-writing relationships I have had was with Jessi. She cruised for a year with her parents aboard *Pair Egrenations* when I was 11 and she was 10. We met them at Highborne Cay in the Exumas, but didn't really get to know them until we were both anchored at Staniel Cay. She and I were both attending the Calvert School (a correspondence school) at the time, she being a year behind me, and we had a lot in common. Cruising kids were fewer then than they are now, and we became inseparable. Our families explored Pipe Creek together, had cookouts, and went on diving expeditions. We sailed to George Town in February, where Jessi and I played on the beach every day with Michelle, one of my oldest and closest friends. We met up again in the Abacos. When we separated for the summer, Jessi and I were both upset, but we promised to write.

Her family moved ashore near Jacksonville, Florida, and kept their boat, but Jessi returned to the life of regular school. When we were anchored in Fernandina, Florida, they came out to *Chez Nous* for an evening. As we quietly swung at anchor, we talked of all our adventures and mishaps of the past year. That was the last we ever saw of them.

That summer, Jessi and I wrote to each other at least once a week. She missed the boat, and I missed the Bahamas, and we shared stories and drew pictures and sent each other little trinkets in the mail. After a year or so, the stream of letters slacked off. I met new people and she grew accustomed to land-life. Occasionally, we would still write when something really important happened, but eventually we stopped altogether.

Last summer when we were in Newport, Rhode Island, and Dad was working at *Cruising World,* a letter arrived addressed to the magazine. It was from Jessi, five years after we had last seen each other. It was evident that she missed cruising, although she was nicely secured in high school life. I wrote her a long letter, and got one back, learning that they still had the boat and still sailed every once in a while. It was great to hear from her.

This goes to show that letter writing can create strong bonds, and also that cruising kids don't forget each other easily, even though they may move on to different places, people, and situations. For kids just starting to cruise, letters from back home ease the pain of leaving, although I've frequently noticed that the kids they write to are too busy mall-hopping to write back. This is sad, and though there are certainly exceptions, the land kids usually never catch on. Sometimes they'll surprise you, though. I have a friend in Virginia who has never been on a boat for more than a week, but he still writes to me at least once a month.

The materials are few and simple—paper, pens, envelopes, and stamps for whatever country you are visiting. These things are a lot less expensive than two minutes on-line, and they hardly take up any space. You'll need to watch the envelopes because they get stuck together from condensation. Putting waxed paper between the sticky part and the body of the envelope will make it last a little bit longer. Or, try to find self-adhesive envelopes with seals over the sticky part. Also, look for self-adhesive stamps. Paper is a matter of preference; I've gotten letters on everything from graph paper to Monopoly money.

Don't be afraid to write first—in most of my correspondence friendships I have been the first one to write. Usually, people will answer. If they don't, it's not a big deal.

I keep most of my letters, because I like to read them over again, and because they are special to me. So are the people who write them. I always thought that I wrote more letters than I received, until recently when I met my match in letter writing. Even I couldn't keep up when I realized that this person was writing me a letter every day!

Out in the islands, I throw my fate to the currents and trust my letters to the weekly mailboats. I walk among pink, blue, and green houses to the little post office and drop my letters into a tiny slit in the wall. Inside, I listen to the faint rustle as they fall to the concrete floor, waiting for the mailboat to come.

▼

▼

(text continued from page 303)

piano. They can have a huge encyclopedia and other research material aboard if yours has a CD-ROM reader. Software changes radically and rapidly, so I won't recommend specific programs. Shortly before you leave, check out the software available in a good shop. I can't emphasize enough how valuable an onboard computer can be.

As we discussed earlier, bring along toys as appropriate.

Hobbies are often overlooked ashore and in the cruising community. If your kids already have hobbies, help them bring them along if practical. If not, work on getting something new that complements cruising. Again, chapter 19 lists many of these, but I can add stamp collecting, sewing, cooking, and more. For years Carolyn caught small fish in the Bahamas and observed them. She kept them in a portable clear plastic tank or cage with a top—very practical for hamsters, goldfish, hermit crabs, and lizards. She caught food for them by dipping up sargassum weed with a fishnet as we sailed along, removing small creatures such as tiny fish, shrimp, and crabs. After a while, she would release her wild pets.

Musical instruments, ranging from keyboards plugged into a computer, to harmonicas, to guitars, to conch horns, can not only be entertaining to your kids, they can help them find friends and a place in the cruising community.

Money-making projects can be fun, too. Melanie long ago began painting T-shirts. Each one is a one-off, hand-painted original—no silk screens or artificial reproductions. Occasionally she sells them on the beach. She also makes jewelry. We've seen other kids making shell jewelry, lemonade for popular cruising beaches, and painted shells.

There is almost always a need for bottom cleaning. If you are in a clean, safe harbor and if your kids swim and dive well, they may find a lot of jobs. (Warn them about barnacle cuts and swimming in clouds of toxins brushed off the boat's bottom. We prefer some current for this job.) You'll need plenty of good brushes and wide paint scrapers, but you probably have them on hand for your own boat. Kids also get odd jobs such as polishing stainless, cleaning hulls, and maintaining teak. Always be careful that you don't run afoul of local laws.

Inherent in all of this is the obvious fact that there must be somewhere for your kids to retreat, to do things, and to store their stuff.

Kids are not an afterthought, their stuff should not be an after-thought, and their spaces on the boat should not be. They need private space, even if it's only their bunk enclosed by a curtain, and they should be allowed to decorate it as they wish. As much as possible, this must be respected as their special place. We occasionally have to disrupt some of our girls' private lockers to get deep down into our forward nether regions for special ground tackle. It has always seemed to be a moment of pain. Privacy is important. Your kids must also have their own private lockers and shelves, just as they would have in a house. Plan for these well before you take off. I heard of one family who began cruising with a ban on books and toys because the father felt that they were too heavy and would impair his boat's performance. The family's lifelong cruise lasted less than a year. Normal human needs don't disappear as soon as you go to sea. If your boat won't allow for privacy, get another boat, rebuild the one you have, or forget some of your stuff.

PETS

In the seminars I give, I always ask for questions from the audience. Invariably, kids ask about pets, and when they do, you can detect a fair amount of anxiety in the question. We have always had pets, though perhaps not the kind we would have had ashore. Many other cruisers I know have pets. If having a pet is important to your kids, try to accommodate them if you can.

Obviously, small pets are the way to go. It's also important that they be able to "go" on the boat in an acceptable place, that they not pose cleanliness problems, and that you can carry enough food to last until you can resupply. I've seen dogs, some quite large, aboard cruising boats. It most cases, all parties, including the dog, are quite happy. *But*, unless you are tolerant and have a trainable dog, or can find a place to walk it, you will have a problem. Along the ICW and its inland waters, you can get ashore to do this, but the people who live ashore would just as soon not have you land on their property to poop your dog, thank you. There are many other impediments to walking your dog. Sometimes the seas are too rough and you can't get to shore. Sometimes there's no place to anchor *and* land the dinghy. If you do get ashore, you may encounter alligators. And, many dog owners tell me (always taking care not to let doggie know) that there are many times when they just don't feel like getting in the dinghy, getting wet and/or cold, and going ashore. If your kids already have a dog, then there is probably no decision to be made. But if they don't, think about alternatives.

Cats make excellent cruising pets. Not only are the generally smaller than dogs, they generally train well. They tend to be more content to curl up in a corner and amuse themselves. Besides, as they see it, they're above dashing around to find something to chase and bark at. They also can come in handy when you inadvertently take on a pet cockroach or mouse or, worse still, a rat. It does happen, even on the very nicest boats. However, both cats and dogs can infest a boat with fleas. Be prepared.

We started with hamsters. They lived in their cage and met all the requirements. Hamster food often came with vermin, so we were careful to store it in airtight plastic containers. Our hamsters loved to escape. They proved particularly adept at this whenever the girls decided to take them out and dress them up in doll clothes. A hamster running loose on a boat is no better than a rat or mouse running loose on a boat. And these creatures hide in the most inaccessible places until they get hungry at night. If they can't find anything better to eat, they will eat hoses (as in below the waterline) and electrical insulation. Needless to say, the thought of setting out a rat trap for that fluffy little pet with a loving name doesn't make for a happy crew. Another problem with hamsters is that they tend to look alike at the pet store, whether boys or girls or pregnant or not. We have had numerous respectable pet store employees guarantee that said new purchase was not pregnant and, besides, was a boy anyway—only to have it off-load a dozen or so babies within a few days of coming aboard. If you get hamsters, be sure to get them well before you set sail so that you can straighten out these matters. Another negative: hamsters don't seem to live long. There are *Chez Nous* hamster graveyards all up and down the East Coast and throughout the Bahamas. All in all, we thought they were relatively good cruising pets.

Goldfish, believe it or not, have made excellent pets. Our first concern was to anchor the bowl, which was no problem. We built a teak rack to hold it. Even though the fish resided in the forward cabin with the girls, and even though it has gotten rough up there from time to time—so much so that the girls squealed as they became airborne when the bow plunged—the water generally stayed in the bowl. This cannot be said for the fish, unfortunately. Once, after we had sailed through a rough inlet, one of the two fish simply wasn't there anymore. We looked all around the bowl, on the shelves, and on the cabin sole with no results. Four hot tropical days later we found Goldie where she had expired, up in the toe of one of Carolyn's shoes.

The major problem with goldfish is treating new water before adding it to the bowl. As you travel from port to port and take on water, changes in the water's chemistry will kill any goldfish. We soon learned to buy water-treatment pellets from the pet store, and to let the new water sit outside a long time, after being treated, before pouring it into the bowl. Reverse-osmosis water (from a water-maker) has always worked fine. If you are debating whether to get a watermaker, this fact will surely be the final pièce de résistance.

Perhaps our most successful pet was Dixie, a budgie. We kept it in a cage, and the girls spent many hours learning how to talk like birds. (They said they were teaching it to talk, but that isn't the way it worked out. The only really human sound I ever heard was "tweet tweet.") Dixie was resilient in many sea conditions and varied temperature extremes. Once, while going out an inlet, we fell

Carolyn and our parakeet, Dixie.

off a huge wave. Dixie's cage broke loose and flew through the air, hitting the deck with a crash six feet below the shelf where the cage had sat. Dixie, although a bit unhappy, wasn't hurt at all. Just a month or so ago, however, Dixie fell off the cage while we were tied up in a flat-calm marina and broke a leg. This proved to be too much, and the bird eventually passed away.

We have always had special burials for our pets—usually at sea with all the trappings. (When you have your first burial at sea, avoid doing it when there are barracuda around . . .) As I noted above, we have frequently buried hamsters ashore, always looking for a nice plot of green grass, such as those usually found behind a Keep off the Grass sign. Alas, Dixie passed on in Ft. Lauderdale during a particularly ferocious northeaster. We couldn't bury the bird ashore in the midst of a city, and we certainly couldn't get out to sea in the storm. The thought of burying Dixie on the beach with the churning waves and churning feet of tourists was equally unappealing. After much thought and discussion, we finally came up with the only answer. We prepared the body in a small cardboard Dixie-brand sugar canister weighted with sand and grass and flowers. We all mournfully walked up the tall Seventeenth Street Causeway Bridge, carrying the coffin. For those of you who haven't been to Ft. Lauderdale, the Seventeenth Street bridge is a major bridge over the ICW, just up from the Port Everglades Inlet and its turning basin, where yachts and ships from around the world enter and maneuver. Huge passenger liners, sometimes even the *Queen Elizabeth II*, come into the basin. At the eastern end of the bridge lies the world-famous Pier 66 Marina and, at the western end, Lauderdale Marina. Some of the most elegant and expensive megayachts of the world pass through the bridge and dock at the marinas, not to mention thousands of other pleasureboats traveling the ICW. The bridge itself has a beautiful mural of a jumping marlin on one of its supports. At the very top (but just to the side of the main span) we said a few words and committed Dixie to the deep.

As the bird plummeted downward, I looked around to see if a megayacht had chosen that moment to pass under that particular span. I was envisioning the scene on the flying bridge of a billion-dollar floating palace as Dixie made contact with a $10,000 chart plotter, or a captain in uniform. But none of this happened, and Dixie found a resting place in the bosom of the outgoing tide. Needless to say, I wouldn't suggest doing this with a dog.

BABIES ABOARD, by Mel

Babies aboard are easier after they are born—you don't have to carry them all the time. They are harder when they become mobile; harder still when they can toddle. The real fun begins when a second or a third arrives and the normal routine is compounded by the sibling thing. I would not have missed any minute of it, although at times I wonder how in the world we all made it through those first years.

We moved aboard *Chez Nous* three months before Melanie was born. She was our first; we had waited long before we decided it was time to have children. We felt the normal parental apprehensions about whether we were doing the right thing for our child and the right thing for ourselves. But we knew the boat was where we wanted to live, and that we would make it work, despite what some friends and family said.

In our circumstances, we would never have had a home birth. If I had been much younger and cruising in remote areas of the world, I might have considered delivering a baby aboard the boat. I was having my first at age 33 while *Chez Nous* was tied up to a comfortable dock close to a large city; it was not worth taking any risk. We brought Melanie from the hospital directly to the boat; less than two years later we brought Carolyn home.

The babies were quite easy to take care of when all they did was lie there and sleep, eat, or cry. For the first few months they each slept in a small basket that we could move around and wedge into different parts of the dinette as the boat heeled. Sometimes I carried them in a baby carrier on my chest. Sometimes we strapped them into a small car seat—a type no longer legal in cars. This seat enabled them to be up and looking around, but they were strapped into the seat as well as to a part of the boat. When they were on deck, we always held them unless they were strapped into the seat. We purchased the smallest life jacket available. It was made by Mustang and had a special support for the back of the head and extra buoyancy on the front of the chest. This kept the head up, supported, and facing the right way. It didn't fit the babies when they were tiny, but it was the best we could do. They were breast-fed in those days, each for most of a year, so I had no baby food to prepare.

Laundry was a problem, but it would be with a baby anywhere. We chose to use disposable diapers; real diapers were more

▼

than I could handle with respect to storage (of dirty ones) and laundry. I don't like to waste trees, but we could not come up with any other solution. Trash disposal was not a problem because we were cruising stateside at first. Where trash, cost, and storage of disposables is a problem, one would have to determine whether laundering cloth diapers would be easier. I know many cruisers who have tried both with mixed results. Where they did laundry by hand—first washing in salt water, then rinsing in fresh—the baby's skin became irritated from the salt and possibly from not getting the diapers as clean as hot fresh water would have. Most cruising boaters cannot not carry enough fresh water to do the whole diaper wash in fresh water. Many laundromats do not have hot or even warm water, so this may not be any better than hand washing. At sea, disposable diapers can be separated by removing the plastic covering for disposal ashore and saturating the biodegradable paper part so that it sinks, thus helping with the trash problem. Obviously, one would not want to do this in coastal waters and/or where it is illegal. Early potty training is desirable aboard cruising boats, for good reason. You also see lots of bare-bottomed babies on cruising boats.

We worried a lot about the babies' safety in rough conditions. During their crawling stage they were strapped into the seat if it was really rough; if the weather was nice, they wore child-size safety harnesses (with careful watching so they did not become tangled in the tether) in the cockpit, which was completely enclosed. If they went on deck with one of us, they wore the life jacket, which fit them by that time, and the harness when we were underway. At anchor they were given a little more freedom to explore, especially at the toddler stage, but always with a life jacket on. We installed lifeline netting that completely surrounded the deck, so safety at anchor involved teaching not to climb up the lifelines.

The most valuable thing we did for the babies' safety and our peace of mind was to teach them to be comfortable in the water in their life jackets and to swim without them as early as was possible. Simple and fun play and splashing around in shallow water was begun as soon as they could hold up their heads. The big hurdle was to get them to enjoy being splashed in the face. Beaches, swimming pools, and friends' bathtubs enabled them to float freely and to feel their own buoyancy. We tried to balance the fun and splashing in the life jackets with real swimming lessons. They had to swim back and forth from one parent to the other, which made it a fun game. They have been excellent swimmers since the time they could walk, but more important, they did not fear the water.

A safe berth for young children is an important consideration. When ours were too big for the basket, we were able to find a small portable playpen that doubled as a berth with the addition of some foam padding around the base. This took a lot of precious floor space, but enabled us to relax with the babies in a safe place. It worked until they could stand up and climb out. The next step was to convert the V-berth area to a child-safe spot. For us this involved fitting a strong fabric from bottom to top between the two bunks to separate them. It is important to make it tight enough so that the child cannot get out underneath or fit its head into the space on top. This could result in strangulation. We next made a fitted net covering (canvas was sewn on the edges and small snap shackles were attached in six places) for the open space of the bunk. We could unsnap it quickly and easily from the top, but it fit tightly all the way around, top, bottom, and sides. It allowed for ventilation and for the child to see out, but made a secure, private place to sleep and play. When you are making a child restraint of any type, it's important to consider the natural curiosity of young kids: they like putting small things in their mouths, chewing, sticking heads and limbs through holes, and climbing anything there is to climb. Always closely observe the child using the item you make before you leave him or her unattended, even if just to sleep. Babies wake up and play at strange times and will try anything and everything.

Buttons, lights, and all the things that parents keep turning and switching, especially on the electrical panel, are fascinating to a child. They can also be extremely dangerous. These also include stove controls and the lighted propane switch and autopilot controls. A steering wheel being turned by the autopilot may be deadly to a small child caught in the wrong place. Watch closely and teach them not to touch until they are big enough and ready to help safely. It may be possible to cover your electrical panel with Plexiglas; with ingenuity you may be able to come up with some type of child-proof solution. Electrical outlets can be plugged with plastic plugs made for household use. Sharp and pointy objects can be smoothed over with silicone or filed or sanded off. Dangling ropes and cords are everywhere on a boat. Watch and teach and make childproof when possible.

We have suggested elsewhere that the child should begin help-ing as early as possible. We don't mean that you should sacrifice sound safety practices for this purpose. But you will find that even toddlers will be fascinated with what is going on, and you shouldn't discourage their curiosity. Make it a part of their learning—not just a big NO. At first, this will take extra time as you teach and watch to see that there is no safety hazard while you're doing your own job (for example, there are no edibles in a tool box). But babies take extra time. Still, you won't have any finer times, and in the long run involving them early will pay off immeasurably for both you and your child.

Take a good look around the boat's interior from a floor-level perspective and see what dangers and also what interesting play-things you might find. You will be amazed at the things we grown-ups don't see because we're always looking from above. We found some sharp edges, for example, under the nav station chair, which were just the wrong height for a crawling baby's head. We covered these with silicone sealant.

You don't need all that baby paraphernalia that society, other mothers, and department stores make you think you need. Babies can get along with very little materially, but need a lot of help and love from their parents. Other mothers based ashore worried that our kids did not have a highchair to eat in. This was just one of the many unnecessary things. Babies are easy to hold when they eat solid food; very early on they like to sit and eat for themselves. I did get a small plastic bathtub and put it in the bottom of the stall shower. The kids had a lot of fun in it when they were old enough to sit up and play with rubber duckies.

A final thought about children: the more you have, the harder it is to watch them all the time, and the more you have to consider the aspect of sibling relationships. When they are very young, they are not capable of looking out for each other and may not want to. Not all of them will mature at the same rate; just because one didn't climb out of the bunk at five months does not mean that the next one won't. They may push each other at unexpected times or encourage each other to take chances or get in trouble in many ways that an only child never would. At young ages, the more children there are, the harder the parents must work; as the children get older they entertain each other, they look out for and help each other, and they have a special closeness that is unusual among siblings.

PERILS OF PARADISE

Cruising is about more parenting, not less. Although I've cautioned about this in preceding chapters, I can't emphasize enough the dangers in developing the attitude that cruising is a vacation from parenting. Although this should be obvious, a number of cruising parents become lulled by the spectacular beauty, by the vacation atmosphere, by the laid-back tenor of island life, and perhaps the misconception that there are no perils in paradise. How wrong they are.

BE VIGILANT

There is a beautiful ocean beach on Stocking Island, the long barrier island of Elizabeth Harbour at George Town. As I mentioned earlier, this is an immensely popular cruising harbor, often with 400 to 500 boats anchored during the winter season. It has thus become a good place for cruisers with kids to stop, because there are almost always boats with cruising kids there. They can walk over the high island to the ocean beach and find good swimming and surfing, although this isn't an officially designated swimming beach. It's just one of the few sand beaches in the area. Rocks with caverns and suction holes at either end are prevalent along this beach.

Year after year, I've seen groups of cruising kids, from just below 10 years old to the upper teens, swimming and surfing here without anyone watching or acting as lifeguard. The parents are usually tending to other pleasurable pursuits in the harbor. Strong rip currents in this area, some of which run parallel to the beach, can suck a swimmer into the rocks. If someone were sucked out to sea or hurt, the others would have to run about a mile down the beach, up and over the high backbone of the island, down to the beach at the other side, get into a dinghy, and go out to an anchored boat to get a VHF radio and call for help. The responding cruisers would have to send someone on foot back over the same route. To reach the scene by water, a dinghy or fast boat would have to travel several miles down the harbor, out the cut (which can be very rough), and then back up the eastern side of the island. In that amount of time it is unlikely that anyone in serious trouble would survive. If a swimmer had been sucked out, he or she would probably no longer be visible. There is no U.S. Coast Guard personnel on regular duty, nor is there any other formal rescue service.

Yet we have repeatedly seen crowds of kids swimming and surfing under these circumstances, the parents nearby but apparently not realizing the danger.

To give the kids some degree of safety to go along with the great fun they are having (and to which they are entitled), all it takes is one sufficiently strong older kid who has the proper training and experience (many do) to act as lifeguard, or a parent with the same qualification. The lifeguard could be equipped with a handheld VHF to call for quick help should it be needed.

Is any of this ever done at this beach? Almost never. Would you send your kids to swim on an ocean beach in the States without a lifeguard or at least a watch? I doubt it. But people often do in paradise, where there are no search planes, no fast rescue boats, no hospitals or doctors—only miles and miles of ocean punctuated here and there by sharp rock. This is but one example of many that we have observed where parents are lulled into a false sense of security.

Another caution: There are many nice walks, some along cliffs towering above the sea. Often these cliffs have been eroded by waves. Warn your kids about these, and know where the safe and unsafe walks are.

DINGHY SAFETY

Don't let your kids operate dinghies with outboards until they know how. Make them drive for a while with you as a passenger so that they learn the skills with your supervision. This doesn't take extra time; you'll be traveling around in your dinghy anyway—just let your child drive. Kids like to take on responsibility. Use this desire to teach them small-boat handling skills. I've seen kids become seriously injured, some killed, when younger people (older too, of course) were running dinghies without training. These accidents often occur when kids are running up to or away from a crowded beach, impressing their friends and forgetful of the spinning propeller. A dinghy that hits a wave at high speed can toss a child out of the boat, and this happens frequently. Kill switches attached to a lanyard that is secured to the driver have saved many lives. Ensure that your outboard has one and that your young driver always has it securely attached.

Teach your kids to swim—and swim well—before you leave. I'm not referring to proficiency in the butterfly stroke or the crawl.

I'm talking about survival swimming and floating, and how to react when you land in the cold, rough drink with no warning. Teach them how to stay afloat in those circumstances for long periods of time. Teach them what to do if they fall overboard, and what to do if you fall overboard. Teach them about maintaining visual contact with the victim, reciprocal courses, and getting people back aboard. Practice these techniques as a family.

CRIME

There is crime in paradise; there is crime around seaports. Don't think that all quaint tropical islands are immune, and don't take the chance and let your kids roam without supervision. If possible, check with local authorities about the crime rate; law enforcement is lax in many tropical islands communities. And don't rely on your guidebook to warn you; it may not. Although crime is less of a problem on the islands than in densely populated mainland areas, the crime rate in island cruising areas seems to be increasing, particularly as you see the TV dishes multiply.

SAFETY EQUIPMENT

With younger kids in particular, it's helpful to have a safety net all around the boat. When our girls were just crawling and then tottering about, we had our netting so snug and secure that they could wander about the entire deck without going over. We never let them wander around without watching them, but the netting made things much safer and less stressful. Now that our girls are 14 and 16, we still have this netting because we found that it does a great job of keeping our abundant cruising stuff on the boat. It isn't as escape-proof as it was in the early days, but it still makes us feel better.

Have safety harnesses and see to it that they are worn at the appropriate times. This will vary with the child's age, your boat, its cockpit, and the conditions—but better safe than sorry. When they were very small, we put our girls in harnesses whenever we were underway and they were out on deck. Obviously, the same goes for life jackets. Spend the money to get quality life jackets, designed for the size and weight of your child. This is no place to scrimp.

We never allow our kids (or ourselves) on deck at sea at night unless they are wearing a life jacket with a personal strobe. If there is a sudden lurch and someone goes over, the odds of being found on

▼

a dark night are extremely slim without this measure. In most conditions while underway at sea in the dark, we don't allow the kids (or ourselves) to venture outside the cockpit without wearing a harness.

NATURAL HAZARDS

Teach your kids early about creatures that bite and sting. The books I mentioned in chapter 19 are a good place to start. Many stings can have serious effects on some people. For example, fire coral can cause respiratory arrest. Stingrays, sleeping peacefully in the white sand where you love to wade, can give powerful, incredibly painful stings and leave their barbs in the victim. Often they are mostly covered by sand, but if you are accustomed to looking out for them, you'll probably be able to spot them. Start pointing them out to your kids early on. Sea urchins, which look like little round black porcupines, give painful stings. Rocks in the shallows have lots of neat things underneath, and most younger kids can entertain themselves for hours looking. They also have bristle worms, which give bad stings and leave the bristles behind. Baby conch, cute in their tiny new shells, love to graze in shallow water near the beaches. This is where we often love to swim and wade. Their shells have very sharp points. When you step on them, they give deep puncture wounds, frequently leaving a part of the point and also organisms inside the wound. These wounds often become seriously infected. Tell your kids to look out for baby conch. Coral cuts can also become infected. A little piece of coral can remain inside the wound and continue to live. If you treat it with iodine, the coral will be in seventh heaven and thrive inside the cut. Iodine is found in the sea, and coral love it. Tell your kids to avoid touching coral, not only for the sake of the reef, but also for their sake.

There is no mystery to safe parenting on a cruising boat. Be as alert and vigilant as you would anywhere else. At sea you need an extra dose of vigilance because you're in a new world with strange and unfamiliar dangers—and strange and unfamiliar beauties and pleasures.

Chapter Twenty-Two
TEACH YOUR CHILDREN WELL

If you have children, there is nothing more important you can do in life than providing them with a good education. Different folks have different teaching abilities and aptitudes. For some, the best thing may be to send the kids to public schools or private schools. But if you have the qualifications and the emotional wherewithal to teach your children yourself, you are blessed with a gift that will make your life meaningful beyond your imagination. If you can do this while cruising, you will have added dimensions to the educational process that make the institutional classroom pale to insignificance.

When we first began teaching our children there were fewer people doing it than today. Some states, arrogantly assuming that a bureaucracy could teach children better than qualified parents, attempted to stop the movement with oppressive Big Brother legislation. To the surprise of no one, many of those advocating mandatory public classroom education were the very ones who had so abysmally failed. They were turning out high school graduates unable to speak proper English (or any other language), unable to do basic mathematics, unable to spell, and unable to write. Their solution, of course, was to lower the grading standards so that it would look like the students were doing well (until you interviewed the graduate as a job or college applicant). They tried to guarantee their own jobs, despite their failed performance, by requiring every child to be "educated" by them. Fortunately this ran so solidly against common sense, our nation's fundamental belief in some degree of freedom, and the Constitution, that the various legislatures began to relax their stranglehold on the continuing intellectual growth of the young.

There are indeed many dedicated public-sector teachers and administrators, and there are many systems that work well, but we did not wish to gamble with the future of our children. Even though a particular English teacher may have been excellent in one system, for example, we wanted excellence in education across the board.

And we did not want our children held back to accommodate those who were unable or not motivated to make the grade. We were ready to fight to teach our kids, even if we had remained ashore.

CAN YOU DO IT?

Teaching your kids at home is an extremely time-consuming, often difficult task. Obviously, you must have the necessary education, although this certainly doesn't have to be a degree in public education. It also requires unrelenting commitment, and if you find that it's too hard or too time-consuming, or if you change your mind, you have no honest choice but to resume public school without delay. This may be a bit difficult if you are in a remote area.

We have seen a few people take off with noble ideas about teaching their kids but then begin to let it slide. They get involved with the typical vacation attitude of many seasonal cruisers, they begin to find more and more excuses, and soon they are saying things like, "Oh, the world is their teacher," or, "They are learning so much by just being out here, we'll have plenty of time to catch up later." While teaching your kids well is the best thing you can do with your life, depriving them of a good education is perhaps one of the worst things that you can do.

Considerably more time is required to teach younger kids. It will probably take, on average, three to five hours a day, five days a week—and more if needed. During these hours, parent and child work together. A good program will begin teaching students to study and work alone. As they reach junior high school level, you may find, if you have been pursuing a good program, that less and less of your time is required, although you must always be there helping and checking to see that the work is done and done properly. A typical school day at this level is five to six hours long, but most of this time does not involve the parent directly. There will be special days—during rough passages or serious storms or major breakdowns—when school will have to take a recess, but these days must be made up.

Although Mel and I met the legal requirements for teaching our kids ourselves, we also chose to enroll them in approved and accredited correspondence schools. We wanted the objectivity that this would promote, we wanted a formal curriculum and schedule, we wanted review by someone outside our family, and we wanted course preparation by true experts in the field. We also wanted our kids to have formal graduation documentation. This has been costly over the years, averaging approximately $700 for elementary school and $1,000 for high school per year per child. Although this has been a significant financial challenge, it has been worth it many times over. In Canada, at this writing, the public school system provides books and course material free, for a while. We have felt strongly that the public schools systems in States should do this also, because we still pay taxes to support our children's schooling. As it is, we are paying double. We pay for the public system's often incompetent efforts, and we pay to get good material to ensure that our kids do receive a good education. Many kids whose parents are on a sabbatical have books and lesson plans from their old school districts and don't have to be in correspondence schools if they are gone for just one school year. They may have to be tested when they return, and the parent may have to do a lot of paperwork, but this may be the best option for kids gone for that length of time.

CORRESPONDENCE SCHOOLS

Most states have lists of correspondence schools they endorse. Most states also have specific home schooling laws to ensure that the students receive an adequate education. If you intend to maintain ties with your state, you should coordinate with your board of education and jump through whatever hoops they have for home education so that certificates of completion or graduation are issued each year. Also, you don't want to find yourself in violation of the law. Compliance with state requirements will provide additional documentation of successful progress. You should do this in some manner even if you are totally cutting loose. Remember that your child will probably have to demonstrate that he or she is a graduate. Home-schooled kids generally achieve test results much higher than kids who attend public schools, and yours will probably do the same. Nevertheless, an official piece of paper can be important.

We used the Calvert School of Baltimore, Maryland, for preschool through eighth grade. Now Melanie and Carolyn, having completed the maximum grade level of Calvert, are enrolled in Brigham Young University, Department of Independent Study (this program is nondenominational). Both of these institutions send thorough teaching manuals for each course, in addition to textbooks and other supplementary materials.

In the early years, Mel and I divided subjects according to our familiarity and background, and we each spent three or four hours a day teaching. The manuals were directed to us and guided our teaching methods. As time-consuming as this was, we still miss it greatly. It was an incredible opportunity to be with our kids and to see and help them learn. We always sent the testing back to the

Melanie doing school in her cabin.

▼

school for grading and teacher comment. This usually costs extra, but we feel it is more than worth the investment.

As our girls got older, the teaching manuals were increasingly directed toward them. They were already accustomed to the concept and use of these manuals because they had used them all along. They were obviously proud to be able to do as much as practical on their own. The manuals address the students as a teacher standing in front of a class would and provide assignments from the textbook each day. The manuals supplement and discuss the text. They include quizzes and tests. But unlike a teacher standing before a class, the manuals are not saddled with many students of varying competency and commitment. Therefore they can go into great detail; students can learn at their pace, spending only the time they need on the questions.

People always ask, "What happens when there is a question you can't answer?" Obviously, this is a concern. But we have seldom had such a problem because the combination of the text and the teaching manual usually gives us enough information to figure it out. Occasionally, though, we have been stumped. But on each of these few occasions, we have been able to quickly find another cruiser who could help. (You'd be surprised at the number of retired professionals floating around at sea.) If there is no one who can help, your correspondence school, if it is a good one, should have a service to help you if you can get to a phone or fax.

With these programs, students learn how to study in college before they go to college. I can't vouch for how it is today, but when I went to college, lectures were often optional in many schools, with the main emphasis on the text and the assignments. You would spend most of your productive hours in the library or in your room learning. Advanced home schooling is similar in many ways.

STUDY HABITS

If your kids are already accustomed to the spoon feeding prevalent in public schools, you may find that they will not be ready for self-conducted learning. If this has been going on for years, your kids may have an ingrained expectation of learning by doing canned tasks and performing to the level of the lowest common denominator. You may, therefore, have to spend much more time with your older kids than would have been the case had you started earlier.

You should be able to gauge some of this from your observations of and understanding of your kids.

Being parent and teacher in one can create some problems. We all know, for example, that sometimes a kid will be more likely to listen to someone other than a parent. It is one of those facts of life that we must all deal with; it can become exaggerated in home schooling. This shouldn't be an insurmountable problem, but it is one that you must recognize. We don't have any magic answer to this. Formal home-schooling courses such as the ones mentioned above certainly help. Mutual support between spouses helps. If one parent is having problems, the other parent should be up to speed and be able to jump in. Basic family stability helps too. Disciplinary action may be needed in some of these situations.

People also ask, "What do you do about lab? How can they cut up their frog?" My kids have been cutting up fish and other creatures for as long as I can remember, and studying the various parts. It comes rather naturally with cruising. Whoever heard of a young kid cutting up a fish and not wanting to see the brains or the eyes or the tummy? Cutting up a frog seems absurdly superficial, a bit like asking a farm kid whether he knows where milk comes from. We also purchased a microscope and related equipment such as slides, and a telescope. We have been able to conduct a fair amount of "scientific" experiments. However, we have noticed that so many of the practical application exercises are ho-hum when compared to the daily activities cruising kids experience. For example, a text discussion of how an internal-combustion engine works may be nothing compared to what your kid saw just yesterday with your diesel or outboard. The elaborate drawings of generators and electric motors will seem silly when they see the real thing pulled apart on the floor of the main cabin. A description of lead-acid batteries will be a bore when your kid remembers what happened to your 4D when you dropped it last month.

Obviously, you must be careful about chemical experimentation aboard. For example, if you use muriatic acid to dissolve calcium in your head hoses, you will be demonstrating all sorts of things that have a lot more meaning than passive bubbling in a test tube. You will, however, have to take the time to explain what is going on for all of this to serve as meaningful education, and to preach and exercise caution.

(text continued on page 329)

"THREE WEEKS IN THE LIFE OF A GENERATOR" by Melanie

Things break on any boat; it's a fact of life. So, during my first semester of eleventh grade I enrolled in a course on small gas-engine repair. It was offered by Brigham Young, and fit nicely into my high school classes, which went something like this: Algebra II, Spanish II, American Literature, U.S. History, Art, and Creative Writing. It took no more time than the rest of my courses, and after reading the textbook from cover to cover I was pretty confident in my ability to fix chainsaws, lawn mowers, and go-carts. At that time, we were in Florida, a few days north of Ft. Lauderdale and coming up on Christmas. Our plan was to spend it tied up at the Las Olas city dock in Ft. Lauderdale.

My final assignment was very specific—I was to disassemble and rebuild any small gas engine. That left me with few options. We have two Johnson outboard motors, but Dad and I decided that they were too valuable for my project. Our old air compressor was out of the question. For

Melanie rebuilding the generator.

some years, through our wind-generator days and beyond, we had maintained a spare Yamaha EF 2500 portable generator. We rarely used it because it was noisy and because the Onan diesel generator always did a fine job, rumbling away in the bilge. This little Yamaha had been sitting on the poop deck for a while. Dad had intentions of selling it, so we nominated it for the project.

The Saturday when we began was beautiful and sunny. Mom was steering the boat south down the Indian River; Carolyn was below catching up on school. We didn't try to start the thing, but attacked it immediately. Off came the gas tank, the carburetor, the muffler, the valve cover, the cylinder head. A few years back Dad had fixed a valve that had dropped out in the Bahamas by bending and reshaping the C-clip that held the spring retainer. We discovered that the valve was seated a little unevenly. I would have to lap it, which I was prepared to do.

There was a lot of carbon on top of the piston, so I scraped it off as Dad instructed. Somehow, I managed to get a fair amount of it into the holes where the lifters were. I tried to clean this up with our vacuum cleaner. No problem. Getting the valves loose without anything to compress the springs was another matter. I held them down with sore thumbs while Dad pried the C-clips off with a shark hook. The first one came off without hesitation, but the second was a little tougher. Dad pried and pried, and then pop!—it was free. The C-clip fell down onto the table, and the spring retainer flew into the air. And it didn't fall back down. We looked and looked, taking up every bit of carpet on *Chez Nous* and checking under every cushion. I went to bed that night dreaming of valve spring retainers turning into airplanes.

Since it was Christmastime, we had our tree all set up and decorated in the corner of the main cabin. It was a big pine, and its branches hung out halfway over the engine-room hatch. It had lights too. The boat smelled like Christmas and gasoline from my project. I had lapped the valves, and was ready to start calling around looking for a valve spring retainer once we got to Ft. Lauderdale. The project was at a standstill. I was working on my academic courses up in the forward cabin when I heard Carolyn say, "Melanie, what did that part you lost look like?" She was standing there, holding the blasted retainer.

"Where did you find it?!" I yelled. She pointed to the top of the Christmas tree. There it had been hanging, shining like a star for all the world to see. Merry Christmas!

But this was just the beginning. We reached Ft. Lauderdale and settled into slip 83. Soon we had befriended some Canadians on a Stamas 44, *Lady of the Island.* They had two kids a little bit younger than Carolyn and I. All of us were excited about Christmas, which was a week away, but, through all our plans and preparations, the generator project continued. That valve was pretty bad off and needed to be professionally ground, so Dad and I found out about a local machine shop. They did in five minutes what was impossible to do by hand, as my blisters proved. That done, I sat down one day to put the whole thing back together while Carolyn and Ashley and Stephen (our new Canadian friends) went to the beach. When they came back they found me trying not to cry. I had broken one of the bolts on the cylinder head (not a head bolt, but a little insignificant one), and I could *not* back it off. The next day found Dad and me back at the machine shop.

Those professional mechanics must have thought the whole thing was pretty darn funny, as the cylinder head of our little Yamaha was about a tenth of the size of the stuff they usually worked on. But they did a fine job, and we were back in business. Christmas, a memorable one, came and went. We had a cold front on Christmas Eve and had to dig out our winter clothes on Christmas Day, but inside the cabins of *Chez Nous* and *Lady of the Island* our kerosene lamps kept us warm. Christmas afternoon, we hopped from one boat to the other looking at each other's presents and sharing stories of past Christmases. It was a wonderful interlude from the reality of that beast on the stern.

Somehow, I got all the parts back where they belonged. On my two-week anniversary with the Yamaha, Dad and I stood over it and prepared to start it. Our patient looked well enough. We pulled the starter rope once, and again. It sputtered and roared into action. I stood over it, dazed, for five minutes. Then it made a horrible rattle and died, just like that. "It's normal for it to cut off. Let's give it another try," Dad said. So we did, and did again, but it refused to start. Nothing we could do would bring it back to life.

We checked the compression and found some, but it didn't seem right. I took the carburetor off three or four times to clean out the jets. By then, I thought I was an expert on carburetors—until I went to put it back on for the final time. Someone once told me that, in order to get the proper torque, you should tighten the bolt until it breaks and then back it out; of course, he was joking. I guess this didn't register with me, because when I tightened that carburetor bolt I got it a little too tight, and it snapped. I couldn't believe my eyes. This time I *did* cry. Luckily, I was able to back the end off, and Mom and I found a Pep Boys auto shop that had the matching metric bolt.

Still it wouldn't start. We cranked it and cranked it and put ether in it and cranked it some more, but nothing happened. Every day, the folks at the dock would ask me if it was running yet, and Ashley and Stephen joked that I would never make a mechanic. Determined to find out what was wrong, I took off the valve cover one day, and was amazed to see the intake rocker arm totally askew. An examination with a flashlight revealed that the intake lifter was not moving at all, although the exhaust valve was operating just fine. There was nothing left to do but open the crankcase. We had to remove the generator unit from the body of the engine in order to do this, and we didn't have the right equipment. We tried, but we didn't want to damage the generator coils. Again, we were lucky: the generator shop from whom we had recently purchased our brand-new 8 kW Onan agreed to let us use their facilities. On the second day of the new year, they came and took it away. I watched it go like a mother sending her kid off on the first day of school.

Dad and I spent an afternoon at the generator shop, pulling the generator and going inside the crankcase. It turned out that the lifter was stuck and not broken, as we had feared. It was a little glimmer of good luck to make up for the bad. The lifter had gotten stuck because of the carbon that I had spilled into the hole on the first day, three weeks earlier. We put it back together and took it home.

That Saturday, on my three-week anniversary with the generator, we got it started. For some reason, I wasn't as excited as I had been the first time. "A mechanic can't get freaked out every time he or she fixes something," I thought to myself as I smiled at the Yamaha purring away. When I reached over to turn it off, it wouldn't cut off. We had to disconnect the spark plug lead in order to shut it down. Obviously, this was a problem, but Ashley and Stephen and everybody else thought it was funny. After I fooled around with the wiring, I was able to get it working properly. The project was over.

The impact something like this can have on a person amazes me. It was my first real mechanical project—easy compared to the things that I'm sure will come. I was obsessed about that generator—it occupied all my thoughts. When it wasn't going well, I didn't want to wake up in the morning; when it was going well, I was eager to serve it. Through it all, I became aware of the insignificance of my little project. Although it was huge to me, it was just a small part of life on the boat—no doubt an important part, but small. More than anything, I began to realize how little I knew and how much I had to learn in order to live this cruising lifestyle. My sister and Ashley and Stephen would get on my nerves because they were ignorant of what was going on, but I learned to control my temper and to take things one day at a time.

A week later Dad and I hauled the thing over to a popular boating-goods consignment store. We passed Ashley's dad on the way in, and he looked knowingly at us without saying a word. To everyone else, it was just another generator, to be set aside with all the treasures in the back of the store. Papers were exchanged and good-byes were said, and now my little generator sits waiting for somebody else to carry it off as a spare. It was sad, but like everything else it was a lesson.

I got an A on the project and a B on the overall course, but I didn't feel like the grades made a bit of difference. What mattered was not a letter on a report card, but the little bit of confidence that came with a little bit of knowledge. Society cares too much for pieces of paper. The project was a stepping stone to higher things—I want to know all I can about the maintenance of boat systems so I can be self-reliant. Just before we left Ft. Lauderdale, I found myself examining one of our outboards, trying to fill an empty space left by the Yamaha. I'm sure that in days to come there will be few empty spaces, as something always needs to be fixed.

▼

(text continued from page 324)

SPEND WHAT IT TAKES

In short, don't even think about home education if you aren't going to be dedicated enough to spend whatever time it takes. You will also probably find it necessary to spend more money than anticipated. Good correspondence schools can be expensive. They have well-written teaching material, they'll send you quality textbooks, and they pay good teachers to grade and comment on the work. In addition to yearly tuition, we spend large amounts on postage, particularly if we are in a foreign country. It is important to get the work to the school, graded, and back again so that the student knows how things are going and will have a feeling of accomplishment. We also spend money, when necessary, on long-distance calls, sometimes overseas, to ensure that the material flows smoothly or to coordinate tests or problems. Equipment such as the microscope and telescope are also expensive, although sometimes you can find good used equipment. If you let people know what you're doing, they may lend you equipment. But you will be saving money on new styles of clothing every year, winter clothes, fancy haircuts, and many other things. And, this money, if you do it right and stick with it, will return your investment a million times over.

Before you begin, investigate thoroughly. Appendix B lists a number of correspondence schools. This is a good place to start, but note that this information changes frequently. Contact several schools and request catalogs. Then telephone those that seem good. Our telephoning quickly weeded out some. Make sure that the school has no hidden agendas with which you do not agree. Some, for example, have a notable religious bent, tailored to specific doctrines with which you may not agree. This could preclude good science courses as well as subjects you feel are necessary.

Talk to the school board in your area. Determine the requirements for home education in your state. If you plan to maintain contact or return, particularly if you think you might later re-enroll your kids in the system, get a written description of the requirements and procedures in your state. Sometimes people report reluctance or even animosity on the part of public school officials. Often they are quite helpful. If they are not, insist that they become so. They are supposed to be helpful to you. You are paying their salary, and you are proposing to do their job for them while still paying their salary.

Many states have home education organizations, established by parents who are doing what you are considering. Find out if there are any in your area and contact them. They can save you a lot of time and provide good information. Ask public school personnel for information about these organizations.

WHEN TO BEGIN THE NEW SCHOOL

Most people beginning this lifestyle take off in the spring or summer, and head south during the fall. They begin home schooling as they head south, shortly after getting aboard. In our experience, it's better to begin home schooling before you begin your cruise.

If you begin while still in your house or tied to your home mooring, you will not have the stress and distractions inherent in this new venture. You will not be worrying as you turn the text pages whether the boat might run aground around the next bend, whether you'll make the inlet before the next low-pressure cell, or whether that clanking noise you hear will result in another overwhelming repair job. Your students will pick up on these stresses and become stressed or unable to concentrate. If you start the process ashore, you won't have to adjust while simultaneously coping with your children's inevitable separation blues as they leave old school chums behind. Best of all, you will have a chance to see if you can do it—and really want to do it—before it's too late.

It's also a good idea to still have a car and access to the land of plenty as you begin to realize all the things you still need in order to do the job right. You'll also learn how well the school you chose is working with you. If a change is needed, it will be much easier to handle it before you're out in the islands.

Often, however, new cruisers aren't able to handle this optimum method of getting into home schooling. You may have a job that you must attend until the very last moment so that you will have enough money to go in the first place. You will definitely find yourselves totally immersed in getting away during the last year or so. Therefore, consider the second-best but still very good alternative. Take off in spring or early summer. This will leave you at least three, hopefully more, months to settle into the lifestyle, learn to cope with the new set of stresses, get over the initial excitement (it is always exciting), and suffer through the inevitable initial breakdowns. Stay close to home, or at least some familiar area, during the warm months. Not only will you be better able to solve problems in easy territory, your family won't face such a precipitous change. By the time school goes into session, many of the first stresses will have mellowed out and the students will probably have begun to wonder about what is in those boxes and books, and what it is going to be like. Anticipation is a great inducement to learning.

Assuming you're on the East Coast, head south in the fall, staying within the ICW most of the time. This will give you many easy days of calm water (it's hard to do schoolwork when you're rolling about, until you get accustomed to it), plenty of nice anchorages, and relatively stress-free cruising. A pattern will evolve as you get up early each morning and head slowly south through marshes, woods, and barrier islands. Parents can take turns steering as each is needed for his or her teaching specialty. For school breaks the students can come up and see natural history and social history passing by. It is a great way to start home schooling.

As you go, you'll find many places to stop that will lend reality to what the kids are, or will be, learning. As you pass places, go ashore, or at least point them out and talk about them (again,

chapter 23 lists good spots to stop along this route). There are
many more; be sure to consult a good guidebook for the area you
are cruising.

HOW TO RUN YOUR SCHOOL

You will be principal, teacher, and parent. This isn't an easy role.
You'll have to do it all, and you will have to take it all. In a public
school situation there's always someone to blame, but there's always someone to turn to for support, too. Someone else can make
the hard decisions. There are several good ways of dealing with this.

Both husband and wife must be involved with the schooling.
Far too often the husband feels he has more pressing matters to attend to, like fixing the diesel or going fishing. If you are going to
teach your kids, very few things in your life should have higher
priority. Sharing the responsibility makes home schooling more
feasible, and discipline becomes a family matter, as it should be.
Also, one parent is not unfairly and impossibly saddled with the
loss of the majority of the productive hours of her or his day. From
the standpoint of mere administration, it is important that both
parents consider teaching their job and responsibility.

From the standpoint of quality teaching, it is also important for
both parents to be involved. There will inevitably be subjects that
are more familiar to one than the other. Students will benefit from
different perspectives and different personalities. Kids may get tired
of that same old teacher all the time. You would.

From a purely selfish standpoint, you should both want to
teach anyway, because the one who doesn't will be missing a rewarding experience.

It will also be important to establish a schedule and a formal
setting for school. The correspondence school, if you use one,
should establish performance standards and schedules for getting
work and tests in, but you should establish a daily schedule, a routine, to which you adhere as rigorously as possible. This gives students a feeling of continuity if they transferred from a public school.
If home schooling is their first school experience, this schedule gives
them an early sense of the seriousness and importance of the en-
deavor. School should usually begin fairly early in the morning,
when everyone is fresh. *Chez Nous* school begins around 8 A.M.
Melanie and Carolyn pledged allegiance to the flag for many years.
This ceased, unfortunately, as they began to do more self-study and

their schedules began to differ. School for us usually lasts until the prescribed lessons for the day are completed. We break for lunch and then do a bit in the early afternoon. Remember, there is no time wasted in waiting for the bus, the bus ride, standing in line, walking to and from class, or waiting for the rowdies to settle down. It should all be quality time. Therefore, the same material is usually covered much more quickly—and successfully.

After the formal school hours, there is seldom homework in the traditional sense because that sort of exercise is usually a part of the regular school day. We have noticed some cruising kids doing work in the evenings, apparently out of habit, but we have found it better to get the scholastic learning over with and then get on with the day and other types of learning. If we are on a passage and there is nothing much to do, the girls will often go into the next day's lesson to build up free time for that special harbor over the horizon.

There will, of course, be exceptions to your schedule. These include rough passages, storms, special field trips, and major repairs aboard that can't be put off. In public schools there are things such as field trips, snow days, and enough public holidays to make work an exception to the rule. In your school, you will have the power to limit the exceptions to meaningful reasons, but you will always have to make up those days. We've noticed over the years that most cruising kids become quite upset if they get behind, and are most anxious to keep up.

If you do not use a formal correspondence school, you will have to do all the lesson plans and achievement structuring yourself, as well as everything else. Parents who wing it are generally not as successful. No one is an expert in every subject. You can't know it all and do it all, particularly when you are as emotionally involved with the students as you should be. For many the cost of formal enrollment in a qualified correspondence school is prohibitive; it has certainly been an extreme burden to us. But I can't imagine a more important place to put your money; and I suggest that if you can't afford this for your child, then you perhaps ought not to do it. We have seen some exceptionally talented, educated, and motivated people try to do it all themselves, particularly those out for only a year or so. Some do it well, others don't. If the local school board helps with books and lesson plans and suggestions, there seems to be a greater success rate. If there is any doubt, get help. This is your child's education. It is sacred.

SUPPLIES AND SPACE

Many correspondence schools include what they consider to be the necessary supplies in the boxes they send each semester. Calvert and Brigham Young University have been thorough in this. But you should examine the boxes and buy whatever extra supplies you think you may need before leaving convenient shopping areas. For example, you may wish to load up on extra brushes, paints, paper, and other art supplies for the artistically inclined. If a student is particularly interested in chemistry, you should get whatever you feel is practical given the spaces on your boat. You'll be amazed at the difficulty of finding school supplies once you leave the States.

It's also important, before you leave, to review the teaching manuals to determine what, if any, special things you may need. These manuals, especially the science manuals, assume that you will teach in a house ashore and be able to get all sorts of commonplace odds and ends. You probably won't have to get much, but make sure you have the necessary items aboard.

Your students obviously need space in which to study, with as little interruption as possible. It should be roomy enough to enable students to comfortably read and write. This sounds obvious, but on a small sailboat with more than one kid, it can be quite a problem. Many cruising kids do their concentration work on their bunks or in their sleeping space. They use boards or special bed desks for writing, and computers. Some cruisers use the dinette table, or put one student at the table and another at the nav station, and so on. Whatever solution you come up with, don't overlook this aspect in the planning stages. If your boat isn't already set up for school spaces, do it before you leave.

THE COMPUTER AND SCHOOL

As you have already gathered, we are sold on the computer as a useful onboard learning tool. You don't want your students to be computer illiterate.

Computer courses given in some public schools can be inadequate because they allow only minimal time on the computer. With a computer aboard, your students will not only be able to use it to learn about using computers, they'll be able to use it to learn about different school subjects, and they will see it used daily in many practical applications that have nothing to do with computer games.

Again, I hesitate to mention specific programs because the market is constantly changing. Before you go cruising, visit a well-stocked software shop with your kids and see what is available. Talk to teachers and anyone else you can find who has used the new programs, and choose wisely. Avoid the mind-numbing joystick games. There are plenty of good educational programs that are also fun.

A computer can serve as an invaluable research tool. As we said in chapter 21, a CD-ROM reader can give your kids an interactive encyclopedia, thesaurus, atlas, and more. The educational (and fun) opportunities alone justify having a computer. In the early days of family cruising you would never imagine being able to provide the same resource materials that you might have in your house, or even a small library; now you can. And with most of this, once your students get going, this is something they can do on their own.

Obviously, there is no affordable access at this time to the Internet from a cruising boat, unless you are plugged into a dock with a telephone line and not cruising. But I'm not prepared to say that this isn't a blessing. Cruisers have access to a world far more meaningful.

Chapter Twenty-Three
OUR NEIGHBORHOOD

We'd like to tell you about our neighborhood. It's a good place to begin cruising, and it's diverse enough to bring enjoyment long after you've become a veteran cruiser. When you take off you should plan the first months of your cruising around easy living and fun places, and our neighborhood is full of them. You'll be barraged with adjustment demands, and there will be many days when your family is alone together on the boat making passages. Don't plan an isolated confinement scenario as soon as you leave. Do some of those decadent weekend cruising things. Stop at places with good dinghy landings and interesting things to do. If you have kids, study the guides for special stops for children. Try historical stops. Here you can begin to use cruising to improve education and turn the kids on to how cruising makes school fun. Below I'll talk about some of my family's favorites.

REGIONS AND SEASONS

Although our neighborhood is pretty big, it's confined enough to be familiar to us. It is the east coast of the United States and the Bahamas. Many people, even those from the west coast of North America and from Europe, choose the U.S. east coast as an ideal place to begin cruising. Its features illustrate what you may want to look for in a shakedown area, and the descriptions I give here will be helpful if you cruise the area.

The East Coast offers almost everything and is relatively easy cruising ground. There are different cultures, geographical areas, weather patterns, and waters. You can spend days offshore, or along rivers or bays, and in the ICW. There are good and convenient anchorages, nice marinas, and easy supply stops. And it's convenient to be approaching lower latitudes while on your shakedown cruise.

THE NORTHEAST

Try the northern section, from Long Island Sound north, in the summer. Explore the Chesapeake Bay in the early fall, generally between September 15 and October 30; it's usually hot and muggy there from late June through early September. You can spend years there and not get bored, and you may want to return next spring; or you could start the Chesapeake in the spring, go north for summer, and finish in the fall. After the Chesapeake, follow the coast southward in time to reach lower Florida before it gets cold. The 1,000-mile trip from Norfolk, Virginia, to south Florida takes from one to two months for the typical sailboat or small trawler making around 6 knots. Your ultimate progress will depend on how often you stop to smell the roses (the more the better) and how often you choose to do offshore passages, which can save a lot of time. The advance of cold weather varies from year to year, but most cruisers want to be in south Florida by mid-December, or earlier if they have a low tolerance for cool weather or if an early winter is developing.

From Long Island Sound north, you'll find many famous yachting centers such as Newport and Block Island, cultural centers such as Boston, and many quiet anchorages ranging from the misty forests and rocky cliffs of Maine to the pastoral Long Island Sound. Radar is helpful in northern regions because of the frequency of fog. We consider it indispensable. Some of the marinas in this area are outrageously expensive, and some harbors don't allow you to anchor. They want to force you to take a mooring for which they also charge an outrageous price. We ask around about such areas and avoid them.

Just to the south of Long Island Sound, you can visit New York City by water, stopping at one of the marinas. The least expensive at this writing is the one operated by the city at 79th street on the Hudson River called, as one might expect, The 79th Street Boat Basin. This is currently being renovated. They have moorings at a reasonable price. Broadway and 79th is only a few minutes' walk, and you'll find good grocery, hardware, and other stores within several blocks of this intersection. A few blocks over is Central Park and the city's museums. A taxi ride of around $7 gets you to the United Nations or Times Square, where you can wait in line at a ticket center and get tickets to Broadway plays for half-price. We don't recommend walking from Broadway to this marina after dark, although we have done so numerous times with no difficulty in the daytime. When you go home at night, you are at home, eating inexpensively, and you have a wonderful moat separating you from the city.

CHESAPEAKE BAY

The Chesapeake Bay is one of the prettiest, most interesting, and most user-friendly cruising grounds we've ever found. You can, within the space of a day's short run, go from deserted anchorages to the finest that civilization has to offer in museums, restaurants, and other diversions. The Chesapeake is also a living history book, and an ideal place to get your kids into the real stuff rather than textbook print and pictures. The anchorages are usually good ones with all-weather protection, good holding, reasonable depths, and an easy shoreline should you drag. Plentiful anchorages also mean that you can cruise the bay and sample its shoreside treats inexpensively. This is true of most of the East Coast ICW, until you reach lower Florida.

FLORIDA

Florida can be an easy place to cruise, and it can be warm in winter if you have reached Palm Beach or, preferably, even more southerly latitudes. Most areas are crowded, but not all. Partly because a few cruisers tend to camp out here on the hook for years, and partly because there are a few narrow-minded people ashore, some communities have in recent years displayed some hostility toward cruising boaters, but we haven't found this in Florida as a whole.

The ICW meanders along the eastern coast of the state, into the Keys, and also up along the western coast. It introduces you, via inland routes, to many beautiful areas. With plenty of good inlets, ocean sailing is always a great option.

The west coast of Florida, particularly from New Port Richey south, offers great cruising that prepares you for the Bahamas and beyond. Uninhabited islands with white beaches and good anchorages are within an easy sail of civilization. The Ten Thousand Islands, between Marco Island and the Shark River, are also great escapes from civilization if you can handle tricky navigation (there are few aids) and shallow waters. They are part of Everglades National Park, off the mainland west coast of Florida. If your draft isn't much more that four feet, the mangrove islands in the Keys provide beautiful isolation. The west coast of Florida is a great place to charter boats if you want to learn about living aboard.

A great feature of the East Coast is the incredible number of fun stopping places for the whole family. Most of these have reasonably good anchorages. Enjoy these spots as you slowly make your way south. This is especially important if you have children. If you don't stop and enjoy you will be missing out on one of the great aspects of this lifestyle, and you will be depriving your children of fun excursions that make it all worthwhile, not to mention fascinating lessons in history, nature, and geography.

WHERE TO STOP

In this section I've chosen to describe a number of specific stops from the Chesapeake south, because of the warmer temperatures

▼

and because I see so many families really getting into their new adventure from here. Each stop is no more than a few days south of the last. The activities I've concentrated on are especially good for kids, so be sure to share this chapter with your children. I haven't left out fun stuff for parents, though, so read on.

CHESAPEAKE BAY

The Sassafras River in the northern Chesapeake Bay is a great place to stop and swim. Surprisingly, there are not many really good places to do this on the ICW because of swift currents, murky waters, and sometimes stinging sea nettles or even alligators. The Sassafras is fresh and clean, and there are many great places to anchor under the trees. From there you can go to small beaches at woods' edge or simply jump off the boat and swim in the heat of the day. In the evening, deer may come to the water to drink, perhaps where you were swimming. There are no stinging nettles in this water, but as you move farther south down the Chesapeake these creatures can make swimming unpleasant in the summertime.

The Inner Harbor of Baltimore, an easy daysail down the bay, is one of the best spots to have fun. An anchorage in the center of the attractions lies in the shadow of the U.S. frigate *Constellation*. The submarine U.S.S. *Torsk* lurks nearby, a shark's red mouth painted on either side of the bow. Live sharks swim within inches of your face in the National Aquarium, which towers over the harbor. This aquarium has enormous circular tanks several stories high. Walkways wind down the center as the creatures of the sea swim around you. Special tanks for mammals and an educational show acquaint you with dolphins. You can explore the steamy paths of an indoor tropical rain forest at the top of the building.

Within walking distance of the Inner Harbor is the Maryland Science Center, which is designed for kids. It houses an IMAX theater that features spectacular nature shows on a five-story screen; 38 speakers deliver the sound. The Oriole's baseball stadium, Camden Yards, is also only a walk away, as are many other museums. You can go aboard and explore the *Constellation* and the *Torsk*, as well a Coast Guard cutter, a lightship, and classic bay sailing vessels among others. Almost every day the harbor amphitheater features free shows. And, if you're missing your favorite mall, there are three huge ones right at the waterside. The stores include a kite

▼

shop, fudge and ice cream stores, and a variety of restaurants. There are also marinas if you wish to tie up.

At St. Michaels on the Miles River, the Chesapeake Bay Maritime Museum shows every aspect of the bay, including live exhibits, shows, and other attractions. The museum entrance fee is inexpensive; this is a fun and affordable way to learn about the bay. Anchor off the museum or tie up. Another interesting bay museum is located in Solomons Island on the western shore, just up the Patuxent River.

Visiting Washington, D.C.

You can visit Washington, D.C., via the Potomac River, and go to all the displays of the Smithsonian and most of the government buildings for free. All are approximately within a 15-minute walk from a great anchorage and two nice marinas, the Gangplank and the Capital Yacht Club.

At the southern end of the Chesapeake, on the northeastern corner of Mobjack Bay, New Point Island stands out from the marshes and sits behind an authentic historical lighthouse. Its solitude, clean white sands, and natural beauty foreshadow what awaits you in the Bahamas. It's a great place for all kinds of beach activities. Anchor off for the day, just southwest of the island, and then take a short run up into the Mobjack to anchor overnight in one of four beautiful and protected rivers surrounded by trees and farms.

If you studied U.S. history and thought it was boring, you must stop near the York River in the lower end of the bay for a change of heart. In Sarah Creek, a few miles up from the mouth of the river, you'll find a good anchorage and a nice marina, the York River Yacht Haven. Here you can rent a car and visit a famous battlefield as well as Williamsburg and Jamestown. All are within an hour's drive.

As you enter the creek, the battlefield of Yorktown will be on the banks of the river behind you. Britain's General Cornwallis surrendered to the Continental Army here, ending the American Revolution. Today you can walk the embankments and trenches and visit the museum at the Park Visitors Center.

At Jamestown, climb aboard working, full-size replicas of the three ships that brought Captain John Smith and other colonists from England. You'll never again think that your boat is crowded once you've seen where—and how—so many people lived while crossing the Atlantic. Then visit a carefully reconstructed Indian village with authentically built lodgings, Indian craftsmanship in progress, and interesting tours. Next pass into the walls of a working replica of the log fort built by the colonists. Throughout the day, colonial militia training and colonial games are conducted. You may be expected to join in. An interesting movie shows the life of the early colonists. The cost of all this is reasonable; there are few other places where you get as much for your money in historical education and just plain fun. If you need a break from all that living history, visit Busch Gardens and Water Country. These two well-known theme parks are also near Williamsburg.

Passing through Norfolk, prepare to call off school. You'll probably never get a better chance to see huge aircraft carriers, nuclear submarines, and warships of all types. They appear to your left as you turn into the Elizabeth River, leaving Hampton Roads, where ironclad warships slugged it out during the War Between the States. Also in Norfolk, mall lovers will find a large waterfront mall and marina called Waterside. Just to the north a large gray and rather strange-looking structure houses Nauticus, a fascinating attraction that includes exhibits on shipbuilding, modern naval warfare, and petting tanks, a well as an IMAX theater. My favorites include an authentic, simulated, modern naval battle and a virtual-reality deep-sea monster hunt in which you sit inside a submarine module. You control the module as it speeds and swerves among undersea caverns to hunt monsters and other ships that are also hunting you. This is a short walk from Waterside.

THE INTRACOASTAL WATERWAY

Just south of Norfolk begins what most people think of as the ICW—you are at Mile 1.0. Take a side trip through the Dismal Swamp Canal, where tall trees form a canopy over your boat as you glide through beautiful and wild forest. Just south of the North Carolina line is a state welcoming station with free docks and a park, all within the swamp. At the southern end of the swamp, Elizabeth City offers free docking and another park. If you go the regular ICW route and pass through the Great Bridge Locks, you'll find a playground including swings, a curlicue sliding board, and monkey bars just to the east of the locks. You will probably be tied to that side while going through, and if there is a delay and it is safe for you to get off, there may be time to have some fun.

Soon comes the Alligator River, with the Alligator-Pungo Cut just to the south. Keep a sharp lookout deep into the thick forest on each side of the northern end of this narrow cut as you pass through. There are bears in there—we have seen them. Once, a big black bear swam across the cut, just a few feet from our boat.

An island with wild horses and a wide beach forms the southerly shore of the Taylor Creek anchorage at Beaufort, North Carolina, and a small park with space to run around or listen to public concerts awaits on the northern side. The Beaufort Town Docks marina runs along the park. It is across the street from a row of stores, including chocolate and ice cream shops, and is near the free North Carolina Maritime Museum.

In Wrightsville Beach, North Carolina, a strip of land and beach separates your anchorage from the sea. On this strip are some excellent surfing shops, pizza and ice cream shops, and other stores. Land the dinghy and go to the beach. Often there is good surfing.

If your dinghy likes long trips and can handle them well, there is a beautiful wild beach with high dunes to the north of the Little River Inlet, on the border of North and South Carolina. This is a good place for beach running, dunes climbing, or ocean swimming (away from the inlet and its currents). Most cruisers anchor just to the northeast of the ICW in Calabash Creek. There is also a marina up the creek.

A few hours later you can tie up without charge to shop in a huge outdoor mall called Barefoot Landing. It's on the southeast side of the cut just after you come out of the Rock Pile, with all of its turtles sunning on the side. Two of our favorite things about this mall are a large carousel and a candy store where they make salt-water taffy as you watch and test their free samples. After this very civilized landing, prepare to anchor overnight in the desolate swamps of the Waccamaw River. With the dinghy, carefully explore the eerie creeks running up among the moss-covered cypress trees. On warm spring or summer days you may see alligators. One good anchorage for alligator spotting is in a loop behind an island to your right (northwest), near marker "29."

McClellanville, South Carolina, has one of the best trees on the ICW for climbing. There is no anchoring here, but Leland's Marine is very reasonable with a great price on fuel. It's a shrimp-boat dock, and it isn't fancy. A walk to the road, a right turn, and a walk of about a block brings you to a live oak tree big enough to walk up if you don't feel like climbing. In the evening, shrimp boats arrive with their catch. Buy the shrimp live, and the entire family can clean them. You will never again have shrimp so fresh, so good, and so inexpensive. While moving along the waterway near here, watch for wildcats along the shore, and, in warm weather, alligators. You may see some more alligators later, in Florida, between St. Augustine and New Smyrna.

Harbour Town, on Hilton Head Island, South Carolina, is made for kids and families, even though there are usually some mega-yachts around. This beautiful marina nestles beneath huge live oaks. An incredible playground has swings, monkey bars, a play steam shovel, slides, and many other attractions, as well as a neat tree house with a bouncing rope walkway strung from limb to limb. You can rent a bike and ride miles of paths through trees overgrown with Spanish moss. Take a walk in the early morning or late evening and you will probably see deer. An ancient tree called the Liberty Oak towers beside the docks. Live concerts are conducted under its branches during the warmer seasons. You can listen from your cockpit, or join the crowds.

Harbour Town also has a pool, sidewalks for rollerblading, shops (including ice cream, candy, and toy specialties) and almost unlimited grassy yard all around the marina. To top off the day's exercise, climb the spiral stairs of the tall red-and-white lighthouse and look down on the grounds and waters from the observation deck. To make things easier for parents who may need a few days of easy living, a complimentary bottle of wine, cable TV, a phone hookup, electricity, and morning newspaper come with the reasonable dockage fee.

Just a few days away is Cumberland Island with miles of dense, almost subtropical forest and uninhabited beach. Within the woods and dunes are wild horses, deer, armadillo, wild turkeys, wild pigs, alligators, and many other animals. The island is protected by the National Park Service, which maintains paths through the woods. There is no charge to explore here, and there are rangers to help.

Accustomed to human visitors, the animals are just comfortable enough to allow close observation in their natural habitat. Anchor just off the pier by the ranger station and land at the dinghy docks there. Use two anchors in the reversing currents, set them well, and feel secure for a stay. Walk softly down the trails and listen. In the springtime, watch quietly as newborn colts and fawns learn to walk. Go in with your family at daybreak. There will not be many people then; the animals, as they prepare to sleep or as they awaken, will be more relaxed as you drift through the mist. Walk southward toward the huge, haunting ruins of Dungeness mansion. Wealthy and famous people once lived here, but now thoughts of their ghosts entwine with the smothering vines. Turn toward the beach and visit the old graveyard as you pass along. Cross the dunes as the sun rises out of the sea. Then run the beach, which stretches for miles, probably with no one else around. If you see large, strange tracks heading from the sea up the beach, there will probably be a nest of turtle eggs buried in the sand where they stop. Walk carefully here, and don't disturb the little ones waiting to hatch and make their way to the sea.

FLORIDA

We'll talk about some good Christmas stops in our neighborhood now, as well as other regular stops, because many cruisers are in this area of the world during the season and want to celebrate in one way or another.

After one or two days' travel in Florida, you will reach the city of St. Augustine—a good Christmas stop. Although the harbor can get quite cold during December, many cruisers like cold weather for the season. A cruising community is usually anchored just south of the Municipal Marina, or in Salt Run, or tied at the marinas. The oldest continuously occupied European settlement in North America, the city has a rich heritage. The pageantry that begins weeks before Christmas emphasizes the flair of the early Spanish empire. Taxis are cheap, and it's easy to reach stores and other shoreside needs. But if you anchor here and expect a norther, prepare for a roll.

Just south of St. Augustine, Marineland awaits with its dolphin tanks, shows, and other displays of ocean life. There is no place to anchor nearby, but there is a marina on the grounds, just off the waterway. The docks are only a few minutes' walk from the main attractions, an ocean beach, and a playground.

By the time you reach central Florida, you should be prepared for things that go bump in the night. These are manatees. They love to peck on your hull if there are some good bites of grass or sea growth down there. You may also hear them breathing. There are many places to see these huge sea cows. Haulover Cut between Mosquito Lagoon and the Indian River is one of the best. If you don't hear bumps on the hull but you do hear mysterious swishing in the water and some sudden gasps, dolphins may be surfacing beside your boat; you may have seen them playing in your bow wave during the day.

When you reach the Indian River you'll see the tall buildings of John F. Kennedy Space Center as you look off to the east. There are many anchorages around Titusville and Cocoa, to the west of the ICW channel, with a great view of the launchings. Launch times are usually announced on the Ham Waterway Net a little after 7:45 A.M. An inexpensive receiver lets you hear this information as well as weather and other cruising announcements.

Disney World and Epcott Center are within 50 miles by land when you reach Titusville, and within 60 miles if you proceed to Cocoa, Florida. You can anchor or tie up at these towns, and buses run regularly to Disney World. In Cocoa, you will be only a taxi ride away from the space center, which has tours and exhibits for visitors.

Less than a day farther south, a huge, green dragon guards a great anchorage. It is so big that several people can fit between its teeth. Cute dragon babies clamber out of eggs near the feet. At Christmas, a Santa Claus sometimes rides on the dragon's back. Lots of folks stop for the season here, although it occasionally gets quite cold (down to freezing) for a few days at a time. The dragon is on a private point to the west of Eau Gallie harbor, at the mouth of the Banana River, which is on the eastern side of the ICW. There are also marinas here, and two large grocery stores about three blocks from the southern end of the harbor. This is a nice place to stop, but not a good place to get off and run around—the shores are crowded. After a day's trip farther south, however, you can rent a mooring inexpensively from the town of Vero Beach and have the run of a park ashore, with great trees for climbing and hundreds of squirrels who want you to feed them. A public ocean beach is within long walking distance from this park. People stop here for Christmas also, but all the moorings are often taken at this time of year if you don't arrive weeks ahead. Lately the town has tried to make cruisers on moorings raft with other boaters. This could be a very nice or very bad experience.

At Peck Lake, south of St. Lucie Inlet, a narrow strip of beach separates your snug anchorage from the ocean. Turn east just south of marker "19" to head into this spot. Go ashore in the dinghy and enjoy the ocean beach. At night, the roar of the breakers will lull you to sleep.

Soon you'll be in south Florida, waiting for good weather so you can cross the Gulf Stream. One great place to wait, Ft. Lauderdale, has city docks up the New River, where you'll be close to a science museum, park, and an IMAX theater. Cruisers can stock up here and find good deals on parts and boat equipment. There are few places to anchor, and these have time limits. But you can call 1-800-FTL-DOCK for docking and mooring information. Lots of boats spend Christmas in Ft. Lauderdale, and there is a huge

Christmas parade of boats, probably bigger than any you will ever see. Come early if you want a dock or mooring during this season.

An easy day's trip south brings you to Miami and, just south, the beginning of the Florida Keys. Many cruisers anchor here, waiting for winter's winds to offer a brief window so they can cross the Gulf Stream. When we wait there, we always hope the window doesn't come a day before Christmas, because it tempts us to seize the opportunity even when doing so may mean a Christmas at sea. But many other cruisers are in the same predicament each year in and around Miami. With the cruising camaraderie, the mixture of Spanish and U.S. customs ashore, the anticipation of the Bahamas, and the excitement of the season, this can be a great place. There are usually several cruising Christmas enclaves. Most cruisers anchor either in or outside Hurricane Harbor on the west of Key Biscayne, or between the MacArthur Causeway and the Venetian Causeway. If you anchor between the causeways, you may land at the public launching ramp nearby or make arrangements at the Sunset Harbor Marina (in a marked channel going easterly from approximate mile 1089.0 of the ICW). Within walking distance are grocery stores and a fabulous food specialty shop, the Epicure.

You may want to explore the Florida Keys, where you can snorkel on protected reefs, or sail around to Florida's lower west coast and anchor behind deserted islands with white sand beaches. This is a good practice area for Bahamas cruising. In Florida, be aware that occasionally some communities seek to impose unfair and oppressive anchoring restrictions. This may change for the better, or worse, by the time you get there, but if you tune in to the VHF radio, you'll probably get the word.

THE BAHAMAS

Many cruisers like to spend a year or so learning to cruise along the East Coast and then jump off to the Caribbean, Cuba (if permissible), or the Bahamas. We love the Bahamas and consider these islands home. We recommend them as a great cruising area that is readily accessible from Florida. But in many areas of the Bahamas it is difficult to get parts without paying a fortune in shipping and duties. In some areas you must pay around 50 cents a gallon for fresh water, and it may not be good (see chapter 14 for prices and availability). In some cruising grounds, such as the Exumas, there are almost no all-weather anchorages. When the wind changes, you have to move. Many anchorages have ripping current and are fringed with reef, which makes anchor dragging a serious problem.

The Abacos is probably the easiest area in the Bahamas for new cruisers to begin, although you will find it cooler in winter than the central and southeastern Bahamas. There are numerous anchorages with good holding and all-weather protection. A fair number of villages can be found, with good grocery shopping and even boat repair facilities. You can also usually buy good drinking water from the marinas at a reasonable price. The trip from the States to western Bahamian waters can be made in a day, and if the weather has deteriorated so that you don't want to proceed across the banks toward the Green Turtle and Marsh Harbour area, you can stop at a marina at West End, around 56 miles from Palm Beach.

New Plymouth, at Green Turtle Cay, is a quaint town with small and colorful buildings, some around 200 years old. The dialect reminds you of the region's colonial ancestors, who came here to worship as they pleased. Cruisers, delighted to have the crossing behind them to find themselves in a safe and easy part of the Bahamas, flock to the broad anchorage off the town streets, to the secure landlocked harbor called White Sound, or to the mooring area in Black Sound. New Plymouth is an ideal place to spend Christmas. The ceremonies ashore, quaint and simple, reflect the deep faith of the people. A few fine eating establishments and good grocery shopping accent the experience. In White Sound you can hear Christmas music with an island beat at the Green Turtle Club. Several establishments rent rooms ashore, so you can invite family members still living ashore to spend the time with you.

Man of War and Hope Town are each perched on their own small island, side by side in the hub of the Abacos. Each island holds a landlocked harbor, and on one side the Atlantic pounds long beaches while on the other the Abaco Banks allow smooth, safe, and easy sailing. Homes line the streets in tiers up the hill on each island. Like New Plymouth's, the towns' first settlers came for religious freedom, and their influence still deeply affects the communities. The harbors are small, and most cruisers rent moorings. Some rent cottages to enjoy the old-world Christmas festivities. Shopping for basics is convenient; if you want fancier goods, a sail over to the bustling town of Marsh Harbour won't fetch a mall, but it will introduce much wider shopping opportunities.

In Elizabeth Harbour at George Town, Exumas, I've seen as

many as 450 cruising boats anchored during the peak of the winter season. While strong southeasterlies and northwesterlies pack boats into the smaller basins, usually they are sprinkled liberally across the harbor between Stocking Island and Great Exuma. Good groceries, imported and local, are available in town, but its out-island characteristics aren't spoiled by fancy stores full of baubles. The big crowd of cruisers usually hasn't yet arrived by Christmas, but those who are there have a very special time. After Christmas, the Bahamian festival of Junkanoo is sometimes celebrated ashore with music, drums, whistles, horns, and dancing in the streets by local people in elaborate costumes. Elizabeth Harbour is one of our favorite places to be for the Christmas season.

Many cruisers like to spend time in Nassau, Bahamas, so I'm mentioning it for that reason. Shopping opportunities are plentiful and moods are especially festive during Christmas with the constant arrival of boats, from huge cruise liners to the smallest of cruising sailboats. The Junkanoo festivities right after Christmas are fantastic. Boaters anchor up and down the harbor; most settle in the area off the BASRA (Bahamas Air Sea Rescue Association) headquarters north of Potter's Cay, and some settle to the south of the Paradise Island Bridge. Many more, of course, tie up at the marinas. However, like most large cities, Nassau has its share of crime. Unsuspecting boats, particularly at anchor, are frequent targets. Dinghies are especially vulnerable. The Bahamians are trying especially hard to make this a good place to visit.

Epilogue
THE WIDENING GAP

One day it's going to happen. You'll be looking back at the water that separates your transom from the shore, a widening gap between your new life and the old one. In the days, weeks, and months that follow, you will wake up in the morning thinking that it's too good to be true. Perhaps you'll say a silent prayer: "Please, let it continue." It can continue, but you'll have to work hard at it, remember the things we've been talking about, and learn on your own.

Your daily life will change vastly. You'll be part of a fluid community—not just because it is on the water, but because its members come and go with the seasons, winds, and tides. Friends show up at unexpected times and share intense reunions, only to sail away the next day. You never know what a new boat coming into the harbor will bring to your life.

Your community will often be touched by a static community that recedes from and reenters your life, sometimes beneficially and sometimes malignantly. It passes by in slow motion as you travel its coasts; its silent presence looms over the horizon as you sail the oceans. You'll see its smog when you make landfalls, and you'll feel its power as you perform meaningless functions to keep its officials happy. But you'll also rely on it for weather reports, law and order, parts, medical treatment, and much more.

Your flowing world will have its own stability. You will always be confronted with unrelenting, raw reality. Ashore, they try to buffer themselves from it; at sea you can't—and you don't want to. And there will always be the stability of change. The Sea is change; it is a constant that always moves. The scenery will vary, and you will be a part of it. You'll be immersed in overwhelming beauty even during the worst of storms. You will feel an intimate relation with nature, from the spinning galaxies to the floating specks of life beneath your keel. And it will be difficult to not feel that you are part of a circle: moving but coming back.

To make it work, you need to impose another kind of permanency on your lifestyle. You're probably reading this book in part because the values and standards that allowed the good things of our civilization to develop are slowly deteriorating. If we don't revive and retain those values in the cruising community, we will lose, to ourselves, the freedom we love. The values are simple; they have to do with fairness, honesty, morality, respect for others, and kindness. They come naturally, and they come back.

And one other thing. When you see *Chez Nous*, give us a hail. But please don't anchor *too* close.

Green Flash

In the west a swirling orange ball
of fire
Kisses the water of the Banks.
The calm blue shows a sparkle of
yellow,
A glint of orange in a moment of
all colors.

Slowly the sun sinks,
Like a ship lost in the dreams of
the vast Banks.
It goes down into a world of
conch shells and sea stars
Untouched by man.

Only a speck of sun remains,
Dreams have swallowed the rest.
Yellow! Then Green!
For a second, then gone, in a
flash of wishes coming true.

The Banks are a gray-blue,
The birds have settled down,
And I am asleep
With memories of the sun.
     —Melanie Sunshine
      Neale (age 9)

▲

Note: The green flash is an optical illusion seen just after the sun
sets over the ocean. When the last bit of red sinks under the horizon on a clear evening, you can sometimes see a sharp flash of
green light for a split second. The cause is a mystery.—Melanie

▼ NOTES

I like to keep fresh herbs growing whenever I can. They make plain dishes taste wonderful, and they are fun and challenging to keep going. Usually I get the ones already started rather than growing my own from seed. I place all the herb pots together in a plastic Rubbermaid tub, which I keep under the dodger. They can get too hot and dry out quickly in warm climates, so they must be watched and usually watered daily. I have had good luck with oregano, marjoram, thyme, and basil. Many friends have done well with parsley and chives, but these have not survived on *Chez Nous*. Cilantro has thrived on many boats. Some herbs grow wild on tropical islands: dill is everywhere in the Bahamas, as are goat peppers; what the Bahamians call sage is actually wild rosemary. Talk to the locals and find out what they use, but be careful of what you don't recognize.

The *Chez Nous* crew has had much experience with sprouts. Many years ago I started sprouting the usual alfalfa and radishes and mixtures when it was fashionable to do so. It was so much fun when the kids were small. I wanted them to eat the most healthy food their little bodies could digest and went overboard with the sprouts. We sprouted everything that was a seed, mainly for the challenge: oats, sunflower seeds, rice, sesame seeds, all manner of beans, lentils, wheat, rye, etc. After eating sprouts three meals a day for months, my family staged a not-so-quiet rebellion and the sprouting ceased for many years. Every once in awhile we start up the sprouting again, but usually without enough enthusiasm to keep it going for long. I think sprouting is a wonderful thing to do for children as a learning experience and as a job to keep up with for the ones old enough. Besides, sprouts are about the most healthy food you can eat. Just don't overdo it!

There are some wonderful sprouters available in health food stores, and you can make a very easy one from a wide-mouth jar, plastic screen, and a rubber band. The basics are that you must soak the seeds overnight, place them in the sprouter (make sure that your sprouter is always clean), spread them out evenly by whatever method is appropriate for the sprouter, rinse them twice a day, keep the sprouter in a dark place until the sprouts sprout and grow, then put them in the sun so they will turn green, rinse the sprouts when fully grown to remove the seed hulls, and refrigerate those you don't consume right away in a plastic bag with holes in it for air circulation. Your kids will love to sprout seeds, and they'll love the taste too.

GRANOLA

▲ 10 cups flaked or rolled oats (or a mixture of wheat, oats,
    and rye)
  1 cup chopped nuts or slivered almonds
  1 cup sunflower seeds
  ½ cup sesame seeds
  1 cup wheat germ (optional)
  ½ cup vegetable oil
  ½ cup honey
  2 teaspoons vanilla
  2 cups raisins

▲ Mix grains, nuts, and seeds together in a large bowl. Heat oil, honey, and vanilla in a small saucepan and pour over dry mixture. Mix well to lightly coat dry mixture. Spread thinly on cookie sheets (no more than ½ inch thick). Bake in hot oven (400°F) till lightly toasted, about 5 to 7 minutes depending on your oven (you may need to experiment). Repeat until all is cooked. Place toasted granola in another large bowl, mix in raisins, and stir a few times until cool. Store in airtight containers when completely cool. It should last about three weeks if stored this way.

Serve with milk and fruit or with yogurt for breakfast, or use as a snack.

For variety: add cinnamon to dry ingredients and experiment with dried fruit, bananas, and chopped apple.

YOGURT

Makes 2 quarts.

▲ ½ cup fresh yogurt for starter (you may use powdered yogurt
culture, following directions on the package)
7 cups water
4 cups (3 packages of 1-quart envelopes) powdered skim milk
(up to 12 ounces evaporated canned milk may be substituted
for the water and some of the milk for added richness—
and calories!)

▲ *Special equipment:* yogurt maker or two 1-quart thermos bottles
(I use thermos bottles) and a candy or deep-fry thermometer

▲ Preheat the thermoses by partly filling them with boiling water before combining the yogurt mixture. Mix the starter with the water and
powdered milk in a large pan. Heat to exactly 110°F and remove from
heat. Pour the hot water from the thermoses into some other container
for later use and fill the thermoses with yogurt mixture. Place tops on
thermos bottles and let set in still place for about 4 hours. If it has not set
up in that amount of time, let it set a few hours more. It will become sour
if it sets too long. Pour into small containers and refrigerate immediately
after it has set. If you do not have refrigeration, make only what you will
use in a day, but you will have to keep it going every day or your starter
will sour.
    Yogurt can be made into cream cheese by placing some in cheese-
cloth and draining the whey for an hour or so.
    If your yogurt separates, the whey can be used in bread or you can
just mix it back in. The concentrated milk mixture should have enough
body so that it will not separate. Save enough of each batch you make to
start the next one, but if you find that it tastes sour or bitter you have
probably kept it too long and it should be discarded. Start the next batch
with fresh powdered culture, a new container of plain yogurt, or some
that you borrow from your friend who has just made a fresh batch (be
sure to pay back!).

SOUR CREAM

This rare treat can be made instantly far away from grocery stores and without refrigeration. It should be used sparingly as it is loaded with fat.

▲ I can Nestle's Cream (available in many stores outside the States
      but not available anywhere in the States that I have heard of)
    I teaspoon vinegar, or lime or lemon or key lime juice

▲ Combine cream and vinegar or juice and mix for a few seconds till cream is thick. Use in recipes or dips. You may want to mix some yogurt with the sour cream to make it a bit more healthy, especially for dips or salad dressings.

WHOLE WHEAT BREAD

▲ *Note:* I make this from freshly ground wheat berries so that it contains the germ and the bran from the wheat. It is very tasty, a bit heavy or dense, but very nutritious and filling. I do not knead it in the usual sense, mainly because I don't like the mess in my galley, which has limited counter space. If you use any other type of flour, you may prefer to knead in the usual manner and use a bit less water for this amount of flour.

▲ 6 cups freshly ground whole wheat flour
  I teaspoon
  2 yeast packets (I use Rapid Rise)
  ¼ cup honey or brown sugar
  ¼ cup vegetable oil
  2½ to 3 cups hot water (it usually takes 3 with the fresh flour)

▲ *Special equipment:* very large bowl and wooden spoon

▲ Mix all dry ingredients together in large bowl. Add liquids and mix with wooden spoon to make a stiff dough. The dough should be stiff enough to form a ball on the spoon when mixed against the sides of the bowl. If it is too stiff, add a bit of water; if too liquid, add flour. Leave the spoon in the dough after mixing. For the next hour give the dough

355

another good mix against the sides of the bowl every 10 minutes. It should become elastic and rise a bit between each mix. After an hour of rising and mixing, if it is too soft to make into loaves at this stage, then add a little flour and knead with your hands directly in the bowl. Place on a board and flatten with your hands. Cut into two pieces and form into loaves. Place in two greased loaf pans. Cover with a damp cloth and place in a warm spot to rise for ½ to 1 hour until double in size. Bake in preheated 375°F oven for 40 minutes. Remove from pans immediately. Let cool a bit before slicing.

I toast it the next morning in a frying pan, either with or without butter. It is delicious warm with honey, and as French toast after a day or so. As with any whole wheat bread, it will not look like grocery store "air bread," but it will taste great and fill you up.

For variety: use some white flour and decrease the liquid; add sprouted wheat berries; make into raisin bread by flattening each piece of dough and spreading with honey, cinnamon, and raisins before rolling into a loaf; top with egg white and sesame seeds; use milk, yogurt, or whey for some of the liquid.

Bread is not magic or mysterious, it can be lots of fun to experiment once you have mastered the basic principles.

BASIC WHITE BREAD

▲ 5 to 6 cups white flour
   1 yeast packet (you may prefer 2 for higher rising bread—
       1 use Rapid Rise)
   1 teaspoon salt
   1½ cups hot water
   ¼ cup sugar or honey
   ½ stick butter or margarine, or ¼ cup vegetable oil

▲ Mix 5 cups flour and other dry ingredients in large bowl. In saucepan, melt butter and mix with hot water and honey if used in place of sugar. Add to dry ingredients and mix to form workable dough. Place on floured surface and knead about 10 minutes or until elastic, adding more flour as needed. Let rise in greased bowl about 45 minutes or until double in size.

▼

Punch down, cut in half, flatten on floured surface, roll up to form loaves, and place in two greased loaf pans. Cover with damp cloth and let rise in a warm place for about ½ hour or until double in size. Bake in preheated 375°F oven for 35 minutes. Promptly remove from pans. Let cool a bit before slicing.

French bread may be made from the same recipe by forming long loaves and stretching them until they are the correct shape and slicing across the top before the dough rises. The loaves should be sprayed with water before putting in oven and again 10 minutes after cooking has started. You may want to decrease the sugar to just a tablespoon for French bread.

BEER BREAD

▲   *Note:* This is a tasty and quick dinner bread; it does not do well sliced for sandwiches, and the beer taste is not appetizing for breakfast.

▲   3 cups self-rising flour (3 cups plain flour with 1½ teaspoons
       salt and 3 teaspoons baking powder may be substituted)
    3 tablespoons sugar
    I can beer (not light)

▲   Mix all ingredients together until moist. Do not overmix. Place dough in a greased loaf pan and bake in preheated 375°F oven for 40 minutes. Remove from pan immediately and serve hot with butter. It may be a bit crumbly.

For variety: mix grated cheese or chopped onions sautéed till browned into the dough.

BANANA BREAD

▲ ⅓ cup water
   ⅓ cup powdered milk
   ½ cup honey
   3 eggs (or egg substitute), slightly beaten
   1 teaspoon vanilla
   3 large ripe bananas (about 1 cup mashed bananas)
   ½ cup butter or margarine (softened or melted), or vegetable oil
   1 teaspoon baking powder
   1 teaspoon baking soda
   2 cups whole wheat flour
   1 teaspoon salt
   optional: ½ to 1 cup raisins or dates, walnuts, or sunflower seeds

▲ Mix water and powdered milk. Mix milk and all other liquid ingredients in one large bowl. Mix dry ingredients together in another bowl (except optionals). Add the dry ingredients to the liquids with as little mixing as possible. Add optional ingredients last. Turn dough into a greased 5 × 9-inch loaf pan. Bake in preheated 325°F oven for 1 hour or until done (testing the center with a knife).

This bread is delicious toasted in a frying pan, or spread it with lowfat cream cheese or ricotta cheese.

EASY PIZZA

Makes two pizzas.

Dough:
▲ 3½ to 4 cups flour
   1 yeast packet
   1 teaspoon salt
   1 tablespoon sugar
   2 tablespoons vegetable oil or olive oil
   1¼ cups hot water

▲   Mix dry ingredients (reserving about ½ cup flour) together in large bowl. Add oil and hot water. Mix well. Turn on floured surface and knead about 8 minutes. If your bowl is large enough, you can do it right in the bowl. Add remaining flour as needed. Let dough rise about a half hour. Punch down and cut in half. Place each piece of dough on greased pizza pan and flatten and shape it into disc about ½ inch thick. Dough will be too elastic to spread out to the edges of the pan. Let it rest about 20 minutes or until you can easily spread it out from center to edges to form the crust.

Sauce:
▲   2 cups prepared spaghetti sauce
        or: 1 8-ounce can tomato paste
    1 cup water
    1 teaspoon each: dried parsley, basil, and oregano, or use
        larger amounts of fresh herbs
    1 clove garlic, minced

▲   Mix sauce ingredients if you made it from scratch. Spread sauce evenly—about 1 cup on each crust. It should go to within ½ inch of the edge all the way around.

Toppings:
▲   Mozzarella cheese (about a pound, sliced thin or grated)
    Parmesan cheese (fresh grated, a 4- or 5-ounce wedge)
    Vegetables: onions, peppers, mushrooms, olives (green and ripe),
        broccoli, tomato slices
    Meat: pepperoni, sausage, or hamburger (precooked), shrimp,
        lobster, conch, anchovies, bacon, or whatever you like

▲   Place grated cheeses evenly on tomato sauce. Arrange veggies and your choice of a meat or two over cheese. Sprinkle with a bit of Parmesan and hot peppers if desired (be careful!).
    Place pizzas in hot oven preheated to 425°F and bake for about 20 minutes or until crust is crispy and slightly golden on the edges. Your boat oven may only take one pizza at a time, and the timing may vary at this high a temperature.

POACHED TURBOT (TRIGGERFISH)

1 large cleaned turbot (enough to feed four), skinned, with head, fins, and tail removed (fillets or steaks of other firm-textured fish to feed four may be substituted)

▲ 1 small onion
    ½ small green pepper
    1 teaspoon butter (optional)
    1 key lime
    salt and pepper
    Crystal brand hot sauce
    2 ounces water or white wine

▲ Place turbot in a large frying pan. Slice onion and pepper on top, Dot with butter, squeeze key lime over, add salt and pepper and hot sauce to taste. Add liquid and cover. Turn heat to high and steam until cooked (usually 5 to 7 minutes). Add more liquid if needed.

    A whole turbot can be served easily because the skeleton is like a plate that separates the two halves and is easily removed. Poached fish is delicious with rice, grits, or boiled potatoes.

GROUPER FINGERS

Substitute: any soft-textured fish

▲ 1 egg
¾ cup milk (approx.)
Crystal hot sauce
flour (or bread crumbs or cracker crumbs or a mixture)
salt and pepper
seafood seasoning (I use Old Bay)
grouper fillets (or any soft-textured fish) cut into pieces about
    2 1 × ½ inches thick—enough to feed your crowd
cooking oil—canola, vegetable, corn, or a mixture

▲ Mix egg, milk, and a few squirts of hot sauce. Place flour, salt, pepper, and seafood seasoning in a Ziploc bag. Pour about 3 inches of oil in a large, high-sided pan. Heat to 350 to 375°F (no higher) using a candy or deep-fry thermometer to determine and maintain temperature. Keep a lid close by and cover the pan immediately and remove it from the heat if the oil smokes. While the oil is heating, dip the grouper fingers in the liquid and then place them about five at a time in the bag of flour, shake, and remove. Put the fingers in the hot oil and cook till light golden brown (just a few minutes). Turn if needed to fry evenly. Remove with a slotted spoon. Drain on paper towels. The fingers may be pan-fried in a smaller amount of oil, but usually are greasier and less tender. Serve with tartar sauce, horseradish sauce, or Crystal hot sauce with key limes.

DEEP-FAT FRYING SAFETY
1. Do not leave hot oil unattended
2. Use a thermometer to check temperature; maintain it between 350 and 375°F
3. Keep a tight-fitting lid handy to place over the pan if the oil begins to smoke or burn
4. If the oil begins to smoke, turn off flame immediately
5. Keep a type B/C fire extinguisher handy (for oil, grease, and electrical fires)

CONCH FRITTERS

▲ *Note:* The number of conch to use in the following three recipes depends on the amount of meat that comes out of the mature conch. Some conch, especially ones harvested from the ocean, have very large shells and consequently, a very large muscle, which may be two to three times as large as the cleaned muscle of a mature conch with a much smaller shell harvested from some shallow banks. Needless to say, you should harvest only conch that are fully mature; these have a well-formed lip that has some thickness to it. A small conch, on average, will feed one person, a large conch, two to three.

▲ 3 to 8 conch, depending on size
    I large onion
    I green pepper
    I tomato
    2 eggs
    thyme, salt, and pepper to taste
    Crystal hot sauce, a few dashes to taste
    I cup Bisquick

▲ *Note:* To grind the conch and chop the vegetables I use a food processor run off the inverter or generator. It uses about the same amount of power as a microwave, but in much shorter bursts. A hand-operated meat grinder is also helpful.

Grind or process conch. Chop vegetables. Mix all ingredients except Bisquick. Mixture will be lumpy and mushy. Add Bisquick about a half-cup at a time. Mix after the first half-cup, and again after the second half-cup. This will probably be enough to give the mixture some body, but not enough to make a very stiff dough. Sprinkle more Bisquick in if needed, but don't add much. Pour about 3 inches of oil in a large, deep pan. Heat oil to between 350 and 375°F, using a candy or deep-fry thermometer to help maintain temperature. Do not let the temperature get any higher; if the oil starts to smoke, cover and remove from the heat immediately. Using two teaspoons, one for the fritter and one for scraping it off the spoon, spoon fritter dough into hot oil, about 8 dollops at a time. Fry until golden brown, just a few minutes. Turn with slotted spoon if needed. Remove fritters from oil with slotted spoon and drain on paper towels. When all are cooked, remove from towels and sprinkle lightly with salt. Serve with key lime slices and Crystal hot sauce, either as hors d'oeuvres with toothpicks or as a main dish. Leftover dough may be saved in the refrigerator and fried the next night. I reuse deep-frying oil a few times, pouring it into an empty jar when cool. Fritter oil stays relatively clean, but grouper finger oil and cracked conch oil don't because of the flour, which falls off and settles to the bottom.

CRACKED CONCH

▲ *Note:* This is just fried conch. It can be tough if not prepared properly. The trick is to slice the conch lengthwise into thin slices and then to pound the slices till they are very thin, translucent, and lacy.

▲ 2 eggs
¾ cup milk (you may need more milk and eggs if preparing
a large amount
Crystal hot sauce
flour
salt and pepper to taste
prepared conch, about one per person, depending on the size

▲ Mix eggs, milk, and a few dashes hot sauce in a bowl. Place flour, salt, and pepper in a Ziploc bag. Dip a few pieces of prepared conch in liquid mixture, then place them in the bag of flour, close it, and shake to cover the conch with flour. Heat oil for deep-frying, as for conch fritters and grouper fingers. Fry conch only until light golden brown. Frying too long will make it tough. Drain on paper towels. Serve with key lime and hot sauce.

CONCH SALAD

▲ 3 to 8 conch, depending on size (small ones are usually more tender
    and better in this recipe)
  5 key limes, squeezed
  I small onion
  I green pepper
  2 or 3 tomatoes
  I stalk celery, with leaves
  salt and pepper
  thyme (if you use fresh, use sparingly)
  Crystal hot sauce

▲ Dice conch into small cubes. Place in shallow bowl with key lime juice
(you can use prepared key lime juice, which is available in stores in the
South, but it is very acidic and must be partly discarded once used for mar-
inating the conch; regular Persian limes and lime juice are not appropriate
for this recipe because they do not contain enough acid). Mix the conch
and juice so that all the meat has been in contact with the juice (the conch
will start to become firm rather than mushy). Place the conch and key lime
juice in the refrigerator for 2 hours. Dice all vegetables. Mix vegetables,
conch, and key lime juice together in larger bowl (if you used prepared key
lime juice instead of fresh key limes, discard some of the liquid before mixing with the vegetables). Add salt, pepper, thyme, and hot sauce to taste.
Some Bahamian cooks slice a small goat pepper (very hot!) into the salad
instead of using hot sauce. Refrigerate the salad for an hour before serving.
It may be kept for a few days in the refrigerator, but it will probably disappear quickly. Leftover conch salad may be chopped in the food processor
and mixed with an egg and Bisquick and made into fritters.

LOBSTER WITH GARLIC BUTTER

▲ *Note:* We are referring to the southern lobster, or spiny lobster, which
has no claws but a sweet, juicy tail and tasty meat in the legs and antennas
(spines). Spiny lobsters, or crawfish as the locals call them, are only shot
with a Hawaiian sling (see chapter 19) and spear, and only when in season.
Occasionally you may get one that is soft and mushy and without taste

▼

when cooked. This is because it has just shed its shell and therefore has a lot of liquid and not much meat filling up its new, larger shell. The shells of these "shedders" may feel soft.

▲   I small or ½ large lobster tail per person
     I inch water in the bottom of the pan for boiling
     melted butter for dipping
     I clove garlic, minced

▲   Cut each lobster tail in half lengthwise on the underside only (use kitchen scissors or a knife). For very large lobsters, you may want to cut the shell all the way in half. Place tails in pan of boiling water. Boil until the meat is firm all the way through and the shells are pink. Melt butter for dipping. Add minced garlic to butter as it melts. Heat butter until the garlic is tender. Remove lobster meat from shells. Serve with butter in a small dish to dip the sweet, juicy meat. Lobster heads (everything but the tail) may be cooked in the same manner and cleaned and dipped into butter or eaten cold as you would crabs. If you use the head, eat only eat the meat from the legs and antennas (this only works with very large lobsters), and be sure to remove all the insides from the body cavity before cooking.

LOBSTER SALAD

▲   *Note:* Use cold, cooked lobster meat, diced into bite-size pieces, about ½ cup per person.

▲   2 tablespoons onion, chopped fine
     2 stalks celery with leaves
     ½ small green pepper (optional)
     2 cups lobster meat, prepared
     ½ cup mayonnaise (low- or nonfat if desired)
     seafood seasoning (I use Old Bay)
     salt and pepper
     I tablespoon capers

▲   Chop onion, celery, and green pepper. Mix vegetables and lobster meat. Add mayonnaise and seasonings to taste. Mix to coat lightly. Add capers and toss again lightly.

LOBSTER BISQUE

▲   *Note:* You may substitute crabmeat or a mixture of crab and fish. A small amount of white wine or sherry may be added at the end of the cooking time, and the same amount of liquid deleted.

▲   I carrot
    I stalk celery
    I very small onion
    dash thyme
    I tablespoon butter
    I can cream of celery soup mixed with I can of milk or water
    I cup leftover lobster meat, diced into bite-size pieces

▲   Slice carrot and celery. Chop onion fine. Melt butter in saucepan, add vegetables and thyme, and sauté till tender. Add soup mixture. Heat through, then add lobster meat. Continue cooking till lobster is heated. Add wine if desired.

STEAMED CRABS

▲   *Special equipment:* Large steaming pot, gloves, tongs, mallets,
        nutcrackers, newspapers, paper towels.

▲   live blue crabs (Chesapeake Bay variety)
    I can beer
    Old Bay seasoning (Marylanders use a mixture of half Old Bay
        and half salt; Virginians use just Old Bay)

▲   Wearing gloves and using tongs (for the inexperienced), fill the steaming pot with live crabs, being careful to put on the lid after each addition or your dinner will climb out and walk away. Sprinkle seafood seasoning over each layer of crabs. When pot is full, pour the beer slowly over the live crabs; they will become very mellow. Sprinkle a last bit of seasoning onto crabs and turn up the heat. Still wearing gloves, hold the lid onto the steaming pot until all activity has ceased and the crabs have been quiet for a minute or two. Continue steaming for about 20 minutes. Shells will be red. Place steamed crabs on layered newspaper and let everyone pick their own. The shell should be removed first, and all the soft parts (known as the dead man) and gills should be scooped out and discarded. Mallets and nutcrackers help crack the large claws, and old pros will probably have their picking knives with them to remove the white meat from the body cavities. Paper towels help keep hands neat. Beer or soft drinks wash it all down.

Leftover crabs should be picked for their meat to make crabcakes later.

CHESAPEAKE BAY CRABCAKES

▲ I pound picked crabmeat (backfin is best)
  I teaspoon prepared mustard
  2 tablespoons mayonnaise
  I egg
  ¼ cup minced onion
  I tablespoon chopped parsley
  I teaspoon Old Bay
  cracker crumbs (10 saltines crushed in a plastic bag; breading may be
      varied to suit taste and amount of crabmeat; it is needed to hold
      the cake together)

▲ Mix all ingredients. Heat a small amount of oil or butter in a skillet. Form patties and fry until golden brown on both sides. Drain on paper towels. Serve with lemon and tartar sauce. Lowfat crabcakes can be made by using egg substitute, low- or nonfat mayonnaise, and then browning the cakes in a skillet coated with cooking spray. Lowfat ones tend not to hold together and to be dry and not as tasty.

This appendix was compiled from a list of schools approved by the State of Virginia.

A Beka Correspondence School
PO Box 18000
Pensacola, FL 32523-9160
1-800-874-3592
Grades: K–12

American School (The)
2200 East 170th Street
Lansing, IL 60438
1-800-228-5600
708-418-2800
Grades: 9–12

Brigham Young University
Department of Independent
    Study
206 Harman Building
Provo, UT 84602
801-378-2868
Grades: 9–12

Calvert School
105 Tuscany Road
Baltimore, MD 21210
410-243-6030
Grades: K–8

Cambridge Academy
1111 S.W. 17th Street
Ocala, FL 34474
1-800-252-3777
Grades: 6–12

Citizens' High School
188 College Drive
PO Box 1929
Orange Park, FL 32067
904-276-1700
Grades: 9–12

Home Study International
12501 Old Columbia Pike
PO Box 4437
Silver Spring, MD 20914
301-680-6570
Grades: K–12

ICS Newport/Pacific High
    School
925 Oak Street
Scranton, PA 18515
717-342-7701
Grades: 9–12

Indiana University
Independent Study Program
Owen Hall
Bloomington, IN 47405
812-855-3693
Grades: 9–12

Phoenix Special Programs
3132 West Clarendon Avenue
Phoenix, AZ 85017-4589
1-800-426-4952
602-263-5601
Grades: 7–12

Southeast Academy
PO Box MM
137 Main Street
Saltville, VA 24370
540-496-7777
Grades: K–12

University of Arkansas
Division of Continuing
  Education
#2 University Center
Fayetteville, AR 72701
501-575-3647
Grades: 9–12

University of Nebraska-Lincoln
Independent Study High School
269 Nebraska Center for
  Continuing Education
Lincoln, NE 68583-9800
402-472-4321
Grades: 9–12

University of Oklahoma
Independent Study Program
1600 South Jenkins, Room 101
Norman, OK 73072-6507
405-325-1921
Grades: 9–12

INDEX